Many thanks for the "exciting" way you combed my fur! Love Buster xx

I will miss you. Thanks for every thing. love Jack xxx

We will miss you lots. Have thoroughly enjoyed your visit. Hope you have wetted your appetite + will return. With all my love Val xx

I will miss you. I hope you enjoyed your time dow here. love malindi

KAPITI

To Chris

The Mentor

We came together from far and wide.
To play the guitar, and how we tried.
Our voices were buggered, and our
cords were reedy.
While over the strings, we were none
too speedy.

But as we played, we talked of
life.
Of its' joys, and its strife.
And while our progress, was often slow.
As we played, my knowledge did grow.
So thanks for your views, your vent
and your time.
It all helped to clear these thoughts
of mine.

Regards
Allan

for
Joan Maclean

KAPITI

CHRIS MACLEAN

THE
WHITCOMBE
PRESS

*Published with the assistance of
the Historical Branch, Department of Internal Affairs.*

First published in 1999

Whitcombe Press
39 Bruce Avenue, Brooklyn,
Wellington
Tel: 0–4–385 1252
Fax: 0–4–389 9354

Edited by Anna Rogers

Designed by
Margaret Cochran & Geoff Norman

Production by Geoff Norman

Printed in Hong Kong by Colorcraft

CONTENTS

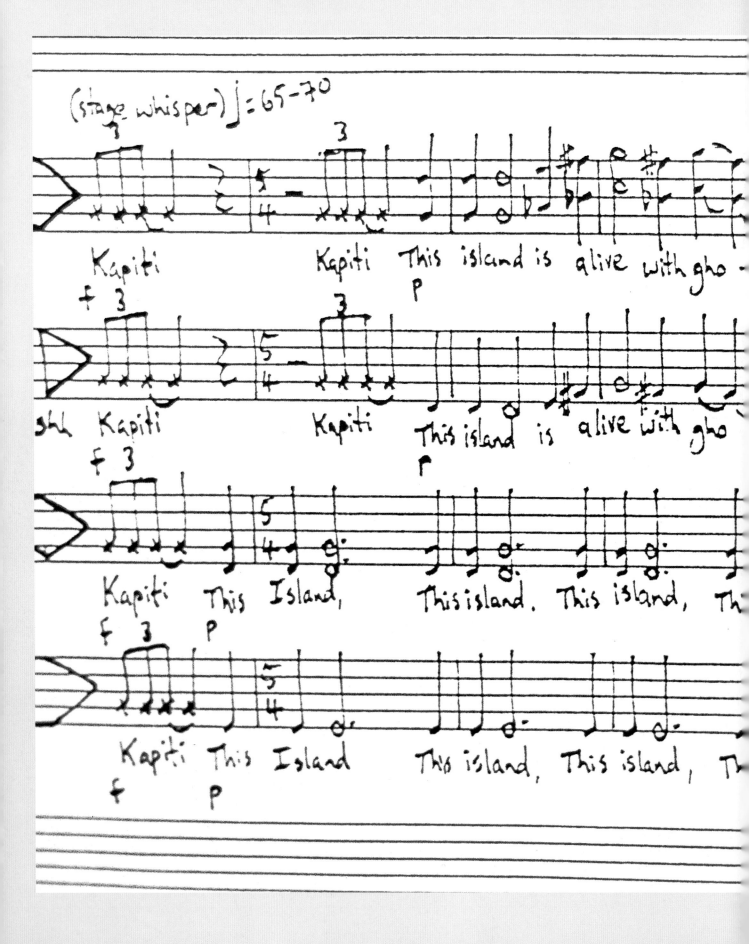

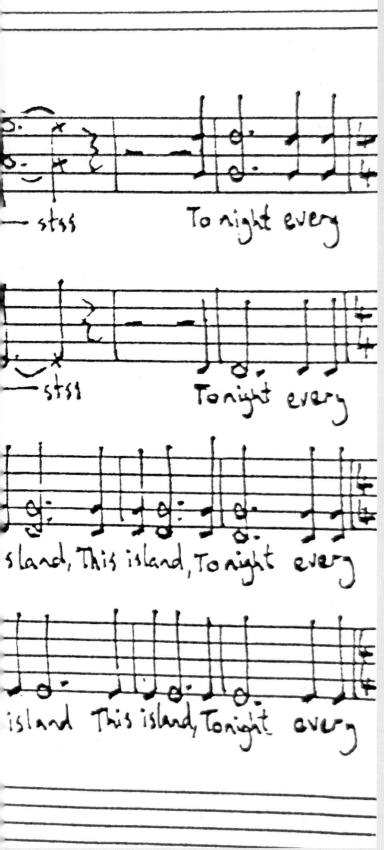

SANCTUARY OF SPIRITS

In past centuries Kapiti was coveted and conquered by a succession of tribes until the most recent, Ngati Toa, lost the bulk of the island to the government in 1897. Since then Kapiti has been a place for birds rather than people. Nevertheless, some of the island's former residents remain, buried in its inaccessible caves and fissures, and their influence lingers on. One of these may be Te Rauparaha. He was buried in the churchyard at Rangiatea at Otaki, but some people believe that his body was secretly exhumed at night, taken to Kapiti, and finally interred there.

His spirit has troubled a number of people on the island, as well as some who live on the mainland. Among them is the poet Alistair Te Ariki Campbell, whose house sits on top of the cliffs at Pukerua Bay, looking across the sea to Kapiti.

In 1963, soon after building the house, Campbell wrote a series of poems entitled 'Sanctuary of Spirits', in which a number of Te Rauparaha's contemporaries recall their memories of him. For Campbell, creating this 'pattern of voices' was an act of personal protection, necessary to quiet the troublesome spirit unsettling his mind. The final voice is that of the poet himself pleading with or, perhaps, commanding the shadowy figure of Te Rauparaha crouched beneath his window on a windy night – 'Madman, leave me alone!'

Campbell's work inspired the composer Ivan Patterson to set the opening poem to music. 'Kapiti' was first performed in 1992 by the Cantoris Choir in the Anglican Cathedral in Wellington. It recalls the Battle of Waiorua, fought on Kapiti in 1824, a tremendous victory that cemented Ngati Toa's hold on the island fortress.

The piece begins the night before the battle with a message to the attackers, assembled on the mainland – stay away!

> This island is alive with ghosts.
> Tonight every leaf is an ear
> attuned to your heartbeat,
> every stick a spear
> gripped by a crouching figure ....[1]

The ancestors of the invaders have come out of their caves to warn their descendants, but they take no notice. Next day, at dawn, they are routed.

ISLANDS can have a fascination born of their isolation, which is sometimes accentuated by dramatic physical features. New Zealand is surrounded by more than 800, but most are small and seldom visited.[2] A few, however, including Kapiti and Rangitoto, have become icons, inspiring generations of poets, painters and photographers. Kapiti is particularly alluring because it combines a dramatic physical presence with a remarkable history and an unusual role as a refuge for endangered birds. To many, it also has a spiritual dimension that exerts a peculiar magnetism.

Maori tribes were drawn to Kapiti for practical reasons. It was a fortress, strategically situated at the northern entrance to Raukawa (Cook Strait), but they also saw that it had underlying power of a more ethereal sort, as a 'sanctuary of spirits'. One who has described that dimension is Marienne de Blois, a personal development teacher from Wellington. 'Kapiti is a training ground for spiritual warriors,' she says. 'People are drawn here to develop the warrior's art of spiritual healing.' The flow of energy that attracts people to the Kapiti Coast, and to the island itself, is particularly strong. 'Kapiti Island is the centre of this flow, which stretches from Paremata in the south to Foxton in the north. There is a spiritual doorway centred here – a stargate.' Apparently, through this opening, one of only a few in the Southern Hemisphere, spiritual energy passes to and from the spirit world. It is discernible, she says, at dusk on a calm, clear evening as a pale blue aura above the island. De Blois herself sees even more. Her sensitivity has been honed since she was a child; her mother was a medium, her father a teacher. 'Kapiti Island, for me, is a gateway like a vast swirling mass of colour. It opens and closes with unfolding energy – it blooms and pulses and is very beautiful to watch.'[3]

Not everyone, of course, accepts this theory, although it could help to explain some unusual experiences people have had on Kapiti. One involved a young couple, Syd Moore and Penny Davies, who sometimes stayed at the north end during the early 1970s. Syd was a scientist and a member of the Skeptics Society.

Paekakariki artist John Baxter is of Maori and Scottish descent. Living in view of Kapiti, he is reminded of his Taranaki ancestors, as well as those of the other tribes that have occupied the island.

The basket-weave pattern symbolises 'the joining of a lot of different iwi,' says Baxter. 'Kapiti is a continuum of history, a place which binds tribes together. The people of Kupe, of Toi and Whatonga, then Ngai Tara, Ngati Ira, Muaupoko and Rangitane then Ngati Toa, Te Ati Awa and Ngati Raukawa.

'The many moods of Kapiti are amazing,' he says. 'There are times when the mist comes and you can't see it at all. Then I say, "Ah Kapiti has gone to visit his relative, Taranaki". Sometimes it's quite haunting.'

TUHIA I RUNGA, TUHIA I RARO. TUHIA I ROTO. TUHIA I WAHO. TUHIA I TE HERE TANGATA.

Penny was more spiritually inclined, identified strongly with a Ngai Tahu fore-bear and found the nights difficult because the presence of Te Rauparaha disturbed her. Even Moore was unsettled: 'I must admit she was so convincing. And the mood of the place was such that on a wild north-westerly night when you could hear the seagulls screaming, the wekas booming, the kiwis calling and the penguins squawking, I could almost feel the ghost myself.'[4] During the day Davies also felt the spirit of the chief near the Okupe Lagoon, where feasts had been held in the 1820s and 1830s. Among the victims were Ngai Tahu prisoners brought from Akaroa aboard the *Elizabeth* to be executed later. On other occasions, when Kapiti's power was understood rather than feared, it could be put to good use as the birth of a child on the island in 1882 showed. The child's parents, Anihaka Park and Matene Tauwhare, had watched helplessly as all their earlier children died in infancy. Finally, Anihaka consulted a tohunga who told her to spend her confine-ment on Kapiti. A daughter, Ripeka, was born there and survived to record the story of her birth, many years later.[5]

These experiences may seem fanciful, but they reveal something of the is-land's spiritual nature, to which some are more receptive than others. Sylvia Lovell (*née* Wilkinson), whose parents were caretakers on the island between 1924 and 1942, was receptive, especially when the weather was stormy and she was alone among the trees:

Standing, listening, I hear the forest breathing, or is it the whispering of the original Maori inhabitants? Are their spirits lurking behind the tall Karakas and Kohekohes? I can feel brown eyes peering at me and brown arms reach out of the past from the green depths. Are they friendly or hostile? I am shuddering, and a heavy melancholy weighs upon me. It is as though spells and strange magic and ancient taboos threaten me.

The mood of the storm and the scary ghosts are too much, and I streak for Rangatira and home as though Te Rauparaha himself were after me.[6]

This perceived spiritual quality may also prevent people visiting the island, or discourage them from trying. Sara Pascoe, a painter who frequently visits Paraparaumu Beach, is certain, for example, that she cannot cross to Kapiti – yet. 'I hold Kapiti in awe. I sense her more than see her. She is mysterious and mystical. Her aura is strong. As I walk on the beach her power permeates my senses. I cannot venture on her till she lets me and she hasn't let me explore her yet. There are many gods hovering and integral to Kapiti.'[7]

Others, however, are drawn to the island as if by a magnet and do not always go there in the usual way, by boat, but more dangerously, by swimming. George Fox, who was the island's caretaker during the 1950s and 1960s, was surprised one evening to see a man emerge from the water near the boatshed. His report records that the man was clearly in great distress. 'Very little sense could be got from him but it appeared he had swum from the mainland. By this time he was in a state of collapse and he was wrapped up in blankets and hot water bags and given a drink. Mrs Fox rang the police and a boat came and took the man away.'[8]

Fox retired in 1968 and was succeeded by the late Peter Rodda and his family. Rodda's strangest memory of his time on the island was the night he was sitting on the beach and heard a splashing sound. 'I thought it must be a fish. Suddenly this body walked out of the water. I asked him what he was doing and he said it was such a beautiful night he'd decided to go for a long swim. He then turned and walked back into the water and swam back to the mainland.'[9]

Curiously, the island has only recently become the emblem of the surrounding district, which is now known as the Kapiti Coast. In the past, the Golden Coast was the community's chosen label. In 1959 the local newspaper reported that 'Approximately 600 loyal subjects of "The Golden Coast" witnessed their Queen being crowned with due pomp, splendour and circumstances at gala Coronation ceremonies performed in the Paraparaumu Hall when the Queen Carnival was declared officially closed.'[10] Later in the evening five knights were invested with the 'Order of the Golden Coast'. In 1973 the district was still known by this name, although there was competition from Queensland's Gold Coast. Perhaps to counter this, there was a publicity campaign 'to promote the Golden Coast as an off-season holiday resort' and a tour of North Island centres by Miss Golden Coast.[11]

Before long, however, realising that Queensland would prevail, local people adopted the island as their emblem instead. The change was partly in response to an emerging sense of community that followed administrative changes in the area. Until 1974 the coast had been part of Hutt County, and it was not until 1988 that it achieved the status of a district. Since then, identification with the island has been widespread. As if to make up for past neglect, Kapiti's distinctive shape now appears in almost every local logo or commercial sign.

PEOPLE AND THE LAND

Until recently, the island's history has also been largely ignored. This is partly because Te Rauparaha has dominated historical accounts and obscured other significant figures and events, and partly because of the emphasis on the island's other role — as a nature reserve. Stan and Amy Wilkinson both published books that described the island's birds, plants and shells in great detail but only briefly sketched its past. Books by Olive Baldwin include vignettes of particular phases of Kapiti's colourful story but do not give an overall account. In 1984, the Director-General of Lands, P. H. Lucas, suggested to his department (which then administered the island) that it should rectify 'the lack of a definitive history of Kapiti Island' but nothing happened.[12] In 1996, with the approach of the island's centenary as a bird sanctuary, the Department of Conservation asked me if I would consider writing a book. I was interested but, although I was not familiar with the details of its 1897 acquisition by the government, I knew enough to understand that the wounds of the owners who were dispossessed of the island, still smarted.

The Department of Conservation planned to celebrate the centenary in a number of ways but the reaction of local iwi soon made it clear that some reconsideration was required. 'This is 100 years of eviction, not celebration,' commented Matiu Rei, chief executive of Ngati Toa.[13] After consultation it was agreed that the occasion would be 'commemorated', rather than 'celebrated'. Clearly, there was a need for greater knowledge of the 1897 legislation and what prompted it. This impression was strengthened when, a few months later, a company based at the north end of Kapiti announced plans to build a lodge on Crown land there. The proposal provoked an impassioned debate, with public meetings, a petition and numerous letters to the newspapers but, despite all this activity, the discussion seemed surprisingly uninformed. Kapiti, it seemed, had no history before 1897. My purpose, therefore, in writing this book has been to try to give a fuller picture of activities on Kapiti before and after that date, in the hope that this might assist the debate over its future.

Surprisingly, it is only in the last 20 years that Kapiti has become the emblem of the district. This painting, entitled People and the Land, *by Raumati artist, Bodhi Vincent, was commissioned in 1993 by the Kapiti Coast District Council. It hangs in the council chambers.*

This painting, by an unknown artist, is based on a sketch by William Bainbridge, which was made in 1846 while Te Rauparaha was imprisoned aboard HMS *Calliope*. Two years later he was released.

The warrior chief's notoriety has obscured much of Kapiti's history and focused attention on only one period of his life. He had other, more diplomatic attributes. Perhaps Te Rauparaha's most significant traits were his adaptability and his readiness to grasp new opportunities in a changing world.

His willingness to migrate, for example, saved Ngati Toa from annihilation at Kawhia. Afterwards, with Ngati Toa firmly established on Kapiti and their enemies routed, it was his readiness to welcome Europeans (and their muskets) that helped the tribe extend their empire to include much of Te Wai Pounamu. By the mid-1830s, however, when Ngati Toa power was at its height, Te Rauparaha was quick to realise that the future would belong not to warriors, but to those who could read and write. He repeatedly asked that one of those agents of literacy, a missionary, be sent to Kapiti.

As Europeans became more numerous and the authority of the colonial government took root, Te Rauparaha's adaptability came to the fore. At Wairau, in 1843, although he was as outraged as Te Rangihaeata by the provocative behaviour of the settlers and surveyors, he urged restraint in the weeks before the fighting and it seems that he would have preferred a diplomatic solution. Later he avoided being drawn into Te Rangihaeata's open war against the colonial government, although he suffered for it.

During his imprisonment without trial (ordered by Governor Grey, who suspected he was secretly

MUSEUM OF NEW ZEALAND/TE PAPA TONGAREWA

supporting Te Rangihaeata) he did not seek utu. In the old Maori world such an affront would have caused inevitable bloodshed; now Te Rauparaha told his people he did not want revenge.

I was also keen to know more of the island myself. I first visited Kapiti as a child and spent my eighth birthday scrambling up to the summit and peering over the dramatic cliffs on the far side. I did not visit the island again for another 16 years, and when I did it was by accident. I had just bought a new fibreglass canoe to replace the wood and canvas kayak I had made as a schoolboy and was keen to try it out. It was a calm, clear, winter morning as I paddled effortlessly away from Waikanae Beach. Soon Kapiti seemed tantalisingly close. I had not intended to visit it, I just kept on paddling. The island drew me closer and within half an hour my canoe grazed the gravel at Rangatira Point. I could not land without a permit, so I immediately turned around and headed back to the mainland. I was foolish to have paddled away without telling anyone but as I would soon be back, I thought no one would have noted my absence.

It did not work out quite like that. I knew nothing of the currents that flow along the island's eastern shore with increasing speed as the tide goes out, sucking Kapiti's waters south towards Cook Strait. I had crossed the channel at high tide when the sea was placid, but now the tide had turned and was dragging me southward with frightening speed. No matter how hard I paddled I made little headway; it was as if the island were determined to keep me a prisoner. The water was creased

Contestants in the annual Kapiti to the mainland swim about to depart from Rangatira, February 1998.

The starting time of this marathon is determined by high tide, when the strong tidal currents are briefly in abeyance. Despite this, as the contestants crossed the channel, they were swept well south of the finish point on Paraparaumu Beach and had to swim 10 kilometres to cover the 5.6-kilometre distance. Only three did not finish.

by currents, and further south, I could see the white caps of waves where the tide raced over the shallow shelf between Motungarara Islet and Kapiti. Beyond lay open sea, and the South Island. It took 30 minutes of frantic paddling to break the island's hold and glide suddenly into calm water. Only years later, when I began research for this book, did I learn that I had been caught in what Kapiti fishermen early this century nicknamed 'The Dardenelles'.[14]

When I started to explore Kapiti itself for this history, I soon realised that I was again fortunate, this time for a different reason. All over the island a network of tracks, cut by possum eradication teams in the early 1980s, spread through every valley and along every ridge. Since then, many had been kept clear of encroaching vegetation to enable scientists to monitor the effect of another programme – to remove rats. By following in their footsteps I was able to explore the island with a variety of companions, each with a particular interest or special knowledge. I also received valuable support from Department of Conservation staff on the island and from the families with an interest in the north end. After two years of regular visits, my fieldwork was complete. Just in time. Once the rats were officially declared to have been eradicated, many of the tracks were no longer maintained and the island quickly became harder to explore.

It was a privilege to be able to wander freely all over Kapiti. I hope this book repays that trust as it presents a picture of the island on the brink of an exciting new era. Now that Kapiti is free of all noxious animals, and an amicable relationship between local iwi and the Department of Conservation seems to be evolving, the island's future looks more promising than at any other time in its history.

PART ONE

ISLAND SHOWCASE

CHAPTER ONE

THE SHAPE OF
THE LAND

When Kapiti is seen from the mainland, as it usually is, only the eastern side is visible; seen from the air, or from a boat, more of its shape and large size are revealed. It is 10 kilometres long, about 2 kilometres wide and is roughly rectangular.

The familiar forested eastern slopes are in sharp contrast to the rest of Kapiti. To the left, on the north-eastern corner, a foreland extends into Rau O Te Rangi Channel and may eventually link the island and the mainland. The nearby Okupe Lagoon, two metres below sea level, has been created by a stream cut off from the sea by sediment sweeping around the northern coast. Further south, on the eastern side, the smaller foreland at Rangatira Point is also visible.

Except on the eastern side of the island, cliffs drop – sometimes hundreds of metres – to the Tasman, their sheer slopes a reminder of the extreme force of the earthquakes that created Kapiti. In a curious way, the contrast between these cliffs and the eastern side seems to symbolise the ambiguities of Kapiti's past: its history of bravery and brutality, cannibalism and Christianity, and farming and nature preservation.

An aerial view of Kapiti from the north, looking south towards Cook Strait, Easter 1997. In the foreground dozens of boats taking part in an annual fishing competition have gathered above a reef to the north of the island.

EARTHQUAKES, sea currents and strong winds have shaped Kapiti, but scientific explanations tell only part of the story of the island's creation. Kapiti's rich human history dates back to the earliest myths of Aotearoa, when ocean voyagers discovered these southern lands. According to Maori mythology, Kapiti owes its shape as much to the actions of ancestors as to the forces of nature. Songs and stories immortalise figures such as the great explorer, Kupe, whose extraordinary feats are recalled in natural features on both sides of Raukawa. Traditions about Kupe often conflict and, even where there is general agreement, details differ, so the stories described here represent only one view of the legendary navigator.

Kupe's journey through these waters nearly ended in disaster. When the huge octopus, the wheke of Muturangi, suddenly surprised his canoe near Te Awaiti (Tory Channel) it was only through quick thinking by Kupe – who managed to distract and kill the wheke – that he and his companions escaped. Kupe then sailed through the narrow channel and round Arapawa Island, before crossing Raukawa to the northern shore, where he found a great sheltered harbour (Whanganui a Tara). Among his companions were his three daughters, one of whom, for unknown reasons, killed herself on the cliffs near the harbour heads. Kupe grieved for her, cutting his forehead, as was the custom, to show his sadness. His blood stained the ground and can still be seen today at the place prosaically known as Red Rocks. He named the two islands in the harbour after his surviving daughters, Matiu and Makaro, before continuing on his journey of discovery.[1]

He travelled north along the west coast, passing between the mainland and the islands of Kapiti and Mana. Tribal tradition says that Kupe created these islands, as well as Arapawa Island, when he severed them from the mainland with a blow from his paddle. The deed is celebrated in a song that was written down, probably from the dictation of Te Rauparaha, when he was a prisoner on board HMS *Calliope* in 1847.[2]

I sing,	Ka tito au
I sing,	Ka tito au
I sing of Kupe,	Ka tito au ki a Kupe
The man	Te tangata
who sliced up the land	Nana i topetope
	Tu wenua
Kapiti stands away	Tu ke Kapiti
Mana stands away	Tu ke Mana
Arapaoa separated	Tau ke Arapaoa
These are the signs	Ko nga tohu, tena
Of my ancestor	O taku tupuna
Of Kupe	O Kupe
Who explored Titapua	Nana i waka tomene Titapua
This land was thrust apart by me.	Ka toroke i au te wenua nei.

The steepness of these islands, especially Kapiti and Mana with their sheer cliffs, evoke Kupe's slicing blade and show the remarkable understanding of the shape of the land that is implicit in Maori mythology. Yet the steep inhospitable slopes of Kapiti are largely unseen for it is the gentler, bush-clad eastern side, visible from the mainland, that is the familiar view of the island. This vista is, however, deceptive. Although forest softens the eastern slopes, people who have climbed them will testify that they are surprisingly steep and some visitors find the trip to the summit an unexpected challenge.

Kupe creates Kapiti *by John Bevan Ford, 1997. This graphite drawing is one of a series that explores the history of Kiwa, the great Pacific Ocean. The overlapping allegorical symbols place Kapiti in its historical and geographical context.*

The early navigator, Kupe, seen here in his canoe, sailed from Polynesia to Aotearoa. During his exploration of these islands he created Kapiti (at the bottom, seen from an aerial perspective) with a blow from his patu, or paddle. Aotearoa is represented by Maui's fish, which is adorned with feathers of the Amokura (above), a wide-ranging bird of the Pacific. Its long tail feathers were prized by the early Polynesians. The line of diamond shapes (top, left) suggests the taniko pattern of a cloak worn by Topeora, a distinguished descendant of a later Pacific voyager, Hoturoa, who guided the Tainui *canoe from Hawaiki to Kawhia. In 1822 Ngati Toa, whose forebears arrived in the Tainui canoe, left Kawhia and migrated to Kapiti.*

GILLIAN AND JOHN THORNLEY COLLECTION

'There is nowhere to go but up,' says Peter Daniel, who spent more than 20 years on Kapiti. As the ranger, he once tramped all over the island but, after three operations on his knees to deal with damage caused by descending these steep slopes, he became understandably cautious. Towards the end of his tenure, trips to the summit were limited to special occasions.[3] He regretted this restriction because no

The view to the south from Rangatira Point. The pale rocks in the foreground are phyllonite, a distinctive pulverised rock characteristic of severe earthquake activity. Phyllonite extends along most of the eastern side of Kapiti, indicating a distinct faultline that has created the steep slopes on this side. The offshore islands of Motungarara and Tahoramaurea are also phyllonite, but low-lying Tokomapuna Island, further to the east, is made of greywacke like Kapiti itself.

other vantage point offers such a clear sense of the island. From the top (521 metres) the true extent of Kapiti is revealed; the island is deceptively large, covering 1965 hectares. A series of rounded ridges and valleys, not evident from the mainland, extend to the north and south. This hidden terrain, parts of which were once cleared for cultivation, explains how the island supported a relatively large Maori population, and also why this was one of the first areas farmed by the earliest European settlers.

Geologically, Kapiti owes its shape to a series of seismic events, the earliest of which probably occurred during the Triassic Age, about 200 million years ago. The island is a massive rectangular block of shattered sedimentary rock, mainly greywacke and argillite, thrust violently upward and then tilted to the east by severe earthquakes.[4] The presence of greywacke suggests that the island was once part of a land bridge, which extended across what we know as Cook Strait. Some plant species found on the island and the nearby mainland are a reminder of this link because they have more in common with the flora of the South Island than the North.

The eminent scientist, Dr Leonard Cockayne, found plenty of evidence on Kapiti to confirm this ancient connection when he conducted a botanical survey of the island in 1907. In his comprehensive report he noted that 'As for the forests of northern Marlborough, including d'Urville Island, they too have in large measure the same species as Kapiti'. He also found earthworms common to the South Island and, intriguingly, the South Island robin. He was doubtful that this small bush dweller, 'being a bird of short flight', could have flown across such 'a considerable stretch of water'. He was also puzzled by the absence of the North Island robin.[5]

ABOVE *An outcrop of phyllonite on Tahoramaurea.*

LEFT *The walking track from Rangatira Point to Waiorua Bay passes through a cave soon after it leaves the beach.*
Evidence of a massive earthquake about AD 1460, which raised the island several metres, can be seen in the wave-cut mark of the old shoreline across the mouth of this cave and the one beside it.

Today some scientists doubt Cockayne's identification and insist that the South Island robin was never present on Kapiti. Conventional lore about the extent and duration of the land bridge across Cook Strait is also being re-evaluated. [6] But Cockayne was not the only person to have seen this bird on Kapiti. In 1876, members of the first scientific party to visit Kapiti noted that only South Island robins were present,[7] and just 10 years after Cockayne's survey the caretaker, J. L. Bennett, described the birds on Kapiti in a letter to the ornithologist, R. D. H. Stidolph. He noted that North Island robins were evident and 'I have occasionally seen the South Island robin here but could never find one when I wanted to show it to anyone – so I do not report it as here'.[8]

It seems likely Kapiti first became an island several million years ago during a period of extreme climatic fluctuations; the sea level rose and fell as a result of temperature changes and periods of mountain building. Land and sea engaged in a ceaseless dance of advance and retreat. The 'North Island' was a series of islands – the mountain blocks we know today as the Kaweka, Ruahine and Tararua Ranges – surrounded by sea. Much of the rest of the land was inundated, including the Kapiti Coast, where the sea came up to the foothills.

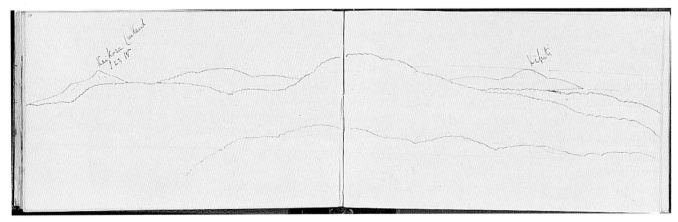

Later, as the climate cooled and great accumulations of ice absorbed more of the sea, the coastline lay 1–3 kilometres to the west of Kapiti.[9] Eventually, this coastline grew to become a vast flat plain extending from Taranaki to Nelson, cutting off Cook Strait from the Tasman Sea. The discovery of 18,000-year-old moa bones on the ocean floor indicates that these giant flightless birds once roamed the now submerged plain, which was covered by cool temperate forest.[10] During the past 10,000 years (barely a moment of geological time), the climate once again warmed, ice concentrations melted and the sea level rose rapidly. The vast Pleistocene plain that once filled the Taranaki Bight and the area to the west of Cook Strait was inundated and Kapiti became an island again.

As the sea continued to rise, it hid further evidence of Kapiti's violent geological past. Below the waves on the eastern side a broad band of pulverised rock, known as phyllonite, extends along most of the island, indicating severe earthquake activity.[11] Kapiti's rectangular shape confirms that it lies between two vigorous faultlines and also explains why it tilts downwards to the east. These parallel faultlines on either side of the island are extensions of the massive fault system that created the Southern Alps and indicate the turmoil beneath the earth's surface as the Indian-Australian and Pacific plates grind away at each other. This evidence of tectonic convergence, together with Kapiti's greywacke composition, show that it is not an island so much as the exposed summit of a submerged mountain range.

This conclusion is reinforced for anyone who looks across at Kapiti from the top of the southern Tararua Range, less than 30 kilometres to the east. From there,

The Taepiro Gorge.

The eastern side of Kapiti is dissected by more than a dozen streams, which fall steeply through narrow curved gorges to the sea. Where they meet the coast, a series of small plateaux made of eroded debris have built up on either side of the stream mouths. These platforms were favoured by Maori as dwelling sites and later also became whaling settlements.

The sharply defined gorges also served as boundaries between different hapu. In 1874, when the Maori Land Court determined individual ownership of land on Kapiti, these natural divisions became the legal boundaries of the new titles.

Kapiti's shoreline is best seen from the air or from the sea. Although the island has extensive shingle beaches at the northern end and around Rangatira, much of the rest of the coastline is difficult to explore on foot because cliffs drop into the sea. Some sections are impassable.

Kapiti's southern coast is rugged and spectacular and includes numerous rocky outcrops isolated from the island by erosion. As a result they have become botanical sanctuaries where rare plants such as Euphorbia glauca and Lepidium oleraceum are found.

Historically, visitors have had considerable freedom to explore Kapiti but today are restricted to the two Trig tracks and the route to the north end. As the Department of Conservation has no plans to broaden the range of options for those on foot, new visitor experiences will probably be based on the sea.

Commercial kayak trips around the southern coast, from the nearby islet of Motungarara, which began in 1997, are an enterprising way to explore Kapiti.

The cliffs of Kapiti are studded with caves ranging from small fissures to large caverns. Cathedral Rocks, beneath Maraetokaroro on the western cliffs (left), contain a number of caves, most of which are only accessible by sea in calm weather. Similar clusters of caves are also found on Kapiti's southern shore and at Arapawaiti, the island's most northern point.

Arapawaiti from the air.

Tareremango, the fin of the shark, is one of the most prominent of Kapiti's headlands. It is one of a series of rocks on the southern coast whose names suggest animals or fish. To the north is a line of rocks known as Ngakuriahinepoupou, the dogs of Hinepoupou. Further east is another headland, Taharirimango, the flank of the shark.

Kapiti from Maungahuka, a peak on the main Tararua Range. The Tararua mountains form part of New Zealand's backbone which extends from Fiordland to the Raukumara Range near East Cape. Kapiti Island, seen here in the distance, is part of this system, although it is separated from the adjacent ranges by the Kapiti Coast and Rau O Te Rangi Channel.

Kapiti appears to be the most westerly of a series of folded ridges receding into the distance. Walking along Kapiti's ridgeline is reminiscent of the tramp across the southern Tararua tops. In both cases sheer cliffs on the western side drop away hundreds of metres, whereas the eastern slopes are gentler, more rounded. Despite these cliffs, both the Kapiti ridgeline and the Southern Crossing have relatively gentle gradients because they are remnants of an ancient peneplain. Later seismic shocks have thrown up chunks of this earlier landform into new configurations, but the gentle contours of the tops of these tilted blocks are a reminder of those distant days when the Wellington region was an extensive plain.[12]

Kapiti's re-emergence as an island, as a result of the most recent phase of global warming, is especially significant. Isolation from the mainland has made Kapiti attractive, first, to generations of Maori seeking the security of this natural fortress surrounded by sea and then, since the 1890s, to conservationists concerned for the survival of birds threatened with extinction on the mainland. Noxious animals such as mustelids and ship rats have never reached Kapiti.

As Kapiti is an island, it has been easier to protect and to modify than the adjacent landmass. In the past it was occupied by a succession of tribes and as one was removed by conquest, another took its place. More recently, wild cattle, sheep, cats, possums and rats have been eradicated and endangered birds have been brought to the island.

Looking north from a clearing at the head of the Te Mimiorakapa Valley towards Tuteremoana.

Kapiti offers some of the finest tramping in the Wellington region. In the past, tramping clubs regularly visited the island but since the 1960s, when restrictions on public access were introduced, only those working on Kapiti have had the freedom to fully explore it.

Although all sides of Kapiti are steep, the undulating slopes of its broad back, especially to the south of the highest point, Tuteremoana, are relatively easy to explore on foot and provide access to the extensive areas of kohekohe forest and the adjacent western clifftops.

A track follows the line of the cliffs and from clearings on several high points there are views in all directions. To the east, the coast of the mainland, from Makara to the Manawatu, lies unfurled with the Tararua mountains looming behind. To the south, the Marlborough Sounds seem tantalisingly close. On a cool, clear day Tapuae-o-Uenuku, Ruapehu and Taranaki can all be seen.
PAUL BRADSHAW

The fact that Kapiti is separated from the mainland has been the single most important influence on its recent history. It is the key to understanding the island's past and its unique role as a nature reserve today.

CHAPTER TWO

THE WITHERING BLAST

Kapiti is an island of extremes. The juxtaposition of a nature reserve and Maori land has provoked a range of opinions, some of them as uncompromising as the shape of the island itself. The island's weather, too, is extreme. The prevailing westerly buffets the island with ferocious gales day after day and only hardy shrubs survive on the exposed slopes facing the Tasman. By contrast, the more sheltered eastern side is clothed in bush and includes some beautiful patches of temperate rainforest. Here nikau palms abound beneath a canopy of kohekohe, pierced occasionally by the crown of a tall rata – a reminder of the mature forest that once covered the island.

Wind-shorn manuka on the northern cliffs of Kapiti. INSET *Nikau and young kohekohe forest, Kahikatea catchment.*

ALTHOUGH geological events, especially earthquakes, have been important in shaping Kapiti, the island also owes its form, particularly the
eastern forelands, to the extraordinary power of the prevailing wind. As
the westerly approaches Cook Strait it is funnelled and bent into a nor'-wester and
the velocity of the wind also increases so that a breeze in Wanganui becomes a
strong wind on the Kapiti Coast and a gale in Wellington.

The prevailing winds are so fierce that Kapiti is surrounded by a vortex of
sea currents, which carry eroded debris from the western cliffs round to the eastern side. In the lee of the island, the currents slacken and drop their load of sediment
which has created a series of beach terraces such as the forelands at Kurakohatu
and at Rangatira.

A similar process occurs on the mainland opposite the island. Kapiti acts as a
windbreak. In its shelter the current that carries debris and sediment southward
along the coast slows down, allowing the material to settle. This, in conjunction
with debris bought down from the hinterland by the Waikanae River, has created a distinctive foreland at the Waikanae rivermouth. The broad bulge in the
coastline was traditionally known as Kenakena, Maori for Adam's apple, a name
that G.L. Adkin, the Horowhenua ethnographer and scientist, regarded as particularly apt. In the *Journal of the Polynesian Society* he described the view from the
summit of the Paekakariki Hill: 'The resemblance of this coastal foreland to that
particular part of the human anatomy is amusingly exact – so obvious indeed that
it is hardly surprising that the simile presented itself to the naturalistic mind of
bygone Maoridom'.[1]

As the foreland has advanced, debris has steadily filled Rau O Te Rangi
Channel between Kapiti and the mainland, until it is now only 55 metres at its
deepest point.[2] If, as seems likely, this process continues, it is possible that at some
time in the distant future Kapiti will once again be joined to the mainland. In that
case the sanctuary will no longer be secure from plant and animal pests.

Strong westerly winds have evidently been a feature of life on the Kapiti Coast
since the earliest times. An early Maori legend tells of the arrival of the chief,
Manaia, in the *Tokomaru* canoe, having been pursued across the Pacific from
Hawaiki by Nuku Tamaroro, who sought revenge for the killing of his brother.
Nuku came across the *Tokomaru* canoe near Pukerua Bay and for two days and
nights he and Manaia fought an inconclusive sea battle between Kapiti and the
mainland. Eventually they agreed to settle the matter on the shore, by single combat.
The powerful tohunga of the *Tokomaru* canoe, Te Aowhaingaroa, had his own
ideas, however, about resolving the conflict. During the night, as the canoes lay
on the beach, he recited a karakia to summon a great gale that not only destroyed
Nuku and his canoes but also blew ashore vast quantities of gravel and sand, creating the sand dunes and stony flats from Waikanae to Te Horo.[3]

The tohunga's gales return to Kapiti each spring, stirring up furious seas and
driving tonnes of sand ashore. For several months life on the Kapiti Coast is trying and the usually crowded beaches are frequently deserted. No doubt the ancient
residents also found the equinoctial gales a nuisance but they also respected – even
worshipped – the wind because, as Te Aowhaingaroa showed, it has the power to
determine the outcome of events. It is probable, for example, that the westerly
played a decisive part in the Battle of Waiorua in 1824 when an armada of canoes,
intent on invading Kapiti, were routed as much by the effects of a rising gale as by
the efforts of the defenders.[4]

Strong winds and high seas in Rau O Te Rangi Channel sometimes isolate the island for days at a time.

Pupils and parents from Solway College, Masterton (seen here listening to ranger Peter Daniel) finally visited Kapiti in October 1996 after five previous attempts had been abandoned because of bad weather.

The wind was deified in a special ceremony by returning warriors a few years later, after Ngati Toa's devastating surprise attack on Ngai Tahu at Akaroa. Te Rauparaha's son, Tamihana, later recalled that when the brig *Elizabeth*, the vehicle of their deceit, returned to Kapiti, her decks piled high with baskets of human flesh for the victory feast, the triumphant warriors came ashore and 'went to the place of offerings to feed the winds'. Tamihana was not present at the ritual so he 'did not know what incantations were used' but recalled that 'when they had finished they came back and put on their clothes and began their laments and speech making'.[5]

Even Tamihana's fearless father found the wind a force to be reckoned with. So, too, did Colonel William Wakefield, who spent several weeks in October 1839 on board the *Tory*, anchored in the lee of the island while conducting land sales negotiations. The spring equinoctial gales were at their height and he found the wind as difficult to deal with as the Ngati Toa chiefs. 'Since we have been here it has never ceased blowing hard,' he wrote in his journal. 'Even in our well equipped ship, the skill and vigour of her commander, which are of no ordinary character, have been often taxed during our short visit.' On one occasion Wakefield was lucky not to lose the young surveyor Charles Heaphy and one of the crew when a sudden violent gust capsized their small boat as it was leaving the island for the *Tory*. A few days earlier, Te Rauparaha had been aboard the vessel when it nearly foundered while changing its anchorage in big seas and high winds. A violent flurry broke the ship's spanker boom and for a moment the *Tory* was caught 'in the trough of the sea and several waves broke over it. At this moment poor Mr Raupero, the King of New Zealand as he calls himself, was in a piteous fright, declaring that the vessel would capsize and muttering prayers most earnestly.'[6] Wakefield's nephew, Jerningham, who was also on deck at the time, later wrote that the chief 'stood trembling with his face to the windward' repeating 'a long, rapid incantation to the spirit of the gale'.[7]

Five years later, when the missionary Richard Taylor and his family visited Kapiti Island, their ship sheltered in the traditional anchorage between the offshore

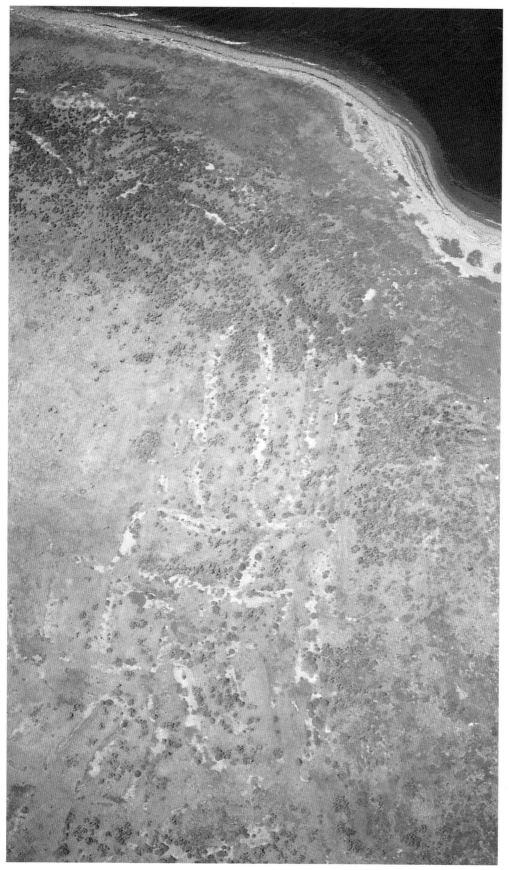

At Kurakohatu, at the northern end of the island, powerful currents, earthquakes and fluctuating sea levels have built a series of boulder banks and, in the process, made the Okupe Lagoon as well as a number of stone mounds which, when seen from the air, look like man-made walls.

This view is supported by an examination of these 'walled gardens' at ground level. They consist of broad mounds of small pebbles. Most are barely half a metre in height, 10 metres wide and up to 30 metres long, quite unlike the structure of drystone walls; also, the ground within them contains little soil.

Debate over the origins of these structures is complicated by another series of stone rows about 100 metres to the north-east, made up of rocks the size of soccer balls, which may well be the remnants of man-made walls.

In the past it has been suggested that these walls were built by Rangitane or Muaupoko or other early residents to shelter gardens but, more recently, this opinion has been challenged. Bruce McFadgen, a Department of Conservation archaeologist, says it is significant that many of the rows lie parallel to the coastline, indicating that sea-borne sediment has created them. The lines that intersect these rows are, he argues, the result of the rise and fall of the shoreline of the Okupe Lagoon.

ABOVE *Westerly gales and driving rain continually erode the exposed western side of the island. In this view, looking down the cliffs at the head of the Maraetakaroro Valley, erosion is more evident on the left side (which faces the prevailing wind) while the sheltered slope, on the right, is more stable.*

RIGHT *Although the western cliffs are arid and exposed, a variety of hardy plants manage to survive there, among them the shrub kowhai (Sophora prostrata). Kowhai usually display a wealth of flowers; here, however, they produce only a few blooms that hang inside the plant where they are protected from the wind.*

islands near the south-eastern shore of Kapiti. Even in this protected spot, they found the wind very disturbing: 'In the night the wind was very high and blew in furious gusts about every five minutes over the lofty land that formed our shelter making our vessel to reel while they lasted'. Next day the wind continued. Taylor visited Brown's Island (Tahoramaurea) nearby, and observed that the wind 'raised the water up in a most remarkable manner especially where it met with the breakers forming clouds of spray 30 or 50 ft high, being regular whirlpools'.[8]

Taylor visited Kapiti in the autumn when the westerly is usually subdued. In spring Kapiti is battered by violent winds day after day. Many years later, Amy Wilkinson, wife of caretaker A.S. (Stan) Wilkinson, lived on Kapiti for 18 years and was a keen observer. In her *Kapiti Diary* she described the effect of the wind on the island:

> For days and days in September the equinoctial gales may rage, lashing the island with furious squalls. The westerly winds strike the barren Cook Strait side of the island, sweep down over the top and swirl around each end, tearing the surface of the heaving sea and carrying spray like steam from boiling water, at a great pace and spraying it across the land. Much damage is done to trees and plants, especially to those bearing their beauteous burden of blossoms. The pure white petals and un-opened buds of the clematis (*Indivisa*) strewn on the floor of the bush, tell of the havoc done to the cascades of beauty hanging from the trees overhead, torn and wilted by the withering blast.[9]

When the wind shifts to the south the change often offers little respite, for southerlies can be equally severe. When gales blow from that quarter the forested

A springtime stroll along the top of the western cliffs reveals a range of flowers including the puataua (Clematis forsteri).

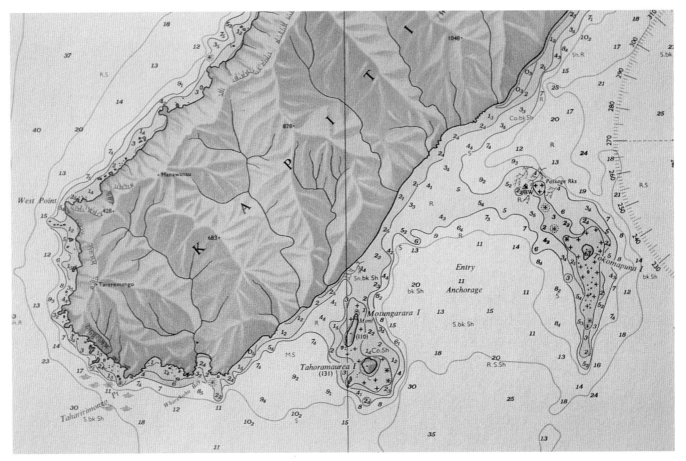

Eroded debris from the western cliffs is carried around the southern end of Kapiti by strong currents. On the sheltered eastern side the currents slacken and the sediment settles on the sea floor, especially around Tahoramaurea, Motungarara and Tokomapuna.

The soundings on this hydrographic map (shown in fathoms) indicate how shallow the water around these islets is. The narrow channel between Kapiti and Motungarara, for example, is barely 2 metres deep.

If sediment continues to accumulate, as seems likely, then it is possible that these rocky outcrops, and Kapiti itself, may eventually be joined together.

PART OF CHART NZ. 4631, (1968) REPRODUCED BY PERMISSION OF THE HYDROGRAPHER, ROYAL NEW ZEALAND NAVY

eastern slopes are battered and scorched by salt spray. Nests are destroyed; birds die.

The Wilkinsons' daughter, Sylvia, who spent her teenage years on Kapiti, later described the impact of such storms:

> The southerly gale is at its height and the waves beat upon the rocky shore with such ferocity that the whole island seems to shudder with the force of the storm.
>
> Driving rain merges with spume from the waves, obliterating the mainland, and it is as though the island were adrift in a million miles of ocean. Wind gusts sweep across the waters and strike the land with an upward thrust causing the bush to become as agitated as the sea.
>
> All around the island the waves torment the battered shoreline – rushing far up the beaches. The undertow is so fierce that the gravel is drawn from the land and then hurled back by the next wave, with the harsh grinding sound of a giant earth moving machine at work, or a great stone crusher, which indeed it is.
>
> The searching waves find their way through every crevice in the rocks, every dark water-line cave excavated by a thousand such storms and with a boom escape through 'blowholes' spouting into the air like geysers.[10]

Southerly storms are less frequent than the persistent winds from the west but they can occur at any time. During the winter of 1836, for example, stormy southerly seas resulted in a disappointing season for the numerous whaling ships drawn to Cook Strait by record catches the previous year. Whales, on their way north from Cloudy Bay, usually brought their calves into the waters of Rau O Te Rangi Channel because they were sheltered from the prevailing westerly wind. But between May

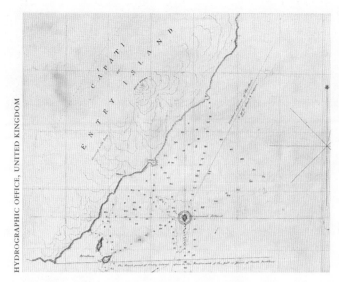

HYDROGRAPHIC OFFICE, UNITED KINGDOM

The first known map of Kapiti was a partial one, showing only the south-eastern shoreline and the offshore islets. It was drawn by George Johnston, the master of HMS *Conway*, which visited the island in 1837.

His map of the 'Anchorage under Entry Island' and Captain Bethune's note on how to approach it, describe the strong winds and powerful currents to which the anchorage was subject. Motungarara and Tahoramaurea are called The Brothers, and Tokomapuna is Hummock Island. The *Conway's* first anchorage was near Rangatira, which Bethune named Robullo Point.

'CAPITI or ENTRY ISLAND is situated on the east side of Cook Straits. The anchorage may prove very useful to vessels bound either way: Conway anchored off Robullo Point, in 25 fathoms. Hummock Island bearing S.°W. We had much difficulty in reaching the anchorage, owing to a strong lee tide, and fearful gusts of wind from the land. A more convenient berth is betwixt Hummock Island and the Brothers; both are open to a SW swell, which occasionally comes in heavy. It may be approached either from the north or south, the only danger being round the islets. The tide or current runs chiefly to the southward – we learnt from the whaling party, that they could seldom tow up a whale killed in that quarter.'
EXTRACT FROM THE REMARKS OF HMS *CONWAY* PUBLISHED IN THE *NAUTICAL MAGAZINE*, 1840
ALEXANDER TURNBULL LIBRARY

In June 1983 a severe southerly storm battered Kapiti. Five finger growing on a ridge more than 200 metres from the sea at Wharekohu, which faces south, shows the effects of prolonged exposure to the salt-laden wind.
BILL COLLINS

Storm by Sylvia Lovell, younger daughter of Kapiti caretakers, Amy and Stan Wilkinson. All three later wrote accounts of their sojourn on the sanctuary and each included a vivid description of the impact of the wind.
RAY LOVELL COLLECTION

and September of 1836 it blew instead, from the south-east, driving away the whales much to the frustration of the waiting boats. Captain Green, who commanded the *Mediterranean Packet*, caught only two whales during the season and reported that when whales did venture into their traditional calving grounds, they were quickly frightened away by the plethora of pursuit vessels. 'When the spout of a whale would casually come within the scope of vision from "the look out point", no less than seventy to eighty boats would put off in pursuit – the monsters, on the approach of such a multitude of boats, became terrified and effected their escape.'[11]

Nor does the island escape the effects of an unseasonable southerly. At Christmas 1934, for example, a severe gale lashed Kapiti. Stan Wilkinson described the damage it caused in an account reminiscent of his wife's description of the nor'-westerly gales in springtime:

> This blow played havoc with some of the trees on the exposed ridges facing south. Even such a tough species as taupata could not stand it, and some of them along the shore were killed outright. The southerly gale came just when the rata was in flower, and it not only destroyed a beautiful picture, but also deprived the nectar-loving birds of their highly esteemed food. Many of the trees are still showing signs of the fury of that gale. On the top of the island leaves and branches were stripped off, and trees uprooted.[12]

Southerlies, as the whalers found, are unpredictable. On rare occasions they can cause freak conditions. Snow, for example, seldom falls on Kapiti because the surrounding sea maintains a relatively warm temperature, but in July 1939 a cold snap resulted in an unprecedented coating on the island. The caretaker reported

that 'for the first time to our knowledge snow was seen falling about our house. However this melted as soon as it struck the ground. Higher up on the island snow was lying about for several days.'[13]

The powerful winds that besiege the island do, however, have a beneficial aspect, for they help to maintain a varied forest. As the Wilkinsons noted, each time a storm batters Kapiti its vegetation suffers. But that destruction benefits the birds because, when a tree is blown down, it makes a hole in the forest canopy that allows a variety of young seedlings to flourish. Such regular renewal is especially advantageous for a bird sanctuary like Kapiti because a varied, young forest can sustain a greater number of birds than a mature forest dominated by just a few types of tree.[14]

The need to preserve a varied forest may put future managers of Kapiti in a quandary since, as the forest gradually matures, it may not be able to sustain the current density and diversity of birds. Will selected areas need to be cleared to create opportunities for new forest to develop, or will natural agencies of renewal, such as wind and fire, keep Kapiti's mantle forever young?

Kapiti from Waikanae.

Most people visit Kapiti in summer but the best weather is usually during winter, when the prevailing wind has abated.

At such times a calm sea, a profusion of forest birds and the relative absence of people make Kapiti especially attractive.

CHAPTER THREE

A VERY VIGOROUS VEGETATION

The earliest known description of the island's forest was written by the German scientist, Ernst Dieffenbach, who visited Kapiti aboard the *Tory* in 1839. 'The very vigorous vegetation' he noted consisted mainly of 'rata, kahikatea and rimu'.

Had Dieffenbach returned 20 years later he might have been surprised to see that most of the forest had disappeared. Clearance begun by Maori in the 1820s quickened towards the middle of the 19th century as European farmers repeatedly fired the bush. Only isolated patches of the original vegetation, protected in moist gullies in the centre of the island, survived.

Today trees have reclaimed Kapiti and although the island is best known as a bird sanctuary, it is also an important plant refuge. One-fifth of the forest is kohekohe, which includes some very old trees. This substantial remnant, together with a similar stand on the slopes of Hemi Matenga behind Waikanae, makes up the largest surviving example in the country of this type of forest that once covered much of the shores of Cook Strait.

The buttressed trunk of an ancient kohekohe ringed by young nikau and kawakawa in a gully on the slopes of Manawanau, south-western Kapiti.
CHRIS LOGAN

The decaying trunk of an old rata on the Trig Track. Despite the almost complete destruction of Kapiti's mature forest early last century, a few surviving northern rata, some more than 35 metres high, can still be found on the slopes above Rangatira and in the adjacent Kahikatea and Te Rere catchments.

DESPITE the strong winds that regularly buffet Kapiti, its climate is warm and moist, especially on the sheltered eastern side and in the hidden valleys that dissect the island's broad back – ideal conditions for the growth of vegetation. Its rapid recovery in the wake of the 19th century clearance is evidence of this.

But growing conditions have not always been so suitable. Earliest records of Kapiti's vegetation (based on analysis of pollen samples) date back tens of thousands of years to the time when the island was part of an extensive plain. Then, Kapiti was clothed with beech forest, the only species hardy enough to prosper in the extreme cold.[1] More recently, as the climate warmed, the island's forests evolved to become the mixed-podocarp type that Dieffenbach admired.

At the time of the *Tory*'s visit Kapiti already had a long history of human occupation, dating back at least several hundred years. Early Polynesian explorers such as Toi and Whatonga, who emulated Kupe's example and braved the unknown ocean to reach Aotearoa, are thought to have visited the Kapiti area about AD 1150. Archaeological evidence suggests that their descendants later settled on the mainland,[2] and it is likely these people also lived on the island because of its strategic location and its value as a fortress. As food was relatively plentiful, these early residents probably did little to modify the land. Seafood from the island's rocky shore, and an abundance of large forest birds such as the easily snared kereru, probably provided a reasonable diet supplemented by limited cultivation of kumara. As the population on Kapiti was relatively small, only the flat areas on the eastern shore would have been used for gardens. Knowledge of this early era of settlement is, however, essentially speculative and will remain so until a comprehensive archaeological survey of the island, which includes some excavations, is carried out.

More certain knowledge charts Kapiti's history from the early 1820s when Ngati Toa captured the island and lived there with their allies. With, perhaps, 1000 people to sustain, there was a great demand for food. New areas were cleared for cultivation and the whole island was a scene of intense activity.

Although wind and waves have sculpted Kapiti, from this time on the most significant influence on the island, especially its vegetation, has been its human

Nopera Te Ngiha.

About 1823, when Ngati
Toa captured Kapiti and
settled there with their allies,
there was a great demand for
food. Cultivations were
established all over Kapiti, on
flat land near the coast and
high on the hilltops at
Pikiwahine, Tuteremoana and
Taepiro. Nopera Te Ngiha
was a young man at the time.
Fifty years later, recalling his
youth on Kapiti at the Maori
Land Court, he likened the
island then to 'a hive of bees
the people were so numerous
upon it'.

But the overcrowding was
brief – no more than a dozen
years. Some hapu left after the
Battle of Waiorua in 1824;
still more left a decade later, at
the close of the Haowhenua
War when tribal territories on
the mainland were reallocated.
The exodus quickened after
the Battle of Kuititanga in
1839. When the Treaty of
Waitangi was brought to
Kapiti for signing less than six
months later, only a few
hundred Maori were still living
on the island.
GILBERT MAIR COLLECTION,
ALEXANDER TURNBULL LIBRARY

inhabitants – and their animals. Dieffenbach's observations are invaluable because
he described the ecological impact of an unprecedented wave of settlement. 'In
the ravines and on top of the hills,' he wrote, 'there is a rich vegetable mould where
plantations of potatoes, cabbages, turnips and Indian corn thrive well.' Elsewhere
on Kapiti he saw 'coarse grass of several kinds affording, with the green bushes,
food for the few head of cattle which were introduced onto the island some years
ago'.[3] Dieffenbach's account reveals the influence of traders and whalers in the cultivation of crops new to Maori and in the use of metal tools such as axes and shovels,
which made the widespread felling of the bush and extensive cultivation possible.
It is likely that the island's occupants also fired the forest to clear land for planting.

Jerningham Wakefield, another of those aboard the *Tory*, was more interested in hunting than scientific observation, but his description of a trip in pursuit

Among those on board the Tory was the New Zealand Company's draughtsman, Charles Heaphy, who drew the first definitive picture of Kapiti, seen here in the centre, as well as other sections of the Cook Strait coastline.

Heaphy's coastal profiles are entitled (from top to bottom):

1. View of Port Nicholson from the entrance.
2. View of Port Underwood, Cloudy Bay (from outside the heads).
3. View of Kapiti or Entry Island. [Seen from the south, looking north. The Tory is anchored close to Tokomapuna which Heaphy recorded as 'Evans's Island', nearby Tahoramaurea is 'Stubb's Island' and Motungarara 'Hiko's Island'.

The 'Coomb Rocks' on the far left of Kapiti are a part of the coastal profile above the island and join it on the extreme right.]
4. View of Cloudy Bay and Cape Campbell (from the entrance of Tory Channel).
5. View of the Two Brothers, Cape Koamaroo, Point Jackson and D'Urville's Island.
6. View of the Two Brothers and Wellington Head (from off Cape Koamaroo).

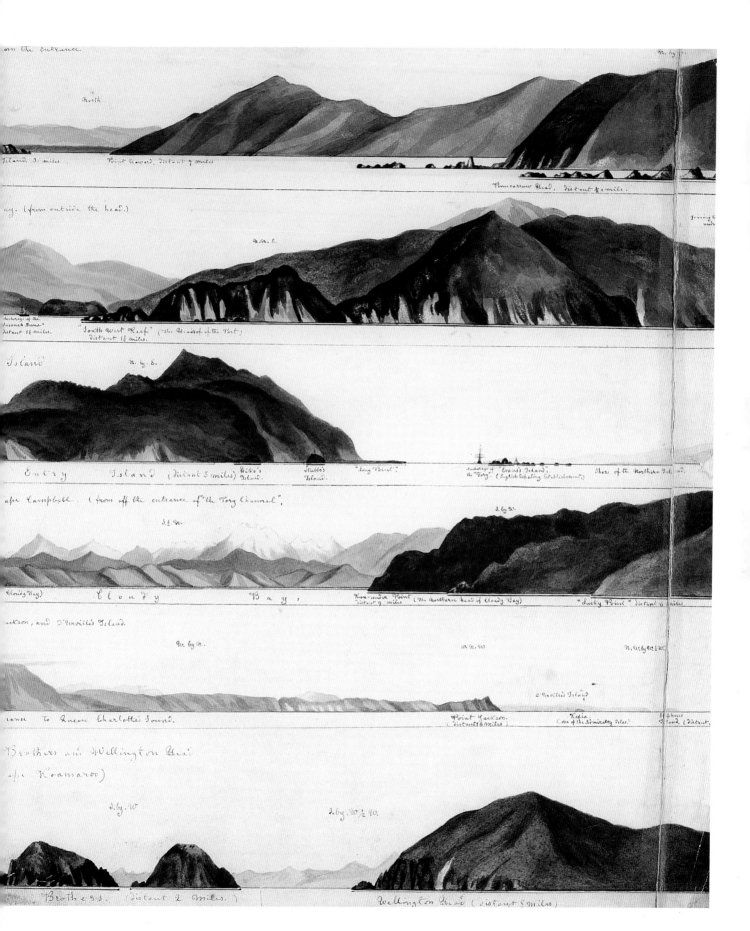

on the entrance

North

Island. 3 miles   Point Howard, Distant 7 miles

Panearrow Head, Distant 4 mile.

ay. (from outside the head.)

Mem. S.

Anchorage of the
Susanah Anne"
Distant 2½ miles.   "South West Reef" (The Head of the Port)
                       Distant 1½ miles.

Island   N. by S.

Entry   Island (distant 5 miles) Kiko's   Stubbs's   "Long Point".   Anchorage of "Evans's Island",   Shore of the Northern Island.
                                    Island.   Island.   the "Tory". (English Whaling Establishment.)

ape Campbell. (from off the entrance of "the Tory Channel",

S.E.W.   S. by W.

loudy Bay)   C l o u d y   B a y,   Vara-under Point   "Lucky Point" Distant 6 miles
                                                     Distant 9 miles (The Northern head of Cloudy Bay)

ackson, and D'Urville's Island.

W. by N.   W.N.W.   N. W. by W. ½ W.

                                                                              D'Urville's Island.

rance   to   Queen Charlotte's Sound.   Point Jackson.   Kafia   Stephens
                                                             Distant 6 miles (one of the Admiralty Isles.)   Island. (distant

Brothers and Wellington Head
(ape Koamaroo)

S. by W   S. by W. ½ W.

Brothers. (Distant 2 miles.)   Wellington Head (distant 8 miles.)

View of [...] island [...] Kapiti, from the North

South

Long Point

E n t

Heaphy's coastal profiles on the previous pages show Kapiti from the south. He also painted the island from a point some 6 kilometres to the north. It shows the bare cliffs on the northern and western sides as well as mature forest on the slopes of Tuteremoana in the centre.
FOLIO 6C, HYDROGRAPHIC OFFICE, UNITED KINGDOM

of wild cattle also mentions, in passing, changes taking place in the island's ecology, especially high on the slopes of Tuteremoana where:

Extensive patches have been cleared of wood by the natives at remote periods and the slaves of the Kawia chiefs still work some nice spots and reside irregularly in picturesque groups of huts among the high grounds. Wherever the land has been cleared a very rich natural pasturage has sprung up among the bleached trunks of the dead trees, chiefly consisting of a grass resembling our 'timothy' and of yellow trefoil; and the presence of the cattle seems to have improved its growth and luxuriance.[4]

The cattle had been sent out from Sydney in 1836 by the trader Captain W.B. Rhodes, who gave them to Te Rauparaha and Te Hiko in exchange for a cargo of flax.[5] Jerningham Wakefield paid Te Rauparaha 5½ sovereigns to hunt one of them, and a party of beaters was included in the price. Despite their help, Wakefield was frustrated by his elusive quarry and managed merely to wound, but not kill, several of them.[6] Other Europeans living on Kapiti, such as the whalers, took great care not to harm the cattle as their owners' displeasure was dangerous. Instead they brought goats and pigs, alternative sources of protein, to the island. Whether they were deliberately released or simply escaped into the bush is not known but a feral population, which bred rapidly, soon became established. Towards the end of the 1830s, sheep were also introduced.[7] The initial flock prospered. Flat land at Waiorua, Rangatira and Wharekohu was cleared and drained to accommodate them but, inevitably, some escaped into the bush where they joined the growing menagerie of introduced livestock.

As whaling declined, farming flourished. The easiest way to make pasture was to burn the bush; periodically fires got out of control and swept the island. The last major fire is thought to have occurred about 1850 but regular, controlled burn-offs continued in an attempt to limit the spread of the manuka and tauhinu, which quickly colonised the new pasture. These fires radically altered the vegetation, especially at either end of the island, where farming was concentrated. In the centre large areas were left to regenerate because they were simply too steep to farm.

South by West.

n° 3.

r y   I s l a n d. — (distant 4 miles)

The legacy of this period was evident in 1876 when the first botanical survey of the island was conducted by the botanist John Buchanan and a group of scientific colleagues from the Colonial Museum. Buchanan's visit is important because it was the first scientific appraisal of the island, pre-dating by 30 years Leonard Cockayne's 1907 survey with which most botanical accounts begin. Buchanan made lists of all plants (including ferns) and birds he and his friends saw, as well as the seaweeds and seashells they collected and the fish they caught. They were, however, 'rather disappointed for the flora of the island is virtually the same as that of the mainland'.[8]

Kapiti's rugged topography and its isolation meant that farming was always difficult. Even so, several generations of the Brown family toiled at Wharekohu until about 1880, and Rangatira and Taepiro were stocked with sheep until the end of the century. Farming continued at Waiorua until the late 1950s, more than a century after whaling had ceased. But Waiorua was an exception. The rest of the island had become a reserve in 1897 and its pastures and pockets of forest had been left to regenerate.

The regrowth that characterised the early decades of the 20th century was, however, quite different from the range of majestic forest species Dieffenbach described. Grassland and scrub now predominated. A surveyor's map drawn by R. P. Greville in 1902 provides a useful picture of the island at the time.[9] His notes show large areas of manuka and tauhinu gradually reclaiming the hard-won grasslands of the early farmers. An analysis of vegetation types 10 years later indicates that half the island was covered by grass and scrub.[10] A further 820 hectares were described as bush but its growth was constantly checked by the browsing of wild cattle, goats and sheep, as well as by other introduced animals such as possums, which had been liberated at the northern end in 1893, only four years before Kapiti became a reserve.[11]

Dr Cockayne's botanical survey, commissioned by the Crown in 1907, was a timely charter of what needed to be done to make Kapiti a functioning sanctuary for endangered birds, plants and insects. Among his recommendations was that

Tawa, the second most common forest tree on Kapiti, is concentrated on the eastern slopes in the middle of the island. Stands such as this one on the Trig Track are a favoured habitat of kokako.

Kohekohe at the head of the Kaiwharawhara Valley, close to the edge of the western cliffs. Kohekohe is an unusual tree; it flowers in winter, in defiance of the season, and the flowers sprout directly from the trunk rather than from twigs or branches.

Kohekohe are especially valuable on Kapiti because their flowers provide abundant food for the birds at a time when other food sources are limited. They flower so profusely that a dense litter of spent flowers and pods collects on the forest floor. Within this decaying layer invertebrates flourish and attract birds that feed on them.

Most of the kohekohe on Kapiti is concentrated in the Te Mimiorakapa and Kaiwharawhara catchments, although there are smaller pockets elsewhere.

Kohekohe litter.

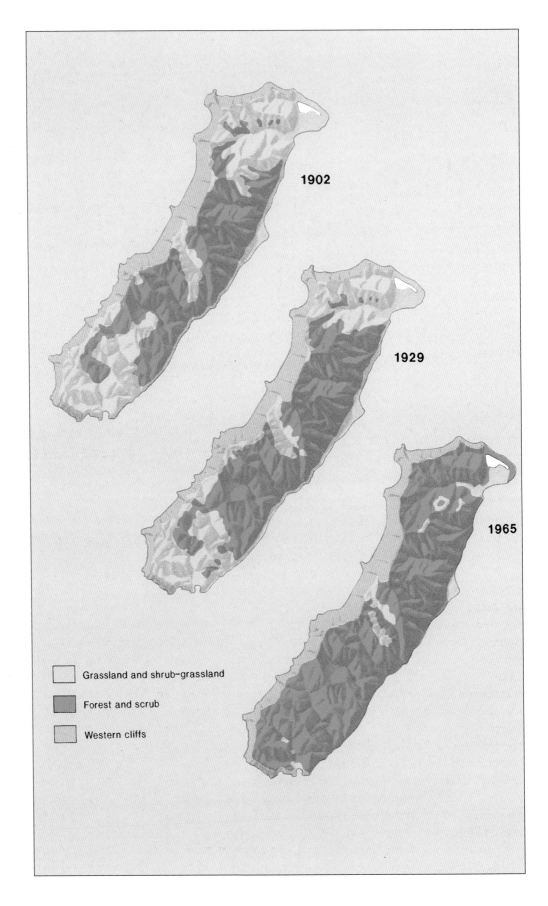

Kapiti Island regeneration based on A. E. Esler's definitive 1967 article on the vegetation of Kapiti Island.
CHRIS EDKINS

1902

1929

1965

Grassland and shrub-grassland

Forest and scrub

Western cliffs

14959

14958

all animals 'foreign to the island' such as goats, cattle, sheep, cats and even the Californian quail should be destroyed and, although there was little evidence that possums were a problem at that time, that they, too, should be exterminated.[12]

The island's managers, the Lands and Survey Department, accepted Cockayne's vision. From then on caretakers were encouraged to shoot wild cattle, cats and goats. When, in 1913, the caretaker, J. L. Bennett, wrote to inform the department that he had shot 138 goats during the previous year, the Under-Secretary replied, noting the 'satisfactory result' but reminding Bennett that 'It is very essential that the island should be free from both goats and cats as early as possible'[13] – an instruction easily written at a desk in Wellington but more difficult to implement on Kapiti. For the caretaker it meant a lot of hard work, even danger; the remaining goats did not present themselves as easy targets but preferred the safety of the inaccessible western cliffs. Undaunted, Bennett hunted them from the sea. Young Norman Elder from Waikanae, while on a fishing trip at the southern end of the island, recalled meeting Bennett 'rowing round the coast in a minute dinghy, his rifle lashed under the thwarts, to hunt out the goats which had formerly overrun the island'.[14] Given the exposed nature of Kapiti's southern and western coasts, and the likelihood of sudden weather changes in Cook Strait, this was evidence of his remarkable determination.

In 1917, at a time when thousands of young New Zealand men were fighting overseas, another smaller war was waged on Kapiti. That year the Lands and Survey Department broadened its campaign to clean up the island: the caretaker was

The surveyor R. P. Greville's map of Kapiti, drawn in 1902, is an invaluable record of the island's vegetation at that time. In this section, which shows the middle of the island, he noted that 'this is the best bush on the island and is worth preserving. Bush consists of rata, tawa, kohekohe, hinau, rewarewa, mahoe, matipo with dense undergrowth in places of kareao (supplejack).'
MAPS 14958 AND 14959, LAND INFORMATION NEW ZEALAND, WELLINGTON DISTRICT OFFICE

also authorised to kill all wild sheep in the reserve. As the job was too big for Bennett alone, the department encouraged hunters and farmers on the mainland to visit Kapiti for shooting expeditions; their reward was the price they could get for the fleeces of the sheep they shot.

The department also decided to act against the opossums (as they were known until the 1960s when the preferred name became possums). Although they had spread only relatively slowly since their release, by 1914 they had reached Te Mimi, more than halfway down the island.[15] The Assistant Under-Secretary wrote to Bennett requesting 'your suggestions upon the best manner of carrying out the work' and asked 'if you can form any idea as to the number that might be caught during the season if trapping were undertaken'.[16] But the proposed extermination campaign was not supported by all interest groups because the threat the possums posed was not universally understood. For example, the secretary of the Forest and Bird Society (an early conservation group with no connection to the current organisation of the same name) suggested that possums should be captured alive on Kapiti so they could be liberated in bush on the mainland;[17] and, in 1916, the possum was accorded the status of a protected species everywhere in the Wellington region, with the sole exception of Kapiti.[18]

Meanwhile Bennett had observed damage to trees on the island and his accounts of the effect of these marauding marsupials were to have an influence well beyond Kapiti. 'This is the first report that has come to hand of any destruction to trees by opossums,' the department noted. 'The information is therefore valuable as the Acclimatisation Societies are asking to be allowed to liberate these animals in a number of districts.' Thanks to the observant caretaker, 'The applications are being refused'.[19]

By 1917 possums had reached the southern end and the island was now completely infested. A trapper was engaged and money for a trappers' hut soon followed.[20] As the war in Europe ended, the campaign on Kapiti gathered pace and for the next 50 years trappers were hired almost every year.

Bennett died in 1924, before he could complete the work of ridding Kapiti of noxious animals, but his successor, Stan Wilkinson, continued his campaign with the same dedication. First, the new caretaker felt compelled to clean up his patch at Rangatira, where the family's dairy cows roamed freely in the bush around the house. He resolved to fence them in. The department supplied some timber for posts but more was needed so Wilkinson scoured the shoreline. As most flotsam ended up on the northern and western coasts, and as the north end was then entirely privately owned, he had no choice but to gather driftwood from the exposed shore beneath the western cliffs. Like Bennett, he found himself alone in a small boat on the far side of the island – always a vulnerable situation. 'The only means of transporting this material was by a small launch with an outdated engine,' Wilkinson recalled. 'Getting the posts off this rocky shore was a tricky business.'[21]

As soon as his cows were contained, the caretaker resumed 'the toughest job on Kapiti'. But it was to be another four years before Wilkinson, the resident trapper, Dick Fletcher, and his dog, Doone, finally got rid of the wild goats – the last six, forced out of their refuge on the cliffs by hunger, were shot as they browsed on the clifftops.[22] The sheep were just as difficult. Local farmers managed to muster only 30, so the remainder – more than 1400 – had to be stalked and shot. It was not until 1930 that hoofed animals were eliminated from the sanctuary. Now, at last, Kapiti could begin to function as a nature reserve. In the 25 years that a succession of caretakers had devoted to this difficult task, several hundred wild cattle, as well as about 8000 goats and 1500 sheep, had been killed.[23]

'Now that there was no fear of plants being eaten by animals we could help Nature to restore the bush,' Wilkinson later wrote, reflecting on his island service during which he, his friends and plant enthusiasts from all over New Zealand laboured to make Kapiti a plant museum. Each year they planted thousands of trees all over the island. Select forest specimens such as kahikatea, kauri, puriri and rimu were planted behind the caretaker's house; coastal species, especially karo, ngaio, pohutukawa and taupata, were liberally placed along the eastern shore from Rangatira to Wharekohu; on the high summit ridge of Tuteremoana, beech trees were set among the remains of the old forest. Seedlings intended for the coast were transported by boat, but those destined for the ridges or the hidden valleys beyond the eastern gorges had to be carried on foot. In dry weather Wilkinson swagged water up to them in special bags slung over his shoulders.[24]

In one year alone, 9582 trees were planted out.[25] This level of activity continued throughout the 1930s, fuelled by the caretaker's ambition to make Kapiti both a plant refuge and a bird sanctuary. His reasons for this dedicated campaign were revealed in a letter he wrote (but never sent) to the secretary of the Native Plant Preservation Society:

> As regards the introduction of mainland and other native species from the NZ area, my opinion about this is that every species that will grow on Kapiti should be transferred. My main reason is that to my way of thinking it is only a matter of time when most of our rare plants and many of our commoner ones as well will disappear. What with animals of all kinds roaming through the bush and on the high country, to say nothing of fires, sawmilling, etc, some species have not a chance of

Karo in flower, Wharekohu. Now that all noxious animals and introduced predators on Kapiti have been eradicated, attention is turning to removing introduced weeds and trees that do not naturally occur on the island. Karo, perhaps the best established of the species introduced by Stan Wilkinson in the 1930s, which was kept in check by rats eating its seeds, may be controlled in the future if it becomes widespead.

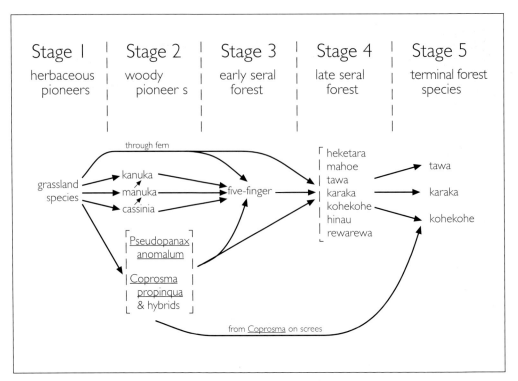

Stage 1 — herbaceous pioneers
Stage 2 — woody pioneers
Stage 3 — early seral forest
Stage 4 — late seral forest
Stage 5 — terminal forest species

through fern

grassland species → kanuka
grassland species → manuka
grassland species → cassinia

kanuka → five-finger
manuka → five-finger
cassinia → five-finger

five-finger → [heketara, mahoe, tawa, karaka, kohekohe, hinau, rewarewa]

Pseudopanax anomalum

Coprosma propinqua & hybrids

[heketara, mahoe, tawa, karaka, kohekohe, hinau, rewarewa] → tawa
→ karaka
→ kohekohe

from Coprosma on screes

This diagram shows the evolution of the island's mantle from the abandoned grasslands of Kapiti's 19th-century farms to the mature forests that will eventually cover the entire island.
ADAPTED FROM 'THE VEGETATION OF KAPITI ISLAND' BY A. E. ESLER, 1967

surviving unless transferred to where they have no enemies. I have seen enough to satisfy me on that point. Go into any forest you like and you can see the enormous damage that is being done. And the damage is not only confined to the forested areas either for on any of the mountain tops you see the same thing.

So with the object in view of saving as much as I could I have planted on Kapiti all the species I could get hold of. During my fifteen years' residence here I have put out something like 250 different kinds. Certainly they are not all rare but most of them are.[26]

More than 50 years later it is interesting to see how these mass plantings have fared. The coastal species have thrived and, in places, karo, pohutukawa and taupata look as if they have always been on the island. The forest trees, now nearing maturity, are evident in the canopy, especially at Rangatira Point. Only the beech trees, to the south of the Trig and at Te Mimi, seem out of place.

But by far the most noticeable feature of these planned plantings, especially those within the forest, is that they have been overwhelmed by naturally occurring species. In hindsight, nature needed less help than Stan Wilkinson and his friends thought. His most valuable contribution was the extermination of hoofed animals. But his strategy of planting endangered species was entirely understandable at the time for, during the 1930s, bush lovers everywhere were becoming alarmed at the unchecked destruction of New Zealand forests by noxious animals, particularly deer. But it was not until the end of that decade that the government started to do something about the deer menace. No sooner had the campaign begun than the Second World War intervened, so it was not renewed in earnest until the 1950s. Stan Wilkinson could not wait. His plantings were as logical as the mass plantings on Mana and Matiu/Somes Islands in recent years. The species planted on these islands have been raised from local seed and from seeds taken from other locations in the vicinity of Cook Strait. Their regional sourcing reflects a vision

of island refuges for species typical of the area, rather than just those known to occur only on Mana and Matiu.[27]

This regional emphasis, not a concern in the 1930s, is a contemporary concept that is part of a new approach to managing restoration. Today the doctrine of 'biological diversity' holds sway. It acknowledges the variety of all living things; more specifically, it emphasises the uniqueness of each locality (and its inhabitants) and recognises that the restoration of specific ecosystems such as islands and regions is a way of rebuilding that variety. So the focus, today, is on maintaining Kapiti's forests in as natural a state as possible. In fact the wheel has come full circle. A few hybrid species, not typical of the island, have been laboriously removed by work parties and some scientists advocate the removal of some of Wilkinson's introduced species. Karo and pohutukawa, for example, which he struggled to establish on the eastern shore, are now flourishing to the point where some consider them pests. Although both species are a useful food source for birds, neither is known to occur naturally in this area, so they may also be removed.

Wilkinson anticipated this criticism. In the same letter he drafted to the Native Plant Preservation Society he defended his strategy by quoting from Cockayne's seminal report: 'As for plants, I can see no reason why as complete a collection of New Zealand forest plants as possible should not be planted in the sheltered valley towards the north of the island when this is finally acquired from its Native owners'.[28] Even if his plantings all over Kapiti might seem to contradict Cockayne's careful qualification – 'Of course the present forest should not be interfered with;

Pohutukawa seedling, Waterfall Bay. The crimson flowers of the New Zealand Christmas tree are cherished by many, but some scientists consider the plant is simply a weed because it has spread to areas where it is not known to occur naturally. For this reason it may one day be removed from Kapiti's shores.

When the Levin artist and children's author, Avis Acres, visited Kapiti in 1956, numerous possums were evident on the island. Possum trapping on Kapiti began during the First World War and continued until 1968, when a moratorium was declared so that the animals' true impact on the vegetation could be assessed. Ten years later evidence of severe damage prompted a resumption of trapping. In 1982 a campaign to eradicate possums began. Four years later, Kapiti became the largest island in New Zealand free of all browsing mammals.
ALEXANDER TURNBULL LIBRARY AND THE ESTATE OF AVIS ACRES

a plant formation is as much a natural object as is a species' – Wilkinson may have been encouraged by the learned botanist's example for, in 1908, Cockayne himself had 'lately conveyed to Kapiti a number of specimens from the far-away Auckland Isles'.[29] Furthermore, the two men knew each other and corresponded regularly so Cockayne presumably knew of the caretaker's crusade although, according to Wilkinson, 'he never mentioned the matter'.[30]

Looking back, it is clear that Wilkinson's plantings were but the most recent of a succession of modifications of the island's vegetation by its human inhabitants. Today's forest is not the same as the one Dieffenbach described. The trees that dominate the forest at present – kanuka, five finger, kohekohe and tawa – represent the progression from the grasslands of the 19th century to the mature forests of the new millennium. The transition is a reflection of human influences: the clearance of the forest begun by Ngati Toa and their allies, the fires of the farmers who followed them and the browsing animals liberated first by whalers and traders, then by acclimatisation societies. Wilkinson sought to remove the pests and to assist the healing of those scars and, at the same time, to create a refuge for plants at risk on the mainland.

At the peak of the possum eradication campaign, Kapiti was covered by a network of tracks totalling more than 800 kilometres, cut by the possum hunters who combed the island.

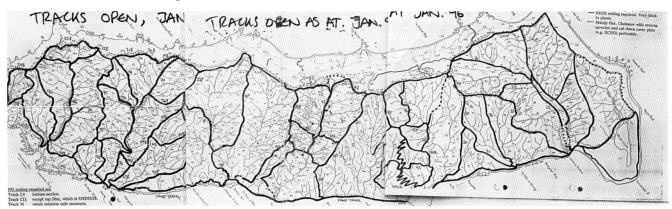

Today only the main tracks are kept open for the work of scientists and volunteers. A glance at a section of the track map suggests it should be easy to move around the island but, in reality, the terrain is so steep and rugged that it is often difficult and surprisingly slippery. Apart from the two tracks to the Trig, which are frequented by the public, the remainder are seldom used and are becoming overgrown. The dense layer of leaves that builds up on the ground, especially under five finger forest and in the cloud zone, traps moisture which creates a greasy layer underfoot. The possum hunters overcame this problem by wearing ice crampons.

Other forms of human intervention, especially pest eradication campaigns, have also influenced the ecology of a number of New Zealand's island refuges in recent times. This is, perhaps, most evident on Kapiti. Of our island sanctuaries it is the most accessible to the public and provides an ideal showcase for the remarkable benefits of eradication. Take, for example, the elimination of possums from Kapiti, which was achieved by a small group of determined trappers between 1982 and 1986. Their efforts have done more than any other recent initiative to allow the island's forests and wildlife to regenerate to their full potential. The trappers' commitment and tenacity were reminiscent of the efforts of the early caretakers to rid Kapiti of wild cattle, goats and sheep.

It has been estimated that each night the possums on Kapiti consumed more than 14 tonnes of plant material.[31] Not only did their rapacity retard regeneration and, in some instances, virtually exterminate species such as fuchsia, but it also denied birds and other species the full potential of the island's forests. Furthermore, growing evidence from elsewhere indicates that possums also raid birds' nests to eat their eggs. Now that the last of the browsing mammals have finally gone, the results are obvious. Everywhere new growth is evident – from the tops of the trees where the leaves are so thick that light barely penetrates, to the forest floor where young seedlings abound. The birds have also benefited. Sightings of kereru, for example, which eat large quantities of berries, have more than doubled since the possums were eradicated,[32] and the greater density of plant species now supports a wider range of birds.

Similarly, the eradication of rats on Kapiti in the 1990s has shown that they also inhibited regeneration by their browsing of flowers, fruits and seeds. Although, at the time of writing, a full scientific assessment of the effects of the eradication of rats had yet to be completed, early indications suggest that their removal, along with the eradication of possums, may allow the island's flora and fauna to reach their true potential for the first time in almost 200 years.

If the first feature of the island that impresses visitors is its bird life, the second should be its forests. Even a short walk in the bush near Rangatira, on either

When parts of Kapiti were farmed, much of the island's vegetation was subdued by fires or erased altogether by sheep, cattle and goats. Once farming was abandoned (with the exception of the northern end), and these animals were exterminated, the island's diverse natural mantle slowly began to reappear. The Kapiti of today offers visitors a glimpse of this variety. They disembark at Rangatira Point where a regenerating wetland and patches of coastal forest are rapidly reclaiming the grassland of an earlier era.

As visitors climb the tracks to the Trig, they pass through an ever changing sequence of forest types. Near sea level, a profusion of kohekohe and young nikau palms create a sub-tropical forest. Higher up, on the steep ridges, tawa, kamahi, kanuka, toro, hinau and rata predominate. Above 300 metres, the greater rainfall is evident in the understorey of tree ferns and the filmy ferns that cling to trunks and branches.

the Trig or Wilkinson Tracks, offers glimpses of a luxuriant world. Young nikau create a dense undergrowth beneath a glossy canopy of kohekohe. Further up the hillside, flowers falling from a grove of young rata make a red carpet underfoot and the noise of birds feeding on the nectar is almost deafening. Although today's forest consists of a different variey of plant species from those described by the scientist aboard the *Tory*, all around are signs of growth and well-being that suggest the return of Dieffenbach's 'very vigorous vegetation'.

Cloud frequently caps the island and often forms a shape similar to Kapiti itself.

The sub-alpine ambience of the cloud forest is quite different from the almost tropical feeling of the bush just a few hundred metres below.

CHAPTER FOUR

A GLIMPSE OF GONDWANA

The kiwi, our most famous bird, is an enigma for it barely resembles a bird at all. It has only vestigial wings and does not fly, relying instead on short, strong legs that enable it to move with surprising speed. The kiwi has a well-developed sense of smell; nostrils near the tip of its long bill allow it to find food on the forest floor, even at night – the time when kiwi are most active.

These curious creatures belong to a family of flightless birds, called ratites, which lived on the ancient super-continent of Gondwanaland. When it broke up to form the world we know, ratites were dispersed. New Zealand once had a range of them, including 11 species of moa, but kiwi are the only survivors today, and even they are in danger of extinction.

When John Gould published this hand-coloured lithograph in the mid-19th century, kiwi were common throughout New Zealand. But the loss of their forest habitat and the ravages of a variety of introduced predators have reduced numbers to the point where their survival cannot be taken for granted.

Fortunately, kiwi were released on Kapiti Island early this century. These liberations have paid a great dividend. Among those released may have been the little spotted kiwi, which is now extinct on the mainland. On Kapiti, however, it has flourished. The island's 1000 birds are now the largest group anywhere, of this, the smallest of the six different types of kiwi.

Little spotted kiwi *(Apteryx owenii) by John Gould, 1848.*

KAPITI'S abundant and unusual bird life offers visitors a unique window on the past, an opportunity to see what our forest inhabitants may have been like before Europeans came. The island is one of three nature reserves that provide endangered forest birds with a secure habitat but the other two, Little Barrier Island (Hauturu) in the Hauraki Gulf and Codfish Island near Stewart Island, are isolated and seldom visited. Kapiti, on the other hand, is just a 10-minute boat journey from Paraparaumu and is visited by more than 10,000 people a year. It is ideally situated to be a showcase for endangered forest birds.

It is also the only island refuge that has both kiwi and weka. Visitors are unlikely to see a kiwi because of its nocturnal nature but an encounter with a weka can almost be guaranteed. The weka's curiosity draws them to people and recent research has shown that the greatest number are found near the public walking tracks.[1] All a visitor needs to do is to pause and remain still and, within a minute or two, a weka (as well as other birds) will soon appear.

The presence of these flightless birds on Kapiti is a reminder that, not so long ago, our forests were populated by a wonderful range of unusual ground-dwelling birds. When the earliest Polynesian explorers arrived here they found birds as strange and exotic as any in the world. The ratites of ancient Aotearoa shared a common ancestry with species found elsewhere in the Southern Hemisphere such as the African ostrich, South American rhea and Australian cassowary and emu.[2]

When Gondwana broke up (about 80 million years ago) the ratites were dispersed. Aotearoa was unusual because it had no mammals (other than bats) and in its isolation new species evolved. The moa, for example, thrived here, its successful adaptation evident in the 11 different species that developed. The tallest stood more than 2 metres high and weighed up to 270 kilograms; the smallest was only one-tenth of that size.[3]

Much later, perhaps as recently as 40 million years ago, moa were joined by other birds when the ancestors of takahe and weka flew across the sea to reach these shores. In the absence of mammalian predators they, too, evolved into new species and took on some of the characteristics of mammals. Because they no longer needed to fly, they gradually lost their wings. Other species, like the moa, became herbivores (plant eaters), foraging for food on the forest floor. Kiwi became like hedgehogs, sniffing out delicacies in the soil, while weka took on the role of rats, adding birds' eggs and the remains of other birds to their diet of invertebrates and fruit. Takahe and kakapo became flightless, grew larger and became mainly herbivorous. Smaller forest species such as kokako, huia and tieke retained the ability to fly although they often foraged on the ground.[4]

The first humans to inhabit Aotearoa found these flightless birds easy to catch and within perhaps 500 years, many species (most notably moa) had been hunted to extinction. Uncontrolled fires, lit by hunters, destroyed large areas of their forest habitat and predatory flying birds such as the giant eagle, which depended on a diet of flightless birds, also became extinct as their prey disappeared. Early Maori continued to hunt the surviving species, often by firing the forest. They brought with them kiore (the Pacific rat) and kuri (dogs), which increased the number of predators, and Gondwana's legacy of birds was rapidly reduced. By the time Europeans began to arrive in the late 18th century it is thought that about one-third of native bird species had become extinct.[5] Even so, what remained was still remarkable. Kiwi, kakapo and takahe were unlike anything to be found in the woods of England or the forests of Europe.

Early European settlement was limited to a few strategic locations, of which Kapiti was one, but the arrival of the first of the New Zealand Company settlers in 1840 marked the beginning of large-scale immigration. Kapiti was one of the first places to be farmed and its bird life, probably already severely depleted by the influx of Ngati Toa and their allies in the 1820s, soon succumbed to the invasion.

We know what the island looked like at this time because Ernst Dieffenbach left a written account and his colleague, Charles Heaphy, painted several views of Kapiti from the sea. Unfortunately, no description of the island's bird life is known to exist so it remains unclear which species were naturally present. The little spotted kiwi is a typical example. Some scientists argue that it was always on Kapiti and has flourished since the island became a reserve, but it is also possible that the species only became established on Kapiti as a result of liberations of kiwi early in the 20th century.

The latter seems more likely because there are no references to flightless birds such as kiwi and weka in the accounts of those who knew Kapiti during the early years of European contact in the 1830s. Jerningham Wakefield, for example, makes no mention of either bird although he went hunting on the island and also shared a Christmas feast, which included roast duck, with the Kapiti whalers.[6] If either bird had been on the menu, Wakefield would have sampled it; on his travels in the Cook Strait region he tried kaka, kereru, pukeko and tui – the latter, he noted, had a 'particularly sweet flavour and was very tender'.[7]

The conspicuous absence of flightless birds in Wakefield's (and Dieffenbach's) descriptions suggests that these species had already been wiped out on Kapiti. As many as several thousand Maori may have lived there in the 20 years before the arrival of the *Tory*. The value of weka and kiwi as easily caught sources of protein would have made their extinction likely.

Eager, young, gun-carrying Englishmen like Wakefield were less of a threat to New Zealand's flightless birds than the array of mammalian predators that accompanied the flood of immigrants brought by the New Zealand Company. As settlement spread throughout New Zealand, flightless birds were ill prepared to survive the onslaught. They were destroyed at an alarming rate by cats, dogs, ferrets, possums, rats, stoats and weasels so that, by the end of the 19th century, many native bird species were in danger of extinction.

This did not worry the majority of settlers who were preoccupied with establishing themselves in their new land, clearing the bush for farms and building houses, bridges and roads. They were probably unaware of the impact of introduced predators, or the effects of deforestation and swamp drainage on native bird life. Among those who did notice, the prevalent view was simply that the displacement of these birds by European species was inevitable, taken for granted as part of the superiority of the Old World. Fortunately, a minority of far-sighted colonists did not accept this imperial notion. They recognised the uniqueness of our birds and lobbied successive governments to set aside a series of islands as sanctuaries where these species might have some hope of survival.

Their campaign coincided with a developing, though tentative, sense of New Zealand's national identity which, ironically, was depicted in images of native birds. Then, as now, an essential element of value seemed to be scarcity. In 1898, for example, a series of stamps featuring New Zealand scenes and birds was issued, replacing, for the first time, the familiar image of Queen Victoria.[8] Just as the term 'Maoriland' became popular towards the end of the century and was used to evoke the romantic notion of a fast disappearing indigenous culture (the Maori population reached its lowest point in the 1890s), so pictures of huia, kaka, kea and kiwi became symbols of the emerging nation.

The major policies of the Liberal government of the 1890s were to continue to create more farmland by clearing native forests and to break up the big estates for the benefit of aspiring small farmers. But it also responded to conservationists' concerns about the plight of native birds. Towards the close of the century, three islands were made bird sanctuaries: Resolution, in Fiordland's Dusky Sound (1891), Little Barrier in the Hauraki Gulf (1894) and finally Kapiti (1897). The last two took some time to acquire because their Maori owners were reluctant to part with them.

Once these reserves had been set aside, the government seemed disinclined to do more. It had more pressing issues to resolve and, as the concept of island sanctuaries was a novel one, there were few – if any – examples to follow. Initially, only Resolution Island was actively managed and then only because of the extraordinary energy and vision of one man, Richard Henry. His transfer of endangered birds from the mainland to Resolution Island was the first such campaign anywhere in the world.

Henry's efforts were not restricted to Fiordland. He also sent birds to more distant destinations including reserves, government departments, botanical gardens, exhibitions and private collections.[9] It seems he did not, however, send any birds to Kapiti. The first known transfer of a flightless species to the island occurred in 1896 when Captain Fairchild of the *Hinemoa* (a government supply ship) brought a pair of Stewart Island weka to Kapiti. The birds were given to Wi Parata, the chief of the Waikanae district, who liberated them on his farm at the northern end of the island. But the weka were in poor condition and only the male survived.

RICHARD HENRY

Born in Ireland, Henry soon moved with his family to Australia, then to New Zealand. He led the life of a colonial rolling stone, drifting from job to job before taking up farming on the shores of Lake Te Anau. Increasingly fascinated by birds and plants, Henry was among those who lobbied for Resolution Island to become a sanctuary. He became an authority on native birds, in particular the kakapo, but his conservationist views isolated him among his peers. Nor was he accepted by scientists, who were sceptical of his theories about kakapo behaviour. Spurned by the woman he loved, he abandoned Fiordland for Auckland, but found little solace there. He even attempted suicide.

His appointment, in 1894, as caretaker of Resolution Island was a welcome turning point in his unhappy life. The job revitalised Henry and he enthusiastically set to work transferring rare native birds from the mainland to the nearby sanctuary. During the next six years he moved more than 700 flightless birds, mainly kiwi and kakapo, to Resolution and other islands in Dusky Sound. He usually worked alone, often in atrocious weather, driven by a determination to ensure that at least some of these remarkable birds survived. Regrettably, they did not.

In March 1900, tourists told Henry they had seen a weasel chasing a weka along a beach on Resolution Island. He thought it a joke but a few months later, he, too, saw one and realised that his efforts were doomed. Even so, for the next 91 days he tried to trap the mustelid, using every strategy he could devise, but the crafty creature eluded him.

The knowledge that Resolution now harboured predators brought back Henry's despondency. Although he remained caretaker for another nine years, his attitude changed. Not surprisingly, he stopped transferring birds and it soon became evident that those already released on Resolution were disappearing. Richard Henry's morale was sapped further by fishermen and hunters who landed illegally on Resolution and brought dogs and guns ashore with them. In 1908 the Lands Department, concerned for his health and mental state, transferred him to Kapiti Island.

Despite the failure of his Resolution Island campaign, Henry's effort was remarkable, a landmark in New Zealand and world conservation history. His was the first programme of systematic bird transfers anywhere and it was another 70 years before anything on that scale was attempted again in this country.

Another female, probably of the local North Island variety, was obtained and released as a replacement, and the many weka on the island today are descended from this pair.[10] Their mixed origins, seemingly unimportant a century ago, are significant today because the birds on Kapiti, one of the few surviving populations of weka anywhere, are hybrid. For this reason the Department of Conservation has been reluctant to allow their transfer to areas where the genetic integrity of other weka might be threatened.

The next liberation occurred in 1907 when Dr Leonard Cockayne released a dozen Antipodes Island parakeets, a similar number of yellow crowned parakeets and some Auckland Island ducks on Kapiti.[11] A year before, Cockayne had prepared for the Lands Department a comprehensive botanical report on the island, which concluded with a strong plea that it be managed as a plant and animal

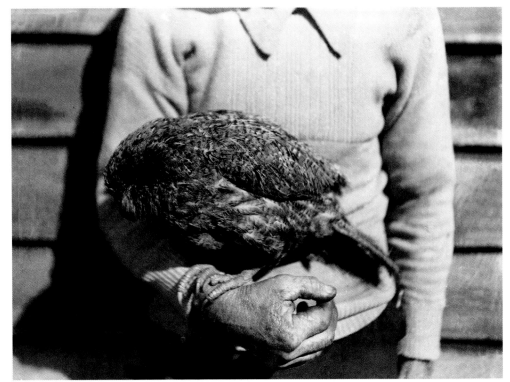

sanctuary. The liberation of these birds, together with the transfer of some rare plants from the Auckland Islands, was Cockayne's contribution. Today, however, neither the birds nor his rare plants are found on Kapiti.

In 1908 Richard Henry arrived to take up the job of caretaker. He brought with him a pair of tokoeka (South Island brown kiwi), which were liberated on the reserve, but that was the only transfer he made. The invasion of Resolution by predators seems to have broken Henry's spirit and his time on Kapiti was as passive as his last years on the southern sanctuary. This was apparent in his approach to noxious animals on the island; he befriended the goats that destroyed the vegetation, arguing that they should not be shot because they kept the grass in check, which reduced the risk of fire.

He also allowed wild cats to roam freely because he considered they kept the rats down. Most human interference was, he argued, misguided. He used Kapiti as an example:

> Both goats and cats have been here for a very long time and yet have left this place nearer to the old order of things than any other place I know. Nearly every turn that we have done towards improving Nature's arrangements in NZ has turned out to be a mistake and that makes me very cautious of interfering where things have been long established and are doing fairly well.[12]

Henry was more concerned at the illegal landings made by local people who came ashore at Wharekohu to steal sheep, and the fishermen who seemed to delight, as their counterparts in Fiordland had done, in defying the caretaker's tenuous authority.[13]

It was not until J. L. Bennett succeeded Henry as caretaker in 1912 that Kapiti really began to function as a bird sanctuary. In that year the Inspector of Scenic Reserves, Edward Phillips-Turner, released three kakapo and five South

Island kiwi on the island. 'The birds were in good heart when let go and should succeed on the island,' he noted.[14] Later he may also have released other species. Wilkinson recalled Phillips-Turner saying that he had also released 'some kiwi that came from the Wanganui district' and, later, several sick kiwi found in the North Island by motorists were also set free on Kapiti.[15] Again, we do not know what species they were but it is assumed that they were North Island brown kiwi.

The fate of these birds illustrates some of the difficulties inherent in transferring endangered species to new locations. Phillips-Turner's kakapo, for example, did not survive, although one lingered on until the late 1930s,[16] but their decline was most likely because only male birds were released on Kapiti. Without breeding partners, they had no prospect of establishing a long-term population. The brown kiwi fared better and today their population numbers between perhaps 50 and 100. But the species that has undoubtedly thrived is the weka, which is present in large numbers. Even so, their existence on the island has been contentious since some consider that weka threaten kiwi by attacking their eggs.[17]

In the 1930s Stan Wilkinson noticed that weka also killed young birds of all varieties. He described how the noise made by young birds in their nests while being fed attracts the weka and 'it will haunt that place until the young birds leave home on the off chance that one or more will fall to the ground'.[18] He also observed that both robins and tomtits were regular victims of weka, which may explain

Weka, by Sylvia Lovell.

The presence of many weka on Kapiti pose a quandry. Although they are part of Gondwana's legacy, their predatory habits threaten insects, lizards and other invertebrates. They may also attack young kiwi and tieke. But it is unlikely that weka will ever be removed because their curiosity and entertaining antics make them popular with visitors.
RAY LOVELL COLLECTION

PETER DANIEL

The saddleback, or tieke, is a wattle bird with distinctive orange jowls on either side of its throat and a broad ochre band across its back, the source of its name. It is a member of the wattle bird family, *Callaeidae*, which also includes kokako and the extinct huia.

Its history is all too familiar. Like the huia, tieke were ill equipped to survive the onslaught of introduced predators that accompanied European settlement. But whereas the huia quickly became extinct, some saddlebacks survived on a handful of islands. The South Island species (not present on Kapiti) came perilously close to extinction in 1964 when a boat accidentally brought rats to Big South Cape Island. Within a year, the number of rodents reached plague proportions and three of four endangered bird species on the island were wiped out. The saddlebacks were saved by the Wildlife Service, which transferred the survivors to predator-free islands. This was the first major translocation campaign since Richard Henry's Resolution Island days. Since that emergency, bird transfers have become an essential part of the management of endangered species.

The North Island variety is more numerous but is still threatened. During the 1970s and 1980s saddlebacks were regularly released on Kapiti but failed to become established because of attacks by rats. Since the rodents were eradicated, however, the number of tieke fledglings has increased significantly, which suggests they will now thrive on Kapiti.

why the South Island robin, recorded by both Cockayne and Bennett as being present on Kapiti Island early this century, is no longer found there.

Weka are wise as other species are naïve. They are, for instance, very protective of their own eggs. 'From the time the first egg is laid until the chicks are old enough to leave the nest, one or both parents are always close to the nest,' wrote Wilkinson in his book on Kapiti.[19] Consequently the island's weka population may number several thousand, although the total fluctuates. But the fact that the population of little spotted kiwi is also substantial suggests that, despite the predatory nature of weka, both birds have found a balance within the island's ecosystem. For this reason, eradication of weka would seem to be unnecessary.

Raewyn Empson, a conservation scientist who has worked with endangered wildlife on Kapiti for more than a decade, cradles a takahe chick in her hand.

Work with endangered species is highly sought after. Empson, who has degrees in zoology and anthropology, first came into contact with rare birds while working for the Wildlife Service. Each year she spent her annual leave as a volunteer on Kapiti and elsewhere, helping with the saddleback and other wildlife programmes. That invaluable experience eventually led to a job with DOC managing threatened species. Such is the attraction of this kind of work that, overseas, it is common for people to pay for the opportunity to work with endangered species.

The greatest threat to Kapiti's birds has been rats. Kiore, the Pacific rat, has probably been on the island since the beginning of Maori occupation and when Europeans began to arrive it was joined by the Norway rat. Fortunately, the most agile rat of all, the ship rat, never made it to Kapiti. Had it done so, the birds would have been destroyed, owing to the ship rat's ability to climb trees and raid nests high up among the branches. But, even without the ship rat, birds have still suffered, especially saddlebacks and stitchbirds. Both species were once known on Kapiti but seem to have died out during the 19th century. In 1925 Stan Wilkinson and his friend, Captain E. V. Sanderson (secretary of the Native Bird Protection Society), visited Hen Island, off the Northland coast near Whangarei, to capture saddlebacks for release on Kapiti. At first the four males and five females seemed to thrive, and Wilkinson even thought he saw signs of successful breeding. However, his optimism was ill-founded; the saddlebacks were vulnerable because they nested and roosted in holes in trees close to the forest floor, which made it easy for rats to

A volunteer, Arnold Heine, spreading rat bait by hand at Waiorua during the eradication campaign.
JAN HEINE

get at them. This was especially so on Kapiti in the 1920s where the young forest provided few suitable cavities. By 1932 saddlebacks were no longer seen on Kapiti.[20]

During the 1980s attempts were made to reintroduce saddlebacks to Kapiti but, again, the liberations were largely unsuccessful because of rats. It was not until Tim Lovegrove, the scientist in charge of the transfers, placed hundreds of specially designed nesting and roosting boxes on the trunks of trees – well above the ground – that the saddlebacks began to survive in sufficient numbers to offer some hope. Even so, the boxes did not guarantee their safety because not all birds learned to use them, or taught their chicks to do so. Those saddlebacks that adapted were still vulnerable to other predators, particularly moreporks, which were able to raid boxes fixed at any height. As a result, mortality rates remained high.

While Lovegrove and his volunteer helpers struggled to outwit the relentless rodents and set up rat control programmes in specific areas, they contemplated what Kapiti might be like if it were entirely free of these predators. But in their hearts they knew it was only a dream.[21] Rats had recently been eradicated from a number of islands but these were all small – just a fraction of Kapiti's size. In the early 1990s, however, the outlook began to change. New, more effective toxins were developed and spreading techniques, especially aerial application, were refined to achieve greater accuracy. But the real breakthrough, discovered as a result of the campaigns on small islands, was that 'non-target' species, in particular rare birds such as kaka and kiwi, were not tempted by the new baits.

In 1990 the Pharazyn Trust of Waikanae expressed an interest in supporting conservation work on the island. Trustee Shane Treadwell had seen a television documentary about the eradication of rats from Breaksea Island (in Fiordland) and wondered whether it might be possible to do the same for Kapiti. The trust gave the Department of Conservation $32,000 for a feasibility study.[22] Conservation officer Raewyn Empson, who had helped Tim Lovegrove with some of the attempts to establish saddlebacks on Kapiti and shared his dream of a predator-free island, spent the next two years conducting trials to see if, and how, it could be done. One of the complications she encountered was finding a way to eliminate two species of rat at the same time while ensuring that all other species remained unaffected.[23] She also consulted extensively with local iwi.

After considerable research, she concluded that aerial eradication was feasible. The Pharazyn Trust undertook to provide $300,000 towards the cost, on the understanding that the government would contribute a similar amount. A further three years were spent planning the campaign in exhaustive detail. All contingencies had to be explored to develop a proposal that would satisfy the

It has sometimes been suggested that the private properties at Waiorua pose an unacceptable risk to the sanctuary because boats landing there may inadvertently reintroduce rats to Kapiti. Although that possibility should not be ignored, it is in the interests of iwi who stay on the island to be vigilant since they know from bitter experience just what a menace rats can be.

Don Watson, who used to stay at Waiorua when he was a boy, later recalled that 'while sleeping in the back you would hear a scuttle and a rat would run across your blankets. There were so many of them they would even appear in daylight.' Now the rats are gone and Waiorua is a different place. Kaka, takahe and other rare birds frequent the gardens that were once the domain of rodents and kakariki and tieke are expected to become established in the surrounding forest.

If rats return to Kapiti they will most probably do so as a result of an illegal boat landing. To protect against this possibility, rat bait stations, marked by white poles, have been placed in likely locations near the shoreline.

Ani Parata lives in two worlds: she is active among iwi on the Kapiti Coast and is a member of the Wellington Conservation Board. For her, the eradication of rats from Kapiti promises far more than just the survival of endangered birds; it is a symbol of better relations between iwi, and between Maori and Pakeha.

'If we didn't get rid of the rats on Kapiti we were going to have rats gnawing at all of us over here. That's how I viewed it, from a spiritual dimension. Rats were causing so much trouble over there in the bird world. If we could get rid of those rats we could stop this nonsense in the human world as well.

'Rats gnaw away at everything. They destroy things. They are a nuisance. This has been happening in Maoridom – we've been gnawed at in different ways.

'Getting rid of the rats on Kapiti will build a better future for all of us. One of the things this country can build on in terms of relationships is conservation. This shows the way, shows that we can work together because we have a common goal.'

scrutiny of the resource consent process. Two trial drops of non-toxic bait revealed that most kaka and kiwi were not tempted by the bait but that several other species, namely brown teal, pukeko, robins, takahe and weka might be at risk – especially the latter, two-thirds of which showed traces of having eaten the pellets.[24] As a result of these trials, robins were transferred to Mana Island, while weka, teal and takahe were caught and held in captivity. Special cages were built in various locations to protect these species during the campaign. About 100 weka were confined at Waiorua and Rangatira and a similar number were removed from the island by volunteers. Half were taken to the Karori Wildlife Sanctuary in Wellington and the remainder were let loose in the Tauherenikau Valley in the Tararua Ranges. The latter liberation was largely a public relations exercise designed to appease some concerned members of the public who feared 'that two to three thousand wekas would die in an era when many endangered species are becoming extinct'.[25]

In September 1996, after five years of planning, research and consultation, Kapiti Island was dosed with toxic bait from end to end. Most of the island was covered by helicopter, although some small areas were done by hand by volunteers on the ground. Then, to make absolutely sure no rats survived, the island was given a second, equally thorough, shower. In total, 32 tonnes of cereal pellets containing the toxin broadifacoum (at a concentration of 20 parts per million) were spread over Kapiti.[26] Eradication on the adjacent islets was done with bait stations.

The Kapiti campaign was a remarkably ambitious undertaking made possible by the support of the Pharazyn Trust and by advances in eradication technology. The use of a helicopter equipped with a satellite navigation system was also crucial, since scientists could monitor its flight path precisely and so be relatively confident that no areas were missed. A decade earlier, teams of trappers had spent years criss-crossing Kapiti on foot to eradicate possums; now a helicopter did the same to the rats in two and a half days.

Takahe, Wharekohu, 1998.
Takahe were thought to be extinct until some were discovered in Fiordland's Murchison Mountains in 1948. Their survival in that location has given rise to the idea that takahe are alpine birds but, in the past, they dwelt at all altitudes in many areas and are known to have lived on the mainland opposite Kapiti.

This pair of takahe chicks, only a few days old, are about to be separated. Takahe rarely succeed in raising more than one chick at a time, so one will be given to another pair of takahe to increase its chances of survival. The chicks' parents, Taku and Squeak, who live in grassland at Rangatira, are excellent breeders with progeny on four island sanctuaries: Kapiti, Mana, Maud and Tiritiri Matangi. But another pair at Waiorua, called Iti and Lyall, have not produced any offspring so they will be given one of this pair.

Kereru play a vital role in the life of the forest on Kapiti and elsewhere because they eat a variety of fruit, the seeds of which they then disperse.

Once, these elegant agents of forest renewal were abundant throughout the country but their tameness, as well as the ravages of introduced predators, have vastly reduced their numbers.

One 19th-century account gives an indication of how numerous these birds were – and how naïve. In 1839, Jerningham Wakefield camped in a grove of trees on the banks of the Pelorus River. As the sun set, 'a great number' of kereru gathered in the branches above his campsite. He shot them 'as quickly as the fowling pieces were reloaded by the natives', noting that the death of one bird did not disturb 'the equanimity of his companion on the same branch'.

Today, since possums and rats have been eradicated from Kapiti, the island's kereru population is increasing.

In 1999 Kapiti was declared to be free from rats. There have been no signs of the rodents and significant increases in the number of young saddlebacks and stitchbirds suggest that the campaign has been successful.[27]

Ridding the sanctuary of rats is a conservation landmark that has raised expectations among conservationists for other islands elsewhere. Codfish Island, home of half the country's kakapo, was cleared of rats in 1998. Raoul Island (2938 hectares) and Little Barrier Island (3083 hectares) seem logical candidates and, in the future, larger refuges such as Campbell Island (11,400 hectares) and even the Auckland Islands may be considered.[28]

The Kapiti campaign has also boosted New Zealand's profile as a conservation innovator, adding to our already considerable international reputation for the successful management of endangered species, especially on islands. It has also been good for business. In the past three years private conservation specialists, based in New Zealand, have organised rat eradication programmes on islands as far apart as Pitcairn (in the western Pacific), St Paul (in the Indian Ocean) and Madeira (in the Atlantic, near Portugal).[29] Both the expertise and the baits have come from this country.

The implications for Kapiti itself are just as profound. Now that the island has been formally declared free of rats, even more endangered species, including bats, birds, reptiles and invertebrates, may be released on the island. This may be especially useful for forest bird species such as the kakapo, which is perilously close to extinction. At present only about 60 of these remarkable birds survive. They are confined to three islands: Little Barrier, Maud (in the Marlborough Sounds) and Codfish. Kapiti may soon offer an alternative location, entirely free of mammalian predators, where these night parrots may eventually develop a self-sustaining population. Kakapo could become the jewel of Kapiti's forest crown.

But before the kakapo or any other species is introduced, Kapiti needs a long-term strategy. The history of earlier liberations is one of occasional well-intentioned initiatives without any overall plan. A restoration strategy is on the Department

In the past, visitors were encouraged to feed kaka on Kapiti – even the caretakers fed them. But when the daily quota of visitors was increased, the kaka came to depend on tourists for their daily diet of dates and other delicacies. At times, according to retired ranger Peter Daniel, as many as 65 kaka would descend on Rangatira when the boat arrived and pester the visitors. Kaka would also target people at the Trig and try to raid their lunches.

Although visitors are now warned not to feed these boisterous parrots, kaka will still sometimes land on a visitor's head, or an outstretched hand, especially if they suspect there is food to be had.
STEPHANIE DREW

Until recently, North Island kokako were on the brink of extinction, like their South Island counterparts, but in the last few years they have become one of the success stories of endangered species management. In 1991, 33 kokako were transferred to Kapiti. Since then, some have bred, which suggests kokako may be becoming established on the island.

Although they are rarely seen, their mournful song is most likely to be heard in tawa forest, their favourite habitat.
DICK VEITCH, DEPARTMENT OF CONSERVATION

A map of listening posts on the Trig and McKenzie Tracks.

Four times a year, members of the Ornithological Society of New Zealand (OSNZ) spend a weekend on Kapiti counting bird calls. Each volunteer is assigned one of six 'lines', or tracks, which have designated listening points marked at regular intervals. There are two lines at the northern end (on the Okupe and Waiorua Tracks), two in the middle (on the McKenzie and Trig Tracks) and another two towards the southern end (on the Te Mimi Spur and Loop Tracks).

The volunteers walk from point to point, pausing at each for five minutes to record numbers of birds seen and heard. They also note weather conditions at the time, as these affect the birds. Strong winds, for example, deter birds so fewer call and those that do are harder to hear.

Visitors using the Trig or McKenzie Tracks may see small OSNZ markers on trees. It is a rewarding exercise to stop for a few minutes and listen. More birds are heard than seen but fantails, robins, tomtits, whiteheads and weka soon appear and will often come close to a patient observer.

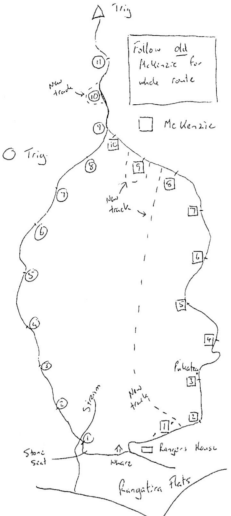

of Conservation's agenda but is unlikely to be completed before the end of this century because time is needed to determine the full range of species on the island; some, such as lizards, may have been severely subdued by rats and will take time to recover.[30] In the meantime, the sanctuary's future can be debated.

Ideally this should include consideration of the island's role in a regional, as well as a national, context. Kapiti's value as a sanctuary for endangered forest birds is well known, but its relationship to the other islands within the Wellington region is still being defined. In recent years, two other islands in the vicinity, neighbouring Mana (off the coast north of Porirua) and Matiu/Somes Island (in Wellington Harbour), have been earmarked for restoration. Both these islands, like Kapiti, are free of rodents but are covered with grassland, not forest. They offer an unparalleled opportunity to create or restore ecosystems; or, a cynic might say, to play God.

Matiu and Mana are being restored as sanctuaries for plants and animals typical of the Cook Strait region, with a particular emphasis on seabirds, invertebrates and reptiles. In 1996, for example, two species of weta were released on Matiu; in 1998 tuatara were liberated there and gecko and rare skinks may follow. On Mana, considerable effort is being made to establish colonies of endangered seabirds such as fluttering shearwaters, fairy prions, diving petrels and gannets. Both islands may also be used to experiment with the replacement of extinct species. One possibility, for example, would be to release alpine rock wrens on the island(s) in the hope that they might eventually evolve to resemble the extinct bush wren, once common at low altitude.[31]

Kapiti, by contrast, is already largely defined. It is covered with forest and already has a remarkable range of forest birds. It seems logical to build on what is already there and to continue to develop it as a forest bird sanctuary. In fact, with little spotted kiwi and weka in abundance, as well as kaka, kereru, kokako, saddlebacks and stitchbirds, it comes closer than any other sanctuary to resembling the pre-European mainland forests of Aotearoa. Together with Mana and Matiu, it offers an unprecedented opportunity to restore the biodiversity of an entire region.

Kapiti is poised on the brink of a new era. During the past 20 years the last of the noxious animals – possums and rats – have been eradicated and the birds and the bush are flourishing. The island offers visitors an antidote to a world in which

Geoff de Lisle (left) and Allan Munro counting little spotted kiwi calls at night, January 1997.

Volunteers play a crucial role on Kapiti. One of the many jobs they undertake is counting bird calls. Sometimes they may focus on a particular species; at other times they record all calls heard. The information gathered is invaluable. It allows scientists to assess the effect of various programmes, such as the possum and rat eradications, on bird numbers.
GARTH BAKER

environmental degradation seems inexorable. Here is a place where people can look back into the past and contemplate the process of 'civilisation' that has led to the conspicuous silence of our mainland forests. Each glimpse of Gondwana is an education. When visitors carry that understanding back to the mainland they add new voices to the growing chorus of concern about the fate of our forests and their inhabitants.

CHAPTER FIVE

THE NEW FRONTIER

The work of making Kapiti Island a successful nature reserve has already been largely achieved. Its future character will be determined by the forests and birds now on the island. There is a little fine tuning to be done – bats, lizards, tuatara and invertebrates may be introduced to broaden the biodiversity – but the island's attractions are already well known and are unlikely to change.

It is the sea surrounding Kapiti that will become the main area for pioneering activity in the years ahead. This vast new frontier was, until recently, largely unknown. In 1991 two areas adjacent to the island were set aside as a marine reserve. As regeneration of the marine life proceeds, these protected areas promise new opportunities for scientists and visitors.

After eight years the signs of recovery are encouraging. If the return of marine life parallels the regeneration of bush and birds on the island itself then, in a century's time, there should be a good deal to celebrate.

SAM MACLEAN

KAPITI'S birds are well known. Many are tagged with small rings of metal or plastic which, attached to their legs in individual combinations, allow scientists to recognise them at a glance. Weka, for example, usually have a pair of bands on each leg which, from a distance, look like ill-matched rugby socks. Some of the rarer species such as kokako and takahe even have names, and their habits are discussed with a familiarity usually reserved for human family or friends.

Our knowledge of the creatures living in the sea around Kapiti is, however, quite sparse. No fish are banded or known by name and, until recently, only local fishermen were familiar with the marine life there. The first official survey of these waters was not completed until 1987, more than a century after the first botanical survey of the island.[1] Interest in the marine environment seems always to have lagged behind developments on the island itself. No assessment of Kapiti's marine life was made until the late 1960s and, even then, it came about through the initiative of a skin-diver rather than a scientific agency or a government department.

Skin-diving competitions can kill a lot of fish. When the national championships were held around Kapiti Island in 1967, for example, more than 870 fish were caught, including hundreds of butterfish, marblefish, moki and red moki, as well as lesser numbers of parrotfish, kahawai and snapper. Among the 150 divers taking part was Peter Rippon, who decided to put this huge fish mortality to good use. He classified the catch by species and by weight, then tabulated the results. He also drew a map of the island's waters showing currents, features of the seabed and the location of various fish species, as well as areas of algae and seaweed.

Three years later, when Kapiti was again the site of a similar contest, Rippon repeated the exercise. Taken together, his two sets of data present an invaluable record of the island's marine world at that time. His observations and statistics also gave credence to the belief, held by generations of locals, that the life in the waters of Kapiti was as rich and varied as that of any marine area in central New Zealand. This was not news to Maori, who were well aware of the abundance of this traditional fishery known as 'he puna kai' (the wellspring of food) or 'he kapata kai' (the food basket).[2]

For almost 20 years, Rippon's results and his undersea map were known only to the spearfishing community until *Dive*, the South Pacific underwater magazine, published them in 1987.[3] The same year, the first official appraisal of Kapiti's marine life also appeared. It was the result of surveys conducted by Andrew Baxter, a fisheries scientist who had spent the previous summer photographing the seascape and studying its recreational use, which had included questioning fishing enthusiasts about their catches. His work was published as two separate reports (an ecological survey and a recreational survey[4]) but, as they were internal reports of the Ministry of Agriculture and Fisheries, they reached only a specialist audience – not the general public as *Dive* had done.

Baxter's ecological report complemented Rippon's research. At long last, a picture of what lay beneath the waves was available. It showed that the forces that had shaped the island, particularly earthquakes and strong winds, also influenced the marine environment. On the northern, western and southern sides, powerful wind-driven sea currents scour the seafloor, which consists mainly of rock. The water on these three sides is clear and butterfish, moki and butterfly perch are common. On the sheltered eastern side, however, where the currents slacken and drop their load of sediment, the water is not as clear and the seafloor is made up of a deep layer of sand and gravel. Some of this is eroded debris from Kapiti's cliffs, which is swept around the island by strong currents, and some is detritus from the Waikanae River. On this side of the island, spotties, eagle rays, goatfish, blue cod

OPPOSITE PAGE *The waters around Kapiti are thought to be the only marine environment near the west coast of the North Island where four distinct habitats are found in such close proximity.*
MINISTRY OF AGRICULTURE AND FISHERIES AND THE DEPARTMENT OF CONSERVATION

THE FOUR DISTINCTIVE HABITAT ZONES FOUND AROUND KAPITI ISLAND
(from A. S. Baxter, 'Kapiti Island – Subtidal ecological survey', Ministry of Agriculture and Fisheries)

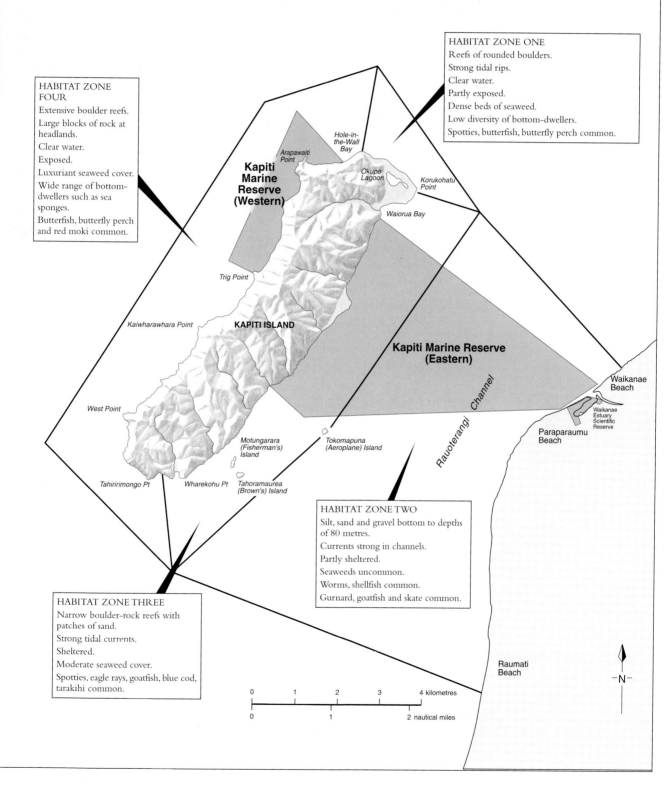

HABITAT ZONE FOUR
Extensive boulder reefs.
Large blocks of rock at headlands.
Clear water.
Exposed.
Luxuriant seaweed cover.
Wide range of bottom-dwellers such as sea sponges.
Butterfish, butterfly perch and red moki common.

HABITAT ZONE ONE
Reefs of rounded boulders.
Strong tidal rips.
Clear water.
Partly exposed.
Dense beds of seaweed.
Low diversity of bottom-dwellers.
Spotties, butterfish, butterfly perch common.

HABITAT ZONE THREE
Narrow boulder-rock reefs with patches of sand.
Strong tidal currents.
Sheltered.
Moderate seaweed cover.
Spotties, eagle rays, goatfish, blue cod, tarakihi common.

HABITAT ZONE TWO
Silt, sand and gravel bottom to depths of 80 metres.
Currents strong in channels.
Partly sheltered.
Seaweeds uncommon.
Worms, shellfish common.
Gurnard, goatfish and skate common.

Kapiti Marine Reserve (Western)

Kapiti Marine Reserve (Eastern)

KAPITI ISLAND

Hole-in-the-Wall Bay
Arapawaiti Point
Okupe Lagoon
Korukohatu Point
Waiorua Bay
Trig Point
Kaiwharawhara Point
West Point
Motungarara (Fisherman's) Island
Tokomapuna (Aeroplane) Island
Tahiririmongo Pt
Wharekohu Pt
Tahoramaurea (Brown's) Island
Rauoterangi Channel
Waikanae Beach
Waikanae Estuary Scientific Reserve
Paraparaumu Beach
Raumati Beach

0 1 2 3 4 kilometres
0 1 2 nautical miles

–N–

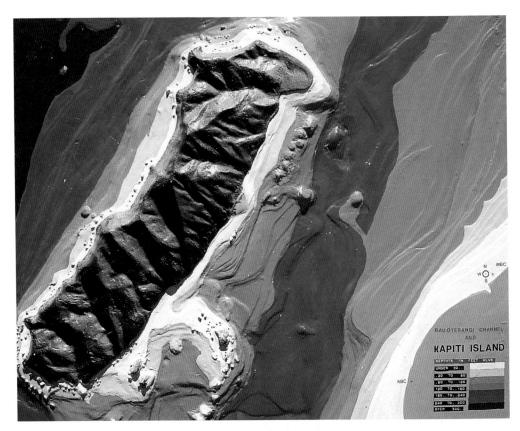

This model at the Waikanae Boating Club shows the underwater terrain around the island.

and tarakihi are common. Further from the shore, towards the middle of Rau O Te Rangi Channel, worms and shellfish as well as gurnard and skate predominate.

The contours of the seascape are an extension of the land. On three sides Kapiti's cliffs continue under the sea, whereas the eastern side is shallower and is fringed by an undersea shelf. In contrast to the forest on the island itself, which is limited to the sheltered eastern side, dense forests of seaweed girdle all sides of the island. In places the weed obscures unusual marine features such as beds of lace coral (bryozoans) that can be found on the western side and communities of calcareous algae (rhodoliths) that occur on the eastern side.

The publication of these marine surveys could not have been more timely since, that same year, Kapiti Island was suggested as a suitable site for a marine reserve.[5] The idea was enthusiastically promoted by some local divers and fishers, who recognised that the once abundant fishery around the island was now badly depleted and that something should be done to halt its decline, which had been confirmed by Baxter's report. He noted, for example, that in 1960 snapper were frequently caught in these waters, but during his 1986 survey he saw only one.[6] Even allowing for the migratory habit of this pelagic species, its absence was still a clear indicator of depletion.

One of the people most concerned about the poor state of the fishery was Peter Daniel, the ranger on Kapiti since 1976. He first came to the island when he was 13. During his teenage years he often visited it and had clear memories of the abundant marine life. But when he came to live on Kapiti he found that the fish simply were not there any more. Once he had merely to cast out a line from the rocks north of Rangatira to catch a variety of fish, but now his catches were too poor to be worth the effort. 'There was nothing there, it was just a desert.'[7]

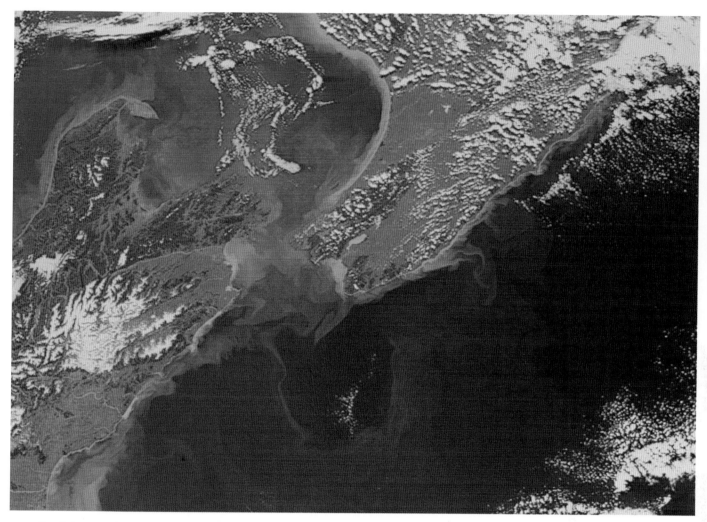

It did not take Peter Daniel long to work out what was happening. In addition to supervising visitors on the island, he was also responsible for inspecting boats fishing around Kapiti to make sure they were observing the regulations. Later he recalled that, between 1976 and 1978, he inspected about 400 boats, 'more than half of which were skin divers' boats. Of these, only about 10 had more than 10 fish but about 5 of those had in excess of 40 fish.' His suspicions were also confirmed by the catches of some line fishermen who 'sometimes had large catches of fish. Of the 175 line fishermen's boats inspected, about 20 caught more than 20 fish and 5 caught more than 40 fish.'[8]

His concerns echoed those of his father, Arthur, who had written to the local paper 20 years earlier about greedy individuals taking more than their share of the abundant sea life. He cited several examples including:

> One man who fishes regularly from Waikanae Beach, is catching up to 50 snapper besides terekihi [sic], hapuka, etc, in a day. A relative of mine caught one hundred and thirty terekihi and other fish one day recently, close to Kapiti. A family from Riki [Reikorangi] dragging, caught four hundred odd flounders and other fish in three nights last week.[9]

But, although the activities of a small group of unscrupulous amateurs clearly contributed to the decline of Kapiti's fishery, the Daniels and others recognised that

Kapiti's marine environment is characterised by the confluence of two currents: the warm, saline d'Urville Current, which flows southward from the Taranaki Bight, and the cooler Canterbury Current, which travels northward through Cook Strait. Because the two overlap, an unusually diverse range of northern and southern species are found in this area.
LANDCARE RESEARCH

G. L. ADKIN, NATIONAL MUSEUM OF NEW ZEALAND/TE PAPA TONGAREWA

FISHERMEN'S HUT ON MOTUNGARARA, 1921
All three of Kapiti's offshore islands have been associated with fishing since whalers lived on them during the 1830s and 1840s. Fishermen returned to live on the two larger islands in the early years of this century. Motungarara became known as Fisherman's Island because of their presence. Fishing families from Paremata and Paraparaumu built rough baches on both islands using a variety of materials, including flattened kerosene tins and stones from the shore. The Johnsons, Watsons and Webbers had huts on Fisherman's Island and the Andrews, Caldwells and Hurrans occupied nearby Brown's Island (Tahoramaurea).

Although fish were plentiful, prices were low so the fishermen had to be self-reliant to survive, especially during the Depression. As a boy, Keith Elliot used to stay with the Johnsons, and he later recalled that 'these fishermen grew all their vegetables on Brown's and Fisherman's Islands. Wonderful gardens – they dug in all their unsaleable fish so the ground was good. They used to make their own nets – it was great to see these fellows. Brave men, earning a living in a tough way with little comfort. At 9.00 pm every night they would be in their whares; dark, dingy, Coleman lamps. Sitting round crystal sets, listening to the weather report. Inside these whares was like "being in the holy of holies". They were interested in only the wind report. You daren't speak, or interrupt them.'[10]

the same destructive practices were also common among the commercial trawlers which regularly passed through Rau O Te Rangi Channel – and their excesses were far greater.

The rape of the resource had, in fact, begun years before, in the 1940s. According to Nolan Best, who fished from Waikanae Beach for many years, 'there's

Eagle rays are common around Kapiti, especially near the eastern shore.
PETER DANIEL

been a big decline in the fishing' which he attributes to the commercial fishing fraternity:

> I used to hop out, for perhaps an hour and a half, and catch all the snapper you'd want and come home. Duck over to the island for a couple of hours and back – fish all over the place. You could catch fish anywhere along this coast in those days, but when the trawlers – it would be during the war – they opened up this inside [Rau O Te Rangi] Channel and the trawlers came in, during the war and right up until three years ago [1984], trawlers would come through and they swept them out.[11]

Other evidence from the post-war period suggests that commercial fishermen exploited the fishery with the same careless disregard for the future as the sawmillers who destroyed virtually all New Zealand's lowland forests in the 19th century. Now the same thing was being done to the sea. In 1957, for instance, the crew of a fishing boat boasted that they had taken 15 tons of fish from the water between Kapiti and Waikanae, and the captain of another vessel admitted that 'having already taken his required catch around Wanganui, he trawled from Te Horo to Paraparaumu, just as an extra, and filled a further 64 cases with fish'.[12] Official records of commercial catches paint a similar picture. In 1952 commercial line fishermen, operating between Raumati and Otaki, harvested 281 hundredweight from the sea; four years later this had increased to 352 hundredweight. Most of the fish caught were snapper.[13]

Not surprisingly, local amateur fishing enthusiasts were alarmed by the activities of some of their commercial colleagues. But when they approached the Marine Department with the suggestion that the water between Kapiti and the mainland be made a restricted fishery (open only to amateurs), the department did not agree. Incredibly, it argued that increasing commercial catches showed the ability of fish stocks to replace those being caught.[14]

Confronted with such myopia, local people had little hope of establishing a protected area. A generation later, however, when the issue re-emerged in 1987,

During the 1980s, Peter Daniel and a number of local diving and fishing enthusiasts led by Mid Beckett wanted to protect Kapiti's fishery but were uncertain how to proceed.

They organised several meetings but made little progress until Daniel came across an article by Bill Ballantine about marine reserves. Ballantine had been involved in the establishment of New Zealand's first two marine reserves at Leigh and around the Poor Knights Island but knowledge of their existence had not reached the Kapiti Coast.

Daniel immediately invited Ballantine to visit Kapiti. He also spoke to a number of local groups – not all of whom gave him a reasonable reception. Nevertheless, his experience allayed some fears and encouraged a wider acceptance of the concept.

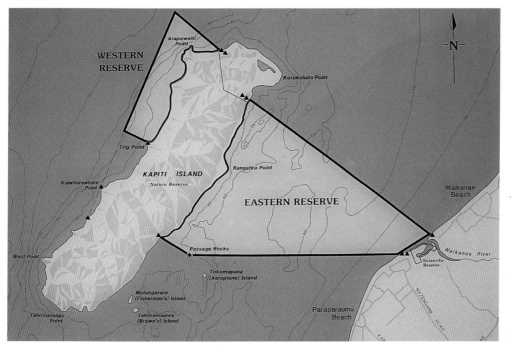

The Kapiti Marine Reserve
consists of two separate
sections: the eastern part (1825
hectares), which extends from
the Waikanae Estuary across
to the island, and the Western
Reserve (342 hectares), which
includes the exposed coastal
waters on the far side of Kapiti
from Arapawaiti Point to just
below the Trig.

The Eastern Reserve
includes rocky reefs and patches
of seaweed on the island's
sheltered shore but out in Rau
O Te Rangi Channel weed is
uncommon because the seabed
is mainly sand and silt. Strong
currents laden with debris limit
visibility.

The Western Reserve is
quite different. It is well
known for its spectacular
underwater scenery: large
boulders, extensive reefs,
luxuriant forests of seaweed,
the submarine 'hole in the
wall' and, on the northern
coast, a series of jumbled rock
stacks that have fallen from
the cliffs above.

the concept of a marine reserve (not just a restricted fishery) was supported by the relevant government agency, the newly formed Department of Conservation.

In the intervening years a new awareness of conservation had evolved. In the late 1960s the struggle to protect Lake Manapouri and, a decade later, a petition to save native forests (signed by more than 700,000 people), were clear signals of an emerging environmental awareness in a nation which, until then, had largely prided itself on clearing forests and taming rivers and lakes for hydro-electricity. Even so, while there was a better understanding of the need for conservation of the land, the application of the same ideas to the sea lagged far behind.

Arguably, this was simply a mental block, for New Zealand's marine environment is as impressive – and as diverse – as its landscape. Fine ocean beaches, wild rocky shores, extensive estuaries, drowned valleys and more than 800 islands constitute a coastal habitat just as spectacular as snow-clad peaks, native forests and geothermal wonders. But, until recently, it was not widely understood that the undersea world, with its kelp forests, sponge gardens, coral structures and shellfish beds, was as vulnerable as any patch of bush. For more than a century the sea was simply a convenient sink into which towns and cities (and their industries) pumped sewage and toxic wastes.

The first sign of an emerging sense of the fragility of coastal marine ecosystems came with the passing of the Marine Reserves Act in 1971. Even then, its primary purpose was scientific. It empowered the Ministry of Agriculture and Fisheries to set aside specific locations 'for the purpose of preserving the area in its natural state as a habitat of marine life for scientific study'.[15]

Four years later, the country's first marine reserve was established near Leigh in Northland. It consisted of a 5-kilometre stretch of coastline between Cape Rodney and Okakari Point which had been a well-known fishing area for generations. Now it was set aside and allowed to regenerate. Twenty-five years later the revitalised marine life in this area has validated the marine reserve concept. Regular scientific monitoring has confirmed that its protection has led to a

One of the duties of the staff on the island is to ensure that the prohibition on fishing in the marine reserve is respected. Few people are found fishing illegally. Of those who are, most plead ignorance. The department's policy, according to coastal marine officer, Bruce Dix, has been focused 'on educating the fishing public' but now that the marine reserve has been established for some years, 'the time has come for us to take a much harder line'.

spectacular recovery. 'Many of the sea animals that had been fished out have returned to enrich the reserve,' states a Department of Conservation paper that goes on to describe how the recovery has benefited not only scientists but also the general public. 'Children can observe crayfish crawling around in shallow water. Red moki, which had been virtually wiped out by the spearfishers, now swim in large groups over kelp beds. Huge snapper also swim over the rocky reefs in search of food. Each year, more than 100,000 people flock to see the abundant marine life in its natural setting, and to swim, picnic and sunbathe.'[16]

A century earlier, when Resolution Island became New Zealand's first reserve for endangered birds in 1892, a rash of reserves followed. In 1894 Hauturu (Little Barrier) became the second bird sanctuary, then Kapiti in 1897. These three well-known islands were soon complemented, after the passing of the Scenery Preservation Act in 1903, by the gazetting of numerous small reserves throughout the country. The marine reserves of the 1980s and 1990s have followed a similar pattern. After Leigh, the waters of the Poor Knights Islands group became New Zealand's second marine reserve in 1981. This was an obvious choice; the archipelago of rocky outcrops surrounded by spectacular underwater scenery and abundant sub-tropical fish was already renowned. Then, in 1990, the sea around the Kermadec Islands (800 kilometres north-east of Auckland) also became a reserve – by far the largest.

Kapiti joined the list in 1991, after extensive public consultation and debate. In making the announcement, the Minister of Conservation, Denis Marshall, noted that 'The water clarity, the impressive big boulders and the wide diversity of flora and fauna together make this an area of very high quality underwater scenery. And it has some outstandingly beautiful natural features such as the "Hole-in-the-wall" on the north-western side of the island.'[17]

These four significant seascapes were joined, within the next three years, by nine further reserves that protected distinctive marine ecosystems from the Hauraki Gulf to Fiordland. Despite this, the total protected area makes up only 4 per cent of New Zealand waters and, if the extensive reserve around the Kermadecs is

deducted, the total amounts to less than 1 per cent of our marine territory. We still have some way to go before the extent of protected sea matches the extent of protected land; more than 30 per cent of the land area is conservation reserve.[18]

Fortunately, at the inception of the Kapiti Marine Reserve an extensive scientific survey was conducted to provide a description of its condition at that time. This will provide a reference point for future studies and will allow the regeneration of marine life to be measured. Since then several limited scientific surveys have added weight to the observations of local divers and fishermen, who maintain that there has been a notable increase in shellfish and a resurgence of heavily fished species such as butterfish and red moki – and that blue cod have doubled in size.[19]

These are encouraging signs. If there are such gains in only five years, what will the reserve be like in 15 or 50 years? Perhaps the rate of regeneration beneath the waves will be as rapid and varied as that on the island and will not only provide a new attraction for visitors but will also be as educational as Kapiti's forests and birds. To offer a natural showcase above and below the tideline will increase the appeal of this already remarkable island.

The Kapiti Marine Reserve may also have other, less obvious benefits. So far it has been managed by the Department of Conservation, with advice provided by a committee of interested members of the public – divers, local fishermen, scientists and the tangata whenua. This involvement is evidence of the department's commitment to consultation with the public and gives effect to its statutory duty of implementing the principles of the Treaty of Waitangi. Not since the heady days of the Tararua Forest Park Advisory Committee (formed in the 1950s in response to widespread public concern about the management of these mountains) and the Kapiti Island Advisory Committee (which was active in the 1960s and 1970s) has the public had such a direct role in conservation management.

What has changed between then and now is that a Maori renaissance has occurred. No longer can local iwi be ignored. Instead, half of the Marine Reserve Advisory Committee must be nominated by the three local iwi most recently

Peter Daniel's (left) experience of patrolling the sea around Kapiti convinced him that a cautionary chat is more effective than a punitive approach. In this instance he advises fishermen from Wanganui that they have been trawling in the reserve. The ranger is also well aware of the practical limits to his authority — he is on his own and, when patrolling on the western side of the island, he is out of radio contact. Prudence is essential.

Little blue penguin, Kapiti.
    These small penguins have always come to Kapiti, especially at breeding time, when they waddle ashore to make their nests in holes in the ground or under fallen trees. Some climb high up the island to return to where they were hatched. The bodies of the casualties of this arduous, instinctive trek are often seen at the bottom of cliffs and waterfalls.
    Since the marine reserve was introduced, the number of little blue penguins has increased.
P. MORRISON, DEPARTMENT OF CONSERVATION

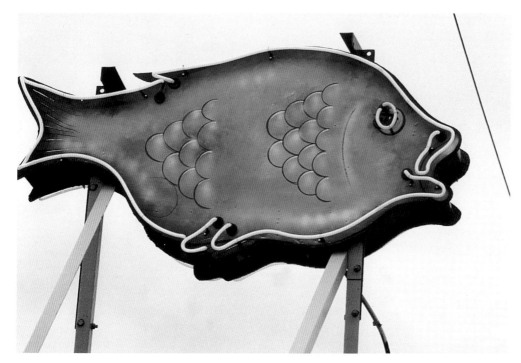

For many years the neon sign above the Kapiti Fish Supply on the main highway at Paraparaumu was as much a local icon as the distinctive statue of the Virgin Mary on a nearby hill. Most of the fish sold there came from Kapiti. At first the shop was owned by Don Watson; later it was bought by 'Kap' and Rewa Webber. It was demolished in the late 1980s to make way for an American fast food outlet.

associated with the island – Te Ati Awa, Ngati Raukawa and Ngati Toa – a requirement that acknowledges 'the special relationship of Maori to the Kapiti area' and their crucial support for the marine reserve in the years of debate before it was eventually established.[20]

Predictably, the involvement of local iwi has not been greeted with universal approval, particularly since it recently became known that the waters around the island are the subject of a Waitangi claim. The issue of who will control the marine reserve has become as provocative as the question of the future management of the island itself. In a letter to the *Kapiti Observer*, Olive Baldwin, secretary of Kapiti Island Watching Interest, asked recently, 'Are we cultivating a healthy regenerating area of coast only to have it swallowed up by some greedy arrogant claimants?'[21] This drew a prompt reply from John Barrett, then chairman of the Whakarongotai Marae at Waikanae. Should the treaty claim be successful, he said, iwi may extend protection to include an area wider than the present reserve, but he was careful to make it clear that he spoke only for Te Ati Awa and he noted that 'Each iwi will have their own view on what the future options might be for the island and the surrounding waters'. In a clear reference to Olive Baldwin's comment he went on to say:

Jim and 'Kap' Webber with hapuka (groper) caught near Kapiti Island, 1933.
REWA WEBBER COLLECTION

> It is obvious to me that some [people] are having trouble understanding the essential elements of our, and other iwi's, treaty claims. People say the Treaty is unrealistic and outdated. The reality is the courts are telling it differently and astonishing those amongst us who give no credence to the claims process.[22]

It is unfortunate that the sometimes acrimonious public debate over Kapiti Island and its waters has obscured the significance of the Marine Reserve Advisory Committee, which is an example of successful co-operative management between the Crown, local iwi and specific interest groups such as boaties, divers and fishing enthusiasts. Although the future of the island remains uncertain, at least until the Waitangi Tribunal has resolved the complex competing claims for Kapiti, the advisory

The Eastern Marine Reserve links the waters around Kapiti with the Waikanae Estuary. This connection has created an unusual, perhaps even unique, sequence of protected areas that ultimately link up with the summit of the southern Tararua mountains.

The distance between Kapiti Island and Mount Hector is only about 30 kilometres as the kereru flies. Within that span is an extraordinary variety of protected areas that form a distinctive continuum: an island sanctuary, a marine reserve, a scientific reserve (at the estuary) and a series of riverside reserves that lead to the Hemi Matenga Scenic Reserve on the coastal foothills. The Hemi Matenga kohekohe forests join up with the Kaitawa Scenic Reserve and the mixed podocarp and beech forests of the Tararua foothills that extend, in turn, to the bushline and open tussock tops of the Tararua Ranges.

The extent of illegal plundering of the marine reserve is unknown but piles of empty undersize paua shells hidden behind the beach at the northern end of Kapiti show that it is definitely occurring.

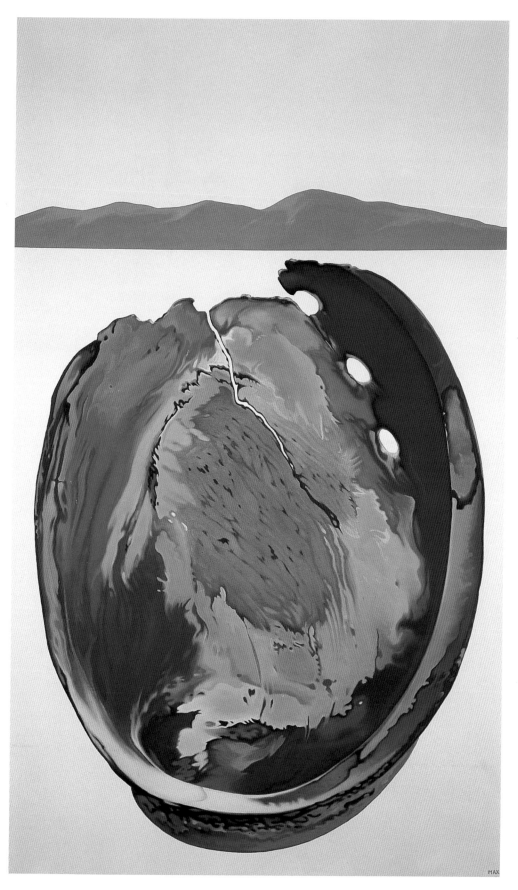

Kapiti/Paua *by Max Tilley, c. 1985.*

During the summer of 1998 a scientific survey was conducted by the Department of Conservation to ascertain what effect the reserve designation had had on the island's marine life. Preliminary findings suggest that regeneration is well under way; butterfish and blue moki, which had been heavily exploited in the past, are once again common and there has been a noticeable increase in the number of rock lobster and paua.

PRIVATE COLLECTION, WELLINGTON

Seal, Rangatira. Seals sometimes come ashore on Kapiti to recuperate rather than to breed. They are frequently observed on the headland at Arapawaiti, where a colony develops during the winter, but they can be seen almost anywhere along the rugged coast, basking on the warm rocks.

committee has got on with the challenging job of forging a working relationship between all the interested parties. In doing so, it has moved beyond a narrow focus on the treaty claims, to establish a successful model for bicultural management that will almost certainly be implicit in any treaty settlement. It might also be useful if a similar group were set up now, to advise on the management of the island itself, rather than waiting for the resolution of treaty claims to require it.

Co-operative management is an idea that has been tested and found to be useful elsewhere, especially in the South Island where the tangata whenua, Ngai Tahu, have used it to re-establish themselves in their tribal area. Ngai Tahu is now in a strong position. Not only does it have a real voice in the management of its traditional resources (achieved in advance of consideration of its treaty claim), but it has also had the opportunity to develop new commercial enterprises based on those resources. The

Like most of New Zealand's coastline, the shores of Kapiti Island are regularly polluted by material from fishing boats.

tribe's success is epitomised by its whale watching business at Kaikoura. Since the settlement of its treaty claim in 1997, Ngai Tahu has moved further ahead because it now has additional money to invest in the natural resources which it is already well experienced in managing. Familiarity and finance create new opportunities.

The sheltered waters of Rau O Te Rangi Channel were also once the domain of whales until they were hunted almost to extinction in the 1830s. Perhaps whales may eventually return to Kapiti. Even if it is too late for that, it is clear that the waters around the island, especially the marine reserve, offer new opportunities. Parties of divers are regularly taken to the north-western tip of

RAU O TE RANGI CHANNEL

The stretch of sea between Kapiti and the mainland (seen here from the north) is known as Rau O Te Rangi Channel. The name celebrates Kahe Te Rau O Te Rangi, of Ngati Toa, who swam from the island to the mainland with her small child, Ripeka, on her shoulders, to warn her people of an imminent attack on Kapiti.

During the 1820s, Kahe lived on Kapiti with her family. Although Ngati Toa defeated its enemies at the Battle of Waiorua, sporadic skirmishes continued for some years. On this occasion, while many Ngati Toa were away tending cultivations on the mainland, a slave warned Kahe of an imminent raid. She had to reach the

mainland to raise the alarm but, as the sight of a canoe would have alerted the attackers, she decided to swim. The current carried her south of Te Uruhi, near the Waikanae rivermouth, where she found some of her people who hurried back to defend the island.

Kahe Te Rau O Te Rangi was a person of considerable mana because she was a member of one of the principal Ngati Toa families and the daughter of Te Matoha, a leading chief. The small settlement and stream on the eastern side of Kapiti, between Rangatira and Waiorua, may have been named after Kahe and subsequently corrupted by successive cartographers to Te Kahuoterangi. On the other hand, the place name may have been in use before Ngati Toa came to Kapiti.

Kapiti by commercial guides who show them the spectacular underwater scenery there and, in 1997, guided sea kayak trips around the eastern and southern coasts began.

In addition to its physical attractions, Kapiti's marine environment also offers an example of how two races living side by side can work together to protect and manage a natural asset both regard as a treasure. Maybe when that idea is accepted by all, and shared management has been extended to include the island itself, the rangatira of the ocean may return to these waters.

Alan Wehipeihana

PART TWO

MOTU RONGONUI

CHAPTER SIX

MOTU RONGONUI

Kapiti was renowned in Maori history as a motu rongonui, or famous island. In pre-European times, a succession of tribes found that it had all the essential elements for survival. From high vantage points, approaching canoes could be seen some distance away and the steep cliffs on three sides made it difficult to attack.

No fortress is invincible, however, without food and water. Kapiti had both. The rocky coastline provided seafood and kumara were grown on the flat fertile ground at Waiorua and Rangatira. Birds were also plentiful. Fresh water was available all year round from the streams that flow down the eastern slopes and there were several springs, including one on Motungarara. Settlements were concentrated on the eastern shore at the mouth of these streams and on flat land at Waiorua, Rangatira and Wharekohu.

John Bevan Ford's drawing Te Hono, The Connections *(1987) places Kapiti in its geographical context: on the left, Te Wai Pounamu, on the right, Mount Taranaki. The artist's perspective is from beyond the Tararua mountains (foreground), which represent the Muaupoko and Rangitane tribes who lived in this region for centuries. The cloak represents the mana of their chiefs, some of whom are buried on the island; the diamonds and triangles are dispersed elements of the cloak's taniko border.*

Early European visitors to Kapiti often remarked on the historic relics that lay strewn about. Nowadays, evidence of Kapiti's long history of human occupation is rapidly disappearing beneath the regenerating bush. Occasionally, however, an historic object is still found.

Geoff Alexander worked on the island in the 1980s eradicating possums. One day, as he stood listening to the ranger talking to visitors, he noticed an unusual stone at his feet. After closer examination he uncovered this greenstone adze.
BOB CAIRNS

TODAY KAPITI is best known as a bird sanctuary, a place of protection, where birds flourish because their needs are given precedence. Visitors are welcomed to the island with an introductory talk which makes it clear that the island's primary purpose is to protect the birds and the bush. A visitor's day on Kapiti is deliberately kept short: the boat arrives from the mainland mid-morning and returns for its passengers five and a half hours later. This allows just enough time for a comfortable climb to the summit and back, a visit to the north end of the island, or simply to enjoy the bird life around the ranger's house at Rangatira. But no other exploration is permitted; most of Kapiti belongs to the birds.

This was not always so. The remains of pa, whare sites and food pits as well as whaling relics such as stone walls, house sites, fireplaces, a grave and trypots show that there has been continuous settlement on Kapiti for hundreds of years. This is confirmed by claims that are before the Waitangi Tribunal in which six different tribes – Muaupoko, Rangitane, Ngati Apa, Ngati Toa, Te Ati Awa and Ngati Raukawa – have registered their interest in the island.

Human habitation began almost 1000 years ago with the Waitaha, the shadowy first inhabitants of the land, of whom little is known. They, in turn, were succeeded by the descendants of early Maori explorers. During the past millennium Kapiti was one of the most sought after living places in the region; it is only since the beginning of the 20th century that people have been excluded from the island.

Yet, despite Kapiti's long record of human habitation, little is known about its archaeology. In the first few decades of this century, observant visitors to the island often found evidence of previous occupants, such as adzes and bones, while they explored the island but, since then, the vigorous regeneration of the bush (which has accelerated since possums were eradicated in the 1980s) has hidden almost all the evidence of Kapiti's past. Only a pair of restored trypots on the foreshore at Rangatira and some whaling remnants on the track to the northern end of the island are visible today.

Neither the Lands and Survey Department, which managed Kapiti for most of this century, nor the island's present custodian, the Department of Conservation (which has a statutory duty to identify and protect historic sites on land under its control), has commissioned a comprehensive archaeological survey of the island. Yet the Resource Management Act of 1991 made the identification of historic sites mandatory and all local authorities are required to identify and assess their significance. Kapiti Island, which is part of the Kapiti District, has escaped such scrutiny because it is a nature reserve.

Given this official reticence, it is fortunate that interested individuals have carried out their own surveys. Without their initiative, crucial evidence of the past would have disappeared. During several visits to Kapiti in the mid-1970s, members of the New Zealand Archaeological Association recorded historic sites. Then, in the early 1980s, two archaeological surveys were carried out; one by an Auckland archaeologist, Nigel Prickett, who documented whaling sites on the island's eastern shore and offshore islets, the other by a possum trapper, Bob Cairns, who made an archaeological map of sites that he found as he tramped the island.

Although these contributions have added greatly to knowledge of the island's past, a comprehensive archaeological survey is still urgently needed – before the evidence is destroyed by the regenerating forest. At present, most of Kapiti's human history is based on oral traditions which record that the island was known to Aotearoa's earliest explorers such as Kupe, who was probably the first to visit

Kapiti. Having severed Kapiti from the mainland, he continued his journey along the west coast of the North Island before returning to his home in Hawaiki. Several centuries passed before his descendants rediscovered and settled Aotearoa, continuing his exploration and naming of the new land. As they dispersed, each group of migrants developed its own traditions which celebrated the actions and achievements of ancestral figures. Prominent features such as rivers, rocks, islands and mountains commemorated their deeds so that the land became the history of the people. Although traditions differ from tribe to tribe, some early forebears, especially those with links to Hawaiki such as Toi and Whatonga, appear in many accounts while others are associated only with a single group or a specific locality.

This account weaves together some of these stories, particularly those of Rangitane and Ngai Tara, and their associated tribes, because they were among the first occupants of Kapiti. But there is no single definitive history and this is ultimately only one person's view.

Settlement of the island began in the 11th century after the *Kurahaupo* canoe crossed the Pacific in search of Aotearoa and landed at Mahia. Whatonga, one of the chiefs who navigated Kurahaupo, set out to explore the new land. Travelling alone in a small canoe, he went south along the east coast to the top of Te Wai Pounamu, where he stayed briefly. He then recrossed Raukawa and paddled past Kupe's islands until he reached the mouth of a large river (the Manawatu). Here he turned inland to follow the river across a plain and through a gap in the mountains to the district beyond, which we know today as the Wairarapa. He then returned to Mahia and shared his knowledge with his people, who were encouraged to travel south.[1]

During later centuries, a series of migrations populated much of the East Coast and the southern part of the North Island. Notable among them was a group led by one of Whatonga's sons, Tara. They settled around the sheltered harbour named Te Whanganui a Tara (the great harbour of Tara) by his wife, Te Umuroimata. As this group was joined by more people, several new tribes, including Ngai Tara

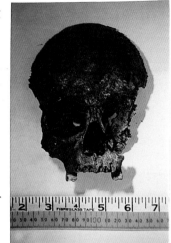

A skull, thought to be that of a young girl, was found by Bob Cairns, a keen amateur archaeologist, while he was working on the possum eradication programme. He measured and photographed it, then re-interred the skull where he had found it.
BOB CAIRNS

The remains of a whaler's hearth is one of several important archaeological relics at the mouth of the Taepiro Stream. Nearby terraces and a stone platform show where whalers' houses stood.

and Ngati Ira, evolved.[2] Later Tara was joined by his brother, Tautoki, who led
another wave of migrants called Rangitane.

According to the ethnographer Elsdon Best, the brothers divided the lower
half of the North Island between them, with Kapiti Island as the westernmost
boundary. Ngai Tara and Ngati Ira occupied the west coast from the Otaki River
south to the great harbour of Tara (including the islands of Kapiti and Mana) while
Rangitane settled north of the Otaki and on the eastern side of the Tararua mountains.[3] Kapiti is said to be an abbreviation of 'ko te waewae kapiti o Tara raua ko
Rangitane', the place where the boundaries of Tara and Rangitane divide.[4]

But the historian of the Rangitane, Jock McEwan, doubts this account. He
points out that, at the time of the division, Tautoki was living in Heretaunga
(Hawke's Bay) and that Rangitane did not occupy the territory described by Best
for almost 200 years. This meaning of Kapiti, he suggests, has continued to be put
forward because it was accepted uncritically by early ethnographers and historians. McEwan's view is reinforced by Joe Tukapua, a Muaupoko kaumatua, who
does not regard Kapiti as a significant name. 'It means nothing,' he says.[5]

Nevertheless Best's version has endured and little consideration has been given
to alternative meanings of Kapiti, although the contours of the island, and its position in relation to the mainland, suggest other possibilities. Kapiti can also mean
'a cleft, a gorge or a narrow pass'.[6] These words are an apt description of the steep
gorge of the Taepiro Stream which, when seen from Pukerua Bay or Paekakariki,
seems almost to cut the island in two, or of the narrow channel between the island and the mainland. The latter possibility is reinforced by the knowledge that
the name Kapiti was originally applied, by Rangitane and Muaupoko, to both the
island and the coastal mainland.[7]

Yet another explanation of Kapiti is based on an alternative meaning, 'to join',
or 'bring together'.[8] It recalls the sea battle between Nuku Tamaroro and Manaia,
fought in these waters many centuries ago. Nuku had pursued Manaia across the
Pacific and came across his canoe near Pukerua Bay. So that the battle could begin, the two long sailing canoes were brought alongside each other (ka kapiti nga

This stone wall, built by whalers, once sheltered the settlement at Taepiro from southerly seas.

Many notable chiefs, including Whatonga and Tuteremoana, have been interred in caves on Kapiti.

Although the island has many obvious caves and caverns, like this one at Wharekohu Point, the bodies of the dead were carefully hidden, often by lowering them through narrow fissures into hidden chambers.

Despite these precautions to protect tapu urupa, visitors to the island in the 19th and early 20th centuries sometimes explored the burial caves and removed remains.

waka i kona) and hand-to-hand fighting took place. The engagement was called Kapiti because the canoes were joined together and the name was subsequently applied to the large island near which the fighting occurred.[9]

Although the meaning of Kapiti is uncertain, traditional place names on the island often provide an understanding of tribal occupation. The names of prominent natural features on Kapiti confirm that Ngai Tara, the descendants of Whatonga, lived here centuries ago. Kapiti's highest point is named after the most famous of Tara's descendants, Tuteremoana, the great chief of Ngai Tara, who was known as 'Te tama whakaete turanga rau, i titi te upoko ki te kura a rangi', 'the young man who forced his way onto a hundred standing places, whose head was adorned with the glow of heaven'.[10] He also lived, perhaps for a long time, at Rangitatau pa on Wellington's south coast, where his name is prominent; part of what we call Barretts Reef was known as 'Te Punga-whangai-o-Tuteremoana', 'the food anchorage of Tuteremoana'. It seems likely, however, that he eventually returned to Kapiti because he is said to be buried beside his wife, Wharekohu, in a cave at the southern end of the island. The nearby bay bears her name. It is probable that Whatonga is also buried on Kapiti. The dead, and the valuable greenstone jewellery that was buried with them, are guarded by an atua, or supernatural being, called Tunui o te Ika.[11]

In later centuries, sections of Ngai Tara, Rangitane, Ngati Kahungunu, Muaupoko and Ngati Apa all occupied Kapiti in a ceaseless cycle of tribal conquest and displacement. There is no clear historical record of these waves of settlement because tribal traditions vary and intermarriage has blurred distinctions between the groups. Nevertheless, by the end of the 17th century, there was a recognisable pattern of occupation within the region. Ngati Ira and Ngai Tara lived on the shores of Te Whanganui a Tara and in scattered settlements on the West Coast and Ngati Kahungunu occupied much of the East Coast, although they shared it with Rangitane, who also lived in the Horowhenua and Manawatu. Muaupoko lived in the lowland forests and around the lakes of the mainland

MARATHON SWIMMERS

Maori women have a remarkable record as long-distance swimmers. The best known is Hinemoa (above), whose swim across Lake Rotorua has become an enduring romantic legend.

Not so familiar, but equally deserving of celebration, are the marathon efforts of the women of Kapiti, especially Kahe Te Rau O Te Rangi and Rangiuira Rakera, both of whom swam from Kapiti to the mainland early last century. Even their feats, however, are overshadowed by the courage and endurance of Hinepoupou, the first person to swim Raukawa (Cook Strait).

Legend relates that, about 1750, Hinepoupou accompanied her husband and his brother on a hunting trip from Rangitoto (D'Urville Island) to Kapiti. As Hinepoupou slept, the men abandoned her and returned home in the only canoe. When Hinepoupou awoke and realised she had been left behind, she was very distressed but resolved to return to her people. From a rock on

Kapiti's south-west coast, she dived into the sea but her dogs refused to follow her and turned to stone.

Hinepoupou was guided across Raukawa by a dolphin named Kahurangi. When she reached Rangitoto, she slipped ashore and stealthily made her way to her father's whare. He was astonished to see her, for he had been told she was dead. Father and daughter planned their revenge.

Her father arranged to take her husband and his brother to a new fishing ground Hinepoupou had discovered during her epic swim. Hinepoupou lay hidden in the bottom of her father's canoe while her husband and his brother accompanied them in a second canoe. When they reached the fishing ground, her father invented an excuse to return home, leaving the unsuspecting pair happily fishing. As she and her father left, Hinepoupou softly sang a karakia to summon a taniwha, which waited until they were a safe distance away, before creating a great storm that overturned the other canoe, drowning both her husband and his brother.

Te Wai Pounamu (the South Island) from Tuteremoana, Kapiti, at sunset.
Rangitoto (D'Urville Island) is on the right.

opposite Kapiti, as well as on the island itself. Ngati Apa, who controlled Rangitikei, also lived on Kapiti.

In the summer of 1769 an event occurred that was to have the most profound implications for all the tribes – the arrival of the English explorer, James Cook. He circumnavigated the North Island and made contact first with Maori in Poverty Bay, the Hauraki Gulf and the Bay of Islands, then at Queen Charlotte Sound and near Cape Palliser. During this last encounter, Maori who came aboard the *Endeavour* asked for whao, or nails, which indicated that word of the new arrivals had spread ahead of them. Aotearoa's isolation was over. But, although Cook later returned in 1773 and again in 1777, Aotearoa remained undisturbed by Europeans for another generation.

About the beginning of the 19th century sealers and traders began to frequent New Zealand waters. Most of their activities were limited to the deep south around Foveaux Strait and the sub-antarctic islands where they quickly depleted the seal colonies. By 1820, the sealers gave way to whalers, especially from America, and traders, usually based in Sydney.[12]

The Bay of Islands became their headquarters, a source of supplies and a place for recreation, as well as a haven for escaped convicts from New South Wales and Norfolk Island. Kororareka (Russell) soon became notorious throughout the South Pacific for its grog shops, debauchery and lawlessness. Traders who called there introduced muskets to the northern tribes who immediately recognised their potential. Women, flax and dried tattooed heads were exchanged for guns that were promptly used against traditional enemies.

Muskets exacerbated intertribal tensions. Their introduction happened to coincide with a period of intense rivalry, especially in the northern half of the North

CHART
of
COOK'S STRAIT
in
NEW ZEALAND

The Dutch explorer, Abel Tasman, was the first European to explore Raukawa but James Cook was probably the first European to sail through the turbulent passage that bears his name. On 7 February 1770, as he left Queen Charlotte Sound, sailing east to confirm that these waters were indeed a strait and not a large bay as some of the crew suggested, Cook recorded the following description of Kapiti Island in his journal.

> I shall not pretend here to assign limets to the length of this Strait a view of the Chart will best illustrate that. About North 9 Leagues from Cape Teerawhitte under the same shore is a high remarkable Island that may be distinctly seen from Queen Charlottes Sound from which it lies NE by E ½ E distant six or seven Leagues. I have called it

Entry Isle and was taken notice of when we first past it on Sunday 14th of last month.

On Cook's return to England the engraver, John Ryland, produced this map from drawings made by Cook and others on board the *Endeavour*. It is the earliest map of Kapiti and shows some of the English names Cook gave to various features, although he retained the Maori names for the main islands, Te Ika a Maui (Eahe ino mauwe) and Te Wai Pounamu (Tawai poe namoo).

Cook's chart was remarkably accurate, but it was not until his second voyage in 1773, when he discovered the great harbour, Te Whanganui a Tara, and recognised Mana as an island, that he was able to complete it.

Tomite : Waka : Nene
New Zealand Chief

Island, as tribes fought over land and resources. These conflicts, made worse by the practice of obtaining help from distant allies, and the relentless demands of utu, spread war far and wide.[13]

The attractions of the region were highlighted one day when a large group of northern chiefs, resting on the shores of Raukawa near Ohariu, watched a European vessel sail through the strait. Fires were lit to tempt the crew to come ashore, without success. This was probably the polar expedition commanded by the

Russian explorer, Bellingshausen, who recorded, as he passed through Cook Strait on 9 June 1820, that 'A great fire was burning on the middle headland as we passed; very likely the inhabitants wished us to visit them'.[15]

The sighting of the Russian ship confirmed to the taua (war party) the strategic importance of Cook Strait and the islands (Kapiti and Mana) that guard its northern approach, and showed that this part of the country was visited by ships. European vessels meant trade, especially in muskets. The Ngapuhi chief Waka Nene is reputed to have encouraged Te Rauparaha to consider bringing his people from Kawhia to Cook Strait to be near the European ships. Ngati Toa could obtain muskets, he suggested, then use them to conquer the local tribes.[16] Te Rauparaha must have valued the advice since he followed it for the next 20 years.

When Te Rauparaha returned to Kawhia, he persuaded his people to accept his vision of a new home near Raukawa. Although they were reluctant to leave the harbour that had been their home for centuries, the tribe recognised that the alternative was annihilation and that the key to their security lay in trade with Europeans – the source of muskets. They therefore made the momentous decision to leave Kawhia.

The heke, or journey, took two years. Accounts vary but it is clear that approximately 1000 people left Kawhia, on foot, to make the dangerous trek southward. They hastened through hostile territory and lingered with allies, especially in Taranaki, where they cultivated crops and recovered from the rigours of the journey, which was punctuated by skirmishes and several battles with tribal enemies. Small groups of allies joined the heke along the way, including Te Ati Awa and Ngati Tama.

News of the heke preceded it and, as Ngati Toa approached its destination, local chiefs in the Rangitikei and further south became anxious, holding a conference on Kapiti to decide how they should respond to the situation. Ngati Apa suspected that Te Rauparaha coveted Kapiti Island; Muaupoko and Rangitane remembered the treachery and slaughter of the taua, two years earlier. 'If Te Rauparaha lives, our land will go,' said the Whanganui chief, Te Paetahi, thrusting his spear into the ground as a sign of his wish to kill the invader. So the decision was made to murder Te Rauparaha.[17]

When the heke reached Horowhenua, the Muaupoko chief, Toheriri, offered Ngati Toa land near Ohau where they built a pa. Toheriri then invited Te Rauparaha to a feast at Lake Papaitonga. Despite the misgivings of Te Rangihaeata and others, Te Rauparaha went, unarmed, with four of his children and about 16 followers. It was a disastrous mistake. After he and his party had retired for the night they were attacked by their hosts and, in spite of a brave defence, all were killed except Te Rauparaha, who forced his way out through a corner of the whare in which he was trapped, and Te Ra-ka-hcrea, who escaped with a spear still sticking in his back.

Three of Te Rauparaha's immediate family, including his eldest son and probable successor, Te Rangi-hounga-riri, were killed, and his youngest daughter, Te Hononga, was taken prisoner. Like his father, Te Rangi-hounga-riri had managed to escape but returned when he heard the cries of his sister, Te Uira. Armed only with a canoe paddle, he fought with great courage but was overwhelmed by the more numerous Muaupoko.

For Muaupoko it was the worst possible outcome. They had tried to assassinate Te Rauparaha and had failed; his escape was their death warrant. From that moment they were hunted without mercy by Ngati Toa and their Te Ati Awa allies. Ngati Toa captured Toheriri, tortured and killed him and sacked his pa. Remnants of the tribe were pursued and killed until, within a short time, only a few small groups of survivors existed miserably in the depths of the Horowhenua forests.

If Ngati Toa had coveted Kapiti before the massacre, their determination to take the island can only have increased after it for, in an unfamiliar area, surrounded by enemies, they were extremely vulnerable. They had fled from Kawhia to escape encircling foes, only to find themselves in the same situation. After several unsuccessful attempts to dislodge Muaupoko and Ngati Apa from the island, it was decided to employ a ruse. A large fighting force was assembled for all to see and marched north, under the leadership of Te Rauparaha, to harry Muaupoko and Rangitane. Meanwhile Te Pehi Kupe, the hereditary chief of Ngati Toa, and a small group of warriors stealthily made their way to Kapiti, where they surprised and overpowered the unsuspecting garrison.[18]

The capture of Kapiti was timely, for Ngati Toa's fears of an attack were well founded. Now that Muaupoko had revealed their true intentions by attacking Te Rauparaha, all three of the local tribes had to strike back, for in the aftermath of Papaitonga, Ngati Toa had made clear it meant to prevail – by fair means or foul. Not only were Muaupoko hunted without mercy but, when Ngati Apa and Rangitane dared to strengthen an old pa at Hotuiti, in the northern Horowhenua, Te Rauparaha immediately besieged it, then invited the chiefs within to visit him to talk peace. Foolishly they did so, and all were slaughtered.[19]

Te Rauparaha and his warriors returned to join the rest of the tribe at Waikanae where they celebrated the capture of Kapiti and success at Hotuiti 'with feasting and rejoicing, little dreaming that any attempt would be made to attack them'.[20] But Ngati Apa and remnants of Muaupoko surprised them with a swift and deadly counter-attack. Sixty Ngati Toa were killed, including Te Pehi's four daughters, as well as Pohe and Tiaho, two wives of Te Pehi's younger brother, Te Rangihiroa. To add to Te Pehi's grief, Ngati Apa seized his musket; it did not matter that they had no ammunition, it was their first gun and a powerful symbol of their success.[21] This unexpected defeat shocked Ngati Toa, who immediately abandoned the mainland and withdrew to the island.

Kapiti provided Ngati Toa with real security for the first time in many years; at the same time, however, withdrawal to the island increased their vulnerability because enemies on the mainland were free to marshal their forces unhindered. An attack was not long in coming. Since Papaitonga, a Muaupoko chief, Te Ratu, had tirelessly canvassed tribes on both sides of Raukawa, urging them to unite and destroy Ngati Toa. Te Ratu's campaign was made easier because Ngati Toa had attacked every other tribe in the vicinity, including Ngati Apa, which had tried to remain apart from the fighting on account of kinship ties – in particular Te Rangihaeata's marriage to Te Pikinga, a Ngati Apa chieftainess. But that fragile alliance had been broken when Ngati Toa murdered the Ngati Apa chiefs at Hotuiti.

The way was now clear to unite and destroy the newcomers. In 1824 warriors from Te Wai Pounamu, the East Coast, southern Taranaki, Whanganui and the Horowhenua assembled at Waikanae. Estimates vary, but the flotilla probably carried as many as 2000 to 3000 combatants to Kapiti. So great was the fleet that one observer said 'the sunlight on the water was obscured'.[22]

Under the cover of night, the armada crossed the channel to Waiorua at the northern end of the island, where the warriors began to disembark. Several differ-

Te Rauparaha *by Edward Abbott.*

Te Rauparaha was born, about the time Cook first visited Aotearoa, into a gifted family that included his elder sister, Waitohi, her daughter, the poet Topeora, and her son, Te Rangihaeata.

Te Rauparaha became a prominent leader of Ngati Toa because of his prowess as a warrior, his authority on tribal and spiritual matters and his shrewd understanding of the opportunities the arrival of the Europeans might bring to his people.

HADFIELD FAMILY COLLECTION

ing accounts of the epic battle exist, reflecting the disparate tribal origins of those who took part. Tamihana Te Rauparaha's version, for example, which was based on his father's recollections, predictably places the great warrior at the centre of the action and imbues the encounter with an almost spiritual quality. His enemies are defeated as much by his mana as by his military power.[23]

Descendants of the other tribes that took part, as well as later European ethnographers and historians, argue that it was those living at Waiorua at the time – including Ngati Toa hapu led by Te Pokaitara, Te Rangihiroa and Tungia as well as a number of Te Ati Awa – who bore the brunt of the initial assault while Te Rauparaha and Te Rangihaeata were some distance away at Taepiro.[24] Stephenson Percy Smith's sources suggested that, after the onslaught at dawn, a truce was called and fighting began again only when Te Rauparaha arrived with reinforcements.[25]

Historians have attempted to explain how fewer than 200 defenders could defeat a force 10 times as large. The secret seems to have been that, for those on the island, it was a fight for their very survival – defeat meant certain annihilation. Their determination may, however, have been aided by practical advantages: terrain that was more difficult to storm than defend and a debilitating division of command among the coalition of attackers. Sheer numbers may also have led to their defeat, as one account suggested that, when the armada tried to land, canoes collided and capsized, creating confusion that was quickly exploited by Kapiti's desperate defenders. An alternative name for the encounter, 'whakapae a tai', meaning 'overturned on the shore', gives this suggestion credibility.[26] Alternatively, the name may have been a reference to the weather. One participant, for example, attributed the real cause of the rout to the wind. During the night, as the canoes converged on Kapiti, a westerly breeze blew up and by morning it was so strong that the canoes were unable to land. Instead, they anchored offshore and the warriors had to swim to the island. When the battle turned against them and they tried to flee, they were trapped and slaughtered on the stony beach and in the sea.[27]

In hindsight, it may be that the encounter had two distinct phases: the initial fighting at Waiorua and then the harassment of the routed armada as its remnants fled toward the mainland. It was probably during this pursuit that Ngati Toa from Taepiro and elsewhere, including Te Rauparaha, distinguished themselves. This is underscored by information given to James Cowan by Wi Parata some years after the event. Parata recounted that a number of fleeing canoes were taken back to the palisaded pa at Taepiro, where the captives were humiliated by Ngati Toa chieftainess and poet, Rangi Topeora. Cowan later told the story in his book, *Pictures of Old New Zealand*, which details the treatment of the Whanganui chiefs, Pehi Turoa and Te Paetahi:

> When the prisoners and their captors were landing from their canoe amid the wildest excitement, Topeora climbed up on the palisade at the entrance and stood on top of the carved kuwaha, the gateway of the pa. She stood with her legs extended, one foot on one side of the kuwaha, and one on the other. All she wore was a rapaki, or mat around her waist. Her breasts were bare; she held a taiaha in her hands; she grimaced, with rolling eyes and protruding tongue – the grimacing of the pukana. She stood in that attitude while Ngati Toa and their prisoners entered the pa, stooping as they did so under the top cross piece of the kuwaha, which was about five foot high. They had to pass between her kuwaha, her thighs as the Maoris expressed it. This was an old Maori custom to whakataurekareka, or degrade and enslave the captured chiefs.[28]

One possible explanation for the remarkable rout, known as the Battle of Waiorua, may lie in the nature of the terrain. The beach at Waiorua (left), like others on Kapiti's eastern shore, consists of a gravel terrace sloping steeply to the sea. The invading warriors, armed with clubs and spears, had to leap out of their canoes into deep water, swim ashore and then struggle up the steep, stony beach, only to be hurled back by the defenders, some of whom had muskets.

Meanwhile, at Waiorua, a victory feast was in progress. Many of the slain were eaten; some were cooked in an oven, Te Umu Paparoa, just north of the bay,[29] while the remains of others lay scattered along the shore and around the Okupe Lagoon. Almost a century later, their bleached bones were still evident.[30] Today the bones are gone, but the Battle of Waiorua remains an enigma. Whatever happened, one fact is indisputable – it was a remarkable victory for Ngati Toa and their allies.

Although, in years to come, there were occasional skirmishes with hostile tribes on the mainland, there was no further serious threat to the dominance of Ngati Toa.

CHAPTER SEVEN

AN ISLAND EMPIRE

Kapiti's location at the northern entrance to Cook Strait meant that whoever occupied the island commanded the sea.

In the 1820s and 1830s the mainland was covered in dense bush, which made movement difficult and dangerous. Ngati Toa travelled instead by canoe, in all directions, to territory held either by themselves or their allies. Kapiti was the perfect stronghold for an empire serviced by canoe.

As Te Rauparaha showed, it was also an ideal base for campaigns further afield. After the Battle of Waiorua his tribe turned its attention to the conquest of Te Wai Pounamu, the source of greenstone, which was as sought after by Maori as gold was by Europeans.

Between 1827 and 1831 Te Rauparaha took war parties to the South Island almost every year, each campaign adding new territory to the Ngati Toa empire. When the victorious warriors returned to Kapiti, they brought numerous slaves and quantities of greenstone back with them. They left behind relatives, such as Te Rauparaha's brother, Nohorua, and allies such as Ngati Koata, who settled in Te Wai Pounamu to ensure Ngati Toa's dominance. The departure of allies also reduced competition for land on Kapiti and the adjacent mainland.

Te Wai Pounamu (left, centre) and Kapiti (right) from Waikanae Beach.
INSET Carved image of Te Rauparaha in his canoe *by G. F. Angas, 1847.*
ALEXANDER TURNBULL LIBRARY

N THE WAKE of the Battle of Waiorua, Ngati Toa was poised to conquer Te Wai Pounamu, with its promise of rich hauls of greenstone, but first the tribe needed to acquire many more of the muskets that were crucial to their success. Fortunately for Ngati Toa, European interest in the region was increasing rapidly. Sydney merchants, in particular, were keen to establish trade in the Cook Strait area because there was money to be made in the exchange of guns for flax fibre, which was used to manufacture rope, canvas and cloth. As early as 1813, the Ngai Tahu chief Tamaiharanui had pioneered the trade in flax with vessels visiting Banks Peninsula.[1] By the mid-1820s it was known in Sydney that the people at Kapiti were also keen to trade and ships began to call there. During the early years of contact visits were relatively few, although when a ship did arrive, Te Rauparaha gave the captain pigs and potatoes and usually received a gun in return.[2] The vessel's hold would then be loaded with flax fibre purchased at the rate of one musket for each shipload of the green gold.

Kapiti was the ideal place for a flax industry. The mainland was a series of vast interconnected wetlands, thick with *Phormium tenax*, stretching from the marshes of the Manawatu River in the north to the Taupo Swamp in the south. But preparation of the flax fibre was a laborious task. First the flax had to be cut and removed from the swampy ground. The fibre was then separated from the leaf by scraping with a sharp shell, washed in water and scraped a second time before it was dried and bundled up. Ngati Toa was not deterred by this tedious work because most of it was done by slaves who had been captured in battle.

Slaves were also an essential element of another Ngati Toa enterprise: trade in the dried tattooed heads that were keenly sought after in Sydney and London. The more intricate the decoration, the higher the price. One of the leading suppliers was Te Pehi's son, the young chief Te Hiko, whose business methods were a reflection of the harsh realities of life. When a ship called at Kapiti, he would assemble a group of his tattooed slaves and parade them before interested buyers. Once a selection had been made, the heads of the unfortunate slaves were severed, dried and presented to the buyers.[3]

The upper Taepiro Valley.

After Ngati Toa conquered Kapiti, they lived on the island with their allies. With so many people to feed, land for cultivation was badly needed. On the flat forelands at Waiorua and Rangatira and at Wharekohu, kumara, corn, potatoes and other crops were grown, but this was not sufficient to supply all the inhabitants as well as visiting ships. The high ridges and valleys were, therefore, also cleared. Tamihana Te Rauparaha later wrote: 'with the need to clear land to grow more food all the trees on Kapiti were chopped down for the island was now overcrowded'.

One of these areas was the upper Taepiro Valley. It made an ideal garden – sunny, sheltered and well watered. Since the 1920s, however, regenerated bush has gradually reclaimed the valley.

Te Hiko, *by Charles Heaphy.*

The young chief's business activities reflected both Maori and European cultures. He was a trader of dried, tattooed heads and was also a whaler for a time.

He bought a whaleboat but later abandoned his new vocation when he became a Christian because 'if it be good to rest for one day of the week,' he explained to a European visitor, 'it must be much better to rest the whole week'.
ALEXANDER TURNBULL LIBRARY

Demand for moko mokai (dried heads) was high in England and Europe after James Cook first brought them back. There was great interest in Maori moko because it was literally the carving of a face, quite unlike other forms of tattooing which involved just pricking the skin. European traders who called at Kapiti were keen to exchange muskets for them; the going rate was one gun for two dried heads.[4]

This gruesome trade was, however, risky, as Joe Rowe, an early European entrepreneur on Kapiti, was to discover. Rowe, whose Maori name was Te Oroa, was one of Te Rauparaha's Pakeha, a favoured trader who enjoyed the chief's protection in recognition of his role as a supplier of guns to Ngati Toa. On one occasion, a party of Whanganui Maori visited the island and recognised the heads of some of their relatives among Rowe's collection, but when they requested their return Rowe refused and 'laughed and made fun of their tears'. His response was not forgotten. Some time later, on a visit to Whanganui, Rowe was ambushed and killed – his head was cut off and dried for display.[5]

But Te Rauparaha's policy of welcoming visiting ships and personally protecting valued traders like Rowe did not satisfy some members of his tribe, who wished to acquire weapons more rapidly. Among them was Te Pehi Kupe, the captor of Kapiti, who was keen to acquire arms to avenge the deaths of his children. His impatience led him to risk the unknown by travelling overseas. He chose his moment well. In February 1824 a sailing ship, the *Urania*, lay becalmed near the western cliffs of the island when it was approached by three canoes. As they drew alongside, Te Pehi leapt aboard. He asked for arms but the captain refused and ordered him back to his canoe. Instead, the chief waved the canoes away, telling Captain Reynolds that he intended to go to England – a courageous ambition. Soon after, a breeze blew up and Reynolds had no choice but to sail away although he tried the following day to put Te Pehi ashore 'near the eastern mouth of Cooks Straits, and in doing so I only just escaped losing the ship, therefore I was obliged, much against my inclination, but to his satisfaction, to make sail and leave for my port of destination – Lima'.[6] During the voyage Te Pehi and Reynolds became friends and Te Pehi rescued him from drowning. In London the captain became mentor and chaperone to 'Tupai Cupa' who became a considerable attraction and, in October 1825, Reynolds nursed the chief through a severe illness. Later Te Pehi left for home with a large supply of clothing, tools, agricultural equipment and presents which, like the Ngapuhi chief Hongi before him, he exchanged for guns in Sydney. He then made a triumphant return to Kapiti.

There is some doubt as to the exact date of Te Pehi's return from his great adventure but it was probably 1826. In his absence European interest in New Zealand had increased markedly and traders were now joined by whalers. As a result, Cook Strait was rapidly opening up to the world. As early as 1794, a disparate collection of hardy Europeans had hunted sperm whales in northern New Zealand waters but, as the whales did not venture near the coast, the whalers remained at sea, coming ashore at the Bay of Islands only to make repairs and for rest and recreation. But, by the mid-1820s, sperm whale stocks had been so severely depleted that the hunters began to turn their attention to the black whale, or right whale as it was also known, because it was just 'right' for exploitation. Not only did it provide high yields of oil and bone, it was also very big, very slow and, most useful of all, it floated when dead. The southern variety also, obligingly, came inshore for weeks at a time.[7]

In winter, the right whales took refuge in sheltered coastal waters to raise their calves. In May they began to appear in Cook Strait, having migrated north from the Southern Ocean in search of warmer waters. During their annual migration, they usually visited Cloudy Bay then swam north through Cook Strait, often passing between Kapiti and the mainland.[8] This predictable behaviour gave whalers the opportunity to hunt whales from the shore in small boats instead of from sailing ships.

The first whalers to frequent Cook Strait were John Guard and his boat crew, who were driven into Te Awaiti (Tory Channel) in 1827, during a storm. There

TE PEHI KUPE BY JOHN SYLVESTER, C. 1826
During his trip to England, the handsome chief sat for a
fortnight, in Liverpool, for this portrait. Te Pehi was
one of the first chiefs to risk the unknown and travel
abroad. During his long stay in England he experienced
life in an industrialised society and was also exposed to
European ideas.

Te Pehi may also have had occasion to consider
the likely effects of further European contact with his
homeland because during his time in London the New
Zealand Company was active. Although its ambitions
were at first commercial, within five years plans for the
systematic settlement of these islands were developed.
Te Pehi almost certainly knew of these because it is
thought that he returned to Kapiti, in the spring of

1826, aboard a New Zealand Company vessel sent to
reconnoitre the Cook Strait region.

What influence he might have had on Ngati Toa's
later dealings with the Wakefields and the early gover-
nors, had he lived, is impossible to guess. His death at
Kaiapohia, soon after his return, was significant, not only
because it led to the near annihilation of Ngai Tahu, but
also because it upset the complex balance of Ngati Toa
leadership. As the senior hereditary chief, his lineage, his
record as a commander and his impulsive nature made
him an effective, though younger, counterpart to Te
Rauparaha. After the débâcle at Kaiapohia, Te Pehi was
succeeded by his son, Te Hiko, who shared Kapiti with
Te Rauparaha. His inexperience, however, was a disad-
vantage in his dealings with the shrewd older man.

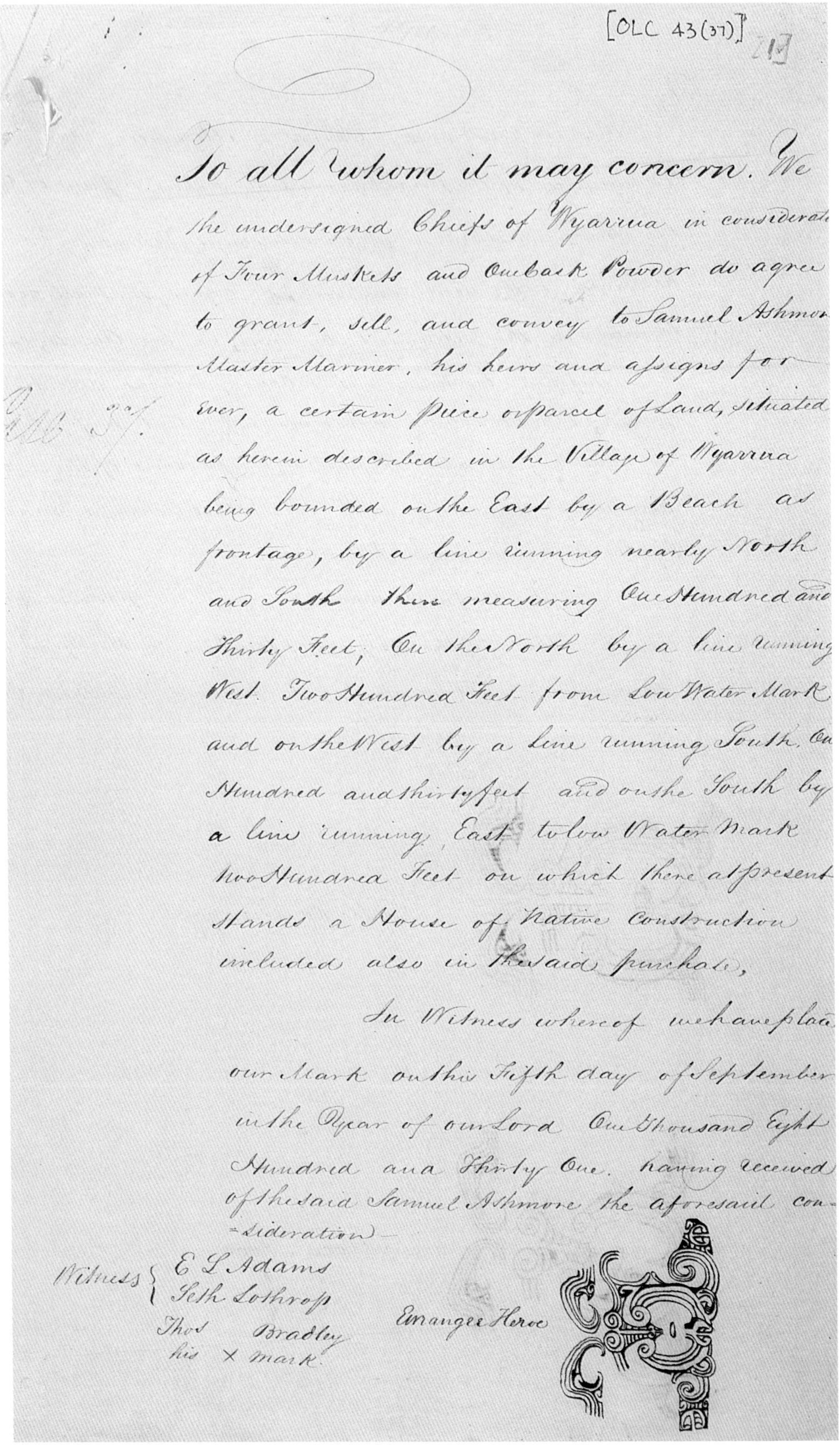

To all whom it may concern. We
the undersigned Chiefs of Wyarrua in consideration
of Four Muskets and One bask Powder do agree
to grant, sell, and convey to Samuel Ashmore
Master Mariner, his heirs and assigns for
ever, a certain Piece or parcel of Land, situated
as herein described in the Village of Wyarrua
being bounded on the East by a Beach as
frontage, by a line running nearly North
and South there measuring One Hundred and
Thirty Feet, On the North by a line running
West. Two Hundred Feet from Low Water Mark
and on the West by a line running South. One
Hundred and thirty feet and on the South by
a line running, East to low Water Mark
Two Hundred Feet on which there at present
stands a House of Native Construction
included also in the said purchase,

In Witness whereof we have placed
our Mark on this Fifth day of September
in the Year of our Lord One Thousand Eight
Hundred and Thirty One. having received
of the said Samuel Ashmore the aforesaid con-
-sideration —

Witness { E L Adams
Seth Lothrop
Thos Bradley
his × mark.

Ewangee Heroe

We the undersigned Chiefs of Wyarrua in consequence of the purchase of a certain piece of ground by Samuel Ashmore in our Settlement, situated as described in the deed annexed, do agree, that all goods landed in this settlement by him, or his Agents, can be reshipped by him or his Order, without detention or fee; We also bind ourselves to protect the property so landed, as also the person or persons of those in any way connected with the Establishment made by the said Samuel Ashmore,

In Witness whereof we have placed our mark this fifth day of September, in the Year of our Lord One Thousand Eight Hundred and Thirty One,

Moko Tungy.

Moco Acco.

Flax trader and mariner, Captain Samuel Ashmore, was probably the first European to buy land on Kapiti. This deed shows that on 5 September 1831 he exchanged four muskets and a cask of gunpowder for a small area on the shore in the 'Village of Wyarrua' which included a 'house of native construction'. Ashmore's deed also included a guarantee that his rights as a trader — and his goods — would be protected.

Three well-known chiefs signed the document with their moko. They were Erangee Heroe (Rangihiroa), Tungy (Tungia) and Accoo (Te Hiko).

This document is of particular value to the descendants of Rangihiroa because it is the only known record of his moko.
NATIONAL ARCHIVES

Ngati Toa chiefs were keen to live on Kapiti's islets because they gave greater security and were close to the anchorage (formed by the islands themselves) used by visiting ships.

During the late 1830s chiefs shared their islands with American whalers. Te Rauparaha occupied the northern beach on Tahoramaurea (right); Captain William Mayhew ran a two-boat station nearby. Later, after Te Rauparaha had left the island, whalers built several stone buildings on the northern side.

Te Rangihiroa and Te Hiko shared Motungarara (left) with Captain 'Horse' Lewis and his crew.

Sketch plan of Tahoramaurea showing remains of occupation.
CAROLINE PHILLIPS/NIGEL PRICKETT

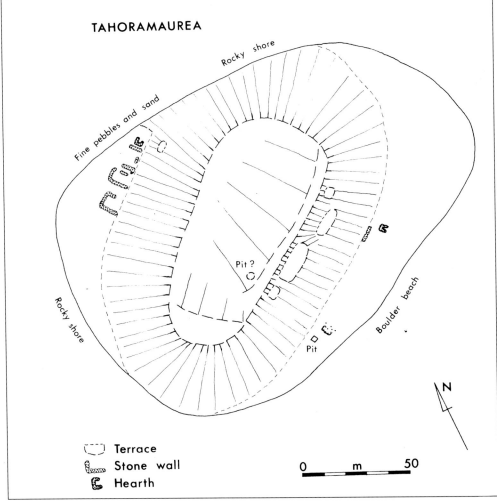

TAHORAMAUREA

Terrace
Stone wall
Hearth

0   m   50

Several stone walls, the remnants of whalers' houses, can be seen on the north-western side of Tahoramaurea.

they settled, near the narrow entrance, living precariously in an uneasy relationship with local Maori, who razed their huts on several occasions. Their facilities were, however, so rudimentary that when a whale was caught only the valuable whalebone was kept and the rest of the carcass was discarded. Guard and his men suffered many privations but stayed on because they were encouraged, no doubt, by the presence of numerous whales nearby and the price of whalebone, which fetched £125 a ton on the London market[9] – big money in those days.

Within a few years whaling spread to Kapiti. The first recorded visit of whalers is 1830, when the captain of a Sydney brig, the *Tranmere*, reported seeing two ships at the island: the *William Stoveld* with 25 tons of oil on board and the *Hind* with 16 tons and a whale alongside.[10] Given that one carcass yielded, on average, about 3 tons of oil, this meant that the two cargoes would have accounted for 17 whales.[11] The value of the whaling business at this time can be reckoned from the English price for a ton of oil, which was £28.[12]

Unlike the southern Maori who harassed Guard, Ngati Toa encouraged the whalers and catered for their needs. They provided them with pigs and potatoes (a legacy of Cook's visit), houses, willing women and, when necessary, protection from attack. Europeans established shore whaling stations and trading bases on Kapiti and its offshore islands. One of the earliest traders, a man named Harvey, set up at Rangatira, and in 1831 Captain Samuel Ashmore bought land on the water's edge at Waiorua.[13] In return, the Pakeha were expected to supply Ngati Toa with guns.

Vessels calling at Kapiti usually anchored in the lee of the island's eastern shore, between the islands of Motungarara and Tahoramaurea. Here they were protected from the wind and were close to settlements on the island. Te Rauparaha lived nearby at Taepiro and on Tahoramaurea, where he was handily placed to welcome

In the late 1820s and 1830s both whalers and Maori lived on Kapiti. There is archaeological evidence of this meeting of cultures at a number of sites on the eastern shore of the island.

At the mouth of the Maraetakaroro Stream, a terraced pa once occupied the steep face on the end of a ridge known as Tuhinapo. On the southern side of the stream, in the foreground, the stone wall built by Maori and whalers to make a platform for their houses is clearly visible.

visiting vessels. Te Hiko and Te Rangihiroa occupied Motungarara. When a ship arrived Te Rauparaha would board it, or the captain would come ashore to visit him. Most Europeans deferred to the powerful and volatile figure, although they did not necessarily respect him, referring to him as the 'Old Serpent', 'Robuller' or 'The Bully' – often with good reason, as accounts from this period include descriptions of Te Rauparaha and his second-in-command, Te Rangihaeata, forcing visitors to make gifts of guns and liquor. Both chiefs drank freely, but did not seem to be much affected by liquor.[14]

On Kapiti, Europeans were encouraged to live with Maori. They were given land, a house might be built for them and some married Maori women and became part of the tribe. The whaler and trader, John Nicol, for example, married Kahe Te Rau O Te Rangi, who was the daughter of a Ngati Toa chief, Te Matoha; the distinguished Pomare family, which included Sir Maui Pomare, are descended from this union. Another whaler, George Stubbs, married Metapere Waipunahau, daughter of Rangihiroa and a chieftainess of both Ngati Toa and Te Ati Awa. Their son, Wiremu Parata, was to become the leading chief of the Waikanae district, a substantial landholder on Kapiti as well as at Waikanae and Porirua, and one of the first two Maori members of Parliament to hold Cabinet rank. According to John Knocks, one of the earliest Europeans to live on the island, 'the Maories treated all Europeans with great respect, offering every encouragement to them to come and reside with them'.[15] This welcoming attitude was, however, well understood by the Europeans who realised that it arose from a realistic assessment of their value. 'Tis for the interest of these natives to keep on good terms with us,' wrote the

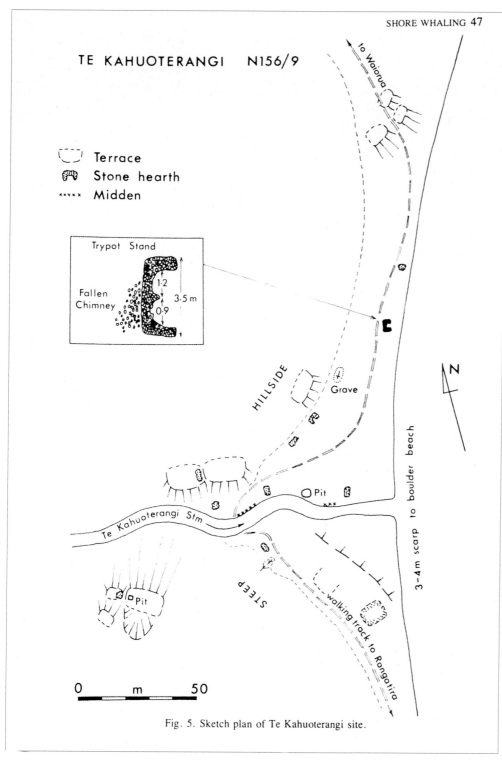

TE KAHUOTERANGI N156/9

⌣ Terrace
🔲 Stone hearth
••••• Midden

Trypot Stand

Fallen Chimney

1.2
3.5 m
0.9

HILLSIDE

Grave

Te Kahuoterangi Stm

Pit

⟂⟂⟂

3-4 m scarp to boulder beach

N

STEEP

walking track to Rangatira

to Waiorua

Pit

0   m   50

Fig. 5. Sketch plan of Te Kahuoterangi site.

On the track to the northern end of the island, visitors walk through the remains of an old whaling station at Te Kahe Te Rau O Te Rangi.

The village, which perched on a beach terrace between the base of the hill and the shore, is now overgrown by forest, but remains can still be found just north of the stream. This is the best preserved whaling site on Kapiti. There are pits, terraces and fireplaces as well as a trypot stand and a whaler's grave.

CAROLINE PHILLIPS/NIGEL PRICKETT

captain of an American whaler, 'as they know that if ships are hindered coming here, adieu to their darling tobacco, muskets and pipes.'[16]

Favoured Europeans were expected to accept Maori custom – even if they did not always understand it, a situation that occasionally led to tension and even violence. The whaler Samuel Bowler, for example, built a whare on the small islet of Tokomapuna without realising that the site had once been a favourite sleeping

An artist's reconstruction of Te Kahe Te Rau O Te Rangi during the 1830s.

The settlement was shared by Ngati Toa and whalers. Its best-known residents were the chiefs Te Matoha and Tungia, both of whom had connections with Europeans through marriage. Te Matoha's daughter, Kahe, lived for a time with Johnny Westcott, then later married John Nicol, and Tungia's daughter lived with Tom Evans who had whaling stations at Rangatira and on Tokomapuna. William Jenkins, who also married a Maori, began his whaling career at this settlement.

CHRIS EDKINS/DEPARTMENT OF CONSERVATION

The remains of a trypot stand at Te Kahe Te Rau O Te Rangi.

This relic, probably the only trypot stand to survive from the early whaling days, along with the other remnants on this site, make Te Kahe Te Rau O Te Rangi one of the best preserved reminders of a colourful chapter in Kapiti's history.

A whaler's grave, Te Kahe Te Rau O Te Rangi.

place of Te Rauparaha and was therefore very tapu – the place where the great chief's head had touched the ground. When Te Rauparaha heard of it, he confronted Bowler, saying, 'Sammy, you are roasting my head', and demanded his gun as compensation for the insult. The gun was handed over but was later recovered by Bowler's fellow whalers and returned to him. When Te Rangihaeata heard of the incident he immediately went to the island and threatened Bowler with a cutting spade, used for slicing whale blubber. This led to a stand-off as the whalers rushed to Bowler's aid and a dangerous situation was defused only by the intervention of Tommy Evans, who was in charge of the whaling station. Having recovered the gun, he presented it to Te Rangihaeata as a gift for his uncle, Te Rauparaha.[17]

In the 1830s Kapiti was a wild frontier, a meeting point of two cultures without the restraints of laws or government. In theory New Zealand was subject, by an act of the British Parliament, to the jurisdiction of the authorities in New South Wales. In reality they were too far away, and in the absence of any means of enforcement there was widespread lawlessness and violence.[18]

In 1830 more than one incident underlined this state of affairs. In August, while the whaling brig *Juno* was at Kapiti buying pigs and potatoes, Peterson, her captain, had an argument with the mate, drew his revolver and shot him dead.

Entrance to the Valley of the Wairau from Cloudy Bay, tinted lithograph by G. F. Angas, 1847.

Although Ngati Toa and their allies often crossed Cook Strait, their familiarity with it never led to complacency. Strong, shifting currents and unpredictable changes in the weather meant that Raukawa was always treated with respect; a canoe crossing was an occasion for ritual designed to ensure survival.

'That part of the ocean called Raukawa was sacred to the people,' wrote Tamihana Te Rauparaha. 'They would not cross it in the ordinary way; all those who had never crossed it before were blindfolded and the figurehead of the canoe was covered with leaves of the karaka. Only those who had previously crossed used their eyes; they acted as pilots, calling out so that those who were blindfolded knew where they were going. When they had crossed and they were close to the beach they would take off the leaves; then the newcomers would be carried ashore by the experienced voyagers, because if they waded a great storm would come up. When everybody had disembarked, the blindfolds would be offered to a tuahu called Tuhinapo.'

The angry crew seized the gun and made Peterson a prisoner, but later, while they were preoccupied chasing a whale, Peterson was released and spirited away by the captain of the *Guide*, which was anchored nearby, and by Captain Ashmore. When the whalers returned, they went after Peterson, who was hiding on Kapiti, but when they came ashore they were confronted by Peterson holding a musket and 'a large body of natives armed with muskets and bayonets'.[19] The crew were driven off and had to return to Sydney – without Peterson.

Any repercussions there might have been were overtaken, only a few weeks later, by the *Elizabeth* affair, one of the most brutal and notorious incidents in British colonial history. It was part of a sequence of events, a chain reaction of attack and revenge, that had begun soon after Te Pehi's return from England when Te Rauparaha, ostensibly to revenge an insult put upon him by the Ngai Tahu chief Rerewhaka, began his campaigns in Te Wai Pounamu. For a time Te Rauparaha and his allies were victorious, inflicting massive casualties on the southerners and taking large numbers of prisoners.

But at Kaiapohia, just north of present-day Christchurch, they were abruptly checked. Here the Ngati Toa chiefs, who pretended to have come in peace, were invited inside the pa by the paramount chief of Ngai Tahu, Tamaiharanui, with the promise of greenstone gifts. Te Pehi, who had met Tamaiharanui in Sydney, accepted the offer, but Te Rauparaha, cautious after his bitter lesson at Papaitonga, was content to remain outside the palisades, trading guns for greenstone. Accounts of what happened inside the pa conflict, although in all versions the outcome is the same: Te Pehi and his escort of chiefs were attacked and killed. Among the dead were Te Aratangata, a half-brother of Te Rauparaha, and 10 other chiefs.

Sorrow and insult of this magnitude had, of course, to be avenged. 'Nourish your children for the time when I come back,' Te Rauparaha called out as he left Kaiapohia, 'because there will be no survivors.'[20] Yet quick retaliation was out of the question, for Ngai Tahu would be on their guard, expecting an attack. What was needed was a new strategy, which would take them by surprise.

The view of Raukawa from Tuhinapo, Kapiti.

A tuahu, or sacred place for the performance of mystical rites, known as Tuhinapo, existed at two locations on the island – near the mouth of the Maraetakaroro Stream and on this vantage point, to the north of Tuteremoana, which has a sweeping vista of Cook Strait.

It was some time before Te Rauparaha found a solution in the European ships that came to Kapiti Island. He first asked Captain Briggs of the *Dragon* to transport him and a taua of Ngati Toa warriors to Akaroa, where Tamaiharanui was known to be, trading flax. Briggs refused. Te Rauparaha then approached John Stewart, captain and part-owner of the brig *Elizabeth*. Stewart also had misgivings about the plan but they disappeared with the promise of an entire shipload of flax fibre as a reward.

When the *Elizabeth* arrived in Akaroa Harbour, Te Rauparaha, Te Hiko and their 100 or so warriors were concealed below decks. The ship's interpreter, a young man named John Cowell, went ashore to invite Tamaiharanui aboard the vessel, pretending it had come direct from Sydney. It seems that the great chief was suspicious, but not suspicious enough. As soon as he and his family came aboard, they were escorted to a cabin where he was seized and bound. Then the Ngati Toa warriors came out of their hiding places and killed the Ngai Tahu who had escorted Tamaiharanui aboard. At dawn the next day the warriors, accompanied, it is alleged, by some of the sailors, went ashore, where they killed hundreds of Ngai Tahu and took many prisoners.[21] Some were eaten, others were cut up and put in baskets stacked on the deck of the *Elizabeth*.

On the return voyage to Kapiti, Tamaiharanui and his wife strangled their young daughter, Roimata, to save her from certain abuse and torture, and threw her body overboard. Tamihana Te Rauparaha later recalled the *Elizabeth*'s triumphant return to the island: 'When the ship anchored at Kapiti the big gun was fired so that the people would know the battle had been won. Then all the inhabitants started off for the shore. The day the ship came in became known also for the thumping of men's feet in the war dance. To us who were at home it seemed like an earthquake.'[22]

Tamaiharanui and his wife were handed over to Tiaia, widow of Te Pehi, and other close female relatives. Both were killed, Tamaiharanui after being tortured but kept alive for several weeks. Alistair Campbell, the celebrated poet of the Kapiti Coast, described his fate in his poem, *Reflections on Some Great Chiefs.*[23]

But Tamaiharanui, what of him?
Pride has seldom had so far to fall.
    Humbled by Te Rauparaha
for Te Pehi's murder,
The brig *Elizabeth* a meat-safe
    stocked with his kinsmen,
his daughter Nga Roimata ear-marked
    for dishonour,
what choice was left him
    but to strangle her?
Hooked up by the chin as punishment,
his body swaying with the ship,
pain was a single fare to Kapiti.
    Claimed by Te Pehi's widow
    as her due,
he became a sexless nothing –
a tailor's dummy that she titivated
    with her mats and jewellery.
But bored with playing cat-and-mouse
    his bankruptcy complete,
        at last she struck…
The fountain she discovered in his throat
quenched her fierce thirst
    and cancelled all his debts.

News of the *Elizabeth* episode soon reached Sydney and London where it shocked the public and caused consternation and disgust in official circles. Until now, intertribal warfare, even when it involved mass murder, was seen as an indigenous matter beyond the authority of the British government. But the involvement of Stewart and other Europeans, coupled with tales of cannibalism on the decks of the brig and the prolonged cruelty of Tamaiharanui's death, convinced officials in New South Wales and England that some action was necessary. Stewart was arrested but released without being tried. Two months later he and the *Elizabeth* were back at Kapiti.[24] Eventually proceedings were begun to bring him and his officers to justice, but the official investigation in Sydney was curiously slow, fuelling suspicion that influential merchants had been able to stall the investigation long enough to allow Stewart to vanish.

Nevertheless the affair did have significant implications. That some form of authority was necessary to curb growing lawlessness in New Zealand was now clear and urgent. The British government approved the appointment of a British Resident for New Zealand and in 1832 James Busby arrived. At the same time the Royal Navy undertook to send a warship to the region to provide visible evidence of authority.[25] A British vessel, the *Zebra*, visited Kapiti in March 1833. According to one of the seamen, C. A. Montrésor, who kept a diary, the European residents of the island were quick to capitalise on the brig's presence:

> Everyone persuading the natives that we came down to redress any injury he may have received. A Mr Harvey, a flax gatherer here, had a hatchet stolen from him some time ago, and although he knew the thief, he could not get it returned. Mr Harvey heard of our being at Sydney, and fancied we might, by chance, visit Capity; so he told the fellow he had written to King William to send a ship down and he would have him killed as soon as she arrived. The man naturally laughed at this; but when, to his great surprise, he saw King William's ship arrive, he immediately went to Mr Harvey with a hatchet and begged forgiveness![26]

Snowy Ilton examines old trypots at Waiorua Bay, 1948.

Until relatively recently whaling relics were a common sight on Kapiti but most have now disappeared. This pair were moved to Rangatira, restored and are now on display in front of the visitors' shelter.

Another pair of pots that once sat on the shore at Wharekohu either rusted away or were removed, as was a trypot on the islet of Tokomapuna. According to an early Waikanae settler, Norman Elder, that particular trypot was 'used as a cradle in which older members of the family would deposit me when they wanted to go fishing'.
FRANK FITZGERALD

Trypot, Rangatira.

HAKOPA TE ATA O TU, 'THE SHADOW OF THE GOD OF WAR'
BY GOTTFRIED LINDAUER

Te Ata O Tu's life was spared by Te Rauparaha at Kaiapohia, adding another remarkable chapter to the already distinguished life of this Ngai Tahu chief.

He was brought back to Kapiti, where he was instructed to keep an eye on the whalers to make sure they did not desecrate sacred places on the island. He is said to have punished an errant European with his fists and few Pakeha on the island dared to cross him. Mrs Brooks, one of only four European women who lived on Kapiti, told James Cowan the Maori she feared most was Te Ata O Tu.

He was a rangatira and a seasoned warrior; tenacity and courage were among his hallmarks, as the following incident suggests. One day a whale (tohora) came in close to the island's eastern shore so Te Ata O Tu and some companions set off in a canoe to pursue it. He succeeded in harpooning the tohora, but fell overboard in the excitement. He could have climbed back into his canoe but chose, instead, to hang on to the harpoon rope. Bewildered by its burden, the whale swam around in circles until it was exhausted. In a final desperate act, it swam straight for the shore, stranding itself on a beach. Despite his ordeal, Te Ata O Tu managed to kill the whale. Amid much rejoicing he was hailed as a taniwha and an atua, or god.

The *Zebra* stayed at Kapiti for a few days, stocked up with pigs and potatoes, then sailed away. It was to be five years before another warship, HMS *Rattlesnake*, visited the island.[27] In the meantime, Te Rauparaha and his people were in complete control.

Only a decade after Te Rauparaha and the taua of northern chiefs had stood on the cliffs above Raukawa and watched Bellingshausen's ship sail by, he had made Waka Nene's vision a reality. Te Rauparaha had led his people away from certain annihilation at Kawhia to make them masters of the greater part of central Aotearoa. It was a remarkable achievement, only partly explained by their access to European weapons gained through the strategic position of Kapiti. Ngai Tahu also had muskets, but that had not prevented their defeat at Kaikoura, Kaiapohia and Onawe in Akaroa Harbour. The crucial factor common to all these engagements was the character of Te Rauparaha – his tactical mastery, his ability to motivate his warriors and to sustain them through hardship, his determination and his ruthlessness. It was this combination that created his mana which, in battle, was often enough to frighten opponents into fleeing.

Yet, despite a ruthlessness that reached its height – or its depth – in the campaigns against Ngai Tahu, Te Rauparaha was a complex man who was capable of unexpected mercy. In the aftermath of the successful siege of Kaiapohia, as Ngati Toa began systematically to kill hundreds of men, women and children, Te Rauparaha asked to see the Ngai Tahu chief, Hakopa Te Ata O Tu. When he was brought before him, Te Rauparaha spoke to him in the most complimentary manner, saying he was too brave a man to be put to death and that his life was to be spared. Te Ata O Tu was taken back to Kapiti and made guardian of the sacred places of Ngati Toa.[28]

This incident should not, perhaps, be overemphasised but it did foreshadow a new facet of the chief's character, which would become more apparent in the years ahead. Te Rauparaha's adaptability and his willingness to accept new ideas, led him to frequently choose diplomacy rather than force. By doing so he was able to hold Ngati Toa's empire together for another decade.

This Indenture made this second day of Sept...
Thousand Eight hundred and thirty Eight Between Rangy...
part, and William Mayhew Jr. of the other part. Whereas ...
full power and right to sell the Lands, hereditaments and ...
have agreed to sell and the said William Mayhew Jr ha...
the considerations herein after mentioned Now this Inden...
consideration of four hundred pounds. of Tobacco. ...
Powder. and three Muskets. amounting together to ...
Sum of sixty five pounds sterling, the receipt whereof to ...
do hereby acknowledge. They, the said parties hereto of the ...
bargain and sell unto the said William Mayhew, Jr. his heir...
called by the natives Towermoury situated on the Eas...
Together with the woods, waters Members Privileges an...
to have and to hold the Said Lands, waters woods Privi...
William Mayhew Jr. his heirs. and assigns forever. free from ...
to the same. And we the said Parties hereto of the first pa...
the said Lands and. Hereditaments unto the said ...
assigns forever.

Witness. James Brice
Francis Williams.
Henry. G. Smith

To Witness the attestation of the parties its being explaine...
Indenture in their own Native Tongue.

No 21.
Entered in Court of Claims New Zealand
5. May 1843

R. T. C. ...
Sec.

Copied ...
W. D. ...
15 Nov 39

5

...bee in the year of our Lord One
Ettie and Robulowe of the first
parties hereto of the first part, having
Premises hereinafter mentioned
agreed to purchase the same for
... witnesseth that for and in
... of Blanket, two casks of
... being equal in value to the
said parties hereto of the first part
...sh party do hereby grant, enfeoff
and assigns all that Island
side of Kapiti or Entry Island
Appurtenances thereto belonging
... and Appurtenances unto the sa...
claim or right of Jurisdiction
... do hereby warrant and defend
... Mayhew & his heirs and...

Rangy Ettie his X mark
Robulowe his X mark
to them the nature of this...

CHAPTER EIGHT

THE CRUCIBLE

During the 1820s and early 1830s Te Rauparaha saw force as the best way of achieving his ambitions but, by the mid-1830s, he exchanged the taiaha for a new weapon, the quill pen. Although neither he nor Te Rangihaeata could write, both used documents to great personal advantage.

This deed, signed by both chiefs, records the sale, in September 1839, of Tahoramaurea to the American whaler, Captain William Mayhew. It was one of a number of similar transactions involving Kapiti, although few of them were valid because Te Rauparaha and Te Rangihaeata sold the same land several times. Disgruntled buyers had no legal remedy.

At the end of the decade, the Ngati Toa leadership signed the Treaty of Waitangi. Their attitude to this important document was not known. Was it just another curious European parchment? Or was its significance understood? What is clear is that Ngati Toa's willingness to accept the compact with the Crown came at the close of an extraordinary period, during which Kapiti had become a crucible for a mixture of whalers, traders, land speculators, missionaries and Maori. In England the convergence of these disparate groups worried the Colonial Office, which eventually realised that intervention was necessary.

When the British authorities did intervene, by means of the treaty, most people at Kapiti welcomed it. They recognised the need for a new order to bring relief from the turmoil of the previous years.

NATIONAL ARCHIVES

THE NGATI TOA empire, the largest Maori had known, was something of a paradox, since it was vulnerable where one might least expect it to be – at its heart, Kapiti. Here tensions between the small tribe and its numerous allies threatened the gains of a decade of conquest.

Antagonism between the tribes became apparent soon after Te Pehi Kupe seized the island and Ngati Toa made it their fortress. The tension was caused, in part, by competition for land, but it was also a response to Ngati Toa's sudden rise to power. The tribes that joined the migration to Kapiti may not have been aware of Te Rauparaha's ambitions; even if they were, they expected to share the new southern lands as equals. But it was Ngati Toa who made the crucial decisions about the land each tribe received, and this was an unwelcome display of power, especially to those who did not fare well in the allocation.

Foremost among these were Ngati Tama, who were confined to Kapiti Island, where they were given a share of a group of settlements on the eastern shore. Resentment at Ngati Tama's failure to secure a part of the mainland created ill-feeling which erupted into fighting in 1827 when Ngati Toa attacked them. There were battles at Maeneene (near the southern end of Rangatira flat) and at nearby Tokokawau. The conflict was brief, but bitter. Among those killed was Pehitaka, a notable Ngati Tama chief. Soon afterwards, they abandoned Kapiti.[1]

For the next few years Ngati Tama were wanderers, briefly occupying land north of Waikanae in a disputed area between Te Ati Awa and Ngati Raukawa, as well as land opposite Mana Island. It was not until the campaigns of Ngati Toa and their allies in Te Wai Pounamu opened up new territory that Ngati Tama found land they could call their own.

Fighting broke out again in 1834 when Te Ati Awa and Ngati Raukawa fought each other in a lengthy and inconclusive campaign, known as Haowhenua, which lasted for two years. Although there was no clear victor, tribal territories were clarified. Raukawa consolidated their control of land from the Kukutuaki Stream (just north of Waikanae Beach) to the Rangitikei, while Te Ati Awa held sway to the south of the stream. The distinct division of territory had one major benefit: members of both tribes living on Kapiti were now able to leave the over-crowded island to settle with relatives on the mainland.

Te Rauparaha's power was also diminished by the increasing European population on Kapiti as whaling prospered and more and more ships visited the island. By the mid-1830s, when shore whaling was at its peak, there were five stations on Kapiti – at Waiorua, Te Kahe Te Rau O Te Rangi, Rangatira, Taepiro and Wharekohu – as well as stations on each of the islets. There were also whaling settlements on the mainland: three opposite Kapiti and others further south at Paremata, Te Korohiwa (south of Titahi Bay) and one on Mana Island.[2] Whalers were not easily intimidated. They were hardy, sometimes violent men, many of whom had lived for years outside the bounds of civilised society. Some were adventurers, others were deserters or escaped convicts. Whaling was a risky business. Every time they put to sea in their small boats they faced danger, possibly death. The most dangerous moment was immediately after the whale was harpooned, as the crew brought their small craft alongside it.

In his book *Adventure in New Zealand* published in 1845, Jerningham Wakefield left an excellent account of this crucial phase of Kapiti's history. He showed that the whalers' lives depended on the judgment of their headsman – and a good deal of luck:

Rangi Topeora *by Gottfried Lindauer.*

Most accounts of Te Rauparaha suggest that he was all powerful. Yet, while he controlled territory from Banks Peninsula to the Manawatu, his power was checked at Kapiti, the epicentre of the Ngati Toa empire, by influential figures such as Topeora, Te Rangihaeata's sister. She was a chieftainess of great mana. The huia feathers in her hair indicate her status.

Her mana was evident in land dealings involving the island. In 1836, for example, Te Rauparaha wanted to sell Maeneene (at the southern end of the Rangatira foreland) to the whaler Tommy Evans, but was prevented by Topeora. Three years later, when Topeora and her son Matene Te Whiwhi sold more than 600 acres at Wharekohu to Captain Mayhew, they did so in spite of Te Rauparaha's disapproval.

Topeora lived on Kapiti for many years. Her authority was acknowledged by Henry Williams, who invited her to sign the treaty. As a demonstration of loyalty and mana, she gave Queen Victoria one of her hei tiki. A few years later, when she was living at Otaki, she was baptised by Bishop Selwyn. Topeora took the name Queen Victoria (Kuini Wikitoria) and was often called 'the Queen of the South'.
AUCKLAND ART GALLERY

The quick obedience to his instant order of 'starn all – lay off!' saves the boat from annihilation, as the whale swings round its huge tail out of the water, and brings it down with a tremendous report. She then 'breaches', or leaps, and plunges in every direction; the headsman continues to direct his crew and boatsteerer, while he poises a new lance, and keeps just out of the vortex formed by her evolutions; the assistant boat and a third one have come up, and, being all of one party, watch outside the splashing for the best chance.

One goes in, and having fixed a lance, receives a blow which smashes the boat and two men's legs; the third boat picks up the men; our first man at last gets steered into the vortex, gives a well-aimed lance in the life, and retreats from the foam, which receives a roseate hue. The monster leaps out of the sea, flourishing her tail and fins, and strikes the water with a noise as loud as a cannon. She wriggles, and plunges, and twists, more furiously than ever, and splashes blood over the boat's crew, who still restrain their excitement and remain collected in all that they do. She is now in her 'flurry' – she is said to 'spout thick blood' and is a sure prize. The boat, by great good management, escapes all accident, and the headsman chuckles as he cuts a notch on the loggerhead, and gives the crew 'a tot all round'.[3]

As the number of whalers grew, so did their determination not be intimidated by their Maori hosts, in particular Te Rauparaha and Te Rangihaeata, with their reputation for bullying Europeans into handing over liquor and guns. An incident involving the well-known whaler and trader, William Jenkins, illustrated the whalers' growing resistance to this practice. Jenkins, who ran a trading vessel between Kapiti and Te Wai Pounamu, later recalled how Te Rauparaha had tried to 'annex' some rum from his schooner. The whaler challenged the chief and a fight ensued. Jenkins grabbed a marlinspike and went for 'Robuller', forcing him to jump overboard and swim ashore.[4] Ten years earlier, Jenkins's action would have been his death sentence, but by the mid-1830s, the balance of power was shifting in favour of the Europeans who could quickly muster considerable support from other gangs. Peterson's station, for example, was said to employ as many as 100 men.[5]

The increasing assertiveness of Kapiti's Europeans (who a decade earlier had been called 'his Pakeha') forced Te Rauparaha to adopt a less aggressive approach

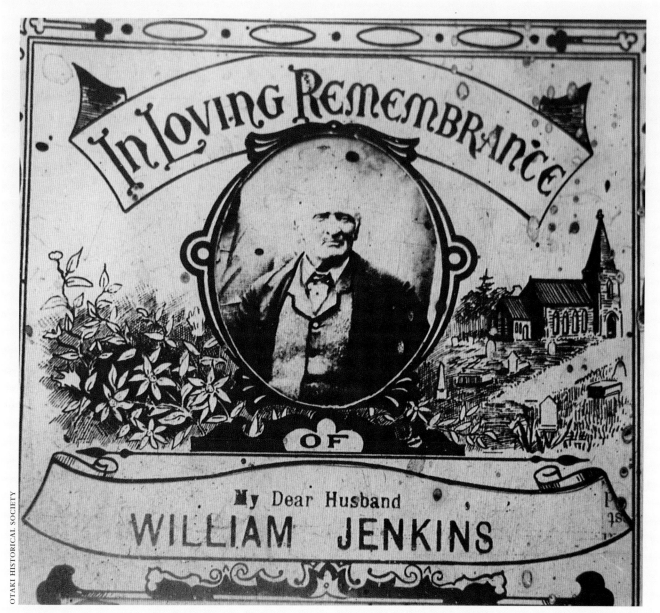

In the mid-1830s, when shore whaling at Kapiti reached its peak, hundreds of whalers lived on or near the island. Most of them remain unknown today but there are a few exceptions, such as William Jenkins.

Jenkins, from Kent, arrived at Kapiti about 1834. He worked first at Te Kahe Te Rau O Te Rangi, then established a whaling station at Waiorua Bay. He also became a trader, running a cutter to and from the South Island. In 1840 he married Paeroke, a Te Ati Awa woman of high rank, retired from whaling and later moved to the mainland where he and his wife ran a farm and an accommodation house at Te Uruhi. In 1853 Paeroke died giving birth to their sixth child, who also died a few months later. Jenkins was heartbroken. For the next four years he was a solo parent, caring for children aged from three to 13.

Paeroke's family hoped that, if he remarried, it would be to one of her sisters, but in 1857 he married a Scotswoman, Margaret Carmont. As a result he was forced to abandon Paeroke's land at Te Uruhi and move to Porirua, where he managed a hotel. In 1869 he and his large family moved again, to Otaki, where he built a house into which he incorporated items salvaged from the *Felixstowe* and the *City of Auckland*; both ships had been wrecked on Otaki Beach in 1878 and, on each occasion, Jenkins risked his life to bring survivors ashore. The same year his 20th, and last, child was born.

In later years William Jenkins became a successful horse trainer. He died at Otaki in 1902, aged 88.

The islet of Tokomapuna has also been known by a series of European names. A chart, drawn in 1837 by the crew of HMS Conway, named it Hummock Island. It was also called Cockatoo Island, although most whalers knew it simply as Evans' Island, because it was the site of Tommy Evans's whaling station.

Evans was an enigma. He ran his whaling station on strict naval lines and, according to Jerningham Wakefield, it 'was always a model of discipline'. Evans's crew wore a uniform: 'red or blue worsted shirts, with white binding on the seams – white trousers, and sou'westers'. And unlike other whaling entrepreneurs, who often paid their men in liquor, Evans paid his men wages, based on an incentive system determined by the amount of oil produced. It was a profitable approach. When Ernst Dieffenbach visited Kapiti aboard the Tory in 1839, he noted that Evans's station produced more whale oil than the other stations combined. Yet Evans's strict discipline seems to have had a malevolent side for Wakefield presented an entirely different pen portrait of the whaling boss in his personal diary. 'Mr Evans would it seems, like to be a little tyrant in Cook's Straits: and having under him in the season a party of 50 or 60 men who will do anything for enough grog, would bid fair to ride roughshod over both native and white people.'

In later years Tokomapuna has also been known as Aeroplane Island, in reference to its profile.

to acquiring the goods he badly wanted. Traders and whalers were keen to buy land, especially on Kapiti itself, and they offered the Ngati Toa chiefs an alluring array of goods in return. The most sought after items were muskets, gunpowder, rum, tobacco, clothing, sugar and rice. Te Rauparaha and Te Rangihaeata, in particular, showed great enthusiasm for this type of deal and towards the end of the decade they had virtually become land agents – without a code of ethics.

A typical example involved the whaler, Tommy Evans, who in 1837 paid the chiefs 500 pounds of tobacco, 100 gallons of rum and 17 pairs of blankets (Sydney value £108) for a slice of the island that included the valuable foreland at Rangatira. Evans built a house on the land and lived there with his wife, the daughter of the chief Tungia, in harmony with his hosts. But Evans was a little naïve not to insist on a record of his purchase. When the Sydney merchant and whaling station owner, Frederick Peterson, bought the same piece of land from the same sellers two years later he made sure there was a written deed. This noted that he 'paid' with two casks of tobacco, one cask of spirits and two pairs of blankets. Meanwhile, the un-suspecting Evans continued to live on the Rangatira block and it was not until he visited Sydney in 1841 that he discovered Peterson was its legal owner. Evans had a lot invested in Kapiti: he owned whaling stations on the island and on Tokomapuna, he had boats and equipment and the island was his home. He had no choice but to buy the land for a second time and pay Peterson £100 for the privilege. This time, however, the purchase was recorded by a legal deed.[6]

These were extraordinary times and Kapiti was an extraordinary place, the meeting point of two very different cultures, neither of them restrained by gov-ernment or regulation. Meanwhile, on the other side of the world, the Colonial Office was becoming alarmed. By 1839 it was clear that the British government would soon prohibit land sales to Europeans in New Zealand,[7] a prospect that prompted a land rush as speculators hurried to make their purchases before the regulations were announced. Foremost among them was the New Zealand Com-pany, whose directors had been watching developments for some time. They planned speculation on a massive scale. Once the rhetoric was stripped away, the

John Stenton Workman.

In his youth Workman, also known as Joe
Stanton, was a shore whaler at Kapiti. He
arrived there in 1839 after some years of
experience on his uncle's ocean whaler, hunting
sperm whales in the Pacific.

'Whaled in Capity for 4 seasons, got an
island from Ruppra called Tupumapuna,' he
noted in a brief outline of his life, now held by
the Alexander Turnbull Library. 'We fortified
the island with four big guns and four shrivels
– this was done for protection against the
natives; but we never had any occasion to use
them. We had several rows with the old chief
but it was always made up again. We the
whalers were always treated well by the
natives.'

While at Kapiti, Workman married
Kokoriti Rewhanga, a Ngati Kahungunu
chieftainess. In 1842 they left for the South
Island, where Workman continued shore
whaling, first at Port Underwood and then at
Kaikoura. Within a few years, whaling
declined everywhere and he turned to farming
instead.

Towards the end of Workman's life he was
described by one writer as 'an old sea-king;
open faced, frank of speech, stately in bearing
and honest as the day. If his story could be
written it would make a book of strange
adventure and eventful life.'

John Workman died in 1904, aged 87.
<small>OTAKI HISTORICAL SOCIETY</small>

Kokoriti Rewhanga.

Jerningham Wakefield was impressed by
the Maori wives of Kapiti's whalers. He wrote
of their 'strong affection for their companion',
and noted that they 'are very quick in
acquiring habits of order and cleanliness,
facilitate the intercourse between the whalers
and their own countrymen; and often manage
to obtain a strong influence over the wild
passions of the former'.
<small>CORAL NICHOLL, NÉE WORKMAN, WAIKANAE</small>

*One of the four guns mentioned by John Stenton Workman has survived and is
on display in the entrance of the Kapiti Boating Club, Paraparaumu.*

Mausoleum for Waitohi on Mana Island by G. F. Angas.

Immediately before the arrival of the Tory *at Kapiti, chiefs from all the local tribes had gathered on Mana Island for the tangi of Waitohi, sister of Te Rauparaha and mother of Te Rangihaeata and Topeora.*

As an adviser to Te Rauparaha and as a recognised leader in her own right, Waitohi had played an important part from the moment the heke (migration) left Kawhia. When Ngati Toa and their allies arrived on the Kapiti Coast and established themselves on the island, it was she who made the crucial allocation of territory and it was her astute diplomacy that contained intertribal tensions. Patricia Burns, biographer of Te Rauparaha, described Waitohi as 'wise in matters of religion and protocol, universally respected and occasionally feared'.

Without her mediation, the fragile peace between the tribes quickly lapsed. Rivalries evident at her tangi flared into violence a few days later at the Battle of Kuititanga when Te Ati Awa and Ngati Raukawa fought at Waikanae.
ALEXANDER TURNBULL LIBRARY

key to the company's 'colonisation system' was quite simple – it intended to buy large tracts of land from the Maori at a very low price then slowly release it on to the market to be bought by the company's emigrants at a very high price. The revenue gained would pay for the development of planned settlements, as well as enriching the directors and their shareholders.

In May 1839, the company dispatched the *Tory* which arrived in Cook Strait in August. On board were Colonel William Wakefield, brother of Edward Gibbon Wakefield, the architect of the 'Wakefield System', and the latter's son Edward Jerningham, usually known as Jerningham Wakefield. The *Tory* called first at Cloudy Bay, then crossed the strait to Port Nicholson, the site chosen for their first settlement. The Wakefields had considerable success in buying land, so that when the *Tory* arrived off Kapiti Island on 15 October, the mood aboard the ship was more than confident, it was ebullient. The next 10 days were spent on Kapiti. In that time William and Jerningham Wakefield began to appreciate the complexities of the country they had come to colonise.

Their arrival was overshadowed by the Battle of Kuititanga, which was fought between Te Ati Awa and Ngati Raukawa the same morning, while Te Rauparaha in a canoe, and a number of whalers in their boats, watched from beyond the surf. The first outing for the ships' company was a visit to the Te Ati Awa pa at the Waikanae Estuary, where they did what they could to help the wounded. Colonel Wakefield remained on board, where he was visited by Te Rauparaha, who was clearly upset and uneasy about the outcome of the fighting. His kin, Ngati Raukawa, had been routed, 50 of their warriors had been killed and he himself was fortunate to have escaped when he had tried to come to their aid. Some accounts suggest that he was largely to blame for the battle, which was the result of his customary tactic of inflaming intertribal enmities.[8]

It is a tribute to his resilience that, within a few days, Te Rauparaha had recovered his spirits and was able to negotiate with the Wakefields using his usual techniques of bluster, charm and intimidation. At first Ngati Toa rejected the

Wakefields' overtures, mainly because they had purchased Poneke (Port Nicholson), which Ngati Toa regarded as their own, without their consent. Eventually, however, the chiefs agreed and on 24 and 25 October signed deeds of sale for large areas in both the North and South Islands in exchange for an array of goods. When these were brought up on deck for distribution, however, a scramble followed that offended William Wakefield.[9] John Knocks, a lad who worked for Tommy Evans, was the colonel's interpreter and described the scene:

> After having negotiated for the purchase of Totaranui, Queen Charlotte Sound, and other parts near there, for which they were paid in goods which was delivered on board the ship, over which there was the most indiscriminate scramble – boxes of pipes all smashed to pieces, pieces of print, calico, and blankets torn to pieces in their wild efforts to get possession, driving us who were on deck into the riging [sic] for fear of being hurt during their mad scramble. The rush was so general, that I doubt whether the rightful owners who sold the land got a due share of the proceeds.[10]

On 29 October the Wakefields sailed away to buy more land elsewhere.

The concern of the British government, and the purpose of its imminent ban on land sales, was to prevent exploitation of the Maori. Whatever may be said about unscrupulous European land buying elsewhere, it is difficult to argue that the inhabitants of Kapiti were deceived. Te Rauparaha and Te Rangihaeata, in particular, were masters of deception who never hesitated to exploit gullible Europeans. And there were many of these among the parade of hopefuls who visited Kapiti in late 1839. Nor is it reasonable to suggest that the chiefs did not understand the real implications of a deed of sale. Ngati Toa had lived alongside Europeans for almost 20 years and several senior chiefs, including Te Rauparaha and Te Hiko, had visited Sydney. More convincing is the suggestion that Ngati Toa had little understanding of the kind of large-scale immigration envisaged by the New Zealand Company. This is confirmed by William Wakefield, who wrote in his diary of rumours that some of those who had signed the purchase deeds believed 'that the sale would not affect their interests, from an insufficiency of emigrants arriving

This memorial cairn, which once stood on Motungarara, recorded the death of George Stubbs, a young whaler from Australia, who was drowned in a whaling accident near Kapiti.

Stubbs was the father of Wiremu Parata Te Kakakura, who became paramount chief of the Waikanae district in the second half of the 19th century. Wi Parata's mother, Metapere Waipunahau, was of Te Ati Awa and Ngati Toa descent. She was a woman of high rank, the daughter of Te Rangihiroa and a niece of Te Pehi.

Stubbs's memorial on Motungarara was originally surrounded by a whalebone fence but when W. E. Bendall visited the islet in 1920 he noted that the bones 'had all fallen down and were buried beneath a mass of undergrowth'.

This photo of the cairn was taken in 1987. A few years later the memorial was dismantled and removed by the branch of the Webber family which now owns the land on which it was built.

on his way to Sydney. Although he stayed for only a day, he saw enough to prompt him to write to the Church Missionary Society in London asking that a missionary be sent to Cook Strait. Marsden's call echoed an earlier plea by Te Rauparaha, who had approached Captain Robertson of the *Bee* when the brig called at Kapiti in 1835.[16] But whereas Marsden was interested in making converts, it is more likely that Te Rauparaha saw that a missionary would teach Ngati Toa how to read and write.

It is probable that Te Rauparaha's interest in the benefits of Christianity had its origins in the missionary work of Matahau, a remarkable young Maori man who was the first to bring the gospel to the Kapiti Coast, probably in the mid-1830s.

Matahau, sometimes also known as Ripahau, was a Ngati Raukawa. As a child, he had been captured by Ngapuhi, who took him to the Bay of Islands and made him a slave. He and his captors were among the first Maori to be influenced by the missionaries. Once freed, he lived with William Williams and then with his brother Henry. When Matahau was old enough, he returned to his people, who now lived at Otaki. His efforts to convert them were not well received so he moved to Waikanae, where he had more success among Te Ati Awa. He introduced them to reading and writing, encouraged them to embrace Christian ideals and inspired them to build a number of small churches.

Te Rauparaha was still determined to obtain a European missionary and twice sent letters to Henry Williams, who was in charge of the Anglican mission at Pahia, with his request.[17] It was not until 1839, however, that the invitation was accepted and it was the Wesleyans, not the Anglicans, who came first. The catalyst seems to have been the knowledge that the *Tory* was about to sail, for the missionary societies were the New Zealand Company's most persistent critics. They knew that colonisation elsewhere had resulted in indigenous peoples being 'despoiled of their lands, demoralised and, in some instances, exterminated'.[18]

In May 1839, the same day that the *Tory* left for New Zealand, the Wesleyan missionaries John Bumby and John Hobbs sailed from the Bay of Islands in the

Hokianga, accompanied by 20 Maori youths who were originally from the Cook Strait region, but had lived most of their lives in the Bay of Islands as slaves, captured by Ngapuhi chiefs of the 1820 taua. As Christianity took hold in the north, they were, like Matahau, freed by their converted captors and became Christians themselves. The Wesleyan missionaries realised that these young people were the key to spreading the gospel among their southern kin.

The *Hokianga* reached Port Nicholson in June, left some of the young men there and crossed to Cloudy Bay. Here Bumby and Hobbs found a keen interest in Christianity among the Maori, but received a rough reception from the whalers, who made it plain that they were not welcome. 'I am persuaded,' Bumby reported, 'if Missionary operations were commenced here, there would be more opposition from civilised Europeans than from the untutored barbarians.'[19]

There was a more encouraging welcome from Te Rauparaha at Mana Island, where he and many of the residents of Kapiti had taken refuge after an influenza epidemic had swept the island, with many Maori deaths. Bumby noted with concern that 'the natives have obstinately refused to take medicine, in consequence of which many have died. Instead of nursing their sick they remove them into the bush to die.'[20] Te Rauparaha repeated his wish for a missionary and a young man called Paul became his teacher.[21] But this was not enough. Te Rauparaha turned his attention once more to the Anglicans. He sent his son, Tamihana, and his great-nephew, Matene Te Whiwhi, to the Bay of Islands to ask Henry Williams to send a missionary to Kapiti. He was gratified when, in November of the same year, Williams himself arrived at Kapiti to install the young Octavius Hadfield. The meeting between Te Rauparaha and Hadfield was to have far-reaching results exemplified almost a decade later by their collaboration in the building of the Rangiatea Church at Otaki. 'He certainly looked more like a chief than any man I have yet seen,' Hadfield wrote in his diary. 'He listened very attentively to what was said, and *appeared* much interested in the gospel message.'[22]

Te Rauparaha *was* interested. He was a perceptive leader and his people owed their survival and their military power to his willingness to consider new ideas. Now, among the tremendous changes in the Maori world caused by the arrival of the Europeans, his extraordinary adaptability was crucial. He recognised that education, which came hand in hand with Christianity, was the key to his people's future. In fact, he had already taken an important step to prepare the ground by acknowledging that a necessary condition of the new order was peace with Ngati Toa's old enemy, Ngai Tahu. It had been negotiated shortly before the arrival of Bumby and Hobbs.[23]

After a few weeks Henry Williams left Kapiti, but returned six months later bringing with him a copy of the Treaty of Waitangi. His 'principal object' was to obtain Te Rauparaha's signature, which he regarded as the key to securing the Crown's 'sovereignty over all the southern districts'. The great chief signed the treaty in the presence of Williams and Hadfield, and Williams wrote to Governor Hobson expressing his 'utmost satisfaction'. The reason the missionary set great store by Te Rauparaha's signature became evident in the next few weeks, when he recorded more than 130 signatures from chiefs in Whanganui, Manawatu, Horowhenua and Otaki as well as parts of the upper South Island.[24]

Notable signatures collected on Kapiti included those of the chieftainesses Rangi Topeora and Kahe Te Rau O Te Rangi – two of only five women who were invited to sign the treaty. This concession was not enough to overcome the indignation

Octavius Hadfield depicted in a stained glass window at St Luke's Church, Waikanae.

Te Tiriti o Waitangi
The Cook Strait Sheet

The Cook Strait Sheet by Max Hailstone, 1990.

Christchurch artist and typographical expert, Max Hailstone, marked the 150th anniversary of the Treaty of Waitangi by producing a series of nine sheets of signatures, based on the original copies of the document that were taken round the country in 1840.

He copied important or graphically interesting signatures from the originals, which were often based on the signatories' moko; the signatures were then enlarged to illustrate his contention that the marks were sometimes similar. Most chiefs were unfamiliar with writing and for many the treaty was their first use of a written mark, so they tended to copy the mark of a dominant figure in their district. This is particularly evident in the Cook Strait sheet, in which Te Rauparaha's mark (fourth from the top on the right) seems to have prompted imitation.

The Herald, *South Island and Kapiti Sheet* by Max Hailstone, 1990.

The signatures of the Ngati Toa chiefs at Kapiti were crucial to the treaty's widespread acceptance elsewhere. Before they made their marks, the signatories were mostly from northern parts of New Zealand, but once the Kapiti leadership had signed, the treaty's credibility was greatly increased. Ngati Toa's co-operation bought central Aotearoa under the treaty and made it a national document.

Emboldened by their acceptance, Major Thomas Bunbury sailed around the South Island on the *Herald*, collecting signatures from Ngati Toa chiefs in distant parts of their empire, and from Ngai Tahu.

of Kapiti's women, who drew Henry Williams's attention to the contradiction of an agreement between a Queen and her subjects being limited almost entirely to men: 'The ladies have expressed some disapprobation in not having a more prominent part in the treaty with her Majesty,' he later reported to Hobson.[25] The island of Kapiti should, it seems, be celebrated as the birthplace of New Zealand feminism.

Williams searched the region for signatures in May 1840; six weeks later Major Thomas Bunbury covered the same ground looking for those who had not signed earlier. Te Rauparaha's support was so important that, although he assured Bunbury he had already signed, he was invited to do so again – the only person to sign the Treaty of Waitangi twice. Bunbury also secured Te Rangihaeata's assent, a considerable achievement.[26]

These men's marks were important, not only to the Europeans who sought them, but also to the Ngati Toa leadership, who hoped that the treaty would protect their empire from claims by other tribes. The treaty recognised land taken by conquest which was still held at the time it was signed. (When the bottle stopped spinning, you kept what you had.) In fact, as later events showed, the dominance of Ngati Toa made the transition to British rule easier than if the Crown had been confronted with a central Aotearoa divided against itself. 'British power on the shores of Cook Strait was inherited from Ngati Toa through the conquest of the conqueror,' wrote the historian James Belich. 'Such occurrences were not uncommon in the history of European imperialism. An intensification of European contact upsets the delicate balance of a fragile pre-existing empire. Europe then inherits its earth, with the help of its own subjects.'[27]

After the treaty was signed, Kapiti's value as a fortress diminished. Ngati Toa, no longer fearing attack, left for their settlements on the mainland. But to ensure their right to Kapiti remained strong, Te Rangihiroa and his family continued to live at Waiorua, as the kaitiaki, or guardians, of the tribe's cooking fires, which symbolised its ownership of the island. Their continuing presence would later constitute crucial legal evidence for, from now on, tribal disputes over land and territorial ambitions would have to be settled through the Land Courts – a new venue for old conflicts.

CHAPTER NINE

THE TRANSIENT NATURE OF ALL EARTHLY THINGS

The exodus of most Maori from Kapiti to the mainland towards the end of the 1830s was matched by the departure of most of the whalers. A decade later, a similar migration of Te Ati Awa, from the mainland opposite the island to Taranaki, further reduced the district's dwindling population.

In 1848 most Te Ati Awa, who lived in three pa around the Waikanae rivermouth, returned to their ancestral lands. The missionary, Richard Taylor, noted that 600 people travelled to various destinations in Taranaki; some went by sea in 44 canoes, others by land on horseback.

The abandoned pa quickly deteriorated. The following year, Hadfield's church in the principal pa, Kenakena, was still standing but many of the whare, and the palisades that ringed the settlement, were starting to collapse. Within a few years, windblown sand began to bury the pa.

Taylor returned to Kenakena in 1854. Hadfield's church was in a poor state, 'the floor rotting, the pulpit broken in pieces, the communion rail partly destroyed, a dead goat laid in the church. The scene was most melancholy and presented a vivid picture of the transient nature of all earthly things.'

Kapiti by W. A. McCleverty shows the island from the north, foreshortened and exaggerated. The setting sun illuminates the western cliffs (right) and the small triangular islet (left) is Tahoramaurea.
REX NAN KIVELL COLLECTION, NATIONAL LIBRARY OF AUSTRALIA

THE FEW MAORI who remained on Kapiti after the signing of the Treaty of Waitangi adopted the new order with enthusiasm. The following year, Jerningham Wakefield stayed with Te Hiko and his family on Motungarara and observed that his hosts prayed three times a day. When Wakefield distributed some prayer and hymn books printed in Maori, he noted in his diary that 'the natives were highly delighted; all laying their hands on their heads in token of gratitude'. Two days later he attended a church service in Te Rangihiroa's clay and wattle house at Waiorua: 'A native teacher preached a sermon after reading a chapter. The audience consisted entirely of Rangihiroa's family and retainers.'[1] Similarly, when the Reverend Richard Taylor visited the island in 1843 he met a small party 'of Xtian natives belonging to Mr Hadfield'. Hearing that he was a missionary, they invited him into their hut 'which in imitation of the European cottages was built of wattle and daub and had a chimney'. Word of his presence quickly spread and three days later he held a service 'in the native chapel at Kapiti' where, he wrote, 'I had full 150 natives present who were very attentive'.[2]

Little is known about this building as no written account or drawings of it exist. It was likely to have been one of the chapels built by local Maori in the late 1830s at the instigation of Matahau. The Kapiti church was of particular significance because it was probably here that Matahau was baptised during Henry Williams's first visit to Kapiti. 'It was an interesting service,' Williams wrote, 'considering that this young man had been made an instrument in the hand of the Great head of the Church in conveying very much knowledge of Divine things to his benighted countrymen.'[3] But although the building was big enough to accommodate 150 worshippers, neither Taylor nor Williams mentioned its location. Today its site is still uncertain, although it may have been on the south side of the Maraetakaroro Stream, not far from the shore. In 1919, a visitor to Kapiti was shown 'a levelled out site built up by boulders above high-water mark on the main Island, and just opposite Motungarara, where Bishop Hadfield had a small church in which services were held on his periodical visits to the Island'.[4] This seems a logical place for a church, close to the islands of Motungarara and Tahoramaurea, which formed the anchorage for visiting ships and were, in effect, the gateway to Kapiti. Since Maraetakaroro was also the site of a large pa, a church there would have been accessible to Maori and whalers as well as visitors. Furthermore, the church site is close to Tuhinapo, a sacred place, so the native chapel would have been part of a spiritual precinct.[5]

Within a few years of the chapel's construction, most of the island's Maori inhabitants had moved to the mainland. Their retreat from Kapiti was temporary (to escape a flu epidemic), but it soon became permanent because the treaty enabled Ngati Toa to live on the mainland without fear of attack. Kapiti was left to the whalers. The missionary John Bumby recorded that there were 'upwards of eighty white men' living on the island at this time.[6] A few Maori settlements remained for another decade, among them the pa at Mangawharariki, which continued to be occupied until 1846 when most of the people left 'so as to be near the churches'. This suggests that, even then, the chapel on Kapiti was no longer standing. Several families remained on the island but 'in 1850 everybody left'.[7]

Nor did the shore whaling industry on Kapiti survive for long. It reached its zenith in the mid-1830s, then declined rapidly. The reason was clear: whale numbers had been depleted by unrestricted hunting of cows and calves without thought for the future of the species, and too many boats were chasing the few whales that survived. The 1838 season at Cloudy Bay was reported to have been 'a total fail-

Deserted pah, Kapiti Island
by W. J. Swainson, 1849.
ALEXANDER TURNBULL LIBRARY

Kapiti from Deserted Pah,
at Kenakena *by W. J.
Swainson, 1849.*
ALEXANDER TURNBULL LIBRARY

ure' and the same was true at Kapiti, where only Peterson's station had any success.[8]

The fickle nature of the whaling boom was illustrated by the change in the fortunes of the Sydney merchants, Wright & Long. In November 1836 their vessel, the *Roslyn Castle*, had docked at Sydney with the largest whaling cargo ever brought into the Australian port, accumulated in Cook Strait during the previous two winters. Yet only a year later, after a poor season in which they managed to acquire just one-tenth of that bumper cargo, the partners went into receivership and their shore whaling stations around New Zealand, including those at 'Capertee', were put up for auction.[9]

Two years later, when the *Tory* arrived at Kapiti, whaling still seemed to be flourishing. Jerningham Wakefield's account presents a picture of lively industry, but that was probably because whaling was now limited to the shore stations, which continued to seem prosperous only because of Tommy Evans's efficiency. During the 1839 season, his six-boat station produced 250 tons of oil, which was more than the combined catch of the 19 boats from other whaling stations in the vicinity. Dieffenbach concluded his more prosaic description of the industry with the comment: 'Like all shore whaling, however, that of Kapiti is on the decline, and I do not suppose that the establishment will be kept up much longer'.[10]

As whaling diminished, the island's remaining inhabitants turned to farming, despite William Wakefield's view that Kapiti 'can never become of great value to the agriculturalist'. He had reached this conclusion when he surveyed the island from its summit, a welcome excursion after several weeks confined on the *Tory* conducting land sale negotiations. From Tuteremoana he noted Kapiti's 'excessive steepness' and later wrote in his diary, 'Its shores are nearly perpendicular and of great height. On the top are occasional table lands on which the timber has been burned and where good pasturage grows. The valleys are narrow and afford no temptation to the settler.'[11]

Among the earliest of Kapiti's farmers was John Nicol who, in 1839, 'drained a swamp there as the whales were getting scarce and I had a heavy family. I trenched this swamp and then planted it with wheat, potatoes, and onions.'[12] Nicol and his wife, Kahe, farmed about 4 acres at Waiorua that belonged to Te Hiko. Not everyone, however, accepted the whaler's right to cultivate the land. Bill Jenkins, a fellow whaler, later recalled a violent dispute that occurred when Nicol began to dig his drain: 'A Maori slave came and knocked him down. I said "You must be a coward to put up with that – knock him down with the shovel!" And he did knock him down. Shortly afterwards Te Hiko came up and marked the piece of land for Mrs Nicol. He put in posts to show the boundaries. Nicol then fenced the place all round, drained it and cultivated it up to the time we ceased to live on Kapiti.'[13] When Richard Taylor visited Kapiti he saw other cultivations. Andrew Brown, the storekeeper on Tahoramaurea, took him to Wharekohu to see his farm 'which chiefly consists of a small swamp which he has drained'. The missionary also met another European who complained bitterly that he had been robbed by 'the natives' because they suspected he had killed one of the cattle on the island.[14]

Wild cattle had been roaming Kapiti for almost a decade, since 40 had been released on the island in 1836 by the Sydney trader, Captain W. B. Rhodes.[15] In the intervening years the herd had grown to about 100.[16] Whether Rhodes still regarded them as his property is unclear, for they were claimed by Te Rauparaha and Te Hiko, who occasionally gave a whaler permission to kill a beast. Livestock, especially sheep, may also have been transferred from Mana Island to Kapiti, particularly after Captain Peterson acquired part of Mana in 1839.[17] Goats were on the island the following year.[18]

What impressed Taylor was the pasture on Kapiti. When he and his ship's captain called at one of the whaling stations they found 'a fertile valley of some extent covered to my astonishment with beautiful rye grass from which hay had been made'. Several days later they visited another whaling site and found 'a beautiful little valley there which to my surprise was in great measure covered with rye grass and forming a sward almost equal to any in England the seed having been bought years ago by some ship. I saw also a neat European garden.'[19]

The first of these farms he described was probably the Waiorua Valley, which was also the site of Robert Jillett's well-known whaling station. It is fortunate that the artist J. A. Gilfillan sketched this village in the early 1840s because his is the only known picture of one of Kapiti's flourishing whaling settlements. Despite the number of visitors to the island, and the 19th century penchant for pen and pencil, the only other images are William Swainson's sketches, but these were drawn in 1849, some years after all the old whaling stations, except Waiorua, had been abandoned. The painter, W. A. Bowring, later produced a watercolour of Jillett's station based on Gilfillan's sketch. No livestock are evident but several of the larger houses have fenced yards, presumably to protect gardens, and a fence can be seen around the perimeter of the village, no doubt to keep out the marauding cattle that often congregated on flat land near the Okupe Lagoon.[20]

The settlement at Waiorua continued for some years as the ex-whalers and their Maori wives cultivated the largest area of flat land on the island. Among them were Bill Jenkins and Paeroke, who lived on the northern side of the stream, and John Nicol and Kahe, who had a house on the southern side. Although both men farmed, they were also traders so were often absent. It cannot have been an easy life for their wives. Each year Kahe had a child and on one occasion Bill Jenkins was her midwife.[21] In 1845 John and Kahe left the island and some of their neighbours also departed at about that time. The valley continued to be cultivated by the remaining whalers, including Bob Jillett who leased the land to the north of the creek from Metapere Waipunahau, the daughter of Te Rangihiroa. John O'Meara shared the southern side with James Cootes and his wife, Waitaoro Te Kanawa.[22]

In 1849 HMS *Acheron* called at Kapiti while on a comprehensive survey of the New Zealand coastline. One of the crew, G. A. Hansard, left a description of the village:

½ past 5 a.m. – saw the Island of Kapiti looming on our starboard bow. Landed and found the shingly beach thickly strewn with the vertebrae of whales ... nearly a foot

Kapiti by *Nicholas Chevalier, 1868.*

The island citadel declined when canoe travel was increasingly being replaced by other forms of transport.

After the signing of the treaty, the mainland became safer for Europeans, who either walked or rode along the coastline from Pukerua Bay to Wanganui.
MUSEUM OF NEW ZEALND/TE PAPA TONGAREWA

in diameter. This has always been the resort of whalers. A beautiful lawn-like piece of land close to the water is occupied by their village, where houses peep forth from knots of trees, and the blue smoke curls upwards; the whole cheered by bright sunny weather, forming a delightful tranquil scene. Meandering through the centre of this grassy spot is a little transparent brook, where, 'turkies' lay basking in the herbage; abundance of common poultry made war upon our enemies the sandflies, and scores of English geese and ducks disturbed by us rushed hurry-scurry into the water.

Everybody seemed engaged in active industry. One party busy at the sawpit; another squaring logs for building; this man repairs his boat; that has killed and is cutting up a wild pig. In front of a cot – a European's, judging by the few tattered books and two formidable harpoons ranged over the fireplace, two or three dark women are busy extracting muttonfish [paua] from their shells. Afterwards they string them up upon strips of green flax, to be dried in the smoke of their wood fires. They cleanse their potatoes by scraping with a broken shell, and wash them by placing one foot in the basket as they dip and shake it about in the water with both hands.

The whalers are well looked after by their Maori wives, who keep the home in nice order. On entering one cottage surrounded with a neat paling, within which was a flowerbed, I saw the Englishman at dinner, assiduously waited on by his wife, a fine specimen of Maori beauty; tall, well-formed and having handsome and intelligent

Jillett's whaling station, Waiorua Bay, 1844 *by W. A. Bowring (after J. A. Gilfillan).*

Robert Jillett, a young Tasmanian farmer and whaler, arrived at Kapiti about 1837. At the peak of the whaling boom, there were five whaling stations on Kapiti and another three on the offshore islets but by 1844 Jillett's was the sole remaining operation. In that year it was as productive as any in the country, operating five boats, employing 40 men and producing 140 tons of oil and 5 tons of whalebone. A year later, however, Jillett's station was reduced to two boats and 16 men.

Within a year or two, whaling ceased and Waiorua became a farming settlement. Robert Jillett continued to live at the village with his Ngati Raukawa wife, Aomarere, and their children, along with other ex-whalers and their families, but by the early 1850s they had all left the island.
ALEXANDER TURNBULL LIBRARY

features. With one hand she covered the table; a beautiful baby, clean and well clothed, was cradled in the other. Her husband, quiet and well mannered, very happy and contented – still more so, if he could procure a few books. They have about 200 goats, 500 fat sheep and thirty head of domestic cattle.[23]

This idyllic life did not last. Within a few years all the whalers and their wives had left the island. Some of them remained in the area, however, earning their living in various ways, especially inn-keeping. Kahe Te Rau O Te Rangi and her husband opened an accommodation house at Paekakariki, William Jenkins and Paeroke built an inn at Te Uruhi on the mainland opposite the island, and in 1848 another ex-whaler and his Maori wife, Thomas Wilson and Hanake, opened the Ferry Inn at the Waikanae Estuary.[24] The inns provided travellers on the coastal highway, the sandy beach that ran from Paekakariki to Wanganui, with food and shelter as they passed through, but the Kapiti Coast and the island itself were no longer destinations in their own right.

For the first time in centuries Kapiti was almost uninhabited. Although local Maori were regular visitors, after 1850 none actually lived on the island. The only residents were the European farmers Cimino and O'Meara, who leased from Wi Parata land at the northern end; and David Brown and his family, who lived at Wharekohu on land his father, Andrew Brown, had bought from Captain Mayhew.

The Browns' involvement with Kapiti dates back to the heyday of the whalers. In December 1839 Captain Mayhew bought Wharekohu from Topeora and her son, Matene Te Whiwhi, for three boxes of tobacco, five cases of pipes, four bags of sugar, one gun and 12 shirts.[25] The sale was opposed by Te Rauparaha but proceeded in spite of him, and he received a share of the goods. The previous year Mayhew had also bought the islet of Tahoramaurea from Te Rauparaha and three years later he purchased Motungarara from Tommy Evans.[26] This made Mayhew the biggest European landowner on Kapiti and a significant player in the island's affairs.

Te Rauparaha and Captain Mayhew shared Tahoramaurea. In 1840, when Colonel Wakefield visited the islet to discuss land sales with the chief, he recorded his impressions of Te Rauparaha's house in his diary:

> A miserable house, tabooed for himself and his wife, with one end parted off for his son, offers no temptation to his enemies nor calls for the envy of his rival allies. Near it are piled up cases of tobacco, of cotton goods and of the various objects which he has begged or extorted from the Masters of vessels anchoring here. These are covered with dead brushwood and are narrowly watched by his slaves.[27]

Andrew Brown and his two sons lived nearby. They ran Mayhew's store and were also busy clearing his land at Wharekohu. The store was still operating in 1843 when Richard Taylor visited Tauhoramaurea. The missionary was no more impressed with the storekeeper's dwelling than Wakefield had been with Te Rauparaha's; he noted that it was 'neatly constructed of reeds built by the natives, but it is kept in a very slovenly manner'.[28]

In 1844 Mayhew left Kapiti to live in the Bay of Islands, where he owned 20,000 acres, and succeeded Captain James Clendon as the American Consul. Before he left, he sold all his interests at Kapiti to Andrew Brown but, unlike Topeora and Te Rauparaha, he was paid in cash, not goods, and he made a substantial profit. He received £200 for the land at Wharekohu, £300 for Motungarara and £500 for Tahoramaurea; the higher price for the latter presumably included the store, its stock and Mayhew's substantial house.[29] In five years Mayhew had converted a miscellany of goods into £1,000.

Brown, on the other hand, paid an enormous sum to buy what was to become a nightmare. The first suggestion of difficulty had become apparent the previous year when the Land Claims Commissioner, William Spain, examined Mayhew's claim to Wharekohu. The star witness was Te Rauparaha, whose ambivalent role in the deal was revealed under cross-examination.[30] Before Spain announced his decision he had to examine many other claims throughout the country, a process that took him two years. In the meantime Mayhew, who probably sensed there would be trouble realising his claims, sold all his Kapiti interests to Andrew Brown. He and his sons had worked for the American captain since they had arrived in New Zealand three years earlier, so they should have been at Kapiti long enough to realise the dubious legality of the rash of land deals that occurred in the months before the Treaty of Waitangi. But Andrew Brown was

W. B. Rhodes 'bought' Kapiti from Te Rauparaha and Te Rangihaeata in October 1839 while on a land-buying spree during which he also acquired large areas on the East Coast.

Although Rhodes's claim to the island was the weakest of all the transactions Commissioner Spain examined, he concluded that a 'bona fide purchase was made' but qualified this with the observation that 'the well known character of Rauparaha and Rangihaeata however hold out a very slight prospect of the claimant being permitted to occupy the land even if he obtained a Crown Grant to it'.

Rhodes, unlike Andrew Brown, did not pursue his Kapiti claim with much tenacity. Instead he put his considerable energy into land deals around Port Nicholson and further afield. By 1850 he owned hundreds of thousands of acres in both islands and was known as 'the millionaire of Wellington'.

ALEXANDER TURNBULL LIBRARY

perhaps naïve, or he may have thought that the signature of the missionary, Henry Williams, gave Mayhew's purchase added credibility. Whatever his thoughts, when Spain made his findings public in 1845 Brown's confidence was repaid – Mayhew's claim was recognised and a grant for 1125 acres at Wharekohu was recommended.[31]

Later events did not, however, favour Brown. Before a title could be issued the land had to be surveyed but, when it was, the surveyors found the block was only 617 acres; this discovery held up the process. In the meantime, Te Rangihaeata had become increasingly irritated at the growing Pakeha presence on the mainland and, in particular, by the Crown's relentless acquisition of Ngati Toa land. In 1846 his frustration flared into open revolt against the government. Seven years earlier, when he had signed the treaty in the belief it would preserve his tribe's land, he had agreed to put aside his warlike ways but, just in case, he had left a cache of gunpowder and bullets with the storekeeper on Kapiti. Now he needed it. One night Andrew Brown awoke to find 'a glaring-eyed tattooed visage' bending over him: Rangihaeata and a group of warriors had come to collect their ammunition.[32] Unfortunately for Brown, he had complied with government regulations and had handed the gunpowder and bullets in to the authorities. Rangihaeata ransacked the store and Brown was lucky to escape with his life. Early reports that the chief had murdered a European on Kapiti were an exaggeration,[33] but the experience was enough to encourage Andrew Brown to move to the mainland.

His son David was not deterred. He continued to develop the farm at Wharekohu while his father pressed the authorities to issue him with the title. He wrote to the Colonial Secretary and Governor Grey, but his efforts had quite the opposite effect from what he intended. In 1849 the Attorney General reviewed his claim but decided that 'the whole affair is suspicious', and recommended that no grant be issued.[34] The Executive Council was more lenient and offered Brown 320 acres, less than one-third of the original claim, because 'the value of the payments made to the Natives at the time of the original purchase were greatly exaggerated in the statement of Mayhew's claim'.[35]

Andrew Brown challenged the council's recommendation. Again he went to the top, making a second approach to his friend, the governor. To no avail. Not only did he fail to sway Grey but, worse, he may have put a grand notion in the governor's mind, for the following year he offered Ngati Toa £5,000 for the whole of Kapiti.[36] The offer was refused by Wi Parata and the other owners, who prized their beautiful and famous island. Grey continued his hunt for an offshore retreat; Arawa declined his bid for Mokoia Island in Lake Rotorua but he eventually succeeded in buying Kawau Island, north of Auckland.

In 1851 Andrew Brown was finally granted title to the land, but his enjoyment of it was brief. Three years later, while returning to Scotland aboard the *William Alfred* to bring out his daughters, he died of cholera.[37]

Throughout these troubles David Brown farmed Wharekohu. He and his father had built a house, perhaps the first timber building on the island, where he lived with his Ngati Toa wife, Rangiuira Rakera. She was a remarkable woman who, on one occasion, is said to have swum from Kapiti to the mainland. But her marriage to David Brown was relatively short. Rangiuira lived at Wharekohu for just four years, during which time she had three children, only one of whom, Matilda, survived. When Rangiuira left Kapiti, Matilda remained at Wharekohu with her father.[38]

In 1859 David Brown remarried. With his second wife, Mary Ann, he raised a large family at Paremata while also continuing to farm at Kapiti where he built a number of drystone walls, a water race and a sheep dip. In 1860 the Provincial Government's sheep inspector reported that Brown had 1000 sheep on the island and his flock continued to increase until it reached a peak of 2000 in 1874.[39] Although there were many larger sheep runs in the Wairarapa, Manawatu and Rangitikei, where flat land was plentiful, Brown's farm and O'Meara's at Waiorua (which carried a similar number of sheep) were among the best stocked in the

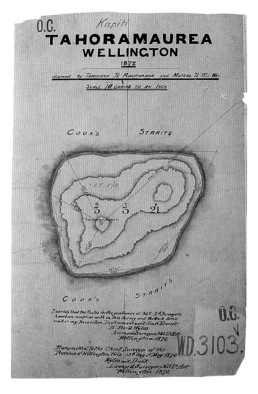

In 1853 David Brown's lawyer wrote to the Executive Council requesting title to the islands. The Colonial Secretary recommended title to Motungarara be granted but declined Tahoramaurea because Spain had not been convinced. The matter continued in a desultory way, without resolution, into the 1870s. Eventually the Crown granted all three offshore islets to Ngati Toa claimants: Wi Parata and his brother Hemi Matenga received Motungarara; Matene Te Whiwhi, Tamihana Te Rauparaha and others, Tahoramaurea; and Ngahuka Tungia and others, Tokomapuna.

Wharekohu from the air, 1998.

When Leslie Adkin visited Kapiti in 1921 he took this photo of Wharekohu from the ridge above the bay. The lined drain, once a creek, as well as drystone walls and a stone sheep dip – the legacy of David Brown's labours – are still evident, although today they are hidden by the regenerating bush.
MUSEUM OF NEW ZEALAND/TE PAPA TONGAREWA

Wellington-West Coast district. Only large sheep stations at Terawhiti and Orongorongo carried more.[40]

Both of the Kapiti farms continued for some years. O'Meara and his partner, Cimino, were active at the northern end until Wi Parata took over in 1870,[41] and Brown continued to farm on Kapiti for another decade. His farm extended well beyond Wharekohu to include most of the southern half of the island, which was leased to him by its Maori owners. Eventually, however, the isolation and the difficulty of ferrying stock to and from the island must have become too much, even for the indefatigable David Brown. Wharekohu and its adjacent blocks were abandoned. The last sheep return for Brown on Kapiti was in 1874; the next entry, five years later, noted that he was farming at Paremata on land he had previously used as a holding paddock for sheep brought over from Kapiti.[42] In the past no more than 100 or 200 sheep had been quartered there but in 1879 Brown had his entire flock at Paremata, which suggests that he abandoned the island in the late 1870s.[43] A visitor to Wharekohu in the 1880s noticed that little remained of Brown's slate-roofed house.[44]

The latter part of the 19th century was a quiet period on Kapiti. Few people visited the island except local Maori who came to fish and hunt. Perhaps the most significant European visitor was the botanist, John Buchanan, who spent Easter 1876

on the island with a party of scientists as the guests of Wi Parata who had just lost his seat in Parliament and was now free to spend more time on the island. One of Buchanan's colleagues noted that Parata was building 'a corrugated iron house, cheerless and miserable in the extreme'. An accompanying sketch shows a one-room shelter, 10 feet square, with a fire at one end and windows in the other three walls. Despite its simplicity, the party seemed content to stay there.[45] This was the beginning of a tradition of hospitality that continues today, almost 130 years later.

They spent their first night in Wi Parata's house at Waiorua, then set off next day to explore the island, climbing up to the trig on Tuteremoana. (The first surveyor's maps of the Wellington region, published four years earlier, show Tuteremoana as a key point of reference with sightlines to all the Tararua peaks as well as Mana Island to the south and prominent survey points in the Manawatu, to the north.)[46]

After a lunch of 'hot cross buns and a weed' (a smoke), they descended along the ridge to the south to 'open grassland, part of Mr Brown's run', most likely the head of the Taepiro Valley, which had been cleared by Ngati Toa and their allies. As they rambled down the valley, they came across the botanical highlight of the trip – 'a grove of mamaku tree ferns, the beauty of which to be properly appreciated must be seen'. Buchanan estimated the grove to contain at least 100 tree ferns and likened them to 'pillars supporting a transparent green-tinted roof, as of a sylvan temple'.

They spent that night at Rangatira Point in a small whare used by 'fishing parties of natives'. It contained a whisky bottle and a book of temperance hymns

This early morning view from the top of Tareremango, at the southern end of the island, looking north to Tuteremoana, shows the succession of ridges and valleys that were once part of the Browns' farm.

WIREMU PARATA TE KAKAKURA WAIPUNUAHAU

Parata, a member of Parliament (1871-76) and of the Executive Council (1872-76), was destined to be a leader. He was born on Motungarara about 1835, the product of the meeting of two different cultures. His father was a whaler, George Stubbs; his mother was Metapere Waipunahau, a daughter of Te Rangihiroa, a younger brother of Te Pehi Kupe, the hereditary chief of Ngati Toa in the 1820s. She also had strong links with Te Ati Awa through her mother.

His high status was clearly defined by his name, Te Kakakura, which was taken from the cryptic dying speech of Te Pehi at Kaiapohia, 'Kaua e hoatu ki te Atua, engari me hoatu ki te Kakakura' (Don't give me up to the European God [Atua], but to the Kakakura). It may also have referred to the ochre-coloured feathers of the kaka, long prized as symbols of chiefly mana.

Te Kakakura, who was usually known as Wi Parata, lived on Motungarara. When he was only a few years old his father was drowned. Soon afterwards his mother took him and his brother Hemi Matenga to live at Kena Kena, the Te Ati Awa pa at the Waikanae Estuary. When Te Ati Awa left the Kapiti Coast in 1848, their land passed to Parata and his brother.

Little is known of Wi Parata's early life or the identity of his first wife. In 1852 he married for a second time, to Unaiki, of Ngati Toa and Ngati Raukawa descent. They had 11 children, four of whom were sons. In 1870 he took over the farm at the northern end of Kapiti which had been leased to Europeans since the 1840s. He developed the property into a sizable farm, carrying 1700 sheep.

In 1871 he was elected to Parliament as the member for Western Maori, a seat which he held for two terms. A year later he and Wi Katene were appointed to the Executive Council, the first Maori to hold Cabinet rank.

'left as an antidote to the whisky' and, as Buchanan and his friends discovered, a lot of fleas. Wi Parata collected the party the next day and brought them back to Waiorua in his boat. On the way they stopped at Te Kahe Te Rau O Te Rangi to fossick among the remains of the Maori village and whaling settlement. The trip concluded with an expedition to the Okupe Lagoon. Buchanan's comment that 'the raised terraces of old beaches are here very noticeable' is especially significant, given the debate as to whether these stone rows have occurred naturally or are man-made.[47]

Although few Europeans visited Kapiti at this time, interest in the island continued from afar. In 1876 John Martin, a prominent Wairarapa landowner and the founder of Martinborough, offered Wi Parata £8,000 for the island but, like Grey before him, was refused.[48] Kapiti's Maori owners had compelling reasons for declining because they had only just established their own legal rights to land on the island, two years earlier, after long and expensive hearings before the Maori Land Court.

Just as the Browns had to mount a determined campaign to convince the authorities of the validity of their claim to Wharekohu, so their Maori neighbours had to prove their hereditary entitlement in court. Regardless of what the judge decided, this judicial process was ruinous for all the competing parties because their lawyers' fees usually consumed much of their equity. Even if an individual or a family were successful in court, land had to be sold to pay the bills. Furthermore, the legal process was contrary to customary Maori tenure, pitting hapu against hapu, to prove exclusive individual ownership. During lengthy sittings of the court, representatives of various families presented recollections of their forebears' occupation of the island, but as the land in question had often been occupied by successive groups, all had valid claims.

In hindsight, it is clear that Maori came and went between Kapiti and other places on the mainland. Some lived only briefly on the island, while others occupied land for more than 20 years, often shifting from one part of the island to another. The court's purpose – to establish individual ownership as a prelude to sale of the land – could not accommodate these complex shifting patterns of successive occupations so the judgments handed down were arbitrary and usually reflected the status quo. In other words, those who were dominant figures within Ngati Toa at the time, such as Tamihana Te Rauparaha, Matene Te Whiwhi and Wi Parata, usually emerged as winners.

The arbitrary nature of the judge's decisions is underlined by the lack of any supporting analysis. English law required judges to explain how they reached their decision but the Maori Land Court operated without explanation. The case of Waiorua-Kapiti No. 5, for example, involved the typically complex history of the occupation of 1645 acres by a variety of different groups, yet its ownership was determined in a single sentence:

> Judgment in favour of Wi Parata excepting 50 acres at Kahe Te Rau O Te Rangi for Ngahuka Tungia, 2 acres for burial grounds about Ngaiopiko for Rene, and 4 acres south of Waiorua for Mary Niccol [sic], daughter of John and Betty Niccol.[49]

Exclusive title to the various Kapiti blocks was established by the Maori Land Court in 1874, although the Kaiwharawhara case was reheard in 1895. By that time the island was attracting attention for quite a different reason – as a possible sanctuary for native birds, which were rapidly disappearing from the mainland and were in danger of extinction.

So, too, was the Maori race. In the 1890s their numbers reached a low point; a decline brought about by disease, loss of land and a fatalism engendered by the relentless expansion of European settlement. Although the government of the day was keen to see some endangered birds survive, the same view did not extend to Maori. Instead it was thought that those who survived would be gradually assimilated into settler society. The gulf between this Darwinian premise, and the determination of Maori to survive as an independent people, would soon become evident as the Maori landowners of Kapiti argued their right to the island before a parliamentary select committee. The different attitudes apparent then still exist today. The tensions that surround Kapiti in the 1990s can be resolved only by understanding the events that led to the Crown's declaration of Kapiti Island as a reserve a century ago.

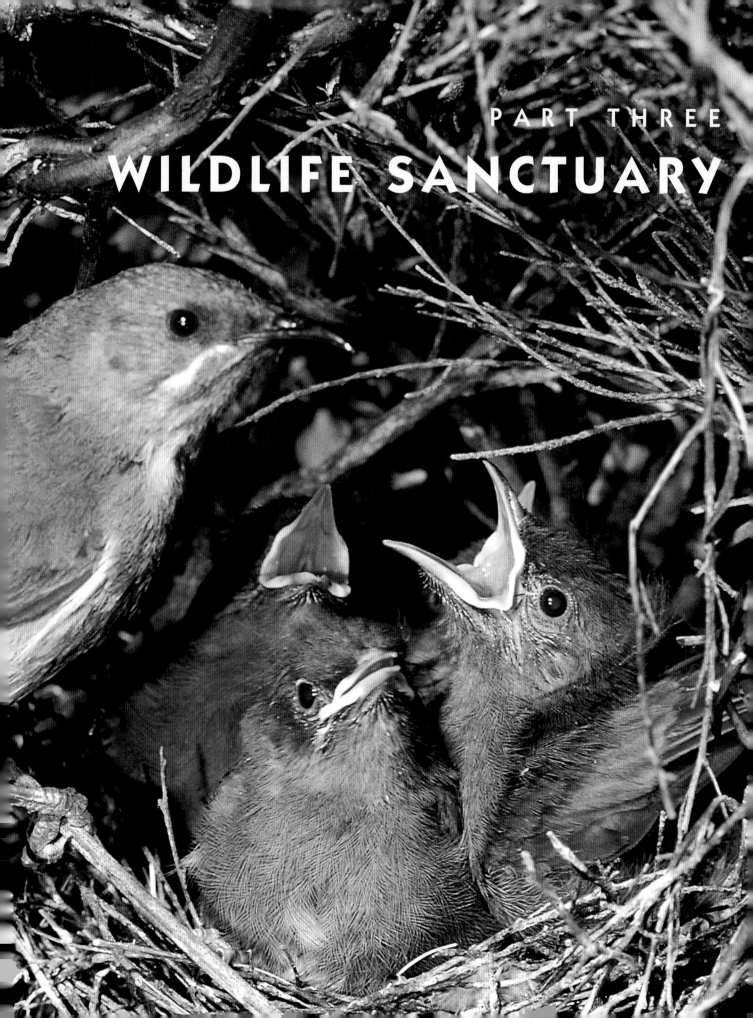

PART THREE

WILDLIFE SANCTUARY

CHAPTER TEN

BIRDS OR PEOPLE?

The idea of island reserves to protect rare birds was first suggested in the 1870s, but by the time several were established 20 years later, birds such as the hihi had all but vanished. Stitchbirds survived only because they were already well established on Hauturu (Little Barrier Island). Even there they were not safe from bird collectors, such as Buller, who supplied, among others, Lord Rothschild's collection which included so many stitchbird skins (more than 80) that eventually Buller was asked to stop sending them.

Island sanctuaries offered endangered birds a reprieve but created another problem. Most of the suitable islands were owned by Maori who, like the native birds, were rapidly declining. Often the only land they had left was on islands such as Hauturu and Kapiti, where historic associations made the owners reluctant to sell. The government's response was to take these islands by legislation. Although the owners received compensation, that did not make up for their displacement.

Stitchbirds, or hihi by J. G. Keulemans for Walter Lawry Buller's A History of the Birds of New Zealand *(1888).*

'I SHOT THEM,' recalled Andreas Reischek, crowing with satisfaction at the capture of his first pair of stitchbirds. Although the lead shot had smashed them to pieces, the mere remains of these elusive birds crowned a four-year search by the Austrian adventurer, who first visited Little Barrier Island in 1880 with the sole purpose of acquiring stitchbirds.

Reischek was determined to succeed because 'the stitchbird,' he wrote, 'is a magnificently coloured rarity which has brighter plumage than any of its New Zealand compeers' and because they were considered to be unobtainable, except on that isolated island. This near extinction excited the professional bird collector, who lived by supplying specimens of rare birds to collectors and museums in the United States and Europe. The rarer the species, the greater the demand – and the higher his fee.

Reischek earned his money the hard way. On his first visit to Hauturu (Little Barrier), he did not see a single stitchbird. On his second he caught a glimpse of one, but a fortnight passed before he found a pair hidden in dense scrub among steep precipices near the summit of the island. The bush was so impenetrable that he had to cut his way through it with a knife, and the noise he made alerted the birds. As they tried to escape he shot them – the first of 150 he 'collected' on this and later visits to the island.[1]

If the stitchbird was dangerously close to extinction before Reischek's visits to Hauturu, it seemed doomed by greed – although he did leave a few pairs alive. But when word of his success reached other collectors, even those few survivors were in jeopardy. They were saved only by the declaration of the island as a bird sanctuary in 1894. Even so, given that wild cats later overran the island, it is a miracle that stitchbirds are still found there today. In the early 1980s a small number were transferred to Kapiti; at first their survival seemed doubtful, but since the rats were eradicated they have flourished.

Andreas Reischek (1845-1902) arrived in New Zealand in 1877 to be taxidermist at the Canterbury Museum. He intended to stay for two years but remained for 12.

Reischek soon became much more than a museum assistant. He roamed the countryside in search of rare birds and Maori artifacts. Here he displays some of the clothing and equipment that he used on his travels. In 1889 he returned to Austria with an extraordinary collection of more than 14,000 items. His haul included numerous rare birds as well as several Maori skeletons and their burial taonga, which he had looted from caves in the King Country.
ALEXANDER TURNBULL LIBRARY

Judged by modern ethical standards, Reischek's actions are indefensible, yet he had no qualms about shooting so many birds. He believed they were going to die out in any case, and at least he was guaranteeing them a future as items of study and curiosity in the world's museums. According to Reischek, the real culprit was 'civilised' man and the predators he brought with him to this 'primeval paradise'. At the same time that he shot his first pair of stitchbirds he reflected on the situation: 'That night, lying there, I experienced a sense of shame, which those who swear by civilisation will certainly fail to understand, that civilised man can be the worst vermin of the whole earth. For wherever he comes, he destroys the wonderful equipoise of Nature, and much as he bothers himself with his so-called arts, he is not even capable of repairing the damage he causes'.[2]

By the 1880s, the development of roads and railways ensured that settlement of the countryside was well under way. Everywhere forest was fired or felled to make way for pasture. In summer the sky was hazy with the smoke of countless bush fires which sometimes got out of control, as they did in 1885–86, when vast tracts of virgin bush were destroyed.[3] As always, the first casualties were the birds. Not only did they lose much of their natural habitat, but they were also confronted by a number of introduced predators such as cats, dogs, ferrets, rats, stoats and weasels, against which they had no defences. Faced with this combined onslaught, the birds dwindled rapidly. Some species, such as bellbird and tui, managed to survive in reasonable numbers but species that were already declining before European settlement, such as the hihi and huia, simply vanished in most cases. For example, in the Wellington region, the last stitchbird to be seen was observed by a surveyor in the Tararua mountains in 1883; and by 1907 the huia, which lingered on in rugged bush country behind Waikanae, had also disappeared.[4]

The loss of these and other native birds was noticed, but without concern. Their displacement was seen merely as an illustration of the evolutionary process, proof that indigenous species were inherently inferior to the European. Ornithologists like Buller and Reischek considered it entirely natural that the blackbird and thrush should replace the hihi and the huia. This prevalent view was seldom challenged. Perhaps the first recorded protest was voiced by Thomas Potts, the Canterbury naturalist who raised the issue of forest conservation in Parliament in 1868. He was ahead of his time and the concept of conservation found little support. It was only in 1873, when the youthful premier, Julius Vogel, became a convert after a journey through denuded parts of the South Island, that the idea of protecting forests for future use gained credibility.

Potts had the satisfaction of seeing this new idea enshrined in Vogel's innovative New Zealand Forests Act of 1874 (which designated 3 per cent of the nation's forests as reserves) but it offered no protection to native birds. During the debate on the bill, he had raised the issue of their decline, but whereas forest conservation was justified on economic grounds (because it protected trees for milling in the future), no such argument could be made for the protection of endangered birds, whose continued existence offered no prospect of profit. If anything, their seemingly inevitable extinction was a commercial incentive for collectors.

The perceptive Potts at once recognised this, and based his pleas on how future scientists might judge his generation as stewards of their new land: 'Let it not be forgotten that our fauna is of very great interest to naturalists and physiologists, the wide world over. We shall justly incur the opprobrium of barbarism if we neglect to use strenuous exertions to avert the fate which seems impending over them. No excuse that we could offer for indifference will palliate our destructiveness in the eyes of the scientific world.'[5] No mere theorist, he had a practical solution in mind. Potts suggested that a series of island reserves be set aside as sanctuaries for native birds, specifically Resolution in the south, D'Urville in the centre and several small islands close to the coast in Northland. These offshore havens, he argued, offered the best chance to save species at risk of extinction.

Potts publicised his proposal in speeches and articles, but gained few adherents in the face of the widespread belief that the extinction of these birds was inevitable. Shrewdly he responded by presenting his idea in England, and the prestige implicit in publication at 'home' gave credibility to his cause in New Zealand. In 1872 the respected English journal *Nature*, for example, published his article

'Help Us To Save Our Native Birds', in which he reiterated the proposal to create island reserves.

His campaign was also boosted by the intervention of Professor Alfred Newton of Cambridge, who had been alarmed by a newspaper report that runholders were keen to import weasels from England to control rabbits. He immediately wrote to leading scientists in New Zealand urging them to oppose this 'disastrous importation': not only would weasels fail to control the rabbits, but they would also destroy what remained of the indigenous bird life. Newton's letter had an immediate effect, indicating the influence of English ideas. A bill to prohibit the import of polecats, stoats and weasels was passed by Parliament but when it reached the Legislative Council, which was dominated by runholders (those most affected by the rabbits), it was thrown out. 'Are there any birds worth preserving in this country?' asked one member, while another explained that, although he was sympathetic to the plight of native birds, farming took precedence. 'He was,' he said, 'very fond of birds, but when it came to a question whether he would have birds or sheep, he would certainly vote in favour of sheep.'[6]

The defeat of Potts and the preservationists seemed complete when, in 1882, the government itself began to import and liberate ferrets, stoats and weasels throughout the country. At this low point, however, when indigenous birds seemed doomed to disappear, the attitude of the general public began gradually to change in favour of preservation. At the same time, a tentative but growing sense of national identity led some New Zealanders to recognise that their country's birds were unique. And there were other factors. The unexpected consequences of almost half a century's relentless modification of the countryside forced the settlers to reconsider some of their assumptions. The widespread clearance of lowland forests, for example, had caused floods that ravaged the newly won farms and alerted their owners to the value of indigenous forests. Trees, it was realised, held the land together; take them away and the land might soon follow.

As the landscape was modified, even the most obtuse settler could not help but notice and some were saddened. Thomas Bevan came to the Horowhenua, opposite Kapiti, as a child in the 1840s. Half a century later he described the changes he had seen:

Only those who saw the country in its virgin state can realise the prodigality of nature, of the beauty that has forever passed away, leaving in the settled districts not a trace behind. Mountains and plains alike were clothed with magnificent forest, abounding with bellbirds, pigeons and tuis, and vocal at sunrise with their music, while the beautiful lagoons swarmed with native ducks. The changes which have followed settlement in this island must be seen to be credited. Since 1855 the woods have gone, and with them the teeming and beautiful bird and insect life to which they gave shelter.[7]

Bevan's nostalgia reflected a growing appreciation of the fast-vanishing 'primeval paradise', which gathered strength as the population became increasingly urbanised. The changing view of the land came about partly because the forests and mountains were no longer the obstacle to settlement they once had been. Instead, their distant beauty began to be celebrated in poetry, prose and painting. Fifty years earlier, their forebears had been confronted on all sides by 'trees of stupendous size' and in the struggle to survive had developed an antipathy to the tangled trunks and vines that made it so difficult to clear the land.[8] Now their rural descendants looked out at neatly fenced paddocks; their urban descendants at suburban backyards. It is not surprising that both viewed the countryside in a different light.

A new romanticism was evident in the popularity of books on indigenous birds, and especially Walter Buller's landmark publication, *A History of the Birds of New Zealand*, which first appeared in 1873 and was republished in a new, enlarged edition in 1888. Buller himself exemplified changing popular opinion. Like Reischek, he was an avid collector of rare birds and rivalled the Austrian in the vast numbers he sent overseas. Both justified their activities with the familiar Darwinian premise that since these birds were doomed to extinction, they were doing the world a favour. But as public opinion began to change, so too did Buller's views, especially when it became clear that prominent politicians were keen to see surviving species preserved on island sanctuaries.

Even Reischek played a small part in the campaign to set aside islands. When he spoke to members of the Auckland Institute in 1886 about the birds of Little Barrier, one of the audience, F. D. Fenton, suggested it be bought by the Crown as a sanctuary. Fenton knew the island well. As the Chief Judge of the Native Land Court, he had presided over hearings to determine its ownership. That very day the court had given judgment in favour of Ngati Wai, and the island, Fenton considered, could be bought from the successful claimants for £3,500. Reischek was enthusiastic and even offered his services as custodian but the government's chief scientist, Sir James Hector, did not support the idea.[9] Later events were to show that this was a rare opportunity the Crown should have seized without hesitation. Nevertheless, the idea of island sanctuaries continued to gain support. It surfaced again in 1891, when Professor A. P. W. Thomas of Auckland University addressed leaders of the country's scientific community at the conference of the Australasian Association for the Advancement of Science. When he suggested an approach to the Minister of Lands, with a specific proposal that Resolution and Little Barrier Islands should become reserves, the conference endorsed his proposal.

Meanwhile the preservation campaign received unexpected endorsement from the Earl of Onslow, Governor of New Zealand between 1888 and 1892, when he chose Huia as the name for his infant son, who was christened soon after the scientists' conference. Although it was the last of the child's four names, he was known throughout his life as Huia Onslow.[10] Lord Onslow's gesture was significant; it popularised the plight of endangered birds and raised the public profile of the campaign in a way no scientist could do. From this time, the extinction of rare birds no longer concerned only scientists and ornithologists but was also a matter of public discussion.

Soon afterwards, John McKenzie, the new Minister of Lands in the Liberal government, declared Resolution Island the country's first reserve for native flora and fauna. McKenzie also started negotiations to purchase Little Barrier Island, but as some Ngati Wai were reluctant to sell and his colleague, the

Sir Walter Buller (1836-1906).

As the son of a missionary raised on a remote mission station in Northland, Buller might have been expected to become a person of piety. Instead, from an early age, he showed a great fondness for the secular rewards of property, prestige and power. He made a number of visits to England where he enjoyed some prominence. In 1886 he was knighted for his contribution to the acclaimed New Zealand display at the Colonial and Indian Exhibition, held in London.

Buller's complex nature was evident in his ambivalent attitude to rare birds. His definitive book, A History of the Birds of New Zealand (1873, 1888), celebrated the diversity of the country's species, yet his relentless trade in endangered birds hastened their extinction. He could have saved the huia, for example, when he was given one of the last breeding pairs, in the 1890s, expressly for their preservation. Instead he took them to England and gave them to a collector.

For much of his life Buller was involved with Maori land, first as a lawyer, later as a magistrate of the Native Land Court. Land was eventually his undoing when he became involved in a bitter and protracted dispute over his purchase of a block of Maori land near Lake Papaitonga. Despite an attempt by the Minister of Lands to rescind the purchase, he retained the land, but at the cost of his reputation. The controversial transaction haunted him for the rest of his life.

Minister of Native Affairs, was reluctant to buy, the talks eventually collapsed.[11] When Lord Onslow heard of the impasse, he consulted his friend and adviser, Sir Walter Buller, in drafting a letter to the government to support the creation of island reserves. Buller, who had been interested in collecting rather than preserving rare birds, now found himself the leading advocate for a cause he did not, in fact, support. He was, as the sub-title of his biography states, 'the reluctant conservationist', but such was his veneration for vice-royalty and his craving for approval, that he threw himself into his new role with characteristic vigour. 'The Onslow Memorandum', as it became known, was all Buller's work. Even if he himself was not convinced, the combination of his persuasiveness and Lord Onslow's prestige convinced others, including the premier, John Ballance.

In spite of all this, progress was slow. Resolution Island had been formally declared a reserve in 1891 but it was three years before Richard Henry was appointed custodian and any preservation work – such as transferring kakapo and kiwi to the island – began. Ballance directed his efforts, instead, toward acquiring the ownership of Little Barrier because its Maori owners (who, in the light of the government's interest, could see that their chances of keeping the island were slim) were busy logging the kauri forest. In December 1892 a court injunction stopped the felling, a custodian was appointed and plans were made to capture and transfer huia to the island.

When Onslow returned to England in 1892, his vision seemed about to be realised but it quickly faded. Soon after his departure Ballance died unexpectedly, negotiations to buy the island again broke down and the custodian, Charles

13

Robinson, who had previously been one of Buller's bird collectors, was rumoured to be shooting – not saving – stitchbirds. Nor did Robinson have much success in finding huia on the mainland to transfer to Hauturu. When he did eventually capture a live pair, instead of taking them to the island sanctuary as instructed, he gave them to Buller, who took them to London (in defiance of legislation prohibiting the export of rare birds) to add to the Rothschild collection.[12] When Buller returned to New Zealand in 1894, Little Barrier was still in limbo. Eventually the government decided that since it could not obtain the agreement of all the Maori owners to the sale, it would acquire the island by compulsion. A bill to this effect was passed by Parliament later that year and the island was gazetted a reserve. Ngati Wai on Hauturu were compensated, then evicted.[13]

The acquisition of Little Barrier and the creation of a reserve on Resolution marked the success of the campaign started more than 25 years earlier by Thomas Potts. Yet at no time had Kapiti Island been mentioned as a potential bird sanctuary. This may have been because the island was being farmed at the time. Compared with islands such as Little Barrier and Resolution, Kapiti seemed to have little bush and few rare birds.

Government records of this period do not reveal whose idea it was to make Kapiti a sanctuary for birds, but when it became known, Buller was quick to promote it. When he addressed the Wellington Philosophical Society in August 1895, Buller began by saying that the creation of island reserves on Little Barrier and

Weka Weka Rock, Little Barrier Island by Hugh Boscawen, 1893, with Great Barrier Island in the distance.

As Lord Onslow's private secretary, Boscawen was familiar with the campaign to establish island reserves. When Onslow returned to England in 1892 Boscawen joined the Lands Department in Auckland. The following year he visited Hauturu and wrote a comprehensive description of its wildlife. He judged it to be 'a nineteenth century paradise for all New Zealand flora and fauna and likely to continue so if left undisturbed by man'.
ALEXANDER TURNBULL LIBRARY

Resolution had been 'the subject of comment and praise all over the world', and went on: 'It will be, I am sure, as gratifying to you as it is to me to learn that the Minister of Lands has decided on acquiring, for a similar purpose, the freehold of the Island of Kapiti, in Cook Strait'.

Buller then listed the reasons why Kapiti would be suitable for a reserve:

> Much of the bush on the island is of exquisite beauty, and the surface is sufficiently diversified to insure the successful cultivation of all our native trees and shrubs. Three species of birds – the wood-robin, the korimako, and the whitehead – which are now practically extinct on the mainland, still have their refuge on Kapiti; and Captain Ross, who has hitherto been occupying the greater portion of the open land as a sheep run, has been most careful to prevent dogs and cats – those great destroyers of native birds – from becoming feral on the island. It is at a convenient distance from the mainland, and seems specially designed by nature for what it will now, we may hope, soon become – the central colonial depot, so to speak, for our birds and plants.[14]

Buller's enthusiastic endorsement of Kapiti (which, it seems, he had never visited)[15] came at a time of growing interest among the general population which Buller described as 'this gradual awakening to the fact that we have animal and vegetable forms of life indigenous to this country which ought to be protected and cherished'.[16] In the case of Kapiti, however, several problems had to be solved before the island could become a reserve. It was almost entirely owned by Maori, and as the government had learnt during negotiations to purchase Hauturu, they were unlikely to part with it willingly. Also European interests on the island were, perhaps, more extensive than the Crown realised and those involved would be no more inclined to part with their stake on the island than the Maori owners.

It was a complicated situation. Captain John Ross did farm on Kapiti, but his land was leased from its Maori owners by a retired surveyor, Harry Field, who lived at Waikanae. He, in turn, leased it to Ross and his sons, Alfred and Arthur. They regularly travelled to the island from their principal farm near Marton. Field did not farm the island himself because of poor health, which had caused him to retire from the government service as a relatively young man. He spent his days doing casual surveying or tending his orchard, but his real interest was politics. In 1893 he was elected to represent the local riding on the Hutt County Council.[17] Three years later he became MP for Otaki. Once in Parliament he did not have the time to maintain his interests on the island; he terminated his leases and sold his sheep on Kapiti to the new lessee, Malcolm Maclean, and his brother, Robert. They lived on the island with their families and farmed the Rangatira, Kaiwharawhara and Maraetakaroro blocks.[18] (The author is not related to this family.)

Whether the Macleans knew of the government's plans for Kapiti when they took up the leases is not known but the termination of Harry Field's leases created an opportunity for others to negotiate with the Maori owners to gain a toehold on Kapiti. His brother W. H. (Willie) Field and the Macleans were each able to purchase prime 12½-acre blocks on the waterfront near Rangatira. The Wellington lawyer, Charles Morison, who was a substantial landowner at Waikanae, also acquired the lease of a block at Waiorua in September 1896, and six months later another Wellingtonian, Charles Lowe, took up a 21-year lease of 1234 acres at the northern end.[19] Field, Lowe, Morison and the Macleans added further small parcels of land to their holdings whenever the opportunity arose. By April 1897, almost all of the island was either leased or owned by Europeans.[20]

The most likely explanation for this burst of acquisition is that they realised this was their last chance to get a slice of Kapiti before the Crown acquired it and prohibited private land deals. It was a risky business. The government might resort to acquiring European interests by compulsion, possibly with inadequate compensation, but lawyers such as Willie Field and Charles Morison were not deterred by that prospect. In any case, there might be a change of plan – or a change of government – that would make the risk worthwhile. Even if the Crown did confirm its plans for Kapiti, established leaseholders or landowners would be in a strong position to negotiate some permanent presence on the island – not necessarily as farmers, but perhaps as ab-

sentee owners with rights to visit and stay on Kapiti. No one understood this better than Field and Morison. Both were experienced land buyers who had been systematically building up their holdings on the coastal plain at Waikanae since land in the area became available for sale in the early 1890s, much later than in other parts of the country.[21]

If the coastal plain was desirable, Kapiti was even more so. From his homestead in Ngarara Road, Willie Field looked out across pasture and wetlands to the island that had been coveted by generations of Maori and Europeans. Field realised that this was his chance. Now that the government's interest was common knowledge, Kapiti's Maori owners might be induced to part with their land. They may have known what happened to Ngati Wai on Little Barrier Island, but even if they were not aware of this particular case, they were all too familiar with official dispossession of their land. In the preceding half-century Ngati Toa had sold more than 20 million acres to the Crown, often reluctantly.[22] Kapiti would be no different. If the Crown wanted it, the island would be taken one way or another.

Willie Field may have seen the matter in a different light. Maori were in decline in the 1890s and lacked political influence, but it would be far more difficult for the government to dislodge a confident European lawyer, especially one with a brother in Parliament. The key to his strategy was freehold title – the

Harry Field moved to Waikanae from Wanganui in 1878 after a career as a surveyor. Fluent in Maori, he was a keen observer of Maori life and sometimes worked as an interpreter. The following year he married Hannah, daughter of the ex-whaler Tom Wilson and Hanake (Wirehana Te Awawa) who had established the Ferry Inn at the Waikanae Estuary in 1848.

Harry and Hannah disliked the life, so they closed the inn, although they continued to live in the building while they farmed nearby land belonging to Hannah. Harry Field also leased land on Kapiti but relinquished his island interests when he was elected to Parliament. He was elected for a second term in 1899 but died four days later. In the subsequent by-election he was succeeded by his younger brother, Willie Field.
ALEXANDER TURNBULL LIBRARY

Malcolm Maclean emigrated from Scotland to Dunedin in 1888. He and his brother Rob made their way north, labouring on farms, and arrived on the Kapiti Coast about 1893. He became engaged to Phoebe Howell of Paraparaumu and the following year Malcolm became a shepherd on Kapiti. In 1896 they married and moved to Kapiti, where they farmed the blocks previously leased by Harry Field. Malcolm Maclean is pictured here with his son Robin on the island.
RITA MACLEAN COLLECTION

A group of hunters with their dogs and guns on the verandah of the farmhouse at Rangatira Point, c. 1890s.

Soon after Harry Field leased a large part of Kapiti in 1881, he built a house there for the farmers to whom he sub-let the land. The first occupant was a man called Robinson. He was succeeded by John Ross and his sons, Alfred and Arthur. They paid Field £500 per annum and ran 4000 sheep on the central part of the island.

On an early map (1880) the building was described as 'Field's house' but it was, and still is, generally known as 'the Whare', in acknowledgment of an earlier shelter on the same site. When Professor John Buchanan and a group of scientists visited Kapiti in 1876 they spent a night at Rangatira in 'a Maori whare that is used by fishing parties of natives'.

ALEXANDER TURNBULL LIBRARY

more land he owned on the island, the stronger his position. Charles Lowe, the new lessee of a part of the northern end, should not, therefore, have been surprised when he received a letter from Willie Field in August 1897, to the effect that from now on he should pay his rent not to the Maori owners but to Field.[23] The letter was couched in legalese but the underlying message was clear: the lawyer now had a lien over the land and it would be only a matter of time before he owned it. Lowe had been finessed. The fact that the mortgage over the property was in the name of Isabel Field, Willie's wife, was a common device that deceived no one – least of all the Liberal government.

Isabel Field's mortgage over land at the northern end of Kapiti is referred to obliquely in this letter from W. H. Field to the leaseholder, Charles Lowe. When the mortgage was registered it came to the government's attention and precipitated the Kapiti Island Reserve Bill.

W. H. FIELD LETTERBOOK, ALEXANDER TURNBULL LIBRARY

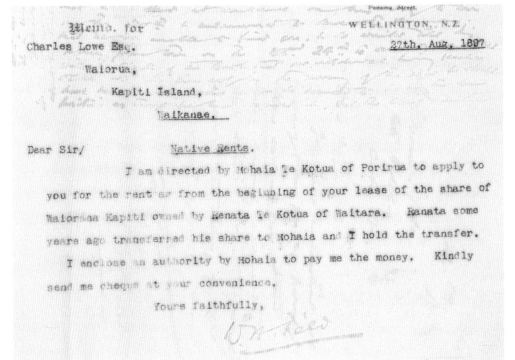

The homestead still stands. It is the most historic building on Kapiti and has recently been restored by the Department of Conservation. Since 1912 it has been used by scientists, administrators and official visitors privileged to stay on the island overnight.

When word of the mortgage (which became public knowledge as soon as it was registered) reached the Cabinet, alarm bells rang. Premier Richard Seddon and his colleagues were well aware of the technique Field was using to acquire land and they immediately realised the implications of Mrs Field's £168 loan to the Maori owner of Lowe's leased land. The Liberals' primary policy was to break up the estates of large landowners to make land available to small farmers, but a new generation of entrepreneurs like Field threatened to undo their work. But Field was more than just an ideological opponent; his Kapiti transactions clearly showed that he did not accept the Crown's stated intention to make the island a reserve for endangered flora and fauna. By late 1897 he owned land at Rangatira, had a hold over some of the best farmland at Waiorua and was also, according to his correspondence, receiving rent for a portion of the Kaiwharawhara block, to the south of Tuteremoana.[24]

As the parliamentary year drew to a close, Seddon drafted legislation to secure Kapiti for the Crown. On 15 December, a week before the House was due to rise, the Kapiti Island Public Reserve Bill was considered by the Native Affairs Committee. A number of Maori landowners who presented a petition opposing the bill were invited to speak and to answer questions. The first speaker, Hemi Kuti, made it quite clear that his people opposed the legislation:

> What we above all things desire is to retain this land in our possession. This land has been the support – the mother's milk – of our ancestors and ourselves from the time of their coming from Kawhia, and it is the only land now remaining to the Ngatitoa. The Ngatitoa hapu still are, as they have always been, supporters of the Government, and they have sold all their other lands to the Government – more than twenty millions of acres – that is, in both Islands. Well, the purchase-money received has been spent.

But in response to a question, Kuti said that 'if the government felt compelled to take this island, we can do nothing but suffer it; we cannot hope to successfully contend against them'.[25]

In the 1890s, when the balance of wealth on the Kapiti Coast began to shift from Maori to European, W. H. (Willie) Field (1861-1944) became as influential as Wi Parata. Although Field (right) was a generation younger than the chief, their lives overlapped; they knew each other and had interests in common.

Field first knew the area when, as a young man, he stayed with his elder brother Harry, at the Waikanae Estuary and was taken to Kapiti Island. Later, as a lawyer in Wellington, he maintained his interest in the district by buying land at Waikanae whenever it became available. He built a house there and commuted regularly between the city and the Kapiti Coast.

He soon became one of the local bankers, an important role in the days before local banking agencies were established. He lent money to European and Maori, including Wi Parata, but whereas the chief was careful to always keep his debt low, others were not so prudent. Many Maori, in particular, obtained loans from Field, using their land as security. Frequently they increased the loans, then could not repay Field, who took their land instead. He soon became the largest landowner in Waikanae.
FIELD COLLECTION

Other speakers repeated Kuti's concern, but the questions asked by members of the committee made it clear that they did not attach the same importance to the island's historic associations. Their interest lay in finding some way of persuading the Maori owners to agree to give up the island – perhaps in return for equivalent land elsewhere, or compensation that would be invested in a fund to provide them with annuities equal to their current lease-based income. Another suggestion was that the island should be made a reserve for Ngati Toa and a bird sanctuary under Crown control. The owners were asked to consult their people and return with an answer the following day.

Seddon sat on the committee throughout, but took no part until just before the end, when he asked a question of Hanikamu Te Hiko (whose interest in the Waiorua No.5 Block was mortgaged to Isabel Field) that indicated his reason for pushing the bill through the legislative process with such haste. 'Are you aware,' he asked, 'of negotiations going on for the sale of Kapiti to other persons than the Government during the last year?' Te Hiko replied that he had not heard that. When Raiha Puaha spoke, Seddon raised the matter again. She was defiant in her opposition:

> I will not agree to this Government Bill which proposes to seize and take from us our land. Of course, it means the whole island, and that includes my land; and as far as I am concerned I will not agree. If everyone else is going to sell, let them sell, but my land I shall keep for my child. I will not accept any money for it. My land will remain mine in the midst of the government land. I need not say anything more to the Committee than this: that nothing will induce me to agree to the Bill.

In answer to a further question, however, she revealed that her land at Waiorua was leased to Charles Morison, who was paying 1s 6d an acre for land he appeared not to be farming.

Seddon was sceptical. 'I should like to get some explanation as to why you love the lawyer better than the Government,' he said.

'That is my business,' Puaha replied.

'Suppose the Government gave you 3s 0d an acre?'

But Puaha was not to be tempted. 'I would not let them have it if they offered me £1. It is a valued possession of our ancestors; and if the Government got hold of it, we should never see it again and my son would never be able to look upon the land and say, "That is the island that belonged to my ancestors."'[26]

The exchanges between the owners and the committee merely showed their irreconcilable cultural attitudes: to the politicians, land was a tradeable commodity; to the owners, it was a link with their forebears and a source of prestige. Both viewpoints were clearly expressed but little understood by the other party. When Heni Te Rei made the final submission, she spoke with passionate despair:

And I may say that, when I discovered the Bill that has been proposed by the government to deal with the island in this way, I have been weeping ever since; and I feel that I cannot, under any consideration, agree to such a proposal. I put it to the Government in this way: that I am absolutely without another acre of land in the world except what I hold in that island; and are they going to take that from me? I am the mother of many children, and the grandmother of many children. That is all.[27]

When the Maori owners left the room, Seddon told the committee that the bill would proceed and the owners would be compensated. He intended to

move a motion to this effect the next day. But when the committee reconvened the following morning it became apparent that there had been some hard talking overnight. It is not known who spoke to Seddon, but the only Kapiti Maori owners absent the previous day were Hemi Matenga and his brother Wi Parata. The latter usually acted for the former (who lived in the South Island) and it seems likely that Wi Parata may have approached Seddon privately to discuss their interests on the island. Harry Field, who was a member of the committee, may also have been involved. A fragment of his personal diary has survived, and although it covers a period before the bill was introduced, it shows that about the time Isabel Field's loan became known, Harry Field visited Seddon and McKenzie several times; Wi Parata also made regular visits to Wellington.[28] If Kapiti was discussed on these earlier occasions, as seems very likely, no doubt the same kind of consultation occurred during the formal passage of the bill. When the committee resumed, the premier withdrew his motion and allowed another to proceed instead; it stated that 'a short Bill be passed this session preventing any private dealing with the land for twelve months, and in the meantime the Government should meet the Natives and endeavour to arrange matters with the owners'.

This compromise was accepted by the committee, which referred the bill back to Parliament. But as the committee met, a letter was delivered from the Wellington law firm, Stafford, Treadwell and Field. Although it was not signed by a named individual, it was clearly the work of Willie Field. If anyone had failed to grasp the immediate purpose of the bill, the lawyers' last-minute appeal made it obvious.[29]

Sir,

Kapiti Island Reserve Bill.

We have just learned that this Bill is before the Native Affairs Committee for consideration this morning. We are unaware what attitude the Native owners adopt towards the Bill beyond the fact that several of them have informed us that they are opposed to it.

We are, however, concerned on behalf of several clients who are interested in the island, in particular Mr Malcolm McLean [*sic*], the present lessee of the larger portion of the island. This gentleman holds leases of practically the whole of the Rangatira, Kaiwharawhara, and Maraetakaroro Blocks. These leases are not entirely complete, for the reason that in some cases there are signatures wanting, but they are valid documents, which the Native Land Court will confirm. Mr McLean has for the past eighteen months been in possession under them, and has made his home there, and effected improvements. It would therefore be grossly unfair that the Bill, if favourably considered by the Committee, should not protect our client's leases.

In respect of all portions of the above land to which our client has not an absolutely confirmable lease owing to want of signatures, he is the holder of the balance of the term therein acquired by Mr H. A. Field, M.H.R., in or about, 1881.

Mr McLean is also the owner by purchase, which has been duly confirmed by the Court, of 12 ½ acres, being one-fourth of the Rangatira Kapiti No. 4a Block.

Our Mr Field is the owner in fee simple, under a confirmed transfer, of 12 ½ acres, part of the Rangatira Kapiti No. 4a Block, which he bought as a building site for the use of his family in the summer. He is naturally averse to this land being taken from him. He also holds a confirmed mortgage over the interest of Hanikamu Te Hiko, containing 100 acres, in the Waiorua Kapiti No. 5 Block, Section No. 2.

We shall be happy to afford any other information which may assist the Committee in this matter.

Yours, & c.,

Stafford, Treadwell, and Field.

Four days later, on 20 December, the bill was given its second reading in Parliament. Seddon himself introduced the legislation and explained that 'it was the earnest desire of the government to conserve the island, and in obtaining possession of the island they would be able to conserve the flora and fauna of the island'. He acknowledged that the bill, in its present form, did not actually acquire Kapiti but that it did suspend any further land deals such as the recent 21-year leases. Long before these were up, 'the private leases would have secured the freehold'. He went on to say, 'That was what always happened. If a person wanted a piece of Maori land he would take out a lease of the land, then the Maori would borrow on the land, and all this person had to do was to reply, "Yes, if you give me a purchasing clause", and the result was invariably the same. He could trace how all the land had been secured. It started with a lease or the lending of money, and it was then only a question of time when the freehold would go from the Natives.'[30]

During the second reading there was only one other speaker, Hone Heke, the member for Northern Maori. Although he took a broader view and acknowledged the Crown's concern to protect native birds, it was, he suggested, a 'sentimental reason', as was the Maori owners' opposition on the grounds that it 'tended to deprive them of all their interests in Kapiti Island, and all the old associations of their ancestors and forefathers'.[31] Later the same day, the Kapiti Island Public Reserve Bill received its third and final reading without any further debate: members were no doubt aware of the amount of legislation yet to be dealt with on the second-to-last day of the session. The most eagerly anticipated debate concerned the Minister of Lands' Horowhenua bill, which promised a discussion of Sir Walter Buller's dubious dealings in Maori land. This, rather than the Kapiti bill, was the prime focus of the politicians, the press and the public, who expected controversy as McKenzie's long feud with Buller culminated in legislation intended to strip him of his land. The minister's determination to see Buller's duplicity exposed had little to do with a concern for the rights of Maori landowners; it was driven by personal antipathy and a loathing of the large landowner.

The following morning, the Kapiti bill was the first of a number to be considered by the Upper House, the Legislative Council. The first reading was a formality without debate; the second reading followed soon after so that the bill could go to the Waste Lands Committee for its consideration. Westland MP James

Bonar 'hoped the Committee would look very carefully into this Bill. As far as he could understand, there were people very largely interested in the matter who were strongly opposed to the land being acquired.'[32]

A few hours later the bill was back before the Upper House. In the interim Bonar had made up his mind to oppose the bill because 'he thought an injustice was being done to the Natives'. The next speaker, Otago's Hori Kerei Taiaroa, was alarmed at the speed of the bill's passage. He protested against 'the manner in which the Government made a practice of leaving all Bills which affected the Natives until the last days of the session'. His criticism, reiterated by another speaker who described it as a 'disgrace', diverted attention from the bill and led to a bout of bickering as to whether such a term was unparliamentary. The debate returned to the subject of Kapiti only when the final speaker, Charles Bowen of Canterbury, spoke of the bill's broader purpose: 'it was a very good thing that reserves of this sort should be made while there was yet time for the purpose of preserving the flora and fauna of the colony, which were disappearing in a lamentable manner'. He, too, recorded his concern at the bill's hasty passage and noted that 'A good deal of the opposition to the Bill would have disappeared if members had been allowed more time to enquire into the matter'. Nevertheless, 'he hoped the Bill would pass'.[33] It did. From that moment private transactions involving land on Kapiti became illegal, and those other

The present-day landowners at Waiorua Bay are all descendants of Wi Parata.

than 'the original Native owners' who had existing interests, were required to forfeit their land or lease in return for compensation. Henceforth, Kapiti was to be a public reserve for the conservation of its 'natural scenery' and for the preservation 'of the fauna and flora of New Zealand'.[34]

Seddon had certainly succeeded in stopping Field, Morison and others from ever owning private land on the island, not just for 12 months as the Native Affairs Committee had suggested. But the Act offered no solution to the problem of Maori ownership. It was, as the original motion passed by the committee noted, 'a short Bill' intended to prevent 'private dealing' while providing a year to resolve the matter of Maori ownership of most of the island. If no agreement was reached, compensation would be determined by the Public Works Act. In the meantime Maori retained ownership of their land, but without the power to sell or lease (except to the Crown), they were denied the essential elements of freehold tenure.

Seddon's failure to resolve this issue at the time of the bill's passage is understandable, given the pressures he faced and the need to move quickly to stop any further private transactions. But once the bill became law, there was little incentive for the Crown to find a solution. Seddon and his colleagues may have thought that nature might do it for them since there was a widespread belief at the time that the Maori people, like the rare birds, would eventually die out.[35] But the Maori race did not disappear; on the contrary, the number of Maori steadily increased and today the descendants of those original owners are demanding recognition of their special relationship with Kapiti.

CHAPTER ELEVEN

MARKING TIME

The Crown showed great determination in acquiring Kapiti. Once the legislation had been passed, however, it no longer seemed interested, and for almost a decade, the island was neglected.

Meanwhile, the inexorable decline of native birds continued, even quickened, and it was clear that the most vulnerable species – such as the huia – were perilously close to extinction. If they were to have the slightest chance of survival, urgent measures were needed to assist them.

An opportunity occurred shortly after 1900 when a Wairarapa farmer, R. B. Sayer, from Dalefield, on the edge of the forested Tararua foothills, captured three live huia: a male, a female and a young bird. He took them home and informed the government, which asked him to keep the birds until arrangements could be made for their transfer to Kapiti Island. Sayer built a large cage for the birds, but as no one ever came to collect them, they were eventually released.

Within a few years this distinctive species had vanished.[1]

Three huia *by J. G. Keulemans, c. 1900.*
MUSEUM OF NEW ZEALAND/TE PAPA TONGAREWA

EVEN IF the three huia discovered by Wairarapa farmer R. B. Sayer had been taken to Kapiti, it is unlikely that they would have prospered because, by the turn of the century, the island had only small, isolated pockets of mature forest left standing. Most of the 'very vigorous vegetation' that Dieffenbach admired had succumbed to a succession of fires, lit by sheep farmers, that swept the island in the mid-19th century.

Huia had flourished in the Ruahine, Tararua and Rimutaka Ranges because their cool, damp forests provided sustenance. The birds used their long beaks, especially the females' long curved bills, to extract grubs and insects from rotting trees and from decaying material on the forest floor. On Kapiti there was probably not enough of this type of habitat to ensure their survival. But at least the island was free of most mammalian predators – the principal agents of the huia's disappearance on the mainland. Kapiti may not have been ideal, but it did offer a slim prospect for the species' survival. On the mainland it was doomed.

After the Kapiti Island Public Reserve Bill was passed, the government was preoccupied with arrangements for compensating the island's aggrieved former owners. By 1901 compensation had been paid to all the Maori owners who had sold their interests; and after members of the Compensation Court, led by the Chief Judge Sir Robert Stout, visited the island, agreement had been reached with all the European leaseholders and landholders, except one. Payment varied according to the identity of the claimant. 'Native owners' received about 12s 6d per acre; Europeans received about £3 5s per acre – five times more than their Maori counterparts.[2]

Only the claim of the lawyer W. H. Field remained unresolved. Field's demand for £675 in compensation for the loss of his 12½-acre freehold section at Rangatira[3] (£54 per acre) clearly signalled his extreme displeasure at the arbitrary forfeiture of his stake on the island. If the Crown wanted his land it would have to pay a premium price for it. But the government ignored Field, which merely increased his sense of grievance.

Although Willie Field supported the Liberals, letters he wrote to the premier do not have the respectful tone that might be expected of a first-term member. Even though his demand was tempered by that of his more reasonable clients, Malcolm and Rob Maclean, who also owned 12½ acres at Rangatira, Field's real intention was clear. In September 1900 he wrote to Seddon: 'I hope you will without fail, see that Messrs. Macleans' compensation is paid next week at latest. It is a matter or urgency *not only to them but to me*.'[4] Seddon promptly replied that he would refer the matter to Cabinet,[5] but a week later Field wrote again in a similar vein: 'You are causing not only my clients, but also my firm, and myself *serious inconvenience* by not attending to this matter. May I ask that you will attend to it today?'[6] It was an imperious message to a Cabinet preoccupied with the Boer War and other important matters.

Soon afterwards, the Maclean brothers received their compensation, but Field's extravagant claim was ignored. Four years later it was still outstanding and it seems never to have been paid. All Field received was £168 as payment for the transfer of his wife's mortgage over Hohaia Te Kotuku's land to the Crown, effectively rescinding the transaction that had prompted the government to take Kapiti by legislation in the first place.

Willie Field was free to show his dissatisfaction but the Macleans had to be more reasonable in their dealings with the Crown because they continued to farm and live on Kapiti at the pleasure of their new landlord – the government. The

brothers and their wives and children lived at Rangatira in the four-roomed farm-house that Harry Field had built.[7] They leased 'the Whare', as it was known, as well as pasture in the central and southern parts of the island, from the Crown for £70 a year.[8] In 1902 Rob and Annie and their family returned to the mainland but Malcolm and his wife Phoebe stayed as the island's first caretakers until 1905.[9] Phoebe Maclean later recalled that they were careful to preserve Kapiti's bird life: 'The only time I tasted bird on the island was when a quail was struck by a hail-stone. I stewed it, it went further that way.'[10]

At this point Kapiti had been a nature reserve for eight years yet nothing had been done to develop it as a sanctuary. The Lands Department's sole initiative had been to send a surveyor, R. P. Greville, to map the island, but although his field-work was completed in 1902, his final maps were not completed until 1912. Despite this delay, Greville's record has proved to be invaluable. His maps are a bench-mark against which later botanical surveys have measured the island's revegetation. They show landforms, relief, fences, houses, tracks and streams, as well as giving detailed descriptions of the bush and grassland. He also noted the effect of nox-ious animals on the forest remnants. The bush on the slopes of Tuteremoana, for example, consisted of 'Kohekohe, Tawa, Hinau, Rewarewa and Rata (the Ratas are for the most part dead) the undergrowth has been dense but has to a great extent been destroyed by the goats which abound on the island'.[11]

That Kapiti was over run by wild goats, sheep and cattle showed the neglect which was largely the result of the confused administration of the island reserves. They were a novel concept, without guidelines for a clear system of management. The three offshore sanctuaries (Resolution, Little Barrier and Kapiti) fell within the sphere of three different government departments. And as no single agency had sole control over endangered species, it was difficult to initiate measures that might offer birds such as huia a chance of survival. Internal Affairs, for example, controlled a wide range of wildlife activities from the regulation of game hunting to the protection of native species because it administered the Animals Protection and Game Act, but it had no authority over the three island reserves that had been

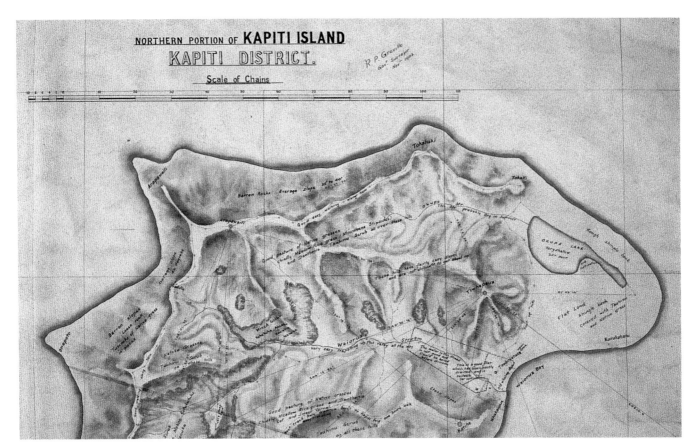

NORTHERN PORTION OF **KAPITI ISLAND**

KAPITI DISTRICT.

Scale of Chains

R.P. Greville
Govt Surveyor
Nov 1902.

A part of surveyor R. P. Greville's map of Kapiti, which described land at the northern end owned by Hemi Matenga and his brother, Wi Parata.
MAP 14958, LAND INFORMATION NEW ZEALAND, WELLINGTON DISTRICT OFFICE

specifically created to preserve rare native fauna. Because Resolution, Little Barrier and Kapiti had been gazetted as sanctuaries under the Land Act they were the responsibility of the Lands Department.[12]

Lands, however, had no experience of managing endangered species and little interest in their survival. This is evident in a letter from the Wellington Acclimatisation Society to the Colonial Secretary which politely pointed out that 'the Island of Kapiti has not been declared an excepted area within the meaning of the Animal Protection Act of 1880'. Without this basic legal protection, the island was not a sanctuary. The letter concluded: 'Our Society is informed that several parties have lately visited the island, and that both Native and Imported game birds are being shot there'.[13] This hint had the desired effect. Less than a fortnight later, the governor issued a special proclamation formally prohibiting the killing of any birds on Kapiti.[14]

Apart from that, the government did little more to enhance the island. In fact, it seems that its future was by no means certain, and its management was even more confused when Lands and Internal Affairs engaged in a struggle with a third Crown agency, the Department of Tourist and Health Resorts, which was rapidly extending its influence, mainly because it administered the Scenery Preservation Act. Under this legislation, representative areas of forest and scenery throughout the country were to be protected for aesthetic and scientific reasons.[15]

In 1904 the same department gained control of Little Barrier and Resolution Islands[16] and, the following year, it cast covetous eyes at Kapiti, even though its superintendent was not convinced that the island was ideal for a sanctuary. In a letter to his minister he wrote: 'I am not altogether satisfied that Kapiti Island is quite suitable for the purpose recommended as I understand the bush is very limited in extent and therefore there must be a comparative shortage of shelter and food'.[17] Nevertheless, he advised the government that if it was intent on making Kapiti a sanctuary, it should acquire the remaining 1400 acres of Maori land under the Scenery Preservation Act. Cabinet approved this recommendation in December 1905.[18] Within 10 days, the Department of Tourist and Health Resorts inspector, James Cowan, was on the island to assess its value 'for the purposes of a bird sanctuary and game preserve'. He scrutinised the island thoroughly, gathered considerable information about its history and concluded that 'Kapiti seems to be an excellent place for a deer preserve. There is an abundance of woodland shelter, with splendid feed and plenty of water. The land is so diversified with gullies and corries and spurs that there is any amount of cover, and the open valleys and flats everywhere carry rich grass.' Cowan saw no conflict between the needs of endangered native birds and introduced game animals so his recommendation reinforced his department's vision for the island: 'I think Kapiti will continue to be an excellent place for the preservation of the makomako and other rarer varieties of birds, so long as the present area of bush is not diminished; and it should be a suitable experimental ground for various kinds of big game'.[19]

Cowan's report was, however, careful not to endorse the other part of his department's strategy – the acquisition of the remaining Maori land on Kapiti. His familiarity with Maori, the legacy of Cowan's boyhood on the edge of the King Country, meant that he also considered the Maori point of view, so he drew attention to earlier, unsuccessful European attempts to acquire the island. He also made it clear that he had talked with Wi Parata and found the chief and his family 'very unwilling' to part with their land on the 'motu Rongonui (far-famed island)'. In a far-sighted recommendation, as relevant today as it was then, he urged the department to 'enlist the services of some reliable Maori at Waikanae as a caretaker or ranger. I think it would be wise to secure the assistance and sympathy of the Parata family in this matter, as they have shown a desire to preserve the native birds and the native bush.'[20]

The question of a caretaker also concerned others, including the tireless conservationist, Harry Ell, who wrote to the Superintendent of the Tourist and

Unlike Cockayne and Ell, who came from Canterbury, journalist James Cowan (1870-1943) grew up in the Waikato on a family farm that included part of the Orakau battlefield. He had a lifelong interest in Maori people and their history.

In 1903 he joined the new Department of Tourist and Health Resorts in Wellington to write reports on scenic and tourist attractions throughout New Zealand. Soon after he completed his Kapiti report in 1907, Cowan left the department to become a freelance writer. He produced more than 30 books, as well as numerous newspaper and magazine articles.
ALEXANDER TURNBULL LIBRARY

Harry Ell (1863-1934) grew up in Christchurch; he spent his youth roaming the Port Hills, which inspired a lasting passion for conservation.

In 1899 he entered Parliament and for the next 20 years advocated the preservation of forests and endangered birds. His efforts culminated in the passing of the Scenery Preservation Act (1903), which enabled forest remnants throughout the country to be protected. Ell also kept a watchful eye on Kapiti.

After he lost his seat in 1919, Ell used his prodigious energy to improve access to the Port Hills; in particular, the completion of the Summit Road and the building of a series of walking tracks and wayside inns. The Sign of the Kiwi and the Sign of the Takahe are still in use today.
ALEXANDER TURNBULL LIBRARY

Health Resorts Department a few weeks after Cowan's visit. His tone was urgent because the country was in the grip of an unprecedented drought: 'I do hope that you will spare no effort to have a caretaker put in charge at once in order to provide as far as possible against injury by fire. Shooting and fishing and camping parties now go to the island and they are at liberty to burn and destroy as there is no one there to check them.'[21] Soon after, in 1906, a caretaker was appointed, not by the Department of Tourist and Health Resorts but by the Lands Department, which was still the actual manager of the island. Whether it was familiar with Cowan's as yet unpublished report is not clear; even if it was, it did not heed his advice to appoint a local Maori and instead engaged E. A. Newson, a 22-year-old European from Otaki.[22]

Newson faced challenges that would have deterred someone twice his age. As there was no boat on the island he was effectively marooned and when he arrived the Whare was barely habitable, its front having been smashed by a severe southerly storm. The following year the Lands Department repaired the house and provided Newson with a whaleboat complete with sails and oars, but by then the effects of isolation were beginning to take their toll and after two years he resigned because of loneliness.[23] His brother, C. E. Newson, took his place and remained until a replacement could be arranged.[24]

The Newsons' presence on Kapiti was significant, less for the island's ecology than as a visible display of Lands' authority. Rivalry with the Tourist and Health Resorts Department had galvanised the department into protecting its preserve, and soon after E. A. Newson's arrival it took a further step to consolidate its control of the island when a well-known scientist, Dr Leonard Cockayne, visited Kapiti to prepare a botanical report for the Minster of Lands. Cockayne spent two weeks on the island, sufficient time to explore all areas except the south-western coast, which was accessible only by sea. Since Newson had not yet been provided with a boat, such an expedition was not feasible. On his return Cockayne wrote a long, detailed account of the island's vegetation, but before it could be published, yet another government department – the fourth – made a bold bid to acquire Kapiti.

Leonard Cockayne (1855-1934), a pioneer in the science of ecology, emphasised the relationship between animals and plants and their surroundings.

Cockayne reported on many of New Zealand's outlying islands, including the Auckland, Antipodes, Bounty, Campbell and Chatham groups, so he was the logical choice to make a botanical survey of Kapiti Island. This was first of a series for the Lands Department, including reports on Waipoua Kauri Forest, Tongariro National Park and Stewart Island.
ALEXANDER TURNBULL LIBRARY

In March 1907 the Minister of Public Health let it be known that his department planned to use Kapiti as a leper colony. This extraordinary proposal was not without precedent. Tiny Mokopuna Island near Matiu/Somes Island in Wellington Harbour, and Quail Island in Lyttelton Harbour, had both been used for the confinement of lepers in the past. But these islands were not sanctuaries for native flora and fauna. Rejection of the idea was swift and universal. When W. H. Field heard the news he sent a telegram to William Howell at Paraparaumu to alert residents of the Kapiti Coast. 'Learned yesterday the Government establishing a leper station on Kapiti. Have strongly protested on ground defilement beautiful historic favourite public resort and close proximity

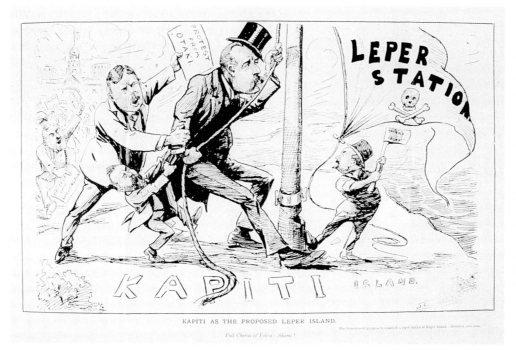

KAPITI AS THE PROPOSED LEPER ISLAND.

Full Chorus of Voices: Shame!

The Government propose to establish a leper station at Kapiti Island.—Dreadful news item.

Blomfield's cartoon in the New Zealand Free Lance *shows the Minister of Public Health, George Fowlds, raising a leper station pennant over Kapiti while Willie Field and the well-known conservationist and politician, Thomas Mackenzie, try to stop him. Wairau MP Charles Mills (right) assists them by chopping at the base of the flagpole. Their protests are amplified by the voices of numerous other objectors.*
ALEXANDER TURNBULL LIBRARY

to Maori population.'[25] The *New Zealand Free Lance* devoted a full page to a cartoon by J. C. Blomfield about the 'Dreadful news item'. In the same issue an editorial entitled 'A Horrible Threat' pointed out that the island was already earmarked as a sanctuary for native species. But the populist weekly's real objection was not about conservation:

> The Government, it is alleged, are going to add a new attraction to the Empire City by turning Kapiti Island, not far from the entrance of the port of Wellington, into a sanctuary for lepers! Most people would naturally believe that this was a ghastly Ministerial jest, for, of all the islands off the coast of New Zealand, none could be found less suitable than Kapiti. The wandering tourist, seeing the distant beauties of Kapiti, will naturally enquire about it, and he will get a shock when told 'Oh, that's the leper island!' He will conclude that the chief city of the colony is so leprous that it is necessary to have a place of easy access to dump the frequent 'cases' on. He won't know that the lepers only number three all told – one Chinaman and two Europeans.

> No protest can be too strong as a means of preventing this intended wrong to Wellington. If the proposal emanated from the Minster of Public Health, it is strange that he did not propose Motutapu, Motuihi or Rangitoto as a fit and proper place for lepers, these islands being quite close to the City of Auckland.[26]

A few days later a large meeting, including residents from various parts of the region, was held at Waikanae. It called on local MPs from Wanganui to Wellington 'to strongly protest against the evil being introduced into our district'. Among the speakers was Hemi Matenga who, since the death of his brother, Wi Parata, was the largest landowner on Kapiti. 'There were natives affected with leprosy before the pakeha arrived in this country, when the white man came here the disease departed,' the *New Zealand Times* reported him as saying. 'Two years ago the Maori Council made a law that all the native villages should be cleaned up, and now the Government has found a way again for the natives to get this disease,' he said.[27] The idea was dropped.

Nevertheless, it was a warning to the Lands Department that its hold on Kapiti was still precarious. Only a month later, Cockayne's report was tabled in Parliament by Robert McNab, the Minister of Lands.[28] In doing so, he reinforced his department's statutory authority over the island and showed that it had its own plan for Kapiti. McNab's political dexterity was crucial, for Cowan's report, which had been completed more than a year before Cockayne's, was still waiting to be presented. By tabling Cockayne's report ahead of Cowan's, the Minister of Lands effectively outmanoeuvred his rival, the Department of Tourist and Health Resorts, and also ensured that there would be no more scares like the leper colony. For the next 80 years the Lands Department's hold over Kapiti was unchallenged.

Cockayne's report was also a considerable success for Harry Ell. While Cockayne was writing his report, Ell was asking questions in the House about the island and urging that the government 'give full effect to the original intention to set it aside as a native bird sanctuary'.[29] Ell and Cockayne were friends and together 'the two were a formidable force in the face of threats to the sanctity of the natural environment'.[30] Cockayne's conclusion included five recommendations intended 'to carry out the purpose of the sanctuary with scrupulous exactitude'. He urged that:

- The greatest caution should be observed in allowing visitors to land on the island. Those permitted to land should be compelled to exercise every care not to destroy anything or disturb the birds in any way.

- It is absolutely necessary that the whole island should be acquired by the Government.

- The animals foreign to the island should be destroyed.

- Such native forest birds as are not present on Kapiti should be introduced. The huia, and all flightless birds of various kinds should all find there a sanctuary.

- I can see no reason why as complete a collection of the New Zealand forest plants as possible should not be planted in the sheltered valley towards the north of the island when this is finally acquired from its Native owners.[31]

For the first time since it became a sanctuary a decade earlier, Kapiti had a charter for its development. This was welcomed by all those concerned for the dwindling bush and birds, but it was far from acceptable to the Maori families who owned the northern part of Kapiti. In 1906, Wi Parata's death had provided the Crown with an opportunity to attempt to acquire his land and it might have succeeded had it not been resisted by his brother, Hemi Matenga, and by Wi Parata's youngest daughter, Utauta. The Crown's intention had been approved by Cabinet in 1905 and was reiterated in 1907 when the chairman of the Native Affairs Select Committee reminded the Commissioner of Crown Lands that 'Because of the Crown's desire to secure all of Kapiti Island negotiations should proceed posthaste to ensure the successful acquisition of Maori owned land'.[32] But Wi Parata's death actually made acquisition more complex because he had left his extensive landholdings, including his interest on Kapiti, to his five adult children. His estate was administered by one of them, his son Hira, and Hemi Matenga, so the government had to negotiate with six people instead of one.

Like Wi Parata, they all had compelling reasons for retaining their Kapiti land. The island was an important source of identity and mana, not merely to the Parata family but also to Ngati Toa and its allies who had shared the stronghold. Cowan

HEMI MATENGA AND UTAUTA PARATA

Hemi was the son of Te Rangihiroa's daughter, Metapere Waipunahau, and an Australian whaler, George Stubbs, who was drowned in a boating accident when Hemi was a small boy. He and his elder brother, Wiremu Parata Te Kakakura, lived on Kapiti, at Motungarara and Waiorua. Later, when most people left the island, they moved to Waikanae with their mother to join her Te Ati Awa kin.

In 1849 most Te Ati Awa returned to their ancestral lands in Taranaki, leaving their Waikanae territory to Metapere. On her death, Wi Parata became the leading chief of the district. Hemi lived at Wakapuaka, near Nelson, and so was less involved in local affairs. As a young man he had been taken there to farm and to marry Huria, granddaughter of Te Puoho. In 1863 the couple became national heroes when they swam through rough seas to the *Delaware*, a brig that had run aground, to help rescue the crew.

Huria's death in 1909 allowed Hemi Matenga to return to Waikanae, where he became the leader of the Maori community in place of Wi Parata. In 1912 Hemi also died. As he and Huria had no children, most of his property passed to Wi Parata's children. Utauta, the youngest daughter, inherited Hemi's land and house on Kapiti.

The Manaaki *was built in Picton to a design based on a model, carved in pumice, by Hona Webber. Its name means 'to show respect and kindness'.*

For 50 years the Manaaki *was an indispensable part of the Webbers' life on Kapiti; the launch took passengers and supplies to and from Kapiti, and it also transported numerous bales of wool to the mainland.*

JIM WEBBER COLLECTION

had said as much in his report. Kapiti was the motu rongonui, the famous island, where these tribes had achieved ascendancy. It was also the place where numerous forebears where buried. Most were hidden in fissures and caves but Te Rangihiroa, the kaitiaki of Kapiti, was buried in the open, on the edge of the beach at Waiorua, in view of anyone who landed there.

Kapiti was also significant for economic reasons. The hills at Waiorua had been farmed for more than 30 years, first by Wi Parata, then by his son Winara. In 1907 the property carried 1400 sheep.[33] Although farming on Kapiti had always been only marginally profitable, the farm there was still a valued part of the Paratas'

Hona Webber and Utauta Parata on their wedding day, at Waikanae, c. 1895. In 1909 they and their six children moved to Kapiti to farm at Waiorua. The families who own land there today are their descendants.

REWA WEBBER COLLECTION

Mahara House, built at Waikanae in 1901, provided 'superior accommodation' for travellers and fishermen. Visitors were also taken to Kapiti on occasions. In the early 1930s it was destroyed by fire.
BRYANT COLLECTION, ALEXANDER TURNBULL LIBRARY

larger sheep operation which was based at Waikanae. Furthermore, Hemi Matenga and Hira Parata owned and operated Mahara House, an imposing Edwardian guest-house at Waikanae.[34] Among the excursions offered to visitors were trout fishing in the Waikanae River, horse racing at the nearby family racecourse and cruises to Kapiti Island.[35]

But if Hemi Matenga and his nephews and nieces wanted to maintain their interests on Kapiti, they saw that they would have to establish a more permanent presence there. Just as the Lands Department had been compelled to appoint a resident caretaker to deflect the unwelcome interest of rival government departments, so the Paratas needed to do more than make visits to muster and shear, or bring over tourists to enjoy the famous island. Someone had to be seen to be living there.

For most of his life Hemi Matenga had lived at Wakapuaka, near Nelson, but in 1909 he returned to Waikanae where he built an impressive house on the foot-hills behind the township.[36] He also built a house on Kapiti to replace the original corrugated iron shelter. Hemi's health, however, was failing, and farming the island was not for him; so Utauta Parata with her husband, Hona Webber, and their six children went to live at Waiorua Bay in 1909.[37]

As the Webbers developed the farm, Utauta also nursed Hemi Matenga, who was a regular guest. Like Hemi and the visitors from Mahara House, the Webbers travelled to and from the island by boat. The trip across Rau O Te Rangi Channel could be deceptively dangerous; sudden changes in the weather sometimes stranded visitors on Kapiti, or the family on the mainland, but the greatest difficulty was the lack of a safe harbour at Kapiti. While Waiorua Bay was sheltered from the worst of the nor'-wester, it was exposed to the south and a severe storm from that direction could tear a boat from its moorings and throw it up on the beach where the waves would pound it to pieces. In their first few years on the island, the Webbers lost two launches.[38]

The Webbers' presence effectively stymied the Crown's plan to acquire the remainder of Kapiti, but the prospect of the acquisition of their land re-

This photo, taken by Richard Henry, shows shearers at Waiorua enjoying a 'smoko' break. From left to right: Hemi Tahiwi (with the banjo), Ruihi (Lucy) Webber, Waru Rae and Hona Webber.
FORMER LANDS DEPARTMENT COLLECTION, DEPARTMENT OF CONSERVATION

mained a threat. Utauta, in particular, devoted much of her energy to lobbying successive generations of officials and politicians to ensure they were able to remain.

In the meantime, Cockayne's plan to make Kapiti a real sanctuary, even if it were to consist of less than the entire island, turned out to be more difficult to implement than the Lands Department may have anticipated. Nevertheless, several early initiatives suggested a promising start. In February 1908, at the urging of Harry Ell, the naturalist James Drummond visited Kapiti to report on its bird life. This was timely, because although both Cowan and Cockayne had referred to Kapiti's birds in passing, a comprehensive appraisal had yet to be made. Drummond spent six days on the island and saw 23 different native bird species, including the North Island robin. His observation that its southern counterpart was not present, despite Cockayne's claim to have seen some two years earlier, tends to confirm the modern view that Cockayne was mistaken. Drummond also noted that the native and introduced birds shared the sanctuary without apparent conflict: 'The English birds do not interfere with the native birds, and the natives take no notice what ever of the intruders. They do not frequent the same parts.' Like Cockayne, he concluded that rare forest birds such as 'the Huia, the North Island thrush and crow, and the saddleback might be liberated on Kapiti'. Drummond also echoed Cockayne's comments about the Maori presence at Waiorua, which he considered:

> will be a menace to the forest and the birds every summer. While I was on the island, a large grass-fire swept over the Maori land, and only stopped at the edge of the forest on the Government land. On another occasion a bush-fire might gain a good hold and sweep over the island. New Zealand birds will not live away from the native forest, and if the trees are destroyed the island will be quite valueless as a sanctuary. In these circumstances it seems advisable to offer the Maori some inducement to relinquish their rights in respect to the land they own on Kapiti.

Drummond, a freelance journalist, had not been commissioned by the Lands Department to produce his report but it must have approved because his disserta-

The caretaker's launch and boatshed, Kapiti Island, 1909.

Richard Henry was an experienced boatman accustomed to sailing alone in the exposed waters of Fiordland; he considered the open whaleboat and smaller rowing boat at Kapiti quite inadequate. What was required was a launch with an engine powerful enough to handle Kapiti's rough seas, yet light enough to be hauled ashore by one man. It was a tall order. When Henry failed to find such a boat, the Minister of Lands gave him permission to have one built to his exact specifications.

The boatbuilders, however, delivered a boat with an unsatisfactory engine and the matter soon ended up in the hands of lawyers. The department insisted that Henry resolve the dispute himself, so he replaced the engine with the Hercules from his boat at Resolution Island and had the launch modified to protect it. 'She would be laughed at in Wellington,' he wrote to his superior, 'but the roof is a necessity here to defend the engine against blowing sand and spray.'

Satisfied at last, Henry noted that at a speed of 6 knots, he could reach the mainland in half an hour, and circle the island in two and a quarter hours.[42]

FORMER LANDS DEPARTMENT COLLECTION, DEPARTMENT OF CONSERVATION

tion was presented to Parliament as an appendix to the annual report of the Commissioner of Crown Lands.[39]

Four months after Drummond's visit, a new caretaker was appointed to replace E. A. Newson. The department may have been pleased to gain the services of Richard Henry, the country's most experienced custodian of rare birds, but his transfer to Kapiti was not, in hindsight, as suitable as it seemed. Henry had pioneered the translocation of endangered flightless birds such as kiwi and kakapo to Resolution Island, but officials in his department (Tourist and Health Resorts) and his doctor were worried about his health and his long isolation on that remote reserve, so they welcomed his appointment to Kapiti which was closer to civilisation.[40]

For a time Henry approached his new position with vigour but, like his predecessor, he had to spend much of his energy organising the basics of survival: shelter for himself and a reliable means of getting to and from the island. On his arrival he found the Whare to be a 'hopeless ruin'. Lands allowed him to buy materials and, with some help, he made it fairly comfortable. Organising a new boat, however, was more difficult and it was six months before he finally had a vessel that satisfied him. Henry then turned his attention to the even greater problem of finding some way to protect his launch while it was moored at Rangatira.

The absence of a harbour worried him and in a letter to the Lands Department he admitted that the big waves stirred up during southerly storms made him anxious about any boat surviving for long.[41] The department was sympathetic and suggested building a slipway and windlass that would enable Henry to haul his launch out of the water, unaided, in bad weather. But when they tried to build it, the constantly shifting gravel beach thwarted every attempt. Henry and his manager, the under-secretary of the department, were not to know that this problem would frustrate a succession of caretakers for years to come.

Henry had to make do with an improved mooring and new anchors and chains to secure his boat. When the barometer indicated bad weather, he hauled the launch out of the water and high up the beach with the aid of a capstan – exhausting work for anyone, let alone a man in his 60s with failing health. Yet the

For many years after it became a nature reserve, visitors were permitted to camp on Kapiti provided they had written permission from the Lands Department. The Webbers also allowed campers on their land. Sydney Higgs's (c.1912) painting shows his friend, Nugent Welch, sketching from the door of their tent on Kapiti.
ALEXANDER TURNBULL LIBRARY

effort was worth it. For the consequences of failing to remove a boat were made plain when Henry visited the Webbers at Waiorua Bay on Christmas Day, 1909. Hona Webber came by water to take Henry to Waiorua Bay for lunch, but the visit had to be cut short when a southerly storm blew up. Returning again from Rangatira, having taken Henry home, Webber did not remove his launch from the sea but secured it, instead, to moorings (which Henry considered inadequate). During the storm, the boat was swept ashore and smashed to pieces.[43] The following year the Marine Department produced plans for a harbour at Kapiti, but it was never built.[44]

On Christmas Eve, 1909, the Webber family called on the Kapiti caretaker, Richard Henry, to invite him to join them for a festive dinner the following day and Henry photographed his visitors. From left to right: Heneti Webber, holding her youngest grandchild, Jim, Arona (holding his hat), Piki, Tuku and behind him, Utauta, Winara and Rangi.
FORMER LANDS DEPARTMENT COLLECTION, DEPARTMENT OF CONSERVATION

Preoccupied though Richard Henry was with the sea for most of his first year, he was also observing the bush and the birds on the island and coming to conclusions that were different from Cockayne's. The botanist had, for example, recommended that all animals be removed, but Henry considered that the wild cats actually helped to protect the birds because they ate the rats which would otherwise have destroyed the birds – especially their eggs and young.

As for goats, he argued that although they ate the trees and shrubs, they also helped to keep the long grass down and so averted the danger of fire. In a paper entitled 'On Kapiti Island – Cats, Rats, Goats, etc', Henry wrote:

> I am certain that there would not be half the bush here now if there had been no goats. They are by far the best scrub eaters for keeping the bush too open to burn. No doubt it would be nicer to have it without goats if we could have it without fires also, but when the latter is impossible the goats are only a trifling harm compared to what fires might be. If the goats were destroyed and the grass and scrub allowed to grow up a fire might do more harm in an hour than the goats have done in a hundred years.[45]

When he first arrived on Kapiti, Henry killed cats but after he noticed that rats caught in traps were half-eaten he left the cats alone. Instead he left food scraps near his house for the cats and bits of fish by the boatshed. He also befriended the goats and became increasingly interested in them. Although he was a prolific writer on a range of subjects, he wrote only one paper on Kapiti and all but two of its nine pages were devoted to detailed observations of the goats' habits and rituals. Henry described their pattern of distribution and their vulnerability to itch as well as the rules that governed the males when they fought. It was curious that these scrofulous creatures, rather than the island's birds, interested this once energetic man whose earlier, dedicated efforts had briefly transformed Resolution Island into an ark for flightless birds. Now, it appeared, he no longer believed in such an approach. The consequence of watching his life's work on the southern sanctuary come to nothing as predators colonised it, and the lassitude of his old age led Henry to advocate a tolerant policy towards noxious animals. Others, such as the ever

Richard Henry's affectionate interest in the goats on Kapiti is clear from his account of male goats fighting. 'They are the most wonderful creatures I have ever heard of, for their real fights are never carried out with spite or bad temper, but strictly on Darwinian principles to prove which is the best. Of course, I have seen bits of bad temper and scrambles amongst the younger ones but the real fights were carried on quite differently. I have watched many of them before my window and I think some of them must have lasted an hour when they were well matched. I have not seen any bloodshed or a sign of cruelty or a sign of resentment that could be avoided. That is what makes them so wonderful to me.

When one of them is defeated he walks away very downheartedly, sometimes cries a little bit but walks very slowly, and the conqueror walks after him or beside him but never attempts to stab him as he could easily do. His manner towards him is more like sympathy than enmity. Thus it appears that Nature does not desire to get rid of the inferior males among the goats for some hidden reason.'
FORMER LANDS DEPARTMENT COLLECTION, DEPARTMENT OF CONSERVATION

During his three years on Kapiti, Richard Henry seems to have taken relatively few photographs, yet they are perhaps, his most valuable contribution for they provide, along with Cockayne's photos, the earliest visual record of the state of the reserve. He photographed the abandoned farm at Wharekohu, for example, to illustrate the fire danger created by 'the tauhinu scrub taking possession of the grassland. It is very inflammable and should be burned next year in December to save a ruinous fire in the dry season. The building and the fence is about the last of the sheep farm that was here.'
FORMER LANDS DEPARTMENT COLLECTION, DEPARTMENT OF CONSERVATION

watchful Harry Ell, were not convinced. 'I do not agree with Mr Henry with regard to the goats' not proving harmful to the vegetation. It is evident that they are eating away at the undergrowth and I think that the winds getting into the open bush retards the growth of the forest.'[46]

Henry was more energetic in his attitude towards obnoxious humans, such as the sheep stealers and bird poachers who regularly raided the island, although the practical limits of his authority, as well as some unfortunate experiences, eventually made him reluctant to act against them. He did not condone their intrusions but there was little one man could do to stop them. Kapiti, Henry knew, was regarded by many sportsmen as a de facto game reserve where good bags awaited those hunters prepared to run the minimal risk of being caught landing illegally: 'Nearly everyone I spoke to asked about the game on Kapiti,' he recalled of his visits to Wellington. 'Even in high places the whole ambition appeared to be to get on to Kapiti to shoot, and they all had the idea that they would be welcome to shoot goats.'[47] A few hunters wrote to the department asking permission, but many more sneaked ashore on some isolated part of the island. 'I found it of no use to go after them in my boat, because they can see me coming from miles away.' Wharekohu, the sheltered cove tucked out of sight at the southern end, seemed to be a particularly popular landing place. On one occasion Henry canoed part of the way from Rangatira, then scrambled over the steep hills to Wharekohu, but failed to find any intruders and the effort exhausted him.[48]

In October 1910 Henry's enthusiasm for enforcing the law was eroded even further when he was told by Hemi Matenga that, at the southern end of the island, he and Hona Webber and several others had come across a party of five rustlers with several sheep they had shot and were about to take away. The intruders were led by William Howell (senior), a justice of the peace, whose sons ran a butcher's shop at Paraparaumu.[49] Henry was shocked at the duplicity of Howell who had recently called on him at Rangatira. He complained to his department, which referred the incident to the police but it was decided that the circumstances did not justify laying charges.

This failure to prosecute encouraged the poachers and they continued to raid Kapiti regularly:

> The sheep stealers have been over about the south end of Kapiti every fine Saturday, Sunday and holiday since I complained to you about them. They have paraded their contempt for me and for the owners of the sheep. Nearly everyone here knows that Howell was caught red-handed and got off scot-free, but most important, they know that he is still the most frequent visitor to Kapiti; and no doubt they say to themselves – Preserving Kapiti is only a bit of a joke'.[50]

Even more serious than the poachers, though, were the persistent efforts of some in the government to undermine the status of the sanctuary by making it something else as well – a game reserve, or a leper station or a sheep farm. Clearly Kapiti's existing designation as a nature reserve was not universally accepted. There were even signs that the Lands Department hoped to make money by converting parts of the island into productive pasture.[51] If the grassland at either end could be put to use, the cost of purchasing and administering the reserve might be recovered and, at the same time, the danger of fire would be lessened. It was a tempting prospect. If this plan succeeded, the sanctuary would be sandwiched between sheep runs at either end. Richard Henry was well aware of this possibility, for in his essay on the island's goats he wrote 'If it is decided to lease the government grass on the south end of Kapiti…'.[52]

Local MP, Willie Field, had campaigned for just such an arrangement for years. He also argued that he and the Macleans should be permitted to build baches there,[53] but when this fell on deaf ears he modified his case to suggest building accommodation on Kapiti, provided that any visitors were 'subject to the most rigid restrictions' to protect the birds and bush.[54] Of existing arrangements he was very critical: 'Up to the present Government policy concerning the island has been more or less one of foolery, for the place might have earned considerable income if the grass were stocked, and the island might have been a source of joy to the public'.[55]

When Richard Henry retired from the government service in the winter of 1911, Kapiti was little closer to being a functioning reserve than it had been in

The dual role envisaged for Kapiti, as a sanctuary and a sheep run, explains the Marine Department's plan for a harbour. Although the drawings do not specify where on the island's coast it was to be built, the configuration of hill, stream and beach can only have been at Waiorua Bay, which raises the question why a government department would want to design and build an expensive wharf for the Webbers. It seems more likely that the proposed wharf was intended to service the Crown's leasehold run(s) at the northern end once the Webbers had been removed, either by negotiation or legislative compulsion.
NATIONAL ARCHIVES

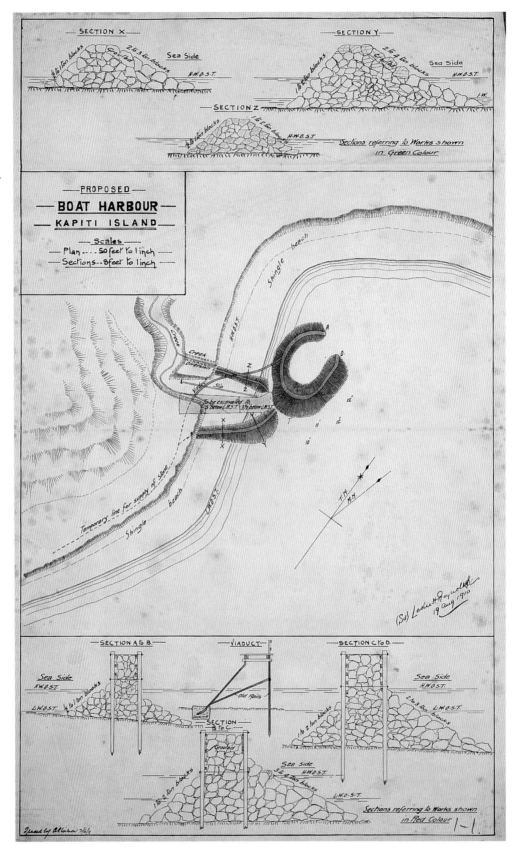

1897. The only steps taken towards creating a sanctuary had been on paper: the island had been mapped by Greville, its history described by Cowan, its botany recorded by Cockayne and its birds listed by Drummond. These surveys were essential, but no real progress had been made on the island itself. Its potential as a sanctuary remained unrealised. Sheep, goats and wild cattle still roamed the reserve as they had in 1897, cats and rats kept the birds in check, and hunters and rustlers still carried out their activities at will. Conservationists like Harry Ell had little to show for their years of persistent advocacy. Few noxious animals had been shot, other than the occasional goat reluctantly killed by Henry for his table. With his departure, a new opportunity arose to actually *do* something to enhance the sanctuary.

Now "FOREST AND BIRD PROTECTION SOCIETY (OF NEW ZEALAND, INC.)"

N. Z. NATIVE BIRD PROTECTION SOCIETY

INCORPORATED

Telephone 43-239

OBJECTS

TO ADVOCATE AND OBTAIN THE EFFICIENT PROTECTION
AND PRESERVATION OF OUR NATIVE BIRD LIFE
UNITY OF CONTROL OF ALL WILD LIFE
ENLISTING THE NATURAL SYMPATHY OF OUR YOUNG
THE PRESERVATION OF SANCTUARIES, SCENIC
RESERVES, ETC. IN THEIR NATIVE STATE

HEAD OFFICE
P. O. BOX 631

WELLINGTON
NEW ZEALAND

MARITIME BUILDING,
CUSTOMHOUSE QUAY,

23rd January, 1935.

CHAPTER TWELVE

GETTING STARTED

On 23 December 1997 a large crowd gathered on Kapiti at the invitation of the Department of Conservation to mark its centenary as a nature reserve. But the occasion was premature for, although the government had acquired Kapiti a century earlier, it did not function as a sanctuary until 1911 when James Bennett became caretaker and began the campaign to rid the island of wild cattle, goats, sheep and cats.

Wherever he went, he took his rifle. In his first three years he killed more than 800 goats; by the end of his term he had shot thousands more and had also eradicated the cattle and cats. At the same time, kakapo and kiwi were released on Kapiti.

Despite Bennett's efforts, some observers were far from satisfied and in 1922 the state of the sanctuary was vigorously debated in Wellington's newspapers. That the controversy reached their columns was no accident, but the result of a carefully planned campaign by a new kind of publicity-minded activist, Captain Val Sanderson. This was his first public foray. In hindsight, it marked the beginning of a national conservation movement. After this successful campaign he founded the Native Bird Protection Society (later the Royal Forest and Bird Protection Society), under whose banner other campaigns have made significant conservation gains.

(INSET) FOREST AND BIRD SOCIETY PAPERS, MANUSCRIPTS AND ARCHIVES, ALEXANDER TURNBULL LIBRARY

JAMES LACON BENNETT, who became caretaker on Kapiti in 1911, was very different from his predecessor. Richard Henry was a high-minded, self-taught, intellectual whose interest in conservation was matched by an enthusiasm for eugenics that led him to observe Kapiti's wild goats rather than to kill them. The Lands Department knew that his attitude had not helped the sanctuary's development, so sought a more active replacement. In Bennett it had a practical man who had worked on sheep stations and been a gold miner.

The department had a clear idea of what he was to do. In 1911, a ministerial visit to the island noted how much damage was being done to the flora by noxious animals, especially goats; the department decided that they must be destroyed, or at least reduced, and Bennett was required to do it.[1] The Commissioner of Crown Lands had no illusion about the difficulties. He noted, prophetically, that 'the last 25 goats will take more trouble to shoot than the first 500'.[2] Bennett began to hunt the animals soon after he arrived, but his first estimate of about 1000 goats on Kapiti turned out to be too low.[3] Ten years later he told a visitor he had shot 7000,[4] and others still eluded him on the western cliffs.

The Department of Lands (which was renamed Lands and Survey in 1913) also hoped to stock Kapiti with endangered birds. The liberation of kiwi and kakapo was to be followed by others, in particular the huia, if any could be found. Numerous searches were organised by the Department of Tourist and Health Resorts, but although there was some evidence to suggest a few might have survived, not one was ever captured.[5]

Bennett was also keen to see tuatara released on Tokomapuna.[6] He wrote to his superiors, who passed his suggestion on to the Department of Internal Affairs but, like Sayer's huia, the idea seemed to vanish into the void between the various government departments with an interest in endangered species. Even if huia and tuatara had been transferred to the sanctuary (and the offshore islet) their survival could not have been guaranteed because of poachers. In 1912 the ever vigilant Harry Ell, now a Cabinet minister, wrote to the Minister of Lands about reports 'that Maoris from outside districts were in the habit of shooting birds on Kapiti Island, one settler alleging that on one occasion a Maori got away with over fifty birds'. Ell suggested that the minister should prohibit anyone from carrying a gun from landing on the island. 'If this cannot be done, then I think the whole island should be acquired.'[7]

A few months later, another visitor to Kapiti, Val Sanderson, heard 'shooting in the bush on the protected area which was not done by the caretaker'.[8] He had first visited the island in 1894 and 1898 as a young man, but did not return again until 1914. He considered that, in the interval, there had been a noticeable decline in the bird life and was shocked into action. In a two-page report to the Minister of Lands, Sanderson made it plain who he thought was to blame:

> The great decrease in bird life is probably caused by cats and other enemies and poaching especially by Natives and it seemed to me the island was a preserve and shooting ground and grazing land for the benefit of Maoris. They should be called on to fence if possible to do so, and kept on their own land. Many rumours are afloat as to poaching by natives from the mainland and there can be no doubt that such occurs. The Island did not have the appearance of being used as a bird sanctuary by any means and it seemed to me the present means of protection are absolutely inadequate.[9]

Sanderson recognised, however, that criticism alone was not enough; he also offered practical suggestions. Because the island was so big, and the job of shooting

out the goats so daunting, the caretaker needed an assistant. And if he was to pa-
trol the island to deter poachers, he needed a better boat. Sanderson thought little
of Richard Henry's pride and joy. 'The oil launch at the caretaker's disposal is a
ridiculous affair, only fit for the scrap heap. He should have something efficient in
this line and should have the best possible launching facilities.'[10]

In a covering letter, Sanderson gave a hint of what might happen if his recommendations were ignored. 'The newspapers have intimated their willingness
to take the matter up and it seems to me great interest is taken by a considerable
section of the public in the island who will be keenly disappointed that better results are not shown.'[11] He well understood the process of lobbying government.
On the same day that he wrote to the Minister of Lands, he sent a copy to the
Prime Minister, W. F. Massey, who forwarded it to the Minster of Internal Affairs.
Suddenly three members of the Cabinet were aware of Sanderson's thoughts on
Kapiti.[12]

Soon afterwards, the Minister of Internal Affairs received several letters about
the state of the island from the New Zealand Forest and Bird Protection Society,
a previously unknown organisation that appeared to be the creation of Harry Ell.
The society's suggestions about improving the sanctuary were remarkably similar
to Sanderson's, although his name was not among the office-bearers and supporters listed on the letterhead.[13] The barrage was effective. Less than two months later,
the Inspector of Scenic Reserves, Edward Phillips-Turner, completed a hurriedly
commissioned report on Kapiti. His findings generally endorsed Sanderson's, although he did not agree that the whole island should be acquired. Buying the
northern end, at an estimated cost of £7,000, would be too expensive, he said; to
recover its outlay, the Crown would have to continue farming the land at Waiorua.
This, in turn, would require more expenditure for fencing, scrub-cutting, building

a breakwater, buying a punt and a launch to get stock and wool on and off the island, and also paying extra staff to run the farm.

Instead, the inspector suggested a land swap with the Maori owners to simplify the existing situation, which was awkward because several blocks within the reserve still belonged to Maori. If these were given to the Crown and it, in return, gave the owners at the northern end an additional adjacent area, administration of the island would be easier for all concerned. Such an exchange, Phillips-Turner noted, would also make clear the delineation between the sanctuary and the Maori land, which could then be fenced to prevent sheep getting into the reserve. Perhaps his most far-sighted suggestion, which Sanderson had not mentioned, was that 'measures be taken to exterminate the opossums that have now become plentiful on the island'.[14]

In August of that year the First World War began and many New Zealanders volunteered for active service, among them the watchful Val Sanderson, whose departure overseas gave Kapiti's managers a breather. The 45-year-old Boer War veteran was considered too old for fighting, so he served instead as a quartermaster in Egypt, until illness eventually led to his return to New Zealand. In his absence, the Lands and Survey Department continued its programme on Kapiti. Despite Phillips-Turner's caution about the cost of acquiring the whole island, that was what it determined to do. An attempt to get an act passed in 1914 failed to make the order paper but the following year the department continued to press for legislation.[15] Its plans, however, were countered each session by Utauta Webber, who regularly visited politicians to ensure that she and her family retained their land. She also invited some of them to stay with her family on the island.[16]

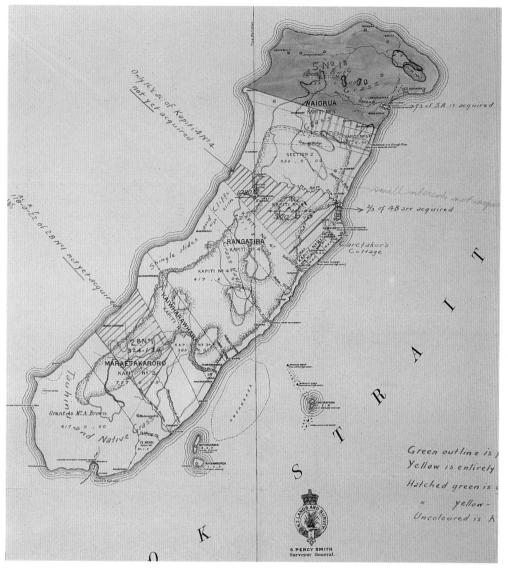

In 1914 the Inspector of Scenic Reserves, Edward Phillips-Turner, visited Kapiti to investigate complaints about the state of the sanctuary. He reported that the reserve included several blocks of Maori land which he marked with parallel green lines on the map that accompanied his report.

This problem, he considered, should be resolved by an exchange of land with the Webbers. The Crown could give a strip of the reserve adjacent to the farm at the northern end (shown here by parallel yellow lines), in return for the inclusion of these Maori blocks into the reserve.

In 1918 the trustees of Hemi Matenga's estate, which owned the Maraetakaroro block, agreed to exchange it for land next to Waiorua although the area ceded by the Crown was greater than Phillips-Turner had indicated and extended right across the island. The Crown had to wait a little longer to acquire Rangatira No. 4, most of which was purchased in 1922.
NATIONAL ARCHIVES

Meanwhile Bennett continued his campaign to eradicate noxious animals on Kapiti. In 1915, possums were added to the list on Phillips-Turner's recommendation and in response to the caretaker's own observation of the damage being done to the bush by the browsing hordes. The department hoped, at the same time, to make money from the possum skins but the war caused a slump in fur prices so they were discarded rather than sold. This made difficulties for Lands because it was still widely believed that possum pelts were lucrative. Nor was it understood how much damage possums did. In 1916, for example, a deputation to the Minister of Internal Affairs asked for their protection. One of the delegation, the Vice-President of the Forest and Bird Protection Society, argued that possums were unlikely ever to become a menace – in fact, they were so easy to kill they might soon be extinct![17] Willie Field, who led the deputation, maintained that a single skin was worth between 10s and £1. Yet, only a few months earlier, the first consignment of skins from the island had sold for an average of less than 2s each.[18]

Given these popular expectations, the Lands and Survey Department looked beyond low skin prices in New Zealand in the hope of better returns from distant markets. R. P. Greville, who was about to visit the United States, was given a batch

On several occasions, Bennett's superiors told him to convey strong warnings to the Webbers about burn-offs getting out of control and their sheep trespassing on the reserve.

If these duties caused a coolness between neighbours it was not apparent. This photograph of Bennett and Utauta suggests a close rapport. It was probably taken by Johannes Andersen on one of his many visits to the island, because it is attached to a copy of Bennett's obituary filed with Andersen's papers.
ARCHIVES AND MANUSCRIPTS, ALEXANDER TURNBULL LIBRARY

When Professor Kirk visited Kapiti in 1919, he was accompanied by a fellow scientist, W. E. Bendall. Later Bendall gave a talk about the island to the Manawatu Philosophical Society in which he suggested that the driftwood on Kapiti might offer unemployed servicemen new opportunities.

'Snugly anchored under the lee of the island a profitable and pleasurable time could be put in by the party sawing up the wood and boating it off to the scow, and the less robust members could keep ship, fish to their hearts content and attend to the commissariat Department. How much better this, than hanging around the Towns waiting for "jobs"; smoking innumerable cigarettes and imbibing the sundry harmful but well meant drinks.'

of possum skins from Kapiti and asked to ascertain their value in New York, the centre of the world's fur trade. His report that most skins were unsaleable, except grey ones, was not encouraging, since Kapiti was infested with the black variety.[19] The department faced a similar problem with the skins of Kapiti's goats, which Harry Ell and others considered to be a potential source of revenue. He hoped that good returns would add impetus to the caretaker's campaign to eradicate goats from the island but, as Bennett found, the skins fetched such low prices that they hardly covered the cost of skinning the carcasses. In any case, bullet holes meant the skins were of little value.[20]

The department continued to consider other ways of raising revenue on Kapiti. For example, when it failed for the third year in a row, to acquire the rest of the island by legislation, it decided that 'if the Native owners still refuse or hesitate to make an offer for their interests, to charge them rental for the sheep grazing upon the portions of the island owned by the Crown'.[21] Similarly, after a summer burn-off at Waiorua that worried Bennett because it might spread into the reserve, the department instructed him to warn the Webbers it would take legal action if future fires caused damage to the reserve.[22]

The Crown's relations with its neighbours deteriorated. The Webbers' lawyer wrote to the department accusing Bennett of shooting their sheep and asked that the two parts of the island be separated by a fence.[23] The official response was to authorise Bennett to kill sheep on Crown land 'for the purpose of obtaining mutton'.[24] But when the caretaker sent sheepskins to Dalgety & Co. for sale, he found that the proceeds had been frozen by the Webbers' lawyer, who contended they were really the property of his clients.[25]

That the problem of wild sheep roaming the island was becoming intolerable is evident in the opening lines of a report on the sanctuary written in 1919 by Professor H. B. Kirk, of Victoria [University] College:

> By far the most important and far-reaching of the recommendations referred to is that the whole Island should be acquired by the Government, that being the only means by which it can be hoped effectively to put a stop to the damage being done by sheep belonging to Native owners. At present the Natives hold about 644 acres. But they have far more sheep than their own holdings could support, and the greater number of these are running wild over the Island. It is safe to say that no less than 800 of these sheep are running on the lands of the Crown.

'Monarch of all he surveys – Mr. J. L. Bennett, the caretaker of Kapiti Island, 1 March 1921.'
Les Adkin's caption was not intended to be ironic. At the time he took the photograph it was true, but later that year a clandestine inspection of the kingdom of Kapiti by Sanderson and others resulted in a sustained campaign of criticism of the government's management of the sanctuary. Although Bennett was not named in the numerous newspaper articles that castigated the Lands and Survey Department, his performance as caretaker was central to the controversy. As a civil servant he was unable to reply publicly, but letters to his superiors reveal both his bitterness and a strong antipathy towards Sanderson.
G. L. ADKIN COLLECTION, MUSEUM OF NEW ZEALAND/TE PAPA TONGAREWA

May and Fred Vosseler with Utauta Webber at Waiorua Bay.

The Vosselers and the Webbers were close friends; Fred and his wife often stayed with the Webbers, and after Vosseler and Willie Field founded the Tararua Tramping Club in 1919, they regularly brought tramping groups to Kapiti. When the Webbers went to Wellington they stayed with the Vosselers at their Kilbirnie home.

REWA WEBBER COLLECTION

Although the Natives have the right to muster over the whole Island, the difficulties of mustering on Kapiti are so great that very many of these sheep have never been docked or dagged; and it may be taken for granted that they have never been dipped. Nearly all are carrying long, filthy dags, very many have wool torn more or less completely from the back by the bushes. It would be hard to find anywhere else in New Zealand sheep that present the marks of neglect more obviously.

These sheep, with the wild goats, are setting a limit to the life of the forest. Not only do they prevent to a very large extent the growth of young trees, but they open up the forest to the sweep of the wind. They prepare it for invasion by grass, tauhinu, manuka and other hardy plants.

Later in his account, Kirk revealed that the problem was not so much the sheep themselves as the question of who should manage them. The government, it seemed, was close to finalising plans for the dual-use strategy that Willie Field and others had advocated for so long.

In the last Estimates there appeared a sum of £1,000 for the purpose of stocking Kapiti Island with sheep. The intention is to fence off the clearing at Rangatira Point and the Taipiro clearing in the middle of the Island, and to run two fences across the Island, cutting off the open land at the Northern and Southern ends. It is intended to make a track from Rangatira to the Taipiro clearing and on to the Southern clearing to enable fences to be erected and to serve as driving tracks in mustering. Sheep could then be run on the open lands with no damage to the bush. Presumably all the Native Sheep would first have been disposed of. The advantages to be gained, in addition to revenue, would be that the danger from fires in the long dry grass would be avoided, and that there would be a sufficient staff, maintained without loss, to care properly for the parts of the Island that would remain a sanctuary.

Kirk himself was not convinced by this pastoral vision and pointed out that the fire danger could be diminished 'by planting the open lands with such Native trees and shrubs as would not readily carry fire'. But he was not optimistic that would happen. 'If the attitude of the Governments of the future is such as we have

In 1921 when Les Adkin, the Levin farmer and scientist, visited Kapiti, he photographed his companions beside the new possum trappers' hut at Waterfall Bay.

It had been built three years earlier by Bennett. The hut was essential, he told his department, because possum skins had to be kept dry if they were to have any value and, as the 'waterfall country' was the most heavily infested area, this seemed the best site.

At the end of the First World War, fur prices improved. Between 1917 and 1920 the Lands and Survey Department made more than £1,200 from the sale of Kapiti possum skins, which more than covered the cost of building the hut (£100) and employing a trapper.

G. L. ADKIN COLLECTION, MUSEUM OF NEW ZEALAND/TE PAPA TONGAREWA

Bennett was very hospitable to Adkin and his friends during their week on the island. He allowed them to stay in the Whare, gave them wild lamb as well as milk, and took them to Wharekohu Bay in his boat.

As they went south along the eastern coast, the caretaker pointed out features such as Lions Mouth Cave, and the old church site beside the Maraetakaroro Stream. When they reached Wharekohu, Adkin wrote, 'Mr Bennett took us to a cave on the hillside which was formerly used by the Maoris as a burial place – we descended into it with candles and found human bones.'

G. L. ADKIN COLLECTION, MUSEUM OF NEW ZEALAND/TE PAPA TONGAREWA

known in the past, the proposal to make revenue by utilising the open sheep lands of the Island will, sooner or later, prove irresistible.'[26]

Kirk's report was commissioned by the Department of Internal Affairs, which was anxious to see the sanctuary developed rather than broken up by sheep farms, because it needed it as a refuge for species that were increasingly threatened on the mainland. For example, the caretaker of the Gouland Downs Reserve, in the mountains of north-west Nelson, feared for the survival of kakapo and kiwi there because of the depredations of rats, stoats, weasels and especially hedgehogs that were spreading throughout the country.[27] But the proposed transfer of South Island species to North Island sanctuaries such as Kapiti and Little Barrier raised complex scientific issues that both Internal Affairs and Lands and Survey wisely recognised were beyond their competence. Consequently, in 1920, Lands and Survey set up an advisory committee to assist it with technical questions regarding the flora and fauna of Kapiti.

One of its members was the Director of the Dominion Museum, J. Allan Thomson, who was a leading advocate of the transfer of South Island species to Kapiti.[28] Two years earlier he had suggested that robins and riflemen from Marlborough be sent to the sanctuary but nothing had come of it, probably because Lands and Survey was still unsure of the island's future and there was also the problem of South Island robins interbreeding with the North Island sub-species.

Other members of the committee were the scientists Dr Cockayne, Phillips-Turner and Professor Kirk, and Willie Field who, together with a local sawmiller and farmer, Arthur Seed, were presumably appointed to provide a broader view. When these men accepted the department's invitation they probably expected to deal with matters such as Thomson's bird transfer proposal; instead, it was their part in the actual management of the island that soon became the subject of uncomfortably intense public scrutiny.

The controversy had its origins in a visit to Kapiti by a group in December 1921. The party consisted of *Evening Post* journalist E. V. Hall, Martinborough farmer Frank Wall, Wellington businessman Fred Vosseler and Val Sanderson. Two days before their departure, Vosseler applied for a permit which was granted on the condition that they report to the caretaker on arrival.[29] At the last minute Vosseler withdrew from the trip. The other three were taken by a fishing boat to the northern end of the island where they stayed in the Webbers' woolshed. The next day Hona Webber, in his launch, dropped them off at the southern end. They made their way back to Waiorua through the reserve, along the western cliff tops.

Four days after their arrival, as they were leaving, the party called on Bennett at Rangatira to present their permit. He had been monitoring their movements since their arrival and had even followed their boat to Wharekohu, but had been too late to intercept them. Very annoyed, Bennett immediately wrote to his superior in Wellington, reminding him that this was 'the same Capt. E. V. Sanderson who wrote to the Hon. Minister of Lands on 19 February 1914 applying for the position of caretaker of Kapiti and, on the same date, sending a ridiculous report on the island'.[30] The department took his complaint seriously and Vosseler and Sanderson were summoned to explain. Their account seemed to satisfy the under-secretary, who wrote a soothing reply to Bennett. Sanderson had apologised: 'the breach of etiquette was quite unintentional,' he wrote, and the party had failed to report to Rangatira on their arrival only because they were 'wet to the skin and were anxious to proceed to the Webbers' woolshed'.[31]

The *Evening Post*, however, told a different story. Under the headline, KAPITI 'SANCTUARY' – FENCELESS THEREFORE DEFENCELESS, the government was taken to task for running the island like a 'comic opera'. The article described the Crown's failure to do its share of the fencing necessary to separate the sanctuary from the Webbers' farm. 'Mr Webber states that he has completed his part of the boundary fence, and investigation on the spot supported his statement.' The *Post* also expressed astonishment that the government tolerated the presence of so many goats, which 'are visible in large numbers from a launch as it coasts down the channel; they exist in flocks inland, and are sometimes tamer than the sheep'. One member of the party that visited the island with the writer was a farmer who estimated that there were about 3000 sheep on Kapiti, and about half that number of goats.[32]

The author's identity was not revealed, but its strident tone suggested Sanderson. Next day the *Post* included an even longer 'contributed' article entitled A THREATENED FOREST – FENCELESS KAPITI, describing how the goats and sheep destroyed the bush, and on the following day there was a third account of the island's birds and offshore islets. The newspaper campaign with which Sanderson had first threatened the Lands Department seven years earlier, was now under way, its purpose 'to arouse public interest in the preservation of a threatened sanctuary'. In the three days immediately before Christmas, Sanderson had secured more than 6 feet of column space in the *Evening Post* but the campaign had some way to go yet: as he was later fond of pointing out, it took more than 42 column feet before a fence was finally built.[33]

New Zealand then shut down for the Christmas break but the matter was raised again in early January by a letter from Vosseler supporting the earlier articles, and published under the headline BUSH PIRATES AND TIMID POLITICIANS.[34] This had the effect of flushing out Willie Field, who publicly asked when the Minister of Lands was going to call the next meeting of the Kapiti Advisory Committee which had not met for 15 months.[35] A meeting was held soon after, but as no account of its deliberations was released, the paper continued to press the Department of Lands and Survey and its minister. In an editorial entitled MINISTERIAL DEAFNESS, it castigated the Minister of Lands, D. H. Guthrie, and suggested that the solution was to remove the Kapiti sanctuary from the care of 'a Department whose chief instinct is land settlement, and place it under a Department whose concern is the preservation of the natural forest on which indigenous life depends'. The public was entitled to know whether the rare birds on Kapiti were safe, it continued, and whether Lands was going to fence off the sanctuary. Guthrie should clarify the situation: 'if he thinks that the remaining bush should be sacrificed and that the island should be treated as a sheep station, then he ought to have the courage of his convictions, and say so'.[36]

Still the minister remained silent, perhaps hoping that if he said nothing the controversy would fade away. If that was his strategy, he underestimated Sanderson, who made it a personal crusade to broaden the affair by approaching other newspapers. The *Dominion* joined the fray, saying it was regrettable that Kapiti was now a sanctuary 'in little more than name'. This was followed by the *Waikato Times* and the *New Zealand Times*, which published Sanderson's detailed schedule of the work required to make the island 'an effective sanctuary'. The most urgent task was the fence, then the eradication of the goats and possums. Once this was done, more birds such as pukeko, kiwi and kakapo should be released on Kapiti, native trees planted on the open grasslands, another lagoon made at Wharekohu and the base of the western cliffs planted with species such as taupata, tutu and karaka. A second caretaker should be established at the south end, a third at the northern end ('should the natives ever change their present attitude') and all three be connected by telephone. There should also be 'a road or track for cycle, motor cycle or horse to enable caretakers to move quickly down the east coast'.[37]

In March 1922 Willie Field and the advisory committee visited the Minister of Lands and persuaded him to publicly commit his department to building a fence.[38] Finally, Sanderson's campaign had achieved its most significant objective. The minister also agreed to visit the island, but when Field took several of the committee to Kapiti a few weeks later, he did not accompany them. They negotiated a fenceline with the Webbers and spent the rest of the weekend inspecting the island. On their return, Field remarked to a *Dominion* reporter that the party was 'agreeably surprised with the state of the native bush' which convinced him 'that the reports of destruction wrought on the island by sheep and goats had been exaggerated'.[39]

This remark provoked an angry response from the Kapiti watchers. They had been sceptical of Field who, until recently, had so ardently advocated farming the island but now seemed intent on their own objectives. His comment suggested his recent conversion to the island's conservation was merely a cynical political ploy. They felt betrayed and their response was immediate. The *Evening Post* published a lengthy editorial attacking Field and also a letter from Sanderson, although it rejected two others 'written against Mr. Field in objectionable terms'. Field, in turn, could not let the matter rest. In a long letter to the editor, he described himself as the saviour of the sanctuary: 'I, and I only, over thirty years ago saved the forest there from destruction. The intention then was to fell all the bush on the easier country and lay it down in grass, and I succeeded, at some sacrifice to myself, in frustrating this intention.'[40]

Gradually the controversy died down as the issues became increasingly obscure and personal. In any case, the battle had been won. Plans to build a fence across the island to divide the sanctuary from the farmland were well advanced.

VAL SANDERSON

Ernest Valentine Sanderson was born in 1866 in
Dunedin, but the family later moved to Wellington
where Val, as he was known, attended Wellington
College. He was a promising cricketer and a keen
hunter and tramper. On leaving school he wanted to be
an engineer. Instead, he went to work for the AMP
Society as a clerk, because his family needed the money.

His father, Walter Spreat, was a talented lithogra-
pher who had made money but became increasingly
erratic and unreliable. He suffered from 'fits', or psy-
chotic episodes, and drank heavily to quieten his demons.
For some time he lived apart from his family and his son
Val took the name of his mother, Jane Sanderson.

Eventually, Spreat returned to the family home on
Mount Victoria, where he lived in a stable out the back.
He frequently threatened Jane but his children never
seemed at risk until one day in 1893 when Spreat

attacked his sons, Louis and Val, with a knife. In self-
defence, Louis shot his father; as Spreat lay dying he
signed a statement absolving his son. 'The Pirie Street
Shooting Affair', as the newspapers called it, culminated
in a sensational coroner's inquest which exonerated
Louis. Nevertheless, the family suffered from the
notoriety. Val's aggressive behaviour in later life, and his
mistrust of others, may have resulted from this experience.

Sanderson served in the Boer War. In 1905 he
used his share of his father's estate to go into the im-
porting business. With a partner, Godfrey Magnus, he
first imported bicycles, then cars. He also married. But
Sanderson's apparently settled and successful life was
disrupted by the First World War. When he came back
from Egypt he seemed uninterested in resuming his
earlier lifestyle. He sold out of the lucrative motor trade
and, in 1921, was divorced. Later, looking back on this
period, he commented: 'Being alive to the fact that the
accumulation of wealth should not be a man's sole aim,
I retired from active money seeking early. At the same
time an idle life without aim or object did not appeal to
me, and moreover, it seemed that a man should do
something for his country to warrant his existence.'

Val Sanderson found this purpose when he visited
Kapiti Island in 1921. During a furtive reconnaissance,
he was shocked to find how little had changed since his
previous visit in 1914. On that occasion, he had complained to the government and his criticism had led to a
new programme to revitalise the reserve. This time, he
harried the Lands Department in the newspapers until
the minister agreed to his ideas for improvements. At
the same time, Sanderson engaged in public dispute
with Willie Field. Although they were the same age and
both claimed to be champions of conservation with the
best interests of Kapiti in mind, Field represented the
exploitative attitude of those who wanted to farm the
island, while Sanderson's campaign was the beginning
of an emerging national conservation movement. When
the Kapiti campaign was successful, Sanderson considered how to use his experience on the mainland, and
with other like-minded people, he founded the New
Zealand Native Bird Protection Society.[41]

At the same time the department began to take steps to exterminate the possums
by employing Kapiti's first permanent trapper, Dick Fletcher of Paraparaumu.[42]
As for the wild sheep, the Webbers were given a deadline by which they were to
remove all their sheep from the Crown's part of the island.[43]

While the department devoted itself to improving Kapiti with a new sense
of purpose and urgency, Sanderson fell silent, though he was far from inactive.
On the contrary, encouraged by his success with Kapiti, he hoped to achieve something similar on the mainland. But here the prospect was different, for there was
no single visible Crown agency to target, nor were the solutions as obvious as

James and Lena Bennett are the only caretakers to have been buried on Kapiti – at Waiorua Bay, near the grave of Te Rangihiroa. The couple must have enjoyed a good relationship with the Webbers, for they could only have been buried there with their consent.

Kapiti's fence. Even if they had been, there was no one to implement them. Internal Affairs, which was charged with protecting endangered species, had no rangers or field staff and other government departments with an interest in the countryside, such as Lands and Survey and the State Forest Service, were committed to exploiting the landscape rather than preserving the birds and the bush. Some progress was made when Parliament revised the Animals Protection Act to include most native birds except 'pests' such as kea, but when Sir Thomas Mackenzie and a few other conservation-minded politicians tried to extend protection to traditional 'game' species such as pukeko and paradise ducks, they were rebuffed. Frustrated, Mackenzie looked beyond Parliament for support but his obvious ally, the Forest and Bird Society, had lapsed into inactivity after Harry Ell returned to Christchurch in 1919.[44] So when Sanderson wrote to Mackenzie in October 1922 suggesting the creation of an organisation devoted to the protection of native birds and forests, Mackenzie was grateful; even more so when Sanderson agreed to organise a meeting of bird lovers to decide what to do.[45]

In an enthusiastic letter to the New Zealand Forestry League, Sanderson sought its support and outlined his plans:

> The exact means to be adopted are not yet decided on but will probably be on the lines of a special Department of the Forest Service or other Department for the protection of our Native birds and sanctuaries, under the direction of a Chief Game Warden with staff of rangers who would control all game through Acclimatisation Societies and other bodies interested.[46]

The Forestry League agreed to give support. In March 1923 a meeting was held and from it emerged the Native Bird Protection Society, with Mackenzie as its president and Sanderson as secretary.[47] The new entity was, however, different from Sanderson's original idea in that it was not a state organisation and therefore required a different approach from its secretary. Rather than hounding a government agency to do what was required, as he had with Kapiti, Sanderson now had to educate and inform.

Ironically, on the island itself he was persona non grata. Or so it seemed. He could not obtain a permit to visit and was forced to write to the prime minister for help – after which he was eventually permitted to return.[48] In the meantime progress had continued on the sanctuary. The fence was finished and plans to plant fire-resistant species along both sides of the cleared boundary were being finalised. At the same time, the department was considering the best way to get rid of the wild sheep. During the previous year Bennett had shot 279 goats and Fletcher had trapped 2292 possums.[49] When the well-known authority on native bird songs, Johannes Andersen, returned from a visit to Kapiti, he told the press that 'it gave promise of becoming a valuable bird sanctuary'.[50]

For Bennett, however, it was a sad time. His wife, Lena, who had lived with him on the island for more than 12 years, became an invalid and died. Bennett himself seemed in good health, but only a year later, he died, at the age of 55 apparently of a heart attack. His death was mourned even by those who had indirectly attacked him in their newspaper campaign.

Sanderson and others were quick to realise that this was the start of a new era for Kapiti. He knew he had no chance of succeeding Bennett but was keen to ensure that the job went to someone of like mind, whom he could influence. The Department of Lands and Survey, deciding it might be better to work with Sanderson than against him, sent him a letter in his capacity as secretary of the New Zealand Native Bird Protection Society, asking if he would like to nominate a candidate. Sanderson recommended A. S. Wilkinson, a member of the society. 'Mr. Wilkinson is a particularly expert bushman of a class now rarely met. He is of a courteous retiring disposition, happy amongst his birds and bush and has the necessary knowledge and ability to make Kapiti a pride and credit to New Zealand and your Department.'[51] Wilkinson was duly appointed. During the next few years he and Sanderson were to become a powerful team whose efforts would transform Kapiti, and achieve the kind of sanctuary that conservationists had so long hoped for.

The Ship-wrecked Mariners

--Xmas Trip----

--Isle

_ The Fleet _

"Once aboard
the Lugger
and the girl
is mine".

_The
"MINOOKI _

-- The Homes

of Lizards.—

— Baby Gulls —

Rotmany, just a few—

— From the Hill-top—

CHAPTER THIRTEEN

THE GOLDEN YEARS

During the 1920s and 1930s, Kapiti developed a reputation as a summer resort. Waiorua Bay became popular, especially with members of tramping clubs, who visited the island each year. There are a number of photo albums such as Phyllis Trimmer's which records the Tararua Tramping Club's Christmas-New Year visit in 1925.

Rangatira also had a summer season, although it was smaller and more studious. During the Wilkinson era, Kapiti was celebrated in prose, poetry, painting and photography. The Wilkinson family's own contribution was remarkable and their creativity made the island known to a wider public.

Nature lovers throughout New Zealand also responded to Stan Wilkinson's campaign to make the island a native plant museum by sending him numerous seedlings to hasten its revegetation.

The golden era lasted, however, less than 20 years, cut short by the departure of the Webbers and the Wilkinsons, who had done so much to foster it, and by the outbreak of the Second World War.

TARARUA TRAMPING CLUB COLLECTION

KAPITI'S popularity with the trampers of the 1920s came about, literally, by accident – after several deaths on the exposed southern Tararua mountain tops. Seen from the island on a cool, clear morning, these mainland peaks seem close, their colours and contours softened in the sunlight. In bad weather, however, they can be deadly. In 1922 two young men died there and, in the aftermath of their deaths, most outdoor enthusiasts were deterred from exploring these mountains.[1]

As an alternative, Kapiti was ideal. It was as steep and rugged as the mountains but had the added attractions of an extensive coastline and a variety of rare birds no longer seen or heard on the mainland. Willie Field and Fred Vosseler were Tararua veterans who, in 1919, had founded the Tararua Tramping Club; Vosseler had been a friend of the Webbers since the turn of the century and Field had been familiar with the island for more than 30 years. The club's first visit took place in April 1924 when a group of 64 members was escorted to the island. They camped at Waiorua, except for five who were unexpectedly benighted on top of Tuteremoana when 'overtaken by darkness'. They spent the long, cold hours singing.[2]

The following year Vosseler began what was to become a tradition of taking a large party to Kapiti in the Christmas-New Year holidays. For the Tararua Tramping Club's younger members, many of whom had recently arrived in Wellington to work in the public service, it was an ideal opportunity to sign on for a mysterious island adventure that offered the prospect of friendship, even romance. For the childless Fred and May Vosseler, it was a time for developing relationships with young people to whom they taught outdoor skills. For the Webbers, it was a chance to entertain people who might become influential in government. A happy holiday on the island made friends who might support the family in its ongoing struggle to retain its land in the face of the Crown's avowed intention to acquire all of the island.

Waiorua Bay became a well-known resort, offering tennis, golf and bowls. Visitors were also taken fishing around the island's spectacular coast in the *Manaaki*. A highlight of these excursions was a visit to the 'Isle of Lizards' (Motungarara) and the two other islets that still had evidence of their occupation by Maori and

Visiting groups camped in the paddock behind the Webbers' house close to an outbuilding, 'the cookhouse' (lower right), in which they prepared and ate their meals.
JOHN BARRETT COLLECTION

by whalers. Also, Vosseler usually obtained a permit for the party to visit the Crown's part of the island, so that the trampers could climb to the trig on Tuteremoana and explore the rest of the island.

The Webber children, now young adults themselves, played their part as guides, taking groups out in boats and on foot around the rocky shoreline. They were also natural entertainers, with great musical ability inherited through their father from the Tahiwi family. In the 1930s their relatives, 'the singing Tahiwis', toured New Zealand and Australia performing Maori songs, many of which were

Bryan Vickerman (left) and Tukumaru Webber in the garden at Waiorua Bay. The Webbers laid out a nine-hole golf course on flat land between their house and the Okupe Lagoon. They also made their own golf clubs.
JIM WEBBER COLLECTION

recorded.[3] On the island, the combination of the tramping club's tradition of singing and the Webbers' musical talents led to many memorable evenings. For the young Webbers, the summer season was a change from farmwork; for the trampers, it was often their first contact with Maori. Photos suggest that these were idyllic holidays full of adventure, friendship and humour. The Webber parents also participated in all aspects of the social season, including pranks, and even Vosseler was not immune. He was a keen amateur archaeologist always on the lookout for an artifact, so Hona Webber, who was an expert carver, made a wooden mere, then aged it carefully by singeing before burying it near the edge of the lagoon for Vosseler to find.[4]

Further south, Rangatira also had its summer holiday season, although it involved fewer people because the Crown did not encourage large groups to camp on the sanctuary. It also had a less exuberant atmosphere because the participants were generally older than the young trampers at Waiorua. Poet and librarian

Rangi Webber was a talented painter. The watercolour below, one of the few to survive, shows her family's house at Waiorua in its heyday.
JOHN BARRETT COLLECTION

*Much of the the Webbers'
remarkable garden was made
by their children, who in
addition to doing many other
jobs, used horses to help them
haul hundreds of large round
boulders from the northern
coastline to Waiorua Bay,
almost half a kilometre away,
to build stone walls and
pathways.*
BOB SPRATT COLLECTION

Johannes Andersen seems to have been the first person to visit Rangatira regularly. During Bennett's tenure he spent his annual leave there each year with his
family and friends, indulging his passion for native bird-song and writing poetry
celebrating the birds and the bush. He was keen to continue these visits, despite
Bennett's death.

Stan Wilkinson arrived to take up his duties in November 1924; his impressions of the reserve, which he was seeing for the first time, appeared in a later

*Rangi was also an
accomplished photographer
whose photos were published
in several magazines.*
BOB SPRATT COLLECTION

JOHANNES ANDERSEN, TURNBULL LIBRARIAN.

JOHANNES ANDERSEN

Johannes Andersen (1873-1962) was born in Denmark but came to Christchurch with his parents as a small child.

He was fascinated by New Zealand's bush and birds and was a keen student of Maori culture. He became an authority on these areas, tirelessly promoting them in books, radio talks, journals and lectures throughout his life.

In 1915 Andersen and his wife, Kate, moved from Christchurch to Wellington, where they lived in a cottage in the bush at Point Howard. He was librarian at the Alexander Turnbull Library (which he gradually transformed from a private collection into a respected research institution), editor of the *Journal of the Polynesian Society* and an active member of the Wellington Philosophical Society. Andersen also wrote poetry and transcribed bird-songs into musical notation.

All these interests intersected when he spent several weeks each summer camping at Rangatira and his observations there contributed to his book *Birdsong and New Zealand Song Birds* (1926), one of the more than 30 volumes he wrote. His favourite place on the island was the Te Rere Valley. To the young Sylvia Wilkinson, Andersen was a 'colourful personality with eyes that glitter with interest in living, hooked nose and long hair brushed back and reaching his shoulders. Early morning sees him,' she later wrote, 'with towel over his shoulder heading for Te Rere for his daily shower and communication with nature. There his poems germinate. With a reed pipe he imitates the birds – a veritable Pan of the forest. He comes back from his bath and meditations telling of the delightful sights he has seen – flowers of Ngaio floating in the water like stars and a fantail taking a shower by flitting in and out under the spray. All these things delight his poet's mind.'

Through his friendship with Stan Wilkinson, Andersen joined the Native Bird Protection Society, and was elected to the executive on which he served for some years until he fell foul of Captain Sanderson, the society's caustic secretary, who engineered his removal.

In 1946 the Andersens shifted to Auckland and his visits to Kapiti ceased. His last volume of verse, *The Tui Cymbalist* (1951), which he wrote in his seventies, included the poem 'Come Away to Kapiti' – an attempt to synthesise images of the island's flowering plants and birds with the excitement of young love.

newspaper article. 'The first thing that struck me was the healthy appearance of the bush,' he wrote in the *Otago Daily Times*, 'and the different shades of green on the trees, ranging in colour from the light, lemon green of the kohepiro and tarata, to the beautiful sap green of the puka and still darker green of the karaka.' After he had explored beyond Rangatira, he noticed 'Another striking thing about the bush on some parts of the sanctuary especially, is the great number of different species of trees to be found in a small area. Thus, on the hill beyond my cottage on an area of perhaps five acres, at least 20 different species of tree can be counted.'[5]

A few weeks later Johannes Andersen and his party arrived for their annual stay. Privately, he wondered what the new caretaker was like – 'Wilkinson is much older than Mr Bennett, who we missed very much,' he wrote in his diary – but within a fortnight, he had come to appreciate Wilkinson. Not only was he more agile than Andersen had first thought (in fact, Wilkinson was 11 years younger than

HOTEL MAJESTIC
PARAPARAUMU BEACH
TELEPHONE 10

22/4/36.

Mr. & Mrs. SPILMAN   ·   Proprietors

Bennett), but he also gave the visitors the same kind of welcome: fresh milk and cream, wild lamb and excursions to other parts of the island in his launch. One day, for example, Wilkinson took them to Waterfall Bay; on another occasion Andersen and his male companions went goat hunting with the caretaker.

Undoubtedly the highlight of Andersen's sojourn was a trip to the head of the Te Rere Valley to listen to the evening chorus of bird calls. Several days earlier, he had found what he thought were signs of kiwi in the Te Rere so he was delighted when the caretaker suggested the excursion. They were accompanied by Wilkinson's son-in-law, Robert Stidolph, a keen ornithologist. As darkness fell, Stidolph attracted several kiwi by imitating their call. Later Andersen described the kiwi's response: 'The cry is like that of the weka, but much shriller and it gets quicker towards the close, being fairly long, 12 or more pairs of notes: it is also uttered more quickly than the notes of the weka'.[6]

The three men were excited to have heard kiwi and weka because the calls suggested that the sanctuary was starting to achieve its purpose. Both species had been released in small numbers some years before; their presence in the Te Rere indicated that they were becoming well established. But it was also clear that the sanctuary's success was limited by the continuing presence of browsing animals, and would remain so until they were all removed. As long as goats and wild sheep checked the growth of the vegetation, it could never sustain more than a limited number of birds.

Wilkinson had already taken up the task of eradication; he had been out hunting goats on most days, and was often assisted by Dick Fletcher who shot any goats and sheep he saw while checking his possum traps. Captain Sanderson was also keen to help; Wilkinson arranged this with the Commissioner of Crown Lands when he visited the island. But it took time for Sanderson to be issued with a permit and, while he waited, he visited the Webbers and used Waiorua as a base, from which he combed the northern end of the island killing any goats he found. Finally, in January 1925, Sanderson received permission to visit the Crown's part of the island.[7] At the same time the reason for the delay became apparent, for the government published a set of regulations concerning the conduct of visitors to Kapiti, turning what had previously been an informal code of etiquette into explicit law. Especially important was the rule that all visitors must report to Rangatira on their arrival and, at all times, acknowledge the authority of the caretaker.[8]

A few days later Sanderson landed at Rangatira and, with Wilkinson, organised an immediate, concentrated campaign against the goats. 'The Captain', as Sanderson insisted on being called, had several strategies in mind and was keen to

In 1923 Frank Spilman built the Majestic Hotel at Paraparaumu Beach in the expectation that the small seaside settlement was about to become 'the Brighton of Wellington'.

His confidence was justified. Two years later, Johannes Andersen recorded his impressions of the flourishing village, although it reminded him of a similar settlement in Christchurch rather than the English resort. 'The beach Paraparaumu is now like early New Brighton, though more up to date than early N.B.,' he wrote in his diary. 'There is a biggish hotel and boarding house, shops, and plenty of residences, sandy streets, with hillocks partly grown with lupin and marram grass.'

The attraction, according to Andersen, was the presence of the Webbers at Waiorua Bay: 'Webber's launch was offshore and took 3 boat loads off to their launch. They run them up to their place for the day at 7/6 or 10/- a head; they must have taken 20-30 aboard.'

Returning to Wellington from Paraparaumu Beach after a two-week holiday at Rangatira, Andersen wrote, 'We saw their launch passing the island pretty well every day. They run a sign up at the hotel – Majestic – when there is a load to go.'

DIANE WOODS COLLECTION

first he was ever sent, barely a month after his arrival, were six whau, donated by Sanderson.

Only a year later 'the Captain' changed his mind, doubting the wisdom of planting seedlings while wild sheep still roamed the reserve. In an internal report to the Committee of the Native Bird Protection Society he was critical of Wilkinson's planting programme. On a recent visit to the island he had been pleased not to have seen a single goat and 'much solid work had been done', but he was disturbed to find seedlings eaten, a horse outside the fenced paddock at Rangatira and evidence that the grassland there had been deliberately burnt. 'There is apparent,' Sanderson wrote, 'a decided lack of organisation in that the Curator, a man eminently in need of direction, is not directed in his work on the spot which fact leads to cart before the horse methods such as planting seedlings for stock to eat and misdirected efforts in various ways.'[18]

Sanderson may once have thought he could influence, even direct, the caretaker, but as Wilkinson became more familiar with his job he grew increasingly independent, to the extent that some of his friends referred to him as 'the king of Kapiti'.[19] It was also evident to Wilkinson that some of Sanderson's own practices fell short of what might be expected. Years later, his daughter, Sylvia, wrote of a revealing incident:

> Captain Sanderson turns up from time to time to see how things are going, bringing with him a large setter, Mack. Dad disapproves of a dog being brought on to the sanctuary, but what can one say to the President of the Bird Protection Society? The Captain is not pleased when told he can't have Mack inside the house, but that he must be kept tied up outside. This causes a certain coolness. However, I save the day by offering to walk Mack. It turns out to be Mack who takes me for – not a walk, but a gallop, and in his joy, he leaps up on me using his tongue on my face like a man using a shaving brush. Setting off at breakneck speed, barking loudly, he pursues an indignant weka. I cling to the chain taking giant strides like the Million Dollar Man. At last, when the quarry is within reach of the drooling jaws, and the weka has nearly recovered his lost powers of flight, I manage to wrap the chain round a handy tauhinu bush which brings Mack up with a terrible jerk whilst I land on top of him. Meantime, the Captain is whistling and shouting to Mack, who takes not the slightest notice. Dad arrives looking thunderous and my mother looks for the weka. 'Now she will leave the nest,' she says, 'and just when the eggs are due to be hatched.'[20]

Relations between Sanderson and those living on the sanctuary deteriorated rapidly when he began a new campaign of criticism, this time about the failure of the caretaker and his trapper to move decisively against the possums. Wilkinson ignored the attack, but Fletcher was provoked by Sanderson's remarks and wrote him an abusive letter, which only strengthened Sanderson's hand.[21] When Sanderson wrote to the Lands and Survey Department and numerous other people, he enclosed a copy of Fletcher's letter.[22] It was a persuasive strategy that convinced even Bob Stidolph – at least until Sanderson turned on him, too, when he failed to repeat the criticisms in his newspaper column. Stidolph was stunned to receive a letter accusing him of being a 'self-seeker' intent on promoting Wilkinson's interests rather than those of the birds. The mild-mannered Stidolph asked for an apology but it was not in Sanderson's nature ever to apologise; in his view, the end invariably justified the means.[23] If native birds were at risk, he was always prepared to upset a few people – in fact, he seemed to gain perverse pleasure from it.

Fortunately for Stidolph, a new issue suddenly arose that demanded all Sanderson's attention. For years the director of the Dominion Museum, J. A. Thomson, had advocated transferring rare birds to Kapiti but the idea had never become a reality, probably because scientists were cautious about the likelihood of interbreeding with similar species already on the island. If, for example, a South Island robin bred with a North Island robin, their progeny would be hybrids. The prospect worried some people but seemed to interest the museum director, who argued that 'In view of the fact that the North Island robin is well established on Little Barrier Island, it is not essential to keep the stock on Kapiti pure, and the experiment of introducing the South Island robin would in itself be a most interesting and valuable scientific experiment, which might throw light on the problems concerning geographical races of birds.'[24]

Sanderson was a recent convert to the cautious camp. As recently as 1922 he had publicly advocated sending kiwi, kakapo and pukeko to Kapiti but as he learned more about ornithology, he changed his mind.[25] J. G. Myers, a scientist whom he respected, was largely responsible. In 1924 he and Wilkinson had made Myers's acquaintance when they scoured the Akatarawa hinterland for huia. Soon afterwards, Myers went to the United States where he learned about ill-considered bird transfers and became anxious for New Zealand's avian sanctuaries. According to Myers, hybridisation had already occurred on Kapiti, with the result that the weka there had the red legs of the Stewart Island variety but the body markings of the North Island species. He did not want to see any more genetic experiments so he wrote to warn Sanderson who, in turn, passed the observations to the *Evening Post*.

Sylvia Wilkinson's sketch of being 'taken for a walk' by Captain Sanderson's dog, Mack.
RAY LOVELL COLLECTION

Kapiti Island
Paraparaumu
5-2-27

Dear Sir,
        I notice in the Evening Post there is some rot,
undoubtedly written by you although you have not signed your
name, a blind man as only to see your rubbish once to recognise
it again. You are hinting behind my back, about all you are
good for, that I am incapable of making any impression on the
opossums. Well I have got £50 to say you or any one like you
cant trap in twelve months and catch 200 where I have got over
2000. I am pretty certain you dont know a opossum from a cat.
When the Advisory board were here, they commended through the
press how much the opossums had been reduced and it is a well
known fact, their letters are taken as much notice of as your
rot is laughed at. A school kid of ten would write a much more
sensible letter than you can. If your brains were gunpowder
and were to go off their wouldnt be enough to raise your hat.
You used to slap at Mr Bennett behind his back, you havnt got
guts enough to do it openly. If I had been him and in his place
I would have given you a damn good hiding. You are also
commented about the trapper leaving the opossums to mister the
sheep if you wasnt so brainless and so thick in the skull you
would understand that one sheep does more harm than four
opossums. If you were to mind your own bloody business a bit
more and stuff pen paper and ink up your arse you might be
thought a bit more of, it puzzles me why the press puts your
lies and rot in. It must be distinctly understood this letter
is strictly personal.
                Yours faithfully   A. FLETCHER.

Captain Sanderson's ability to provoke everyone who came his way is apparent in this letter he received from Dick Fletcher. The handwritten original was almost illegible, so Sanderson typed a version of it and sent copies to a number of people.

Fletcher's letter was ostensibly a response to one he believed Sanderson had written about possums on Kapiti; it appeared when Sanderson was campaigning to have Fletcher replaced. He considered the trapper's efforts to be inadequate and also insinuated, in letters to others, that Wilkinson and Fletcher were soft on the possums because they were sharing profits from the sale of the skins. Wilkinson wisely ignored Sanderson's intrigue but Fletcher allowed himself to be provoked.

As it happened, Fletcher did leave the island but not until 1934, when he had a serious accident, as Sylvia Wilkinson later explained: 'Dick is very fond of my mother, who asks him in for many a meal and also gives him pots of jam. One day when she was busy making jam she ran out of jam jars, so Dad goes down to the Waterfall hut to bring back those she has given to Dick. It is providential that he did so, for Dad enters the hut to find Dick lying helpless on his bunk with a broken back. Had Dad not gone down when he did, Dick would undoubtedly have died. The poor fellow had fallen out of a tree nearby and just managed to crawl to his bunk. After lying there all day and all next night, he realised that if he did not get assistance, he would die. So he managed to drag himself to the top of the cliff and down the perilous track to the beach. There, gathering as much wood as he could, he lit a fire to attract the notice of fishermen on the nearby islands. They did not see it. Eventually he hauled himself up the track again, deciding, I suppose, it was preferable to die on his bunk than down on the cold, bleak beach. Then Dad arrived, got help, and Dick was taken over to the mainland. An ambulance rushed him to Wellington Hospital where he stayed for months. He never returned to Kapiti.'

A North Island robin on Kapiti.
PETER DANIEL

With the growth of sanctuaries in New Zealand I should like to see a warning issued against the introduction of one race or species into the habitat of another, as
has happened, for instance, in the case of the wekas on Kapiti, which are apparently all hybrids. This is a most deplorable thing. I have seen several cases. For instance there were quail on the island of Cuba found nowhere else in the world.
Actuated by some ridiculous idea of 'improvement', the inhabitants introduced quail
of a related form from Florida. The result is that it is now impossible to find a single
pure native quail – all are hybrids with the imported blood predominating.

In New Zealand, while probably all our bird species have been described, the distribution of the geographical and other races into which they are divided has never
yet been worked out. In some other countries well-meaning introductions, even
of one apparent species from one part of its range to another, has rendered this
impossible. In New Zealand there is yet time, and no irreparable damage of this kind
has yet been done; but it must be remembered that we want to protect species and
not bastards.[26]

In April 1927, while Sanderson was busy criticising Fletcher, Stidolph and
Wilkinson, he learned that the Departments of Internal Affairs and Lands and Survey had agreed to transfer one dozen pairs of kakapo to Kapiti.[27] His concern was
heightened when he found that a permit had already been sent to Wilkinson au-
thorising him not only to bring back kakapo but also any 'Crow, Thrush, Robin,
Creeper and Bush Wren' he found on his excursion to the Gouland Downs Reserve.[28] Suddenly it seemed as if the Kapiti sanctuary, to which Sanderson had
devoted so much energy, was about to become an ark full of bastards.

As secretary of the Native Bird Protection Society, he immediately started a
campaign to cancel the transfers. Letters were sent to Internal Affairs and the
Commissioner of Crown Lands, to no avail. In desperation, Sanderson organised
a deputation from the society to call on the Minister of Lands. Wisely, he did not
join it himself. Its members, Johannes Andersen, Dr Robert Falla and Mrs Perrine

Moncrieff, were unable to change the minister's mind. Finally Sanderson wrote to Sir Thomas Mackenzie, who had helped him to found the society, but he was unable, or unwilling, to intervene.[29]

Ironically, had Sanderson not lost Stan Wilkinson's confidence, he might have known about the proposed transfer in time to prevent it. But Sanderson did not even write to Wilkinson. In less than three years, Sanderson had managed to alienate all the key players on Kapiti itself, as well as the staff of two government departments and their ministers. Now, when the secretary of the Native Bird Protection Society desperately needed influence, he found he had none.

So complete was Sanderson's isolation that no one told him he had been outfoxed. Wilkinson had been to Gouland Downs before Sanderson even knew of the trip. While 'the Captain' was preoccupied with Kapiti gossip and intrigue, his old friend was out in the beech forest and tussock looking for kakapo. But, after 10 days searching in unfavourable weather, Wilkinson wrote in his field diary: 'having satisfied myself that kakapo were not to be found without a lot of trouble and that the tree creepers were very high up and therefore impossible to capture, I decided to return to Wellington. I never saw any of the other birds mentioned in my permit.'[30] On his return, Wilkinson reported to both the Commissioner of Crown Lands and the director of the Dominion Museum and it was agreed that he would make a second trip, this time to Taranaki, to procure kokako. So while Sanderson was campaigning against his going to the South Island, Wilkinson was actually at the Ratapihipihi Reserve, near New Plymouth, stalking kokako. He spent 12 days following first one bird, then another, but never got close enough to catch one. He resolved to return in the spring when the mating season might offer a better opportunity.[31]

Soon after he returned to Kapiti, he received a letter of congratulations from Sanderson, who had concluded that Wilkinson had contrived to return empty-handed. In fact, Wilkinson's field diary suggests he would have caught birds if he could, but he needed no lessons in dealing with Sanderson. In reply, he wryly observed, 'Thanks for the congratulations, they don't often come my way', then added, 'As long as I have anything to do with it there will be no mixing of closely allied species on this island.'[32]

Knowing that his influence was negligible, Sanderson made only a few desultory attempts to direct events on the sanctuary during the next decade. Instead, the 61-year-old devoted his energy to creating his own sanctuary on his section at Paekakariki, planting numerous native trees to attract birds. According to his daughter, Nancy Jordan, he was very successful: 'You would walk up the path at night and the birds would rise with a deafening flutter and the path had to be scrubbed constantly. Starlings used to come to roost and we had some quite rare native birds; long-tailed cuckoo, tui, bellbirds, fantails and wax-eyes. And we had wekas .... until someone left the gate open.'[33]

Sanderson seldom visited Kapiti. When he did, he stayed with the Webbers and rarely visited the Wilkinsons at Rangatira. Instead he devoted himself to realising the Native Bird Protection Society's national strategy, which he called 'Unity of Control', meaning the concentration of all conservation management under a single Crown entity, directed by an advisory council of independent experts. This far-sighted concept, which he had first suggested in 1923, was not put into practice, however, until the Department of Conservation was formed in 1987, many years after his death.

On a personal level, Sanderson's many bitter campaigns to convince others of the rightness of his views had come at a cost to his own motivation: 'It would please me exceedingly could I be relieved of this Secretary work as it is not possible to do a public good without treading on someone's toes,' he wrote in the wake of Wilkinson's trips to catch rare birds for Kapiti. 'It takes me a lot of time and much money. Then after all I am only the Secretary and not the Executive but everybody blames me for things they do not like.'[34]

On the island itself, the feeling was one of optimism. Almost all the goats and wild sheep had been shot and, with Sanderson in retreat, Wilkinson's challenging apprenticeship was over. Now he truly was the King of Kapiti, at liberty to implement his ideas for enhancing the sanctuary without interference.

As if to celebrate, in the spring of 1927 the Wilkinsons hosted the first vice-regal visit to the island; Lady Alice Fergusson, wife of the Governor-General Sir Charles Fergusson, and her retinue, escorted by W. H. Field. With the Webbers, the official party also visited the three islets aboard the *Manaaki*. During her stay, Lady Alice tramped to the Trig, where she planted a tree, and 'made a number of pretty sketches and paintings of the bush scenery'.[35]

The visit was a great success. 'Lady Alice still talks of her trip and your kindness,' Field wrote to Wilkinson. Field, for years a critic of the Crown's management of Kapiti, was also enthusiastic now that the island's restoration was really under way. He became a regular visitor and sent the Wilkinsons rare plants for their 'rockery'.[36] Lady Alice enjoyed a number of other holidays on the island, although without the fanfare of her first stay. When she discovered that the Wilkinsons had moved out of their home to make way for her, she was very upset and insisted on staying in the Whare.[37] Years later, when asked to contribute the foreword for the Wilkinsons' book, *Kapiti – Bird Sanctuary*, she wrote from her home in Scotland: 'There are very few places in the world which I have visited of which I have happier memories than Kapiti'. The Whare was central to her recollections:

Memories of turning out of bed at first call of the bellbird, of standing in scanty attire outside the whare, scanning the 'drop-scene' of bush in front of one, and watching the flight of a dozen or so kakas from one point to another; of strenuous climbs to the top, of expeditions along to the south side of the island to look at the trypots, to the north end to call on the Webber family, of collecting and trying to memorise the names of the immense variety of ferns, of cooking delectable meals at night in the whare and, after a day spent in the open, of sleeping the deep sleep of the properly tired, in a comfortable bunk.[38]

As well as painting the bush, Lady Alice painted watercolours of the garden the Wilkinsons had made around their house. Amy Wilkinson was a keen gardener but her interest extended beyond her rose garden and rockery to the island's birds, flowers, insects and plants, which she recorded on film. She showed great persistence in getting photos, especially of birds on their nests; sometimes she had

Lady Alice Fergusson's watercolour of the garden at Rangatira, looking across the foreland to Waikanae in the distance.

As soon as Amy Wilkinson arrived on the island, she set to work to create a new garden. Rocks were brought down from the hillside behind the house for a rockery and there was also a rose garden. Much of the hard labour was done by her husband, who used Sylvia's horse, Jimmy, and a sledge to get the boulders and also to bring the seaweed that was used as fertiliser.

In 1927 Amy broke her leg while gardening. Stan built a fire on the beach to summon help and she was away on the mainland for some time. When she returned she was not as nimble as she had been and used a walking stick.

to wait several years before she was successful. Her husband helped, often building her a stage on timber scaffolding so that she could position her camera close to a particular nest high in a tree. Then Amy would wait, with infinite patience, for the bird to return.[39]

Stan Wilkinson, too, was an expert photographer, although he did not have as much time – or patience – as his wife. He frequently took his camera with him as he went about the island. When the Wilkinsons were on leave, they often camped in the marshland around the Waikanae Estuary, where they photographed

'Although they had the latest equipment available at the time, Mother always preferred her old Thornton Pickard on its tripod,' recalled her daughter, Sylvia. 'With black sateen cloth to shut out the light, she focused on the spot which, from long observation she anticipated the bird would come, one of us holding a matchbox on that spot. I have seen the hand which held the shutter release trembling with anticipation when the bird would appear and land on every branch but the desired one. Then away it would go. Sometimes a whole season, or even years might elapse before the desired picture would eventuate.'

the many and various birds. Back on the island, the family bathroom doubled as a darkroom; if Stan Wilkinson didn't like what he saw emerging in the chemicals he would seize the glass plate, stride down the corridor, muttering, 'Godstruth – another failure!', fling open the front door and throw the offending negative out over the garden into the swamp beyond.[40]

Both husband and wife sent prints of their work to journals, magazines and newspapers; Sanderson often included them in the Forest and Bird Society's magazine and the Department of Lands and Survey used them to publicise the island. In 1935, the Wilkinsons' expertise was acknowledged at the highest level when both received Certificates of Merit at the International Exhibition of Nature Photography at the British Museum. One-third of the 18 photos selected from New Zealand were pictures of Kapiti's birds by the Wilkinsons.[41]

Their chief reward, however, was the sheer pleasure of living on the island. One of Amy's favourite quotations, from Shakespeare's *As You Like It*, expressed her feelings:[42]

> And this our life, exempt from public haunt,
> Finds tongues in trees, books in the running brooks,
> Sermons in stones, and good in everything.

Years later, when they had left Kapiti, the Wilkinsons recorded detailed observations of the island in separate books. These were family affairs, illustrated with their own photos and drawings by their daughters, Nora and Sylvia. Nora's husband, Bob Stidolph, arranged their publication.

All four of the Wilkinson children inherited a talent for drawing from their father but only the two daughters, Nora and Sylvia, developed their talent. Their styles were quite different: Nora concentrated on accurate representation, whether of a bird's egg or a landscape, whereas Sylvia's watercolours and sketches were impressionist, characterised by quick-drawn lines and bold gestures of colour.

Amy Wilkinson's photo of a kereru on its nest.
RAY LOVELL COLLECTION

Nora Wilkinson was an accomplished painter. When she visited her family on the island her father often brought her birds' eggs to paint: 'he would carry them from the nest in a teaspoon, I'd sit down, quickly paint them and he would get the eggs back to the nest while they were still warm'.
DIANA STIDOLPH COLLECTION

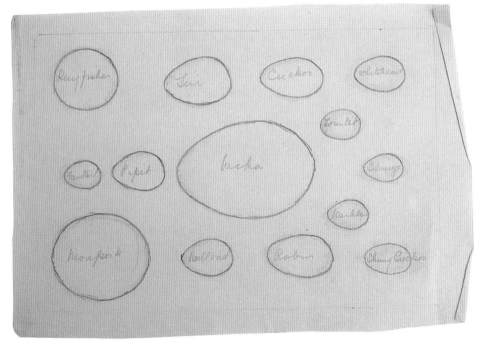

Memories of living on Kapiti remained vivid in Sylvia's mind, inspiring her later to write and illustrate her own account of those years. Her typescript is an invaluable evocation of life on the island from an unusual perspective. So much of Kapiti's history is a chronicle of the doings of middle-aged men – Maori chiefs, whalers, ships' captains, farmers, caretakers and scientists – that Sylvia's story is a reminder of the women and children who sometimes accompanied them.

From the moment Stan Wilkinson collected the 13-year-old Sylvia from Paraparaumu Beach to take her to their new home, she was entranced; as they neared the island and it loomed over the small boat, she said, 'Kapiti cast a spell

Sylvia with Dick Fletcher's dog Doone.
SYLVIA LOVELL COLLECTION

over me which will shade my thinking and feeling for ever after'. Life was exciting, full of exploration and discovery, but she also found it lonely. Sylvia had reluctantly left her horse, Jimmy, in Masterton and there were no companions of her age on the island. Her father arranged for a coastal steamer to bring Jimmy to Kapiti. This changed her life, although the only areas available for riding were the grassy paddock and beach at Rangatira. Her father also taught her to row so that she could take their small dinghy to Waiorua to visit the Webbers. She got to know both the Webbers' daughters, Piki and Rangi, and her elder brother, Ray, was a friend of Kap Webber, with whom he shared an enthusiasm for tennis.

The view to the south from Rangatira, with Motungarara (right) and Tahoramaurea in the distance, by Sylvia Lovell (née Wilkinson).
PETER DANIEL COLLECTION

By the mid-1930s the original fence between the sanctuary and the Webbers' farm had fallen into disrepair. Stan Wilkinson arranged for it to be rebuilt. In his 1936 annual report he wrote 'It gives me pleasure to announce that the boundary fence between the Crown and native owners is now fixed up. This is a great relief to me. I have already planted some trees in the Waiorua Valley on the sanctuary side of the new fence. The species put out were Kahikatea, Poroporo and Parataniwha. I intend putting out some more Kahikatea and Rimu as soon as I get a chance.'

Now, more than 60 years later, most of the fence has disappeared. A few of the original posts, such as this one on a rocky point just south of Waiorua Bay, can still be seen from the track to the northern end.

For Sylvia, a trip to the Webbers was a glimpse of a different world:

> Good neighbours are always precious, but here doubly so. They are always ready to help in times of emergency, which here, can and do occur at any moment. Their warm friendship alleviated the intense loneliness which at times could have become unbearable. Their lighthearted humour, typical of their race, soon banishes depression. Their laughter is infectious. They have a pleasant, well kept home and garden, but the most interesting feature is the 'cook house'. This large semi-detached room houses a ping-pong table where many friendly battles are fought. The walls are covered with pictures from the 'Auckland Weekly' and the 'Free Lance'. Each week new pictures are pasted up which make a very interesting, contemporary art gallery. An enormous open fireplace is used for cooking for the crowd of family and guests which are usually there in the summer. Hospitality is part of their rich culture which is a new experience to me and I enter into it whole-heartedly. We are given a warm welcome and after a cup of tea, everyone sees us off at the beach with laughter and invitations to come again soon.[43]

The two families also kept in touch by telephone, using a single line strung on poles between their two homes.

One of her mother's sisters tried to lessen Sylvia's isolation by sending her film and fashion magazines which she pored over, although they accentuated her loneliness. 'Here I am while all my girlfriends are going out with their boys and I've got nobody. I've got no one but the penguins to look at me!' She found comfort sitting on the cliffs of Paripatea, just to the north of Rangatira. From her perch high above the sea, on a clear, still day, she could see the mainland and hear the distant sounds of trains passing or dogs barking while she dreamt of Rudolph Valentino – 'Oh, isn't it wonderful to be in love!'[44]

Meanwhile, at Waiorua, there was real romance in the 1930s as the Webbers found spouses among the many visitors. Their courting worried Hona and Utauta, who realised that the marriage of their children would mean their departure from the island – and the loss of these farmhands on whom they depended. Utauta had

been determined her children should marry Maori but love is unpredictable and her wish was not fulfilled. Her eldest son, Tukumaru, was the first to leave. In 1933, he married Sarah ('Sadie') Blair, who had come to Kapiti with the Hutt Valley Tramping Club, and they went to farm at Wakapuaka.[45] The second son, Winara, did not tell them of his plans to marry, but slipped away in a dinghy, rowed to the mainland and made his way to Otaki where he married Aromea Udy at Rangiatea. Meanwhile his parents, having discovered his escape, set off in pursuit but arrived too late to prevent the ceremony.[46]

In 1936, Rewa Webster spent her 17th birthday visiting the Webbers with her parents, well-known racehorse trainers in Otaki; she met Kap Webber and they fell in love. Rangi Webber later married Percy Russell, who managed a farm at Waikanae for the estate of Hemi Matenga, and Piki married Leo Barrett. He, like Rewa, met his wife through his parents' association with Hona and Utauta.

No sooner had all their children married and left the island (except Kap and Rewa, who stayed to help on the farm), than Hona Webber died. His death brought a distinctive era to a close for, as his longtime friend Fred Vosseler wrote in an obituary, 'Mr Webber was a link with the old-time Maoris, and his hospitality to those who visited the island will remain long in the minds of those who experienced it'.[47] Utauta moved to her other house at Paraparaumu Beach. Although she continued to visit Waiorua, often crossing the channel by herself in her small boat powered by an Austin Seven engine, she never again lived there.

With her departure, Waiorua Bay was no longer a magnet for visitors. Although she and Kap tried to keep the farm going with the help of casual labour, the outbreak of the Second World War made that even more difficult, as more and more young men went overseas, and crucial commodities such as fuel were rationed. Kap and Rewa left the island to run a hotel in Otaki and the farm was virtually abandoned for the duration of the war.[48]

At Rangatira there was a similar decline. Stan Wilkinson would probably have been happy to continue on Kapiti for the rest of his days but his wife was finding the isolation increasingly onerous without her children. Their son,

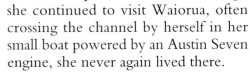

Ray, had been a semi-permanent resident during the worst years of the Depression but he eventually left for a career on the mainland; so, too, did Sylvia. She realised her departure would be difficult, especially for her mother, but knew she had to leave. 'I felt like a criminal to go away to get work but when I looked into the future I saw myself as a middle aged lady with no job, no money and two elderly parents to look after – and what was going to happen to me?' Both Stan and Amy had suffered from lumbago for some years, and Amy also had other increasingly persistent health problems. As her mobility became restricted, she grew more lonely. Eventually, her depression was of such concern that they decided to leave the island.[49]

After the Wilkinsons left, the possum trapper, G. W. Hughes, who had succeeded Dick Fletcher, was appointed caretaker. He was a pragmatic man and one of his first actions was to dismantle the Wilkinsons' elaborate garden – no doubt because he could not maintain it.[50] At Waiorua Bay, the ornate stone-lined creek had fallen into disrepair and was filling up with weeds, and the formal plantings had become overgrown. The desolation of these once-splendid gardens was a sign that Kapiti's golden years were over. Although Hughes remained, there were few visitors during the war years. Not for the first time, the buzz of humanity died away and Kapiti once again became the domain of the bush and the birds.

In an obituary in the Dominion, *Fred Vosseler wrote of Hona Webber's love for the birds of Kapiti, especially the wild ducks: 'At his wonderful home at Waiorua, he had dammed up the stream that flowed through the middle of his garden, and here could always been seen numerous wild ducks, behaving with the same tameness as well-treated domestic varieties. In winter, and to a lesser extent in summer, "Jack" would feed these birds and very often they would take food out of his hands. To some of these birds he gave names to which they would respond, leaving the flock and coming to him. He seemed to have gained the confidence of the tuis and parera (grey ducks) to a greater extent than the other birds, but even the parakeets, whiteheads, weka and robins allowed his close approach with unconcern.'*
BOB SPRATT COLLECTION

CHAPTER FOURTEEN

HOME, HEART AND SOUL

In the 1950s and 1960s, government policy on Kapiti was driven by a resolve to acquire the entire island. Although it was largely successful, the purchasing campaign highlighted fundamental differences inherent in Maori and Pakeha attitudes to land.

Throughout the 20th century, a number of Maori families maintained their interests on the island because of its association with their forebears. Those who kept the cooking fires of ownership alight were often women. This is acknowledged in this painting, *Home, Heart and Soul – Series 1*, by Hariata Ropata-Tangahoe. The female kaitiaki, or guardians, watch over an ancestral landscape that is symbolic rather than strictly representational. The river in the foreground, for instance, is both the Otaki and the Waikanae.

The kaitiaki also suggest the three tribes that most recently occupied Kapiti – Te Ati Awa, Ngati Raukawa and Ngati Toa. The artist grew up on the Kapiti Coast and has links with all three.

By 1967 the Crown owned all except 30 acres of Kapiti but, from the tangata whenua's viewpoint, this meant little. 'We know who owns the island,' says Hariata, 'not DOC. On paper they might, but to me, Kapiti is ours – it belongs to all the iwi who have lived on the island.'
MUSEUM OF NEW ZEALAND/TE PAPA TONGAREWA

AFTER THE DEATH of Hona Webber and Utauta's withdrawal to the mainland, the Webbers' presence on Kapiti was greatly diminished, despite her regular visits to Waiorua. The Crown's policy of acquiring all the island for a sanctuary had been quietly shelved since Utauta Webber's successful appeal to the Governor-General; now it was revived.[1] In June 1939 the Wellington Acclimatisation Society recommended to the government that it should take over the Webbers' land, telling a meeting of its members that 'The time was particularly opportune, as the owner of the North End had died recently'. According to the chairman, 'there was a serious fire risk' on the Webbers' farm and 'people were going across from the mainland with dogs'.[2]

Others were also eyeing the island with renewed interest. Captain Sanderson, for one, judged that the time was once again right for him to become active in determining Kapiti's future. In 1940 he corresponded regularly with the Department of Lands and Survey, this time in an attempt to prevent transfers of blue duck and kiwi to the sanctuary. He warned the department to take notice of his advice:

> Kapiti flora is now showing good regeneration; thanks being due, the writer would remind you, to an exposure of the mismanagement of the sanctuary some fifteen years ago when forty-two feet of newspaper writings were necessary to induce the Department to erect a fence between the Maori land and the sanctuary, and to shoot the trespassing goats and sheep. The writer now considers that this society has not been given a reasonable opportunity of expressing its views in this connection [the proposed bird transfers] and is of the opinion that it is time to re-open public criticism.[3]

In the event, a new campaign in the press was not required because one of Sanderson's supporters, J. W. Heenan, Under-Secretary of Internal Affairs, persuaded the Department of Lands and Survey to shelve the idea.[4]

That spring Sanderson and his second wife and two daughters were Utauta Webber's guests at Waiorua but the visit did not turn out as expected. His younger daughter, Nancy, later recalled that they were stranded on the island without food. 'We went to Kapiti with a fisherman, and Mrs Webber went back with the fisherman to get supplies but a storm came up. We were on the island and she was on the mainland – unable to get back. We were there for two weeks, which was longer than we planned to be. Each day Dad had to go fishing and he also went around the sheep.'[5]

Sanderson was worried by what he saw when he checked the stock and on his return home wrote to Utauta:

> Personally I cannot see what good the hill country is to you or anyone else for farming purposes, and I think the best purpose to which it could be put would be to allow it to return to that condition in which your ancestors knew it. If you so desired you could retain ten or twenty acres around the house. This would give you an association with the past and adequate occupation for your active and industrious nature. The present effort to farm the whole, although very courageous, appears to me to be doomed to failure, and likely to be detrimental to your health. Surely after the years of uphill battling you are now entitled to a peaceful and congenial exisence.[6]

Utauta's reply showed that Sanderson's assessment of the situation was accurate: 'Captain,' ran her letter, 'I am going to take your advice. I am already finding the work a bit heavy, after shearing the rams and a few dry sheep it took a few days to get over it. I forget I am getting old. However, I am leaving the whole business to you, whatever it is, so you can go ahead.'[7]

He did so, with his usual efficiency. Within six weeks he wrote again to Utauta, to pass on a valuation of her property from his old friend, Frank Wall, a Martinborough farmer, who assessed the land at £7 an acre, and the buildings at £2,000.[8] Sanderson encouraged her to write to the Minister of Native Affairs 'informing him of your desire to sell'. At the same time he made an informal approach to the Department of Lands and Survey, suggesting it should lease the land as a prelude to its eventual purchase. In a memo to the department he described a sad state of neglect:

Utauta Webber was a keen worker. As she grew older she became an important figure in the local Maori community, with the aristocratic bearing of her father, Wi Parata. 'When she walked into a room, or into a tangi you could hear a pin drop,' recalled her daughter-in-law, Rewa Webber. 'She was a wonderful woman – she could plough, she could shear sheep but she was an awful cook!'
BOB SPRATT COLLECTION

The hill country is at present carrying about twice the number of sheep which ought to have been allowed to winter there, and the remains of many dead sheep bear evidence of this. The flats were also over-stocked. One horse is said to have died of starvation. The house, property, gardens and the launch are all going to rack and ruin. The house requires painting; the rear wall is rotted, but the timber is there to replace it. The guttering is rusted through, and I could see it would take at least £200 to put it in decent order. Apart from all this, it is probably saturated with T.B. from which several of the children have suffered. The dogs are at times short of food, and one of them at least will worry if it gets the chance.

To me the whole attempt to farm the country on the part of Mrs. Webber appears to be an absurdity, but we must however, have consideration for the feelings of the Maoris under the circumstances. Much of the late Mr. Webber's handiwork is there. A Maori grave and such like. It is perhaps difficult for a Pakeha to realise the reverence which Maoris have for such things. I approached Mrs. Webber and pointed out the absurdity of the position and suggested that she should lease the hill country and hold on to the house and some of the surrounding ground. She assured me that she was agreeable to this. I should like to point out that it is a common practice in dealing with the Maoris to first of all lease in order that they may lose their personal interest in the matter, and then later to purchase. Personally I believe that the Department would be well advised if they left the matter to me to suggest to the Webbers a basis upon which a deal may be made with the Department.[9]

It is not known whether Utauta Webber ever wrote to offer her land to the government, or whether the Department of Lands and Survey ever approached her, but nothing happened. It was wartime; money was short and so, presumably, were the staff of government departments. Whatever the explanation, the opportunity passed. Utauta Webber continued to try to run her farm and Sanderson turned his attention to other matters.

In 1942 the waters round the island became the scene of great activity as the American Marines, who were based at Camp McKay near Paekakariki, used the local beaches to practise amphibious landings as training for the Pacific war. Con-

With no husband or children to help her run the farm during the war, Utauta Webber had to depend on casual labour. She would inveigle local lads across to the island on some pretext, then put them to work. Sometimes they stayed for a month or more. Most had happy memories of these times for, although Utauta worked them hard, there was also fun and friendship. Relaxing on the Manaaki, from left to right, are Jimmy Randle, Bill Campbell, 'Baby' Ropata, Goshin Ropata, Dick Ropata and an unidentified Pakeha.
JOHN BARRETT COLLECTION

sequently, civilian use of the channel between Kapiti and the mainland was almost impossible. 'Kapiti became very remote,' according to Nancy Jordan. 'We weren't even allowed on the beach. They had landing exercises all the time. The big ships would be way out to sea and the sea would be almost black with landing craft doing exercises.'[10]

Bobby Jones
SYLVIA LOVELL COLLECTION

Kapiti itself does not seem to have been used for military purposes, presumably because it was made up of nature reserve and private land, neither of which was suitable for military exercises. Nor was there any need to use it; the nearby beaches were more like the Pacific Islands where the Marines would be fighting and bush warfare training was carried out in the Tararua Ranges. The only time that troops visited the island seems to have been in November 1943 when Air Force personnel recovered the bodies of two airmen who were killed when their Harvard plane slammed into the western cliffs, below the head of the Te Rere.[11] The plane had been carrying aircraft spare parts from Wigram to Ohakea when it crashed. Most of the wreckage was removed, except for the

badly compressed alloy engine block, which still lies among the boulders on the beach far below the Te Rere bluff.[12]

Members of the Kapiti community were deeply affected by the war. Today's visitors, walking on the Trig Track, may be reminded of this when they come to the stone seat built by the parents of Bobby Jones, who died when the plane he was delivering from England to the Far East crashed in the Himalayas. Bobby and his parents had been regular summer visitors to Kapiti since he was a child, camp-

Captain Sanderson and one of his dogs, at Waiorua, where he usually stayed when he visited the island. Some of the mature pohutukawa and rimu in the grounds of the original Webber homestead may have been planted by him.
JOHN BARRETT COLLECTION

The Forest and Bird Society showed its appreciation of Sanderson's long interest in Kapiti when, in 1940, Bernard Sladden, a member of its committee, presented him with this painting (c.1898) of the island, seen from Rangiuru near Otaki, by C. D. Barraud. The mast of the wrecked ship Weathersfield *is apparent in the foreground.*

ing on the site where the war memorial now stands. Sylvia Wilkinson was devastated by the death of this 'exceptionally delightful child' who had grown into 'a beautiful young man'.[13]

After the Wilkinsons left the island in 1942, G. W. Hughes took over as caretaker until, in March 1945, he became ill and was taken to Palmerston North hospital. Captain Sanderson, who had originally arranged for Hughes to work on the island, wrote expressing his sympathy, but also chided him: 'Am sorry to learn your illness has been so bad and judging by its nature am afraid you have been unduly exposing yourself to wet and cold, and possibly failed to quickly change into dry clothes. In my opinion getting wet and keeping the body warm with exercise is beneficial if the clothes are promptly removed before the body warmth starts to lessen. It is then that evil starts.'[14]

Sanderson does not seem to have followed his own advice. He was now 80 and although he remained active as president of the Royal Forest and Bird Protection Society, he spent most of his time at Paekakariki, in his garden or workshop. The keen inventor was preoccupied with perfecting a unique sprinkler system for his garden using perforated brass door knobs. Sometimes while adjusting them, he got rather wet. In December 1945 he caught a chill, developed pneumonia and died.[15]

His successor at the Forest and Bird Society received letters of condolence from a number of people, including the Minister of Internal Affairs, W. E. Parry, who shared Sanderson's enthusiasm for the concept of the unified management of wildlife, or 'Unity of Control'. Like everyone who had known Sanderson well, Bill Parry had experienced his wrath. On one occasion Parry had been ordered out of the Forest and Bird office with Sanderson's shouted denunciation 'hypocrite' ringing in his ears.[16] Nevertheless the minister wrote:

> For many years he strived valiantly for the welfare of our native birds and forests, challenging vigorously any measures which he considered would re-act to their disadvantage. To his work and that of his associates can be attributed much of the increased public interest now shown in these matters.

Captain Sanderson saw the forest, its avian inhabitants, and the clear running water of our forest streams, as one unified natural phenomenon and never ceased striving to impress on the people that destruction of the natural covering of vegetation had far-reaching effects. Birds and forest, he realised, had definite utilitarian as well as aesthetic values, and he stressed both. He was a bitter opponent of vandals of all types.[17]

Among the vandals, in Sanderson's view, were the administrators who neglected Kapiti, the politicians who wanted to farm it and the scientists who tried to populate it with avian hybrids. For more than 30 years, Sanderson made the restoration of the sanctuary a personal crusade. Rightly, his name is associated not only with Kapiti but with the birth of the modern conservation movement in New Zealand as a whole. At the national level his achievements were considerable; on the island, he might have achieved even more – and enjoyed those gains with more regular visits to the sanctuary – had the darker side of his nature not prevailed. As it was, he had been unwelcome at Rangatira for most of that period.

From the Webbers, Sanderson learned a great deal about Maori culture at a time when many Pakeha had a dismissive attitude. He considered that Maori had been better stewards of the environment than their European successors and he always referred to birds and plants by their Maori names.

The influence of Maori design was evident in a small whare he built and lived in until his house at Paekakariki was finished. This later became his workshop. Visitors to the Pingau Avenue sanctuary entered through an ornate gateway reminiscent of a pataka or storehouse, which indeed it was, since it also functioned as a feeding box for birds.

Ironically, in the three years before his death, Sanderson had more influence on the island than ever before. After the Wilkinsons' departure he was Utauta Webber's trusted adviser and his protégé, G. W. Hughes, was now in charge of the sanctuary. But it was too late. Sanderson was old and world-weary. When Hiroshima and Nagasaki were destroyed by atomic bombs he said to his family, 'This is the end of the world.' He did not live long afterwards. As for Hughes, he recovered but never returned to Kapiti. For several months the sanctuary was unattended until W. A. Lindsay was appointed caretaker.

At Waiorua, the end of the war offered new possibilities. Utauta's son, Winara, who had been farming on the mainland, now returned to the island to resuscitate the family farm. Barely a year after he returned, in September 1946, an electrical fault in the Webbers' house started a fire which completely destroyed it. The blaze also destroyed many family treasures, including carvings by Hona Webber, as well as ornaments and photograph albums.[18] Utauta Webber was devastated by the loss of the house that had been the main focus of her life, and the heart of Waiorua Bay in its heyday.

The end of the war also raised the hope that something might now be done about the possum problem, in particular. It seemed this was about to happen when the newly established Wildlife Branch of Internal Affairs (which, in 1945, become responsible for noxious animal control on Crown land) offered 'to exterminate' the possums on Kapiti, adding that 'this Department could possibly make available the services of a small party for several months in an all out effort to rid the Island of the opossum'.[19] Despite this suggestion, nothing happened for the next five years and the possums continued to proliferate.

When a new ranger, George Fox, succeeded W. A. Lindsay in 1951, he was not impressed. In a report to his department Fox wrote, 'It appears that the opossum has been allowed to increase too much',[20] an observation he repeated with increasing emphasis for several years. But still nothing was done. Between 1950 and 1956, the Wildlife Branch's role in the control of pests such as deer and possums was under review by the Public Service Commission. The responsibility was then transferred to the Forest Service, but by that time, the long period of uncertainty had seriously undermined the Wildlife Branch's efficacy.[21] This was all too evident on Kapiti, where it took the Wildlife Branch 10 years to cut trap lines and get some traps to the island. Even then, there was no one to actually use them, so the branch recommended that the Department of Lands and Survey should encourage private trappers to do the work instead. Schoolboys from Scots College trapped during their holidays; so did various adults, including a man who caught kiwi in his traps and had plans to lay cyanide poison – which would have been as lethal for birds as it was for possums.[22]

In the winter of 1955, just before the Wildlife Branch lost its responsibility for possum control, it organised a campaign on the island; 2600 possums and 400 rats were killed by six trappers and two field officers who spent two and a half months on Kapiti. Their morale was sapped, however, by bad weather which made getting on and off the island difficult, but it was a start. Fox, the caretaker, suggested that if more campaigns were mounted regularly the possums might be controlled.[23] As this did not happen, the benefits of the exercise were short-lived, and it was left to Fox to do the trapping himself, in addition to all his other duties.[24]

Meanwhile, at the north end of Kapiti, Mike (Winara) Webber was confronted by numerous possums as well as rats, which had almost reached plague proportions around Waiorua. The fertile valley produced a great crop of potatoes but these had to be stored in a tin-lined shed or the rats would have eaten them all.[25] There was also a major problem with wild sheep. The flock that had survived

abandonment during the war was in poor condition, as were the farm's fences which were broken in many places. Some of the unshorn, unkempt sheep had escaped and taken refuge on the western cliffs and in the reserve. Worse still the Webbers' bull roamed the sanctuary for some time. 'Do you think the bull is likely to be dangerous to visitors to the sanctuary?' the Commissioner of Crown Lands asked Fox anxiously.[26]

The early 1950s were a repetition of the time when first Richard Henry, then James Bennett, had had to cope with the Webbers' sheep invading the sanctuary. Now George Fox found himself having to deal with the same problem.[27] Mike Webber, however, was a great supporter of the sanctuary and he quickly resolved the difficulties with his neighbour. The fence was repaired in 1953 and a strenuous effort was made to muster the wild stock. Webber was assisted by his son-in-law, Doug Williams, who still has vivid memories of retrieving rogue sheep from the western cliffs – in a dinghy. Once an animal was captured, its feet were tied and it was hauled into the boat, but if it managed to free its feet, the consequences could be dangerous. Williams recalls being kicked out of the boat by a sheep and nearly drowned as his heavy workboots dragged him under.

After several years' hard work, it was apparent that the farm would always be difficult to maintain; even if its isolation could be lessened, the profit was not enough to support two families. So Webber and Williams had to supplement their income in other ways. Visitors were brought to the island at weekends for the day at £1 each, and the *Manaaki* was hired to fishing parties for £10 a day. During the week, Webber and Williams went fishing themselves and sold their catch, mainly snapper, to Kap and Rewa Webber who ran the Kapiti Fish Supply. They also cut manuka, which was shipped to Paraparaumu Beach and sold as firewood at Jack McLean's store. But it was a demanding and tenuous existence, with no great prospects of improvement, so the decision was made to let the farm go.

After the war Mike Webber revived the tradition of inviting large groups to stay at the northern end of Kapiti. The caretaker at Rangatira, W. A. Lindsay, was not enthusiastic. He remembered the difficulties there had been in 1950 when 30 members of the Catholic Tramping Club were stranded at Waiorua for five days by bad weather. Three successive air drops of food were required, always a potentially perilous exercise for both the pilot and those on the ground, and the caretaker's radio-telephone was clogged with calls from journalists keen to cover the story.

Before the war, large groups had usually been from tramping clubs; after the Webbers left, most of the trampers shifted south to the sanctuary instead. Nevertheless, some big parties continued to stay at the north end. In 1958 a large contingent of Youth Hostel Association members camped at Waiorua and the following year 56 school children from Wanganui had a holiday on the Webbers' property under the supervision of the Forest and Bird Society.

FRANK FITZGERALD

The wind-down was gradual. For several years, in the mid–1950s, sheep were rounded up and removed, buildings dismantled and equipment taken back to the mainland.[28] Without the browsing sheep, the hilly pastures quickly reverted to tauhinu and manuka.

The unsuccessful struggle to revive the farm had not gone unnoticed by the Department of Lands and Survey and when Mike Webber withdrew, the Crown resolved to acquire the land. At first, it considered taking all the remaining free-hold land by legislation but this option was rejected by the Director-General, D. M. Greig, who favoured a more diplomatic approach.[29] Given the bitterness the Crown's original 1897 legislation had caused, this was a wise decision, but it meant that considerable patience would be required. It certainly was, for it took almost 10 years for the Crown to conclude the purchase of the first of the six remaining blocks of private land. The sale was complex because it required the agreement of all of the surviving children of Hona and Utauta and two of their grandsons, Jim and Jack Webber, whose father, Tuku, had died. In return for the sale of a signifi-cant part of the farm, each received a one-fifth share of a specifically created 30-acre block on the shore at Waiorua Bay, an interest in a one and three-quarter acre section at the southern end of Motungarara and a small cash payment. Mike Webber's right to continue farming the land the Crown bought was also acknowl-edged, even though he had long since given up the attempt.

The new foreshore block at Waiorua would be divided between the five descendants (and their heirs) when they had agreed how this should be done.[30] To the Crown, the partition was vital because it would create individual titles that the owners could then sell, if they chose, to the government. In fact, the proposed division did not happen because there was no agreement between the people in-volved. The department did not facilitate a consensus; nor did it ensure that the land, once owned by the Webbers and now registered as Crown land, was for-mally designated as part of the nature reserve. At the time this did not seem important, for Crown land was inviolate, and the Waitangi Tribunal did not ex-ist; but the Crown's failure to complete these legal niceties later caused real difficulty.

George Fox was appointed caretaker on Kapiti in 1951. He and his wife, Margaret, and their daughter, Barbara, were used to an isolated life, having earlier worked as lighthouse-keepers at Nugget Point, Farewell Spit, French Pass and Stephens Island. George retired in 1968 after 17 years on the island.

Perhaps the most noticeable change during this period was the increasing number of small boats fishing near Kapiti. 'Their occupants require strict supervision,' Fox wrote to his superiors. 'Many of them attempt landings to boil the billy and at all times are a worry to the caretaker especially during the dry season. The weekends are sometimes very hectic as well as interesting to the caretaker.'
FORMER LANDS AND SURVEY DEPARTMENT COLLECTION, DEPARTMENT OF CONSERVATION

At the time, an internal review of the agreement suggested that the Crown might have been too generous: 'Reading the file it may appear that we played into the Webber estate's hands in arranging this deal. There are now 6 titles in place of one and we have not gained much except land which the Webbers did not use in any case.'[31] In hindsight, the department may have been luckier than it realised, in that some of the descendants were prepared to sell to the Crown and had persuaded the others to do the same. As later events were to show, this was quite a feat.

The next purchase was even more of a challenge. The block in question was a 16-acre segment of a much larger section in the middle of the island. It was not owned by the Webbers but by Marion D'Ath (née Wallace), a descendant of Te Rauparaha. Marion was a small, feisty woman with a big voice and a passion for acrobatic flying. Fiercely proud of her heritage, she was not to be trifled with. One

Studies of tui on Kapiti, by Avis Acres.

Towards the end of the 1950s, the world began to discover Kapiti. Knowledge of the island came partly from cine film and radio. In the spring of 1956, artist and author Avis Acres spent a week on the island, which she later described in her radio programme, Country Newsletter, and in her books for children. The following spring, Peter Morrison, a photographer from the Wildlife Branch, made several short films about the birds on Kapiti.
ALEXANDER TURNBULL LIBRARY AND THE ESTATE OF AVIS ACRES

Margaret Fox continued a tradition begun by Amy Wilkinson of feeding the birds, especially the kaka. A pamphlet given to visitors noted that 'Mrs. Fox can whistle birds from the bush and both she and her husband feed the increasing number of birds coming to the homestead for their supplementary rations – last year 400 lbs of dates, 180 lbs of sugar and 20 lbs of honey were used'.

The feeding routine was popular with visitors, since it allowed them to see rare birds, such as kaka, at close quarters. The practice was discontinued in the late 1990s because it made the birds dependent on people and aggressive towards visitors.
BARBARA ANDERSON COLLECTION

of her favourite favourite pastimes was decapitating daisies with a stockwhip from the verandah of her Otaki home.[32] In 1922 the government had appropriated most of Kapiti-Rangatira No. 4, as the land was known, with the consent of the Maori Land Court. Marion D'Ath had opposed the enforced sale of her share so the court had subdivided the block, most of which went to the Crown, although she retained her share. At various times during the next 30 years the Department of Lands and Survey approached her to buy the land but the offers were always firmly rejected. When Marion D'Ath died in 1955, departmental officials waited for a decent time, then approached her family, hoping that they might be more agreeable. They

During the 1950s, film crews from the United States, the Soviet Union and Japan visited Kapiti. Here, George and Margaret Fox pose with members of the Japanese photographic team and their escort outside the caretaker's house. The photographers spent several days on the island gathering material for a magazine article.

Of such visitors, George Fox observed, 'It is very noticeable that when anyone visits the island to work on the birds, they usually have to wait a day or so until the birds allow them to use cameras and tape recorders.'
BARBARA ANDERSON COLLECTION

were not, and her son, Wallace, alarmed them by saying that the family planned to build a casino on the land.[33]

To anyone familiar with the block, this notion could only have been a jest because the steep, unstable hillside on the southern side of the Te Rere would have been inaccessible and useless for such a purpose. Perhaps for this reason, and after continuing pressure from government officals, her children eventually agreed to sell their interest on the island but they asked a premium price of £100 – more than twice its assessed value – which the department reluctantly paid, in the knowledge that this might be its only chance.[34]

With a resolution Sanderson would have admired, the department pressed on with its programme of acquisition. Only three blocks still remained in Maori ownership: a 35-acre remnant of the Webbers' farm and two, tiny separate sections known as Waiorua 5A₂ and Rangatira 4B₂. Their legal descriptions exemplified the difficulties inherent in Maori land transactions, and were evidence of earlier subdivisions, similar to that granted to Marion D'Ath. But whereas she had been the sole owner of 16 acres, 5A₂ (which was just over two acres) had 45 owners, only one of whom was known; 4B₂ (which was little more than three acres) had 15 owners. Faced with the task of tracing so many owners and then persuading them all to sell, the department instead applied to the Maori Land Court for permission to acquire the blocks by compulsory purchase, under the Maori Affairs Act. The court granted the request in the case of Rangatira 4B₂ but could not do the same for Waiorua 5A₂ because one of the owners, Te R. Pomare, objected.

The Ngatea *served a succession Kapiti caretakers for 40 years, providing a vital link with the mainland as well as a means of patrolling the island. On one occasion Stan Wilkinson and his son, Ray, took her north to the Manawatu rivermouth, in a storm, to rescue the crew of a boat that had capsized.*

The kauri-hulled launch was built in Thames and named after a nearby town. Before she came to Kapiti, the Ngatea *was a survey vessel in the Piako swamps, then towed flax barges on the Manawatu River. When she was sold by Lands and Survey the new owner, Reg Saunders, restored 'the gracious old boat', which is still in use today. Ngatea is usually moored in Ivey Bay near the Paremata Bridge.*

He was a descendant of Kahe Te Rau O Te Rangi and wished to remain an owner because of his family's historical association with Kapiti. In discussions with the department, Pomare was adamant 'that while he did not wish to use or even visit the land and strongly favoured the Crown's intended use of the land he would oppose any move that would remove his name from the title and so break his sentimental and historic link with the island'.[35]

Pomare's stance was not new. The same attitude had been apparent in hearings before the Native Affairs Committee in 1897, but now there was greater understanding of the Maori view of the land and a compromise was made. The Crown would lease the land rent-free for the next 50 years but Pomare's name would remain on the title.[36]

Now the Crown had only two pieces of land to acquire: the new 30-acre Webber family block on the beach at Waiorua, and the last part of their old farm, which consisted of steep hills and cliffs on the northern tip of the island. In 1967 Mike Webber sold the latter to the government because he wanted to see the whole island become a nature reserve.[37] With this purchase the Crown concluded a 15-year campaign that enlarged the sanctuary to include all of Kapiti except the small family allotment at Waiorua Bay. The department confidently expected that it, too, would eventually come to the Crown because Mike Webber and at least one other owner were thought to be sympathetic to the idea of a nature reserve. So negotiations began.

All that was needed was agreement among the branches of the Webber family as to their respective portions, but it was five years before a meeting was held to divide the land into individual lots. In that time, significant social change, prompted by black American civil rights campaigns in the United States, led to a greater awareness of the disadvantaged position of indigenous peoples. New Zealand was just one of many countries influenced by these events. As the legacy of Martin Luther King and others spread rapidly around the world via the new medium of television, elements within Maoridom started to reassess their situation. Consequently, when the Webber family meeting finally took place, the reason for calling it had changed. It was arranged by Piki Barrett, who was keen to see the partition proceed so that her son John could build a house at Waiorua Bay.

This was not what the Crown had in mind at all. The Commissioner of Crown Lands tried to find a legal mechanism

> by which the existing owners can be prevented from increasing their assets on the Island and so prolong the purchase of the remaining Maori interests by the Crown. It should also be borne in mind that the increased activity brought about by permanent structures on the Island increases the number of unauthorised landings on the Crown portions and the danger of fires and the introduction of noxious plants and animals by people landing on the parts of the Island over which we have no control.[38]

At this point it was realised that Kapiti was a conundrum. Although the island, topographically, was part of the Kapiti district (which was then administered by the Hutt County Council), it lay beyond its jurisdiction because it was a nature reserve. Lands and Survey turned to the Ministry of Works, which implemented the Town and Country Planning Act, in the hope that its authority might extend to Kapiti and the matter seemed settled when Works replied that it could intervene under the act 'to prevent any building on Kapiti Island'.[39]

A few months later the Minister of Lands was returning to Wellington from Rotorua when his plane flew over Kapiti. Looking down, he saw what he thought

John and Susan Barrett's house was the first of several built on the Webber family block at Waiorua Bay. Later, Fred (Boysie) Barrett, left, also erected a dwelling. Since 1996 he has been a permanent resident on the island.

were 'stopbanks under construction near the north-eastern tip of the island'. He asked for a report, which revealed that the stopbanks were, in fact, a ditch being dug 'some 20 ft long in preparation for the house proposed by Mr. and Mrs. J. Barrett'. The minister was reassured that Works would redesignate the land, under the 1897 legislation, as 'proposed reserve' and so prevent any building.[40]

When the ministry took a closer look, however, the situation did not seem so straightforward. The Commissioner of Works found that while one government department (Lands and Survey) was encouraging the partition of private land into individual titles, at the same time it was asking another department (Works) to deny 'such partitions their logical use – a situation that might not stand the scrutiny of an appeal to the courts'.[41] While officials discussed their response, they were presented with a fait accompli: the Barretts had built their house.

The Department of Lands and Survey may have considered that it fell at the final hurdle. Yet had the Crown delayed its campaign of land acquisition on Kapiti for only 10 or 20 years, it is unlikely – given the change of attitude toward Maori land – that it would have been as successful as it was. It had acquired all but 30 acres of the island, which it was now able to administer as a complete entity. The fact that Kapiti could now be treated as a whole would make remarkable changes possible in the years ahead.

CHAPTER FIFTEEN

WINDOW ON ANOTHER WORLD

'What the Maori people had when they came to New Zealand was amazing, almost unbelievable in today's world. The birdlife, the forest life, was not matched anywhere else in the world. The birds were definitely quite strange,' says Bob Cairns, who spent five years on Kapiti during the 1980s eradicating the possums. He likens the island to 'looking through a window back into that world'.

'It's not a perfect view, it never will be, but it's as close as we'll get to see. Its clarity depends,' says Cairns, 'on how the island is treated. We can clean that window (that's partly what exterminating possums did, and it was another step further to eradicate the rats) or, if we aren't careful, we can smash that window. If we do, we won't ever be able to repair it again.'

During the 1970s, the window almost cracked as the possum population was allowed to increase to an unprecedented level. During the 1980s, Kapiti was again at risk as tension between the ranger and the owners of private land at Waiorua increased. In 1990 differences were discussed in a crucial court case involving those owners, the outcome of which reversed the Crown's policy of the previous 90 years.

From then on, Kapiti's future required some sort of partnership between the Department of Conservation and the island's private owners, as well as with local iwi. The nature and extent of that partnership is still evolving, as is understanding of the issues involved.

BOB CAIRNS (MIDDLE AND RIGHT INSETS)

THE BIRDS were in good form that day,' wrote George Fox in April 1962 when Gerald Durrell, the English naturalist, visited Kapiti. He was accompanied by two BBC cameramen to film him talking about the island's birds. Fox heard that when the film was shown on English television it was 'well received'.[1] Durrell had already publicised the natural world in *My Family and Other Animals* and other books which were widely read in the 1950s and 1960s. The popularity of his writing and his television appearances reflected people's increasing interest in the environment.

This interest was apparent on Kapiti. In 1963 Fox noted that 'once again our number of visitors took a sharp rise upwards. Some 600-odd visited the sanctuary.' Ten years later there were 2500.[2] For the caretaker, this increase created difficulties. In the past, supervision on the island had been straightforward: the caretaker greeted visitors, talked to them and could spot any potential problems with behaviour. Stan Wilkinson, for one, had become adept at this. 'Any amount of people write to me and say they are greatly interested,' he remarked. 'Some of them come over here and do not take any interest in the trees or birds at all. I can soon tell.'[3] Thirty years later, George Fox found the supervision of large parties a challenge, especially in the bush. He asked the department to limit visitors to a maximum of 25 per group and this was agreed.[4] Thereafter Fox had fewer problems, although there were still some surprises: 'I had to request one couple to do their copulating off the beaten track'.[5]

Of much greater concern were some visitors to the north end who sneaked into the sanctuary without a permit. Fox reported that he often found people walking around without his knowledge, and the problem worsened as the number of small boats frequenting the waters around Kapiti continued to grow.[6] In 1973 the Commissioner of Crown Lands appealed to the public to abide by the regulations:

We realise there is great public demand to visit the reserve, and we want to see it appreciated by as many people as possible within the maximum numbers permitted on the island at any one time.

In 1969 Peter Rodda, seen here on the bow of Kapiti Ranger, *took over as caretaker. Like Fox he was a lighthouse-keeper, but he did not share his predecessor's concern about large groups visiting the island. Instead he invited local boating and diving clubs to hold their annual picnics at Rangatira. Sometimes more than 200 club members were there at the height of summer, increasing the risk of fire and creating a different ambience. The Lands and Survey Department did not learn of these gatherings until Rodda left the island in 1976; not surprisingly, it put a stop to the practice.*
FORMER LANDS AND SURVEY
DEPARTMENT COLLECTION
DEPARTMENT OF CONSERVATION

However, during the summer months particularly we are haunted by the prospect of a fire on Kapiti. An incident as simple as a cigarette end dropped into a patch of leaf mould could wipe out years of work on the reserve and destroy one of New Zealand's most valuable areas for the preservation of flora and fauna.

Our primary responsibility is the sanctuary's preservation and we are determined that visitors should enter the reserve only at the approved landing point – where they can be made aware of the regulations applying to the area – and only by permits.[7]

The commissioner was not to know that the island was about to suffer a setback as damaging as any fire could have been, and it was caused not by some careless visitor but as the result of a carefully considered decision, made by

The brushtail possum causes far less damage to vegetation in its native Australia because its density is usually less than one per hectare. In New Zealand it is far more numerous. The possum population on Kapiti Island may have been the highest per hectare in the country. It grew from 13,000 in 1950 to 20,000 in 1980, an average of 10 per hectare.
BOB CAIRNS

those charged with protecting the sanctuary, to suspend the trapping of possums on Kapiti.

In 1967, botanist Alan Esler, of Massey University, had published the first complete account of Kapiti's vegetation, in which he warned that 'The present opossum population is high and is causing considerable damage to the vegetation'.[8] Sanderson had said the same thing in the past but this was the first time a professional scientist had drawn attention to the problem and it was taken seriously.[9]

At the same time the Crown finally acquired all of Kapiti, except for the 30 acres at Waiorua belonging to the Webbers and so, for the first time, the sanctuary's managers were able to make plans for almost the whole island. Now was their chance to mount a sustained campaign against the possums. Instead, in 1968, trapping was stopped altogether to assess 'whether or not opossums without control will in fact increase or harm the vegetation and birdlife.'[10] The plan was approved by the Kapiti Island Advisory Committee and the Department of Lands and Survey and, in 1975, the DSIR (the Department of Scientific and Industrial Research which was undertaking research on possums) began a research programme to evaluate its effects.[11]

Within a few years, the consequences of suspending control measures were evident. When Peter Daniel arrived at Rangatira in 1976 to take over as ranger, he was shocked:

> The most obvious thing when I first came here was the number of possums. I can still remember that in the mornings the decks and railings of the house were covered with faeces and urine. At night, if you shone a torch out through the windows, you'd often see half-a-dozen sets of eyes looking at you from the trees.

> It was very frustrating for me. In the old days I really was a 'hunting, shooting, fishing' sort of Kiwi. I'd grown up in Waikanae, where we used to go out possum hunting, so shooting possums was a big deal. It was incredibly frustrating for me, who was well armed, to look out and see all these creatures looking at me and I wasn't allowed to touch them![12]

His frustration was shared by the Forest and Bird Society and prompted scientists Ben Bell and Ian Atkinson to write an article for the society's magazine in an attempt to allay members' anxiety. The authors were adamant that the policy 'was not an "experiment" to see if opossums will find a natural level with the bird life on the island as has been suggested. The work is designed to measure trends in opossum numbers, their breeding performance, and movements as well as to monitor their effects on the vegetation. From this information the committee can reach an informed decision on future opossum control.' This was not how the study was perceived, however, by some scientists. The following year at the first national symposium on marsupials, the doyen of ornithology, Sir Robert Falla, who was a member of the Kapiti Advisory Committee, responded to the question 'whether there was any indication that discrete populations [of possums] were settling to levels well below the sustaining capacity of the environment'.

> I do have the impression that the very interesting study that is going on at Kapiti Island is likely to provide quite useful information on this aspect at the end of 5 or 6 years' work. This is being done at the request of the Lands and Survey Department's District Office in Wellington, who are responsible for Kapiti Island's welfare; it is also being done against a very steady pressure to drop the research altogether, and to get on with the job of exterminating the possums on the island. I think there is some room for encouragement of research of this kind, and discouragement of well-meaning but otherwise quite misdirected criticism of the work going on in the Kapiti sanctuary.[13]

In 1977 a report by Ian Atkinson of the DSIR recommended trapping be resumed in a number of areas and noted that, although vegetation damage had generally not been irreversible, some species such as fuchsia were being destroyed and might disappear: 'Out of a group of twenty trees along the Trig track, three were already dead and every second tree had been browsed. Damage to the crowns was in the vicinity of 90-100% and there were no signs of revegetation.' Atkinson was confident, however, that the fuchsia would survive 'if precautions were taken such as the attaching of sheet metal around the trunks. Fuchsia was a quick-turnover species with a 100-150 year life.' He added that the island's forest habitat could well be changing. 'In another 100 years the species may have vanished as part of the natural forest cycle.' Atkinson's colleague, Dr Bob Brockie, suggested limited trapping should be resumed along the summit 'to ensure the fuchsia survived' but he also considered that 'at least one further year of research was essential'.[14]

As it happened, the moratorium continued for a further three years. Although trapping did take place at several locations to protect specific species, most of the island remained unprotected. In 1979 the policy was again reviewed. Once again, Atkinson suggested that control be reintroduced in most parts of the island.

Veteran possum control specialist, Les Pracy, was asked to report on how this should be done. When he visited Kapiti the following year, he confirmed that the damage to the vegetation was severe: 'the patterns of defoliation were the worst that I had observed since my official association with the island in 1948'. He also found that more species had been eaten than when he inspected the island in 1970: 'tree, shrub and vine species mainly affected are kohekohe, kamahi, titoki, toro, rangiora, five-finger, wineberry, tawa, rata vine, mamaku ferns and rata trees,' he reported to the department.[15]

Although Pracy did not see it as within his brief to make recommendations, his observations on the decline of the bird life – the noticeable reduction in the

Kohekohe forest defoliated by possums, Maraetakaroro, 1983.
BILL COLLINS

number of parakeets, pigeons, tui, bellbirds, robins, tomtits and whiteheads – were worrying. With the blessing of the advisory committee, the Department of Lands and Survey resumed possum trapping throughout the island.

In hindsight, the suspension of possum trapping for 11 years was a major setback for Kapiti. From the scientific viewpoint, it did produce useful evidence of the growth of an unfettered population of possums in the finite location, and the impact on the bush and birds – but at the cost of severe damage to the island's ecology. But that was not as obvious then as it is now. According to Ian Atkinson, 'If we had known then what we know now about possums as predators, that decision would not have been made. But the predatory impact of possums did not become clear until the 1990s. In the 1970s possums were seen only as unwanted herbivores.'[16]

At the time, however, the exercise did have one good result: it focused attention on the possum problem as never before. When trapping began again in 1980, it quickly reduced the possums; in two years 15,000 were killed.[17] Despite that impressive tally, however, it was assumed that a residual possum population would require control. Records showed that trapping would always be expensive, only partially effective and difficult to supervise; for instance, Peter Daniel found a pair of trappers about to apply cyanide, which was strictly prohibited on the island. He sent them packing and hired a replacement, Geoff Alexander. A carpenter by trade, he had no knowledge of trapping, so went out with the other commercial operators on Kapiti to learn the job. He was surprised to find that, although traps were often sprung by possums, they escaped, which meant there would always be a residual group of veterans too cunning to be caught.[18]

At the same time, investigations elsewhere in New Zealand were starting to confirm what had long been suspected – that possums not only damaged and ate the vegetation, reducing the birds' food supply, but also disturbed birds on their

A crucial step in the eradication of possums on Kapiti was an improvement in the way traps were used. All traps had to be set above the ground to prevent birds such as kiwi being caught. To avoid this, traps were placed on round wooden posts, known as 'sets', which were propped up against trees or vertical posts at an angle. This protected the birds but was less than effective at catching possums.

Geoff Alexander noticed that possums often climbed up and down sets without triggering the trap, so he altered the design. By using square-cut timber instead of round posts, and placing the trap in a groove cut into the wood, slightly to one side of the centre, he created a much more successful device that invariably caught a possum.
BILL COLLINS

nests and even ate their eggs. It also seemed likely that they competed with kiwi for nesting sites.[19] The implications of this unfolding knowledge were important for Kapiti. It was the only refuge of the little spotted kiwi; and it should also be able to accommodate other rare species in safety if it was to really fulfil its potential as an avian sanctuary. Ideally, the possums should be eliminated, but the prospect was daunting. In the past, the Forest Service (which was responsibile for noxious animals on Crown land) had tried to remove possums from several locations on the mainland and was convinced that eradication was impossible.

Or was it? In 1981 Dick Veitch, a Wildlife Service officer, visited Kapiti and did not think so. He had just completed a campaign to clear Little Barrier Island of wild cats. At 3000 hectares, Hauturu was larger than Kapiti and was also extremely rugged, but the greatest challenge, according to Veitch, was psychological rather than physical: those involved had to believe eradication was possible. Veitch had a suggestion for Kapiti's ranger: 'Peter, you've got to get the idea of control out of your mind, think of eradication instead'.[20]

Peter Daniel was convinced, but with his various other duties could not do the work himself, so he asked Alexander. He was enthusiastic and together they planned the campaign. Alexander would co-ordinate the workers while Daniel would arrange the supply of materials, organise the funding and liaise with the various Crown agencies.[21]

Eradication began in 1982. As on Little Barrier, the first requirement was to cut tracks to allow traps to be laid along 'lines' about 100 metres apart. While Alexander and Collins spent two years cutting tracks, Cairns followed in their wake with a succession of Wildlife Service trainees, who laid traps along the freshly cut routes. The team started at the southern end and worked their way up the island until, in 1984, the 'rolling front', as it was known, reached the northern coast. In that time 3933 possums were caught.[22] Despite the intensive nature of the campaign, the team knew some possums had eluded them, and until the last of these were killed, all their efforts were certain to be ultimately ineffective.

Bob Cairns (left) and Geoff Alexander led the successful campaign to eradicate the possums on Kapiti.

Cairns is carrying a load of sets. This, he later recalled, was a job no one liked because 'they stuck up above your pack and they stuck down to about your knees. You would load a pack frame with as many sets as you could get on, then lift the pack frame onto your back and crawl along the ground on your hands and knees until you got to a tree then you could pull yourself up.

'You walked to where you were going and dropped them off, which was a huge relief, because everytime you walked through the bush the sets would hit the trees above your head and you'd get these jarring effects. If you were going down a steep hill they dug into the back of your legs. Then, if you had the misfortune of falling over, or "turtleing" as we called it, you lay on the ground on your back and because the pack straps were pulled up tight, you wouldn't be able to take the pack off. You'd be lying there with your legs and arms shaking out sideways with nothing really happening – that's why we called it "turtleing".'

EVENING POST

Nevertheless, signs of improvement in the vegetation and bird life were soon apparent, which encouraged the workers.[23] In 1982 Atkinson noted that the northern rata were recovering and that new foliage growth, as well as flowering and fruiting of the kohekohe, was spectacular. Other species such as tawa and toro were less resilient; some were recovering but others had died. In general, however, the vegetation was much healthier.[24]

At this stage, the trapping operation was still officially a 'control' exercise because the Forest Service, which was nominally in charge and was paying for part of the programme, remained unconvinced that eradication was possible. Those actually working on the island did not agree and it was their attitude that really mattered. At times it seemed as if the Forest Service did not want the operation to succeed; requested equipment took months to arrive and funding was often uncertain. In desperation, Peter Daniel turned to the local MP, Margaret Shields, for help. After she wrote to the Minister of Forests, and asked questions in Parliament, funding was restored. But all this disagreement had its emotional cost, for the approach of the Forest Service was now tinged with personal enmity.[25]

Fortunately, Daniel and the eradication team enjoyed the support of the Commissioner of Crown Lands, Tony Phillips, and Phil Cowan, a young DSIR scientist, whose report advocating eradication (written at the outset of the campaign) gave it sufficient scientific credibility to counter the Forest Service's scepticism. At the end of the sweep up the length of the island, Cowan estimated that only between 200 and 600 possums remained.[26]

In 1985 the exterminators returned to the south end and, once again, worked their way up the island, this time with dogs specially trained to hunt possums. During this second sweep the island was divided into 45-hectare blocks, which were searched on a 40-metre grid pattern. As three adjacent blocks extended from one side of the island to the other, they constituted a narrow band, a variant of the original rolling front, which progressively moved northward. Each of the dog-

*Orchids (*Earina autumnalis*) on the Taepiro ridge.*
As Bill Collins cut tracks and Bob Cairns trapped possums, they also photographed flowers and plants, especially orchids. Cairns also recorded on a map all the archaeological sites he came across. This informal survey is now invaluable because, since possums were eradicated, the regenerated vegetation has obscured or destroyed many of these sites.
BILL COLLINS

handlers – Kerry Brown, Bob Cairns and Marcus James – had his own block within the band, which was searched exhaustively for about a week, before swapping with his neighbour. At the end of three weeks, each cross-section of the island had been thoroughly scrutinised by three different men and their dogs – a highly effective procedure which ensured that all the surviving possums were found. Actually killing them was sometimes extremely difficult because they lived in inaccessible lairs and they were clever. It was work that required remarkable persistence.[27]

By March 1987, the dogs had scoured Kapiti from end to end and in two years only 48 possums were caught,[28] which showed how effective the original rolling front had been. The island was now free of a pest that had been there for almost a century. The work of the eradication teams was officially recognised by the Minister of Lands, Koro Wetere, who presented their leaders, Geoff Alexander and Bob Cairns, with citations at a special ceremony on the island. Their real reward, however, was the revitalisation of the bush and the increase in bird life all around them.

This had been evident for some time and, coupled with the low number of possums, it gave scientists sufficient confidence to transfer stitchbirds to the sanctuary.[29] In anticipation of the disappearance of the last remaining possums, investigations began into the eventual release of kokako.[30] The arrival of new bird species, as well as the appearance of plant species not previously known to be on Kapiti, such as two types of the rare native mistletoe,[31] were exciting evidence that a new era had begun.

This was reflected by the increase in visitors. Between 1973 and 1986, the annual total had been relatively static but two years after the end of the campaign it had risen by more than 30 per cent.[32] As if in anticipation, the last job that Alexander and Collins did before they left the island was to build a new viewing tower to replace the old trig on top of Tuteremoana.[33] It was an imaginative way to communicate the results of their years of hard work because the 8-metre platform enabled visitors to look out over the recovering forest. Ten years earlier, the view from the summit had been of a expanse of treetops stripped almost bare by hungry possums. From the new tower visitors looked out over the thriving canopy and, in summer, at the crimson crowns of the flowering rata.

At first it was thought that the western cliffs would have to be excluded from the eradication team's close scrutiny because the steep, unstable slopes would be too dangerous to work on. Instead, the cliffs were dosed with an aerial drop of 1080 poison in baits. But that could never guarantee all the possums were killed, so it was decided to work the cliffs. The men moved cautiously at first, but with increasing confidence, as Bob Cairns's account of the pursuit of one particular possum suggests.

As possums are nocturnal, the dog teams searched their blocks at night as well as during the day. One night, Cairns's dog picked up the scent of a possum on the cliffs near Kaiwharawhara Point. Cairns caught a glimpse of it in the beam of his spotlight, fired his shotgun, but it was out of range, so he and his dog chased the possum down the cliff to its lair, which was 'in a big scree face that had a 90 foot bluff beneath it dropping down to boulders on the beach. The scree face was at an angle of about 45°, maybe more, and somewhere in that face was the possum. I started digging my way in, moving rocks aside, until I realised if I pulled the wrong rock about a tonne of rocks would come down on me and push me over the cliff. I had a bad spotlight, it was one o'clock in the morning, not the time to be out there, so I had to call it quits and head for home.'

The following night Cairns looked for the possum without success so, during the day, he followed and mapped its night-time trails. After two weeks he had built up an accurate record of its territory: where it ate, which trees it visited and when. 'It came to me that if we couldn't catch this possum we weren't going to eradicate the possums on Kapiti.' He considered a number of options, including dynamiting the scree slope, but he would never know for sure that the possum had been killed. Instead, he used an army smoke bomb to try to flush the possum out of his hole.

When that failed, all three dog-handlers returned to the scree slope at night and made another attempt to dig the possum out by shifting rocks – again without success. By this time, Peter Daniel had become concerned that Cairns was 'rock-happy', so he asked him to take a week off. When he returned, Cairns intensified his scent-trail mapping until it was clear that the possum regularly visited a small grassy patch in an area of the cliff face that was not as steep as the surrounding terrain. This was their chance.

'I decided we would use all three dog-handlers and their dogs. We would come down different parts of the cliff and catch it on the only easy territory, if you can call any of the cliffs easy.

'So we came down, spread out, with shotguns and a .22 to give us the range, on top of the possum. My job was to get underneath him and cut off the route to his hole, Marcus's job was to come down on top of him and Kerry was to come down on the far side so he wouldn't run in the opposite direction.'

The first night they tried this strategy they were too early; the possum was still making its way to the feeding ground and, when spotted, scampered back home. Their next visit, on another night, was an hour later.

'This time we caught the possum out feeding. My dog went directly to the possum's hole to prevent it returning, Kerry's dog came down through the middle and the possum – knowing it was surrounded – headed down to the beach and up on to a rock. Kerry's dog took him out on top of the rock.'

BOB CAIRNS

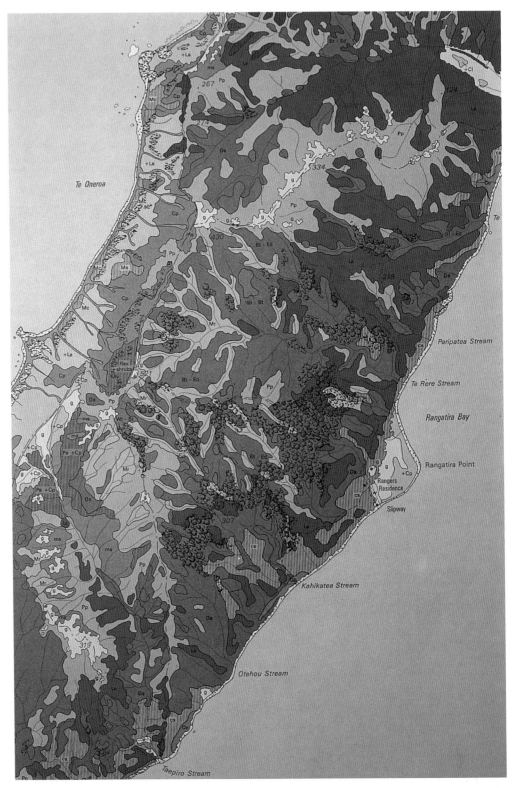

As the eradication campaign proceeded, it became clear that the island's vegetation was beginning to change. A record of the various species and their distribution would be an invaluable benchmark in the future, so a young scientist set out to describe and map the vegetation.

Stephen Fuller spent several years exploring the island and the map that resulted was informative and attractive. Several thousand copies were printed but a year or two afterwards the Department of Survey and Land Information, in accordance with Treasury advice, shredded all the remaining copies. It is now unobtainable.

LAND INFORMATION NEW ZEALAND

At last, 90 years after it became a sanctuary, Kapiti was close to realising the vision of generations of caretakers and conservationists. Yet, ironically, just when problems in the island's ecology were being solved, human relations on Kapiti reached an all-time low. During the 1970s and 1980s, the legacy of friendship between the Webbers and a succession of caretakers steadily evaporated. Perhaps this was inevitable

because life on Kapiti was now quite different. In the past, the caretaker and the Webbers had been neighbours on an isolated island. Each knew and sometimes depended on the other. When the Wilkinsons first came to Kapiti, for instance, they had a dangerously unreliable launch, known as the *Slug*, which frequently broke down, so the Webbers usually collected their groceries and mail from the mainland.[34]

The view to the south-west from the trig tower, 1998.

The different relationship was also caused by the changing nature of the Webber family. By the 1980s Hona and Utauta's family of five children had increased to more than 50 direct descendants, 30 of whom were great-grandchildren who had never known Waiorua in its prime. It was their birthright to come and go from their land on the island as they pleased and to invite friends and relatives to visit or stay on Kapiti. At times some of the family lived at Waiorua. Inevitably, with so many people involved, behaviour varied. Drunken parties and rubbish left lying around angered Rewa Webber, who remembered the bay in its heyday.[35]

The ranger, Peter Daniel, was also troubled by what he saw at Waiorua. He considered that the uncontrolled access of a growing number of people, who were not necessarily aware of the special nature of the island, was a threat to the bird life because of the increased risk of ship rats coming ashore. The island was already overrun by two other species of rat, the kiore and the Norway, but neither was as adept at climbing trees as the ship rat, which is lethal to birds. Should one pregnant ship rat slip onto the island it could mean the end of the sanctuary. Daniel was also worried about dogs being brought ashore, the number of new buildings being built at Waiorua (which increased the risk of rats coming onto Kapiti with building materials) and the risk of fires spreading to the reserve.

When Rewa Webber first visited the Webbers at Waiorua in 1936, their garden reminded her of the Botanical Gardens in Wellington. Looking back, more than 60 years later, her feelings are rather different: 'Now, it's heartbreaking. It's horrible. It's years since I've been there.'

On her last visit, in the early 1980s, she saw 'Beer bottles, paper, rubbish everywhere. Grandma Webber would have whipped them if she could have seen that.' She was so upset by the situation that she resolved to sell her land to the government but was prevented by the decision of the Maori Land Court.

In 1984 Daniel tried to arrange a meeting with the family through Jean Webber but she reported there was little interest in the idea. He later succeeded in arranging a special screening for the extended family of a Wildlife Service video about the invasion of Big South Cape Island by rats. Not everyone, he found, appreciated his educational campaign: 'one older landowner was incensed that I might even suggest that she would allow rats on to the private land, and consequently did not go to the viewing'.[36]

Daniel's ally in his dealings with the family was Jean Webber, a daughter-in-law of Utauta, who clearly remembered what Waiorua had once been. Now, when she went back to visit, she was saddened by the decline. On one occasion Peter Daniel accompanied her and later wrote of her reaction:

> She was so upset with the treatment that the private land had been receiving that she was almost in tears the whole time we were there. (The loss of the big pohutakawa trees, the bits of buildings attached to other buildings, the scruffy appearance of everything, rubbish heaped up everywhere.) No doubt the people who were doing it all would feel a great sense of achievement, but to her and to me the place looked little better than a slum – all the worse as both of us could remember clearly just how beautiful this area had been. She told me that she had told various members of the family that if they abused the property, they would lose it. She kept saying to herself, 'They have lost it.'[37]

In reality, neither Jean nor her sister-in-law, Rewa Webber, who shared her sadness at the state of the settlement, could influence what was happening at Waiorua. They were infrequent visitors and, in their absence, development continued. In 1985 three more slipways were built and soon afterwards the ranger reported another new project:

> An outdoor commercial freezer has now been erected on Piki Barrett's land at the north end so that an Otaki fisherman can carry out his operations using Kapiti Island as his

base. There are some days when Waiorua Bay reminds me a little of Ngawi, the fishing settlement on the south Wairarapa coast. I cannot help but think of rats on fishing boats.[38]

The ranger's close scrutiny did not go unnoticed, especially by Mike and Aromea Webber's daughter, Rarangi Howard, who resented these efforts to regulate what the family did on their private land. She made her displeasure plain at a formal meeting between the family and the Department of Lands and Survey and again, soon after, in a letter to the *Kapiti Observer*, in which she said: 'We are getting rather fed up with this man [Peter Daniel] who thinks he has the authority to ask us to tear up our slipways and even to tell us who we have in our homes on Kapiti Island'.[39]

Her use of 'we' implied unity but in fact there was considerable dissension among the landowners themselves. Several were keen to get the Waiorua block surveyed into individual titles. Rewa Webber would then be able to sell her share to the government so it could be added to the reserve, while Lorraine Spratt, Rangi Webber's daughter, and her husband, Bob, would be able to build a house on land they knew was their own. They were supported by Jim and Jack Webber, who also wanted to be able to identify a specific part of the land as theirs. Rewa Webber and Lorraine Spratt were opposed by the other two branches of the family. John Barrett, in particular, was worried that the partition would pave the way for the land to be sold to the Crown. In February 1989 the government offered him $85,000 for his share, presumably to encourage him to drop his opposition to the partition, but he declined it.

During his 22 years on Kapiti, Peter Daniel developed an interest in photographing the birds and pioneered a technique that enabled birds, such as the kakariki in this picture, to be recorded, frozen in flight.

In 1990 he was awarded a Queen's Service Medal for his photography and his contribution to the possum eradication programme.
PETER DANIEL

Six months later, Rewa Webber and Lorraine Spratt applied to the Maori Land Court for a partition order. In opposing the request, John Barrett tabled a management plan for the land with the court. It proposed:

> The establishment of a trust with a management structure comprising representatives from each branch of the family, with possible representation from Raukawa trustees and the Department of Conservation. The primary purpose of the trust is to assist in the retention of the block in Maori ownership. In addition, the principal objectives of the trust include co-operation with the Department of Conservation on conservation matters; the protection of all sacred and historical sites on the land and the traditional fishing areas around the Island; control over the use of the land for building or recreational or commercial purposes; and the encouragement of the use of the land for traditional Maori Arts and Crafts and cultural activities.[40]

When Judge H. B. Marumaru released his decision, it was clear that the management plan had been a crucial factor.

> Kapiti Island holds a special place in the history of the Parata family, and indeed in the history of the tribes which settled along the southern west coast of the North Island in the early 1800s. Waiorua Kapiti No. 6 of 30 acres is the last piece of land on the Island still owned by all of Utauta's descendants. In my view, the concern of the objectors to retain the whole block as one for development and protection under the management plan reflects a Maori customary preference which in this case must prevail over the wishes of some of the family for individual ownership.[41]

The decision to decline the request for partition was very significant for Kapiti. In effect, it ended the Crown's long campaign to acquire all of the island for the reserve and it meant the Department of Conservation (which took over the island in 1987) had to recognise that from then on, the private landowners at Waiorua would be a permanent part of the island.

Judge Marumaru's response was also an acknowledgment of the remarkable reversal of the prospects for Maori. More than 100 years before this case was considered, the Native Land Court had been established to partition communally owned Maori land so that it could be sold to European settlers. In 1990 the court's decision was exactly the opposite. In the interval, most Maori had lost their land and even those few who had managed to retain some of it had joined the migration to the cities in the years after the end of the Second World War.

In the urban environment, the disadvantaged position of Maori was far more obvious than it had been in the countryside. As the children of these post-war migrants grew older, they looked for redress. Central to their aspirations was the retention of remaining Maori-owned land, such as the block at Waiorua Bay. The Maori renaissance of the late 20th century also encouraged tribes to consider ways of regaining traditional land lost by confiscation or sale. Kapiti was a typical case. It had been taken by legislation against the wishes of its owners, who had made their attachment to the island plain at the time.

In 1988 Muaupoko filed a claim with the Waitangi Tribunal, which included Kapiti. The next year Ngati Raukawa, Ngati Toa and Te Ati Awa followed their example.[42] By 1991 six tribes had registered their interest in the island — a reflection of its long occupation by a succession of different groups. Not all these tribes accept that Ngati Toa has the strongest claim because Kapiti was part of the Ngati Toa empire at the time the treaty was signed. It may be some time before all these claims are heard, but it is possible that some of the island will be returned to Ngati

This view of Mount Taranaki from Tuteremoana illustrates the close association of Taranaki and Kapiti, which is evident in the history of the Te Ati Awa tribe.

During Ngati Toa's escape from Kawhia, Te Ati Awa gave them food and protection and some hapu also accompanied Ngati Toa when they continued their journey to the Horowhenua. Several later migrations added to the Te Ati Awa presence on the Kapiti Coast.

The main Te Ati Awa settlement was on the mainland but some also lived on Kapiti, especially at the northern end. When most of the tribe returned to Taranaki, those who remained continued their association with the island.

Today Ati Awa Ki Whakarongotai of Waikanae regard themselves and Ngati Toa as the kaitiaki, or guardians, of Kapiti.

Toa. Alternatively, if an injustice is acknowledged, it may be compensated with cash, as has happened in other treaty settlements.

This is, of course, only speculation, but it has already influenced the management of Kapiti. So has Judge Marumaru's decision. Since then, the landowners at the northern end, and the descendants of the Maori owners displaced in 1897, have played a crucial part in the two main initiatives of the 1990s: the establishment of the Kapiti Marine Reserve and the eradication of rats from the island. Both succeeded, in part, because of support by local iwi. In return, they have been given a much greater role on Kapiti. When birds are transferred to or from the island, for example, they are usually accompanied by local Maori, and rare birds are now routinely released at the north end.[43] In fact, because the people living there sometimes feed them, rare species are more visible at Waiorua than at Rangatira; takahe and weka are often seen near the houses and kaka and kereru perch in the surrounding trees.

Some of the Maori at Waiorua have been interested for some time in taking a greater part, commercially, in bringing visitors to the island. In 1976, advertisements for 'Kapiti Island Tours' to take visitors for day trips, fishing trips and weekend camps caused a flurry of concern at the Department of Lands and Survey. The tours were organised by John Barrett but since he planned to take visitors to the north end, and from there onto the reserve only if they had permits, the department was powerless to prevent him.[44] What Barrett offered was not new; he was merely reviving a practice of earlier times when the *Manaaki* took boatloads of visitors to Waiorua from Mahara House at Waikanae and the Hotel Majestic at Paraparaumu.

In 1989, the possibility of restoring the *Manaaki* and returning it to the Waiorua run was considered. The idea alarmed Peter Daniel. 'Another very disturbing change is occurring at Waiorua,' he reported.

The old totally abandoned slipway once used for the old motor launch *Manaaki* is going to be rebuilt, and *Manaaki* is to be put back in service. It means clearing all boulders and vegetation and installing new rails and a new winch system, and it also means that not only runabouts but a launch will be being brought from the mainland and pulled up on the island, thus increasing tenfold the chances of ships rats arriving on Kapiti.[45]

As it happened, the restoration did not eventuate, nor did another plan, to build a lodge on Crown land at the north end, but both were signs that some of the landowners were keen to be commercially involved.

The proposed lodge was for members of the public who wanted to stay overnight. Set in bush at the entrance to a secluded valley about 500 metres from Waiorua Bay, it would have accommodated 20 people. At present, visitors are not permitted to stay overnight. In the past, a polite letter to the Department of Lands and Survey indicating an interest in ornithology, or an invitation from the Webbers, gave a number of people the opportunity to hear the famous chorus of birds at dusk and dawn.

In 1952 Frank Simpson spent a night on the island and later wrote:

So I waited, impatiently, ears alert to every sound in the dark forest with its mysterious rustlings.

Slowly the bird songs emerged with the growing light before the clear sunrise, stumblingly at first like a great orchestra rehearsing.

The sun rose over the mainland, lighting the whole eastern bush face of Kapiti. All along the face were white patches denoting the breasts of fat pigeons preening themselves in the early sunlight, and there were smaller patches against the green of the forest, patches of purer white, darting about as white-tied tuis searched for morning nectar.

The noise grew, discordant for a time, then in a strange harmony. A thousand bellbirds tuned their cymbals to the famed chime-in-unison.

Pigeons added a throbbing base. Robins joined with shrill medleys and tuis provided throaty drum-beats. The forest awoke.

This was the dawn chorus of old, the chorus that once could be heard in every bay and on every tree-studded hilltop on the 500-mile coastline from Kapiti to the fiords of Western Southland, the chorus that civilization stamped out, and which civilization has now brought back to secluded Kapiti.[46]

During the 1960s, as the number of daytime visitors increased, the department became stricter and declined most requests for overnight stays. This did not, however, lessen the demand. In 1965 George Fox conducted a 'Gallup poll' of visitors as to the buildings they would like to see on the island and included the results in his annual report. 'You would be surprised how many people are in favour of extra buildings being erected so as to enable them to stay on the Sanctuary overnight. Some of them would be prepared to pay for the use of the buildings. Overall the general opinion of many, or most, of the visitors is that they can see no reason why they cannot camp at the Sanctuary.'[47] The department and its caretaker could see several reasons: the risk of fire, difficulty in providing water and removing sewage and also the problem of visitors being stranded by bad weather. Above all, the department considered the island was primarily a place for birds, not people.

Thirty years later, the demand remained. In 1996 Kapiti Waiorua Tours Limited announced plans for a lodge to be built on Crown land in 'recognition of latent

demand' based on a survey of visitors conducted two years earlier. A sample of 461 visitors had been asked if they were interested in staying on the island overnight and 61 per cent replied that they were.[48] The proposal created a furore, especially on the Kapiti Coast, where feeling about the island is strong. Critics were worried that the lodge would endanger the reserve by increasing the risk of reinvasion by rats; others found the idea of commercialising Kapiti abhorrent. Nearly all objected to the use of Crown land for such a purpose. The reason for siting the lodge there was that some of the owners did not want it at Waiorua. Rewa Webber was one: 'You open any area up to the public and, unless it is very strictly controlled, it will end up a pigsty. And that's exactly what Waiorua was like the last time I was there.'[49]

Because the proposed site was Crown land, Kapiti Waiorua Tours applied to the Commissioner of Crown Lands for permission to build. At the same time, a local group, Kapiti Island Watching Interest (KIWI), organised a petition opposing the proposal, which was signed by more than 13,000 people. It also lodged an application with the commissioner to have the Crown land at the north end (formerly the Webbers' farm) reclassified as nature reserve, as had been intended when the Crown acquired it in 1963.

The two applications brought the question of the competing claims of conservationists and Kapiti Island Maori to a head. Both had compelling cases and they seemed irreconcilable. To help him make a decision, the commissioner, Sam Brown, requested two reports: one to investigate the implications of the Treaty of Waitangi on Kapiti, and the other to analyse the likely environmental effects of the lodge. The latter confirmed a number of potentially damaging consequences,

Kapiti Waiorua Tours proposed building a lodge in a small, sheltered valley at the far end of the Okupe Lagoon.

in particular the risk of fire, the return of rats and an inadequate water supply. Even if these problems could be overcome, the probable demand for use of the lodge would almost double the number of visitors on the island.[50] This, on its own, was a serious issue, since part of Kapiti's attraction has always been its wilderness character.[51]

The implications of the treaty were not as clear-cut; more research was needed but, even so, the existence of arguable claims was evident. Should a claim be successful, the Crown land might be needed as part of a settlement and, for that reason, the land should not be reclassified – at least until the treaty process was complete.[52]

When the commissioner released his decision, the reasons for it were made clear:

> On balance there are more disadvantages (and risks) associated with the lodge application (on the Crown land) than there are reasons to support it. My conclusion is that in this specific case, the natural values of the island are so significant that they should be given greater weight, even to the extent that these values take priority over the possible Treaty argument that a Maori Kapiti Islander should be permitted to establish a lodge on the Crown land to provide an economic base for his whanau.

> My further conclusion is that there are prima facie Treaty issues to be investigated and the status of the land should not be changed irrevocably (to a nature reserve) until those issues have been considered and reported.[53]

The two applications were declined but the status of the land was altered, not to nature reserve, but to government purpose reserve (for wildlife management) as an interim measure, so that its day-to-day management could be transferred from Crown Lands to the Department of Conservation.

In essence, Brown's decision maintained the status quo. No lodge would be built, but neither would the land in question be irreversibly placed beyond its possible use in a treaty settlement. Opponents of the lodge breathed a sigh of relief, not knowing, perhaps, that a lodge had been operating informally at Waiorua for some years without any kind of official scrutiny. Although the Kapiti Waiorua Tours proposal worried many people, it was, at least, an operation that would have

Today visitors have the choice of travelling to Kapiti aboard either Te Aihe *(left) or* Kiwi Express *(right). The latter belongs to Ross Leger, who originally worked with John Barrett in the 1960s and 1970s, taking visitors across to the north end. He now shares the Department of Conservation concession with Kapiti Waiorua Tours, which is a joint venture between Te Ati Awa and Ngati Toa; the first major partnership between these groups since their alliance in the 1820s and 1830s.*

had to comply with the most exacting environmental safeguards. As a consequence of its rejection, those interested in providing accommodation turned their attention back to Waiorua, where freehold rights gave them a certain freedom. In 1999, at the time of writing, two proposals to provide accommodation were being considered.[54]

Some degree of Maori involvement in the commercial activities of the island seems inevitable. Already local iwi have a new boat on the run and Kapiti Waiorua Tours has a Department of Conservation concession to provide talks to visitors on their arrival. What other activities may involve Maori is not yet clear, but a new spirit of co-operation will be needed to take Kapiti into the new millennium. The Department of Conservation and iwi at Waiorua will have to work together, as they have done in the 1990s, but the relationship also involves the general public, for if any arrangement is to be successful in the long term, it will require widespread support.

That support may be some way off. A worrying divisiveness was apparent in 1997 when two separate occasions were organised to mark the centenary of Kapiti as a nature reserve: a commemoration on the island on 20 December and, two days later, a banquet at Southwards Museum. The former was arranged by local iwi and the Department of Conservation, the latter by the Kapiti Island Watching Interest group. Speaking at the KIWI function, Sam Brown made a plea for unity, which he repeated several months later. He intended to recommend to the Minister of Conservation that there be greater community involvement in the management of Kapiti Island: 'I have seen previously disparate groups pushing and pulling in different directions forced by community involvement to recognise a common direction. I am confident it can happen here.'[55]

The Commissioner of Crown Lands' comment echoed those of the government's representative, MP Tutekawa Wyllie, at the official event on the island:

> There are so many tribes and so many people throughout New Zealand who are looking to the Kapiti people as a model as to how we can move forward as a nation in protecting some of the beautiful spots we have left in New Zealand.

John Barrett of Kapiti Waiorua Tours talking to visitors on Kapiti, 1999. He sees the company's takeover of the introductory talks to visitors as a mutually beneficial arrangement. 'It releases DOC to its original scientific and monitoring role while establishing, through iwi participation, a cultural delivery of important information on conservation on the island.

'This marriage will also impact on the iwi. We have to "walk the talk", as the very same process that legitimises Maori with conservation, will demand that iwi safeguard this mana. We will have to protect our financial resource and our public responsibility as guardians of Kapiti's ecology.'

'We have to get it right. The fact that Kapiti is home to a national and international nature reserve has put the spotlight on us.'

There are a number of tribes looking at Ngati Toa, Te Ati Awa and Ngati Raukawa to see how they interrelate, to see how they fulfil their obligations. And there are a number of communities who are looking to the Kapiti community to see how you have managed to resolve differences in the wider interests of this beautiful treasure that we all have. I urge you, and encourage you, to continue to work together to protect this island. In the words of a Maori blessing 'may the shimmer and glisten of summer dance across your pathway'.[56]

One way to achieve this would be through the establishment of a guardians' group, kaitiaki of Kapiti. Little Barrier, Mana and Tiritiri Matangi Islands all have such groups, which involve volunteers in a variety of ways. More contact between concerned members of the public and local iwi might lead to greater understanding – a process which would also be assisted by a greater understanding of the island's past. Many of the people on the Kapiti Coast who object to attempts by island Maori to share some of the sanctuary's economic opportunities are recent arrivals, who do not always know of Kapiti's rich history before it became a nature reserve, or of the tradition of hospitality associated, in particular, with Waiorua Bay.

A kayak glides on a swell through a cathedral-like arch in a small island off Kapiti's south-western coast. Tamarillo Sea Kayaking began in 1997, with the assistance of John Barrett and the late Jack Webber who drowned in a boating accident near Kapiti in 1999. Founder Anthony Norris and his team of guides offer the more adventurous visitor an unusual experience of the island.

In a sense the situation on Kapiti reflects the challenge facing the nation at the end of the 20th century. Maori equity on Kapiti is minimal, only 12 hectares out of a total of 2000, which is roughly equivalent to Maori land ownership nationally. Yet it is Maori history and culture that gives the island much of its interest.

If unity on Kapiti can be found through knowledge and understanding,

Matiu Rei, chief executive of Ngati Toa (left), talks with New Zealand First MP, Tutekawa Wyllie, and other visitors to Kapiti after speeches to mark the island's centenary as a nature reserve.

In the early 1820s the Ngati Toa leader, Te Pehi, and a small group of warriors captured Kapiti when they surprised its Ngati Apa occupants. Most of the island remained in Ngati Toa possession until the government took it in 1897. Exactly a century later, Ngati Toa reconquered Kapiti, in a symbolic sense, when a series of carvings on the visitors' shelter were unveiled.

The Department of Conservation commissioned the carvings and asked that they depict atua such as Tane, the god of the forest, and Tangaroa, god of the sea. But when the three faces were unveiled at dawn on 20 December 1997 the moko were those of Te Rauparaha, Te Pehi and Nohorua – all Ngati Toa chiefs who lived on Kapiti.

then it may serve as an example to other communities facing the same issues. In the process, the island will return a double dividend – as an invaluable sanctuary for endangered species and as a model for the nation.

One of the pleasures of working on this book has been the people I have met in the course of researching it. I am grateful to the following people with an interest in the island who tolerated my tape recorder and camera and gave me information. For this, I thank Geoff Alexander, Tudor Atkinson, John Barrett, Fred (Boysie) Barrett, John Baxter, Bob Cairns, Nellie Carkeek, Amo Clark, Bill Collins, Marienne de Blois, Peter Daniel, Jean Dobson, Albie Edgington, Raewyn Empson, Diana Ferris, Frank and Betty Fitzgerald, Arnold and Jan Heine, Kevin Jones, Nancy Jordan, Ray Lovell, Sylvia Lovell, Colin Miskelly, Jim McIntyre, Syd Moore, Ani Parata, Bruce McFadgen, Bob Spratt and the late Lorraine Spratt, Alan Saunders, Hariata Ropata Tangahoe, Shane Treadwell, Joe Tukapua, Tony Walton, Jim Webber, Rewa Webber, Doug Williams, Wayne Williams and Geoff Wood.

This book would not have been possible without a familiarity with Kapiti which was developed during a number of exploratory trips. I am grateful to friends who accompanied me, not only for their companionship and ideas, but also for waiting patiently while photographs were taken. Garth Baker, Paul Blaschke, Paul Bradshaw, Toby Gee, Vladimir Halama, Josie Johnston, Chris Logan, Geoff Norman, Jock Phillips, Jeremy Rolfe, Pauline Rodgers, Paul Thompson, Alan Wehipeihana and Scott Wilson shared in many adventures.

Other people helped me by providing information and encouragement including Barbara Anderson, Olive Baldwin, Phil Barton, Grant Birkinshaw, Margaret Brown, Neil Brown (Waikanae Boating Club), Ron Brown, Kate Camp, Alistair Te Ariki Campbell, Ian Campbell, Chris Cochran, John Daniels, Murray Douglas, Tony Dreaver, Lois Easton, Scott Elliffe, Alan Esler, Peg Fleming, Blair Gibbs, Nici Gibbs, Isobel Gabites, Lindsay Gault, Sheila Hailstone, Rod Hay, Lois Hope, Ross Leger, Geoff de Lisle, Allan and Colleen MacIntyre, Jean Maclean, Gordon McKenzie, Warwick Marshall, Daphne Meyer (Otaki Historical Society), Tony Morgan, Allan Munro, Brenda Neill (Tararua Tramping Club), Barbara Perryman, Kath Petrie, Miria Pomare, Ron Pynenburg, Geoff Roberts, June Rowlands (Kapiti Environmental Action), Rosemary Rutherford, Reg Saunders, Diana Stidolph, Janet Suter, Geoffrey W. Swainson, Liz Treahy, Bryan Vickerman, the late Jack Webber and Dave Woodcock (Kaumatua Tramping Club).

Successful research often depends on the staff of libraries, government departments and independent agencies. My task was made easier by the assistance I received from the following members of the Alexander Turnbull Library: David Colquhoun, Marsha Donaldson, Margareta Gee, David Retter and Diane Woods (Archives and Manuscripts); Mary Cobledick and Kate Olsen (Cartographic Section); Walter Cook, Joan McCracken, Heather Mathie and John Sullivan (Photographs); Barbara Brownlie and Marian Minson (Drawings and Prints) and especially from Matiu Baker (Takawaenga-a-Rohe) whose contribution was invaluable.

I am also grateful to Scott Elliffe and Nigel Prickett (Auckland Institute and Museum); Bronwyn Dalley, Kathryn Hastings, Megan Hutching, Claudia Orange and Jock Phillips (Historical Branch, Department of Internal Affairs); Peter Burke (Kapiti Coast District Council); Martine Backhouse (Kapiti Public Library); Stephanie Allan, Nigel Canham, Teresa Cox and Jenny McDonald (Land Information New Zealand); Peter Ireland (National Library); Susanna Whiteman (National Institute of Water and Atmospheric Research); the Kaumatua Council, Ngati Toa; Pat Stodart (Porirua Museum); Athalie Dreadon and Ian Speden (Institute of Geological and Nuclear Sciences); Mike Kennedy (The Film Archive); Tony Fraser (Terralink); Tessa Barry (Waikanae Public Library) and Ben White (Waitangi Tribunal).

The following members of the Department of Conservation generously gave their time to increase my understanding of a number of issues: Andrew Baxter (Nelson), David Bishop, Te Waari Carkeek, Herb Christophers, Mark Coghlan, Ian Cooksley, Peter Daniel, Bruce Dix, Murray Douglas, Chris Edkins, Raewyn Empson, Kaye Green, Pearl Hewson, Kevin Jones, Michael Kelly, Bruce McFadgen, Colin Miskelly, Pim de Monchy, Richard Nester, Jeremy Rolfe, Hugh Robertson, Tony Walton, Ann Williams (Wellington) and Barbara Walter (Tiri Tiri Matangi).

I would also like to thank the following authors and publishers for permission to reproduce extracts from: *Pocket Collected Poems* by Alistair Te Ariki Campbell, Hazard Press, 1996; *Symmes Hole* by Ian Wedde, Penguin Books, 1986.

Joan Maclean read the initial draft; her suggestions made the text clearer and more concise. A number of people read and improved part, or all, of the final version. I am indebted to Ian Atkinson, Matiu Baker, Paul Blaschke, John Barrett, John Baxter, Alistair Te Ariki Campbell, Chris Cochran, Bill Collins, Peter Daniel, Bruce Dix, Raewyn Empson, Ross Galbreath, Diana Litton, Ray Lovell, Jim McIntyre, Shona Pengelly, Pauline Rodgers, Jeremy Rolfe, Jim Webber and Rewa Webber for their helpful suggestions and encouragement. Any errors are not theirs. Angie Guy typed the initial draft, and Diana Litton the final version with patience and a perceptive eye for the implausible. Anna Rogers edited the final draft, skilfully making it more accurate and readable.

Kapiti was designed by Margaret Cochran and Geoff Norman, who was also responsible for layout and print production. Margaret's strong sense of design did much to enhance *Kapiti* and I am particularly grateful to Geoff whose interest and ideas have added much to this book.

My greatest debts are to the Historical Branch of Internal Affairs, for providing the grant without which this book would not have been written; to my mother, Joan Maclean, for her editing and encouragement and to my partner, Pauline Rodgers, whose interest and support gave me the time to research and write *Kapiti*.

Many people allowed me to see their photo collections and to copy material, some of which is reproduced here. My thanks to Geoff Alexander, Barbara Anderson, Garth Baker, Olive Baldwin, Paul Bradshaw, John Barrett, Bob Cairns, Bill Collins, Peter Daniel, Jean Dobson, Stephanie Drew, Ray Lovell, Sylvia Lovell, Frank Fitzgerald, Arnold and Jan Heine, Coral Nicholl, the Otaki Historical Society, Howard and Nancy Smith, Bob Spratt, Diana Stidolph, the Tararua Tramping Club, Jim Webber and Rewa Webber.

I also acknowledge the help of Martine Backhouse (Kapiti Public Library), Stella Belliss (Landcare Research), Paul Bright and Debbie Francis (Waikanae Pharmacy Photo Lab), Nigel Canham (Land Information New Zealand), Isobel Gabites, Brian Groshinski, Ross Hansen (Wellington Photographic Supplies), Suzanne Knight (Museum of New Zealand/ Te Papa Tongarewa), Ferne McKenzie (Department of Conservation Image Library), Joyce Maclean, Anthony Norris (Tamarillo Sea Kayaking), Jeremy Rolfe (Department of Conservation), Marcia Shaw (Tinakori Gallery), Geoffrey W. Swainson and Scott Wilson.

Finally, my thanks to John Baxter, Anne and John Bevan Ford, Chris Edkins, David and Mary Hadfield, Sheila Hailstone, Nancy Jordan, Hamish and Jim McIntyre, Ivan Patterson, Caroline Phillips and Nigel Prickett, Bodhi Vincent, Gillian and John Thornley, Hariata Ropata Tangahoe, June Tilley, Barry Woods and Alan Wright and Marie O'Leary for permission to reproduce their drawings, music and paintings.

Except where otherwise stated, photographs were taken by Chris Maclean using a Yashica Fx-3 Super 2000 35 mm camera with 28 mm, 50 mm, 35-70 mm and 70-210 mm lenses, on Fujichrome 100 ASA film.

Images from the collections of the Alexander Turnbull Library and the Museum of New Zealand/Te Papa Tongarewa are identifiable by a reference number listed below:

Alexander Turnbull Library, National Library of New Zealand/Te Puna Mātauranga o Aotearoa
22 (F147893½), 43 (F73836½)), 56 (E-502-018), 61 (PUBL-0026-6-03), 105 (E-205-q-026), 107 (833aj [ca. 1780] Acc.422), 108 (A-255-019), 114 (105352½), 117 (PUBL-0011-04-2), 128 (PUBL-0029-271), 138 (F12¼MNZ), 142 (PUBL-0014-10), 150 (C-020-005), 155 (top) (½-015637-F), 155 (bottom) (½-015631-F), 158-9 (D-018-012), 161 (A-114-023), 162 (F18602⅓), 166 (G-20616⅓), 172 (F300¼MNZ), 174 (C-23025), 177 (C-22932), 179 (F37898½), 180 (F2798½), 183 (F112008½), 184 (F-161-35mm-D), 186 (F-96331-½), 193 (top) (F42994½), 193 (bottom) (F-188-35mm-C), 194 (F18377⅓), 195 (B-040-015), 199 (15037½), 202 (A-090-038), 207 (A-253-033), 212 (top) (F45121½), 212 (bottom) (F32147½), 214 (C22863), 230 (F52303½), 236 (MS Papers 0444-152), 259 (E-502-007), Back cover (A-292-051)

Museum of New Zealand/Te Papa Tongarewa
10 (B37105), 80 (B22216), 151 (B37509), 159 (B22202), 184-5 (B36764), 207 (B22214), 211 (A5910), 213 (top) (B22225), 213 (bottom) (A5789), 214 (B22219), 244-5 (B37029)

National Archives/Te Whare Tohu Tuhituhinga o Aotearoa (Head Office, Wellington)
120-1 (OLC1/43), 134-5 (OLC1/929), 206 (M27 MD3677), 213 (IA 1, 52/71)

BIBLIOGRAPHY

Key to Abreviations

AJHR   *Appendices to the Journal of the House of Representatives*
ATL   Alexander Turnbull Library
DSIR   Department of Scientific and Industrial Research
DOC   Department of Conservation
IA   Internal Affairs Department
LINZ   Land Information New Zealand
MAF   Ministry of Agriculture and Fisheries
MD   Marine Department
MONZ   Museum of New Zealand/Te Papa Tongarewa
MS   Manuscript Papers
NZPD   *New Zealand Parliamentary Debates*

Primary Sources

Adkin, G. L., Diary, January, February 1921, MONZ.

Aitken, Graeme, 'Kapiti Island – Overview of Treaty of Waitangi claims on Crown land', 1997.

Andersen, J. C., Diary 1924, 'Kapiti', MS-0053, ATL

Anonymous, 'Kapiti Island', MS papers 1101, ATL.

Atkinson, I. A. E., 'Kapiti Possum Study: Vegetation Surveillance 1978-1982', Botany Division, DSIR 1982.

Baxter, A. S., 'Kapiti Island: Sub-tidal Ecological Survey'; 'Kapiti Island: Marine Recreational Survey', Central Fishery Management, Internal Reports, 87/2, 87/3 1987, MAF.

Boffa Miskell, 'Assessment of Environmental Effects of Proposals on Crown Land at the Northern End of Kapiti Island', 1997.

Brown, Margaret, 'Andrew Brown of Kapiti', New Zealand Society of Genealogists, MS papers 4280, ATL.

Buchanan, J., Notes of a Ramble at Kapiti', MS papers 292, ATL.

Cairns, Bob, 'Notes on an Archaeological Survey on Kapiti Island, 1982-1987', Archaeology Section, Science and Technology Division, DOC (Wgtn).

Cockayne, L., 'Report of a Botanical Survey of Kapiti Island', *AJHR*, 1907, C-8.

Commissioner of Crown Lands, 'Report on applications for use of the Crown Land at the northern end of Kapiti Island', November 1997.

Cowan, James, 'Kapiti Island – Origin of the Name', MS papers 39(40), ATL.

Cowan, James, 'Kapiti Island', Report to the Tourist Department, *AJHR*, 1907, C-8a.

Cowan, P. E., 'A proposal for the eradication of possums for Kapiti Island', Ecology Division, DSIR, 1982.

Department of Conservation, Kapiti Caretakers Correspondence collection, 1912-1969, 1976-1989, DOC (Wgtn).

Department of Conservation, 'Kapiti Marine Reserve', Draft Conservation Management Plan, 1997.

Drummond, James, 'The Kapiti Island Bird Sanctuary', Annual Report of the Commissioner of Crown Lands, Appendix V, *AJHR*, 1908, C-1.

Elder, Norman, 'Waimahoe', MS papers 699, ATL.

Empson, Raewyn, 'The Eradication of Rats from Kapiti', Statement of Evidence, undated, DOC (Wgtn).

Field, H. A., Survey Notebooks, MS 740, 742, ATL.

Field, W. H., Letterbooks, Volumes 3, 4, 6, 13, 16, 19, 29 & 30, MS group 60, ATL.

Forest and Bird Society, Foundation Members, Obituaries, MS papers 116, 868, ATL.

Forest and Bird Society, Kapiti Island 1924-27, 1928-45, MS papers 0444/152, 152A, ATL.

Greville, R. P., 'Kapiti Island', SO plans 14958, 14959, 1912, LINZ (Wgtn).

Hansard, G. A., 'An account of the work of H.M.S. *Acheron* in New Zealand waters', MS 157, Hocken Library, University of Dunedin.

Henry, Richard, 'On Kapiti Island – Cats, Rats, Goats etc', 22 June 1911, MS papers 387, Hocken Library, University of Dunedin.

Hughes, G. W., Miscellaneous Papers, Olive Baldwin collection (courtesy of the late Colin Cochrane).

Internal Affairs Department, file 52/71, National Archives.

'Journal of the Reverend Octavius Hadfield, 1839', MS papers 896, ATL.

Kirk, H. B., 'Report on Kapiti Island as a Plant and Animal Sanctuary', 16 January 1919, Lands and Survey 4/53(1), DOC (Wgtn).

Knocks, J. A., Reminiscences of Early Wellington and Mana Island', MS papers 1117, ATL.

Lands and Survey Department, 'Kapiti Island', series 4/53 (Volumes 1-6), DOC (Wgtn).

Lands and Survey Department, Discussion Paper, 'Opossum Control, Kapiti Island', 1981, file 8/5/359/1, DOC (Wgtn).

Love, Ripeka Wharawhara, 'In Retrospect – Autobiographical Notes', MS papers 1162, ATL.

Lovegrove, Tim, 'Interim reports to the Wellington District Office of the Department of Lands and Survey on the present status of the Stitchbirds on the Kapiti Island Nature Reserve', 1983, 1984.

Lovell, Ray, 'Descendants of John Stanley Crighton Wilkinson', Ray Lovell Collection.

Lovell, Sylvia, Kapiti typescript, Ray Lovell Collection.

Maori Land Court, Aotea District, 'Chronology of Wairoua – Kapiti', 1998.

Maori Land Court, Aotea District, Minute Book, September 1990.

Maori Land Court, Otaki Minute Book No. 2, April 1874; No. 10, March 1890; Wairarapa Minute Book, April 1874.

Map of the Principal Triangulation in the Province of Wellington, 1872, ATL.

Matenga, Hemi, will.

Native Affairs Committee, Minutes of Evidence, *AJHR*, 1897, III, 1-3c.

New Zealand Parliamentary Debates, 100, 1897.

New Zealand Statutes, 'Kapiti Island Public Reserve Act', 1897, (28).

Old Land Claims, 1/43(37); 1/129(70a); 1/185(90) and 1/928(383a), National Archives.

Parata, Wiremu Te Kakakura, will.

Pracy, L. T., 'Opossums: Kapiti Island 1980', 7/5/2, DOC (Wgtn).

Rhodes, William Barnard, 'Log of the Eleanor, 1839-41', MS micro. 59, ATL.

Seddon, R. J., letters to Field, W. H., Field Family Papers, MS group 60, ATL.

Sheridan, P., Chief Native Land Purchase Officer, 'Return showing particulars in respect of the Island of Kapiti', *AJHR*, 1904, G-8.

Stidolph, R. D. H., Letters received from Kapiti caretakers (Bennett and Wilkinson), Diana Stidolph Collection.

Swan, Jamie, 'Creating a Sustainable Visitor Experience', Massey University, 1997.

Taylor, N. H., 'Map of Kapiti Island – showing Geology, Distribution of Bush and Sites of Historic Interest', 1929, ATL.

Taylor, Reverend Richard, 'Journal and Register of Baptisms, Marriages and Burials 1842, 1843', MS papers 2000, ATL.

Tourism Resource Consultants, 'Kapiti Island Nature Lodge', Concept Plan, 1995.

Wakefield, Colonel William, Diary 1839-1842, MS papers 2102, ATL.

Wakefield, E. J., Diary, MS papers 2208, ATL.

Wilkinson, A. S., Diary 1925-26; 'Kapiti Island Plants 1924-1942' and miscellaneous papers, Diana Stidolph Collection.

Wilkinson, A. S., Diary, 1927, MS 2403, ATL.

Secondary Sources

Articles

Bell, B. D., and Atkinson, I. A. E., 'Opossum Research on Kapiti Island', *Forest and Bird*, February 1976.

Best, Elsdon, 'The Land of Tara', *Journal of the Polynesian Society*, 26, 1918.

Bevan, Thomas, 'Reminiscences of an Old Colonist', *Otaki Historical Society, Journal*, (5) 1982.

Browne, Cyril, 'Bill Jenkins, Kapiti Coast Pioneer', *Otaki Historical Society, Journal*, (7) 1984.

Buller, Sir Walter, L., 'Notes on New Zealand Ornithology with an Exhibition of Specimens', *New Zealand Institute, Transactions and Proceedings*, (28), 1895.

Campbell, D. J., 'The Effects of Rats on Vegetation', in *The Ecology of Rodents in New Zealand Nature Reserves*, Department of Lands and Survey, Information Series No. 4, 1978.

Dingwall, Paul R., 'Harry Ell's Vision in Nature Conservation', *Landscape*, (10) 1981.

Esler, A. E., 'The Vegetation of Kapiti Island', *New Zealand Journal of Botany*, (5) 1967.

Fuller, Stephen, 'A History of the Flora and Introduced Fauna on Kapiti Island', in Baldwin, Olive (ed.), *The Celebration History of the Kapiti District*, Kapiti Borough Council, 1988.

Galbreath, Ross, 'Founding Forest and Bird – The First Meeting', *Forest and Bird*, February 1998.

Gregorie, David, 'Jurassic Island', *Kapiti Observer*, 1 September 1997.

Johnston, Judith, 'The New Zealand Bush: Early Assessments of Vegetation', *New Zealand Geographer*, 37(1) 1981.

Jolly, Jim, 'Little Spotted Kiwi: Paradise Regained or Paradise Lost', *Forest and Bird*, 16(1) 1985.

Joyce, Horiana and Dennis, Jonathan, 'The Singing Tahiwis', *Otaki Historical Society Journal*, (21) 1998.

Moore, P. R., and Francis, D. A., 'Geology of Kapiti Island, Central New Zealand', *New Zealand Geological Survey*, Record, 28, 1988.

Rippon, Peter, 'A Survey of Kapiti Island', *Dive*, 9(6) 1987.

Roche, M. M., 'Securing Representative Areas of New Zealand's Environment; Some Historical and Design Perspectives', *New Zealand Geographer*, 37(2) 1981.

Books

Adkin, G. L., *Horowhenua*, Department of Internal Affairs, 1948.

Alpers, Antony, *Maori Myths and Tribal Legends*, Longman Paul, 1985.

Arnold, Rollo, *New Zealand's Burning: The Settlers' World in the Mid 1880s*, Victoria University Press, 1994.

Baldwin, Olive (ed), *The Celebration History of the Kapiti District*, Kapiti Borough Council, 1988.

Baldwin, Olive, *Weka Rescue*, Fields Publishing House, 1997.

Barratt, Glynn, *Bellingshausen – A Visit to New Zealand: 1820*, Dunmore Press, 1979.

Barrett, Alfred, *The Life of the Rev. John Hewgill Bumby*, John Mason, London, 1843.

Belich, James, *Making Peoples – A History of the New Zealanders*, Allen Lane – and the Penguin Press, 1996.

Bishop, Nic, *Natural History of New Zealand*, Hodder & Stoughton, 1992.

Buick, T. L., *An Old New Zealander*, Whitcombe & Tombs, 1911.

Buller, Sir Walter, *A History of the Birds of New Zealand*, edited by E. G. Turbott, Whitcombe & Tombs, 1974.

Burns, Patricia, *Fatal Success – A History of the New Zealand Company*, Heinemann Reed, 1989.

Burns, Patricia, *Te Rauparaha – A New Perspective*, A. H. & A. W. Reed, 1980.

Campbell, Alistair Te Ariki, *Pocket Collected Poems*, Hazard Press, 1996.

Carkeek, W. C., *The Kapiti Coast*, A. H. & A. W. Reed, 1966.

Cowan, James, *Pictures of Old New Zealand: The Partridge Collection of Maori Paintings*, Whitcombe & Tombs, 1930.

Day, Kelvin, *Shore Whaling*, Porirua Museum History Series (1) 1986.

Dieffenbach, Ernst, *Travels in New Zealand*, John Murray, 1843.

Downs, T. W., *Old Whanganui*, Parkinson & Co., 1915.

Gabites, Isobel, *Wellington's Living Cloak – A Guide to the Natural Plant Communities*, Wellington Botanical Society and Victoria University Press, 1993.

Galbreath, Ross, *Walter Buller – The Reluctant Conservationist*, GP Books, 1989.

Galbreath, Ross, *Working for Wildlife – A History of the New Zealand Wildlife Service*, Bridget Williams Books and the Historical Branch, Department of Internal Affairs, 1993.

Heath, Barbara and Balham, Helen, *The Paremata Story*, Paremata Residents Association, 1994.

Hill, Susanne and John, *Richard Hill of Resolution Island*, John McIndoe, 1987.

King, Michael, *The Collector : Andreas Reischek – A Biography*, Hodder & Stoughton, 1981.

Maclean, Chris and Joan, *Waikanae – past and present*, Whitcombe Press, 1988.

Maclean, Chris, *Tararua – the story of a mountain range*, Whitcombe Press, 1994.

McEwan, J. M., *Rangitane – A Tribal History*, Reed Methuen, 1986.

McNab, Robert, *Historical Records of New Zealand*, Government Printer, 1908-14.

McNab, Robert, *The Old Whaling Days*, Golden Press, 1975 (original edition 1913).

Montresor, C. A., *Leaves from Memory's Log-Book*, Allen, London, 1887.

Orange, Claudia, *The Treaty of Waitangi*, Allen & Unwin and the Port Nicholson Press, 1987.

Phillips, W. J., *The Book of the Huia*, Whitcombe & Tombs, 1963.

Rogers, Lawrence, M., (ed), *The Early Journals of Henry Williams*, New Zealand 1826-40, Pegasus Press, 1961.

Sherley, G. H., *Eradication of Brushtail Possums on Kapiti Island, New Zealand: Techniques and Methods*, Department of Conservation Science and Research Series, (46), 1992.

Simcox, F. S., *Otaki*, A. H. & A. W. Reed, 1952.

Simmons, D. R., *The Great New Zealand Myth*, A. H. & A. W. Reed, 1976.

Smith, S Percy, *Maori History of the Taranaki Coast*, Memoir of the Polynesian Society, 1910.

Stevens, Graeme, *Lands in Collision – Discovering New Zealand's Past Geography*, Science Information Publishing Centre, 1985.

Stevens, Graeme, *On Shaky Ground – A Geological Guide to the Wellington Metropolitan Region*, Geological Society of New Zealand, Guidebook No. 10, 1991.

Te Rauparaha, Tamihana, *Life and Times of Te Rauparaha*, (ed.) Peter Butler, Alister Taylor, 1980.

Towns, D. R., Daugherty, C. H., and Atkinson, I. A. E. (eds), *Ecological Restoration of New Zealand Islands*, Conservation Science Publication No. 2, DOC, 1990.

Travers, W. T. L., *The Stirring Times of Te Rauparaha*, Whitcombe & Tombs, 1906.

Wakefield, E. J., *Adventure in New Zealand*, John Murray, 1845.

Wedde, Ian, *Symmes Hole*, Penguin Books, 1986.

Wilkinson, A. S., and the late Amy, *Kapiti Bird Sanctuary – A Natural History of the Island*, Masterton Printing Company, 1952.

Wilkinson, Amy, *Kapiti Diary*, Masterton Printing Company, 1957.

Wilson, James, G., *Early Rangitikei*, Whitcombe & Tombs, 1914.

REFERENCES

INTRODUCTION
SANCTUARY OF SPIRITS

1 Campbell, Alistair Te Ariki, *Pocket Collected Poems*, Hazard Press, 1996.

2 Daugherty, C. H., Towns, D. R., Atkinson, I. A. E., and Gibbs, G. W., 'The Significance of the Biological Resources of New Zealand Islands for Ecological Restoration' in Towns, Daugherty and Atkinson (eds), *Ecological Restoration of New Zealand Islands*, Conservation Science Publication No. 2, Department of Conservation, 1990, pp. 9-21.

3 *Kapiti Mail*, 21 November 1996; conversation with Marienne de Blois, 22 January 1998 (tape).

4 Conversation with Syd Moore, 4 August 1997 (tape).

5 Love, Ripeka Wharawhara, 'In Retrospect – Autobiographical Notes', MS papers 1162, ATL.

6 Lovell, Sylvia, Kapiti typescript, 'Storm', Ray Lovell Collection.

7 Pascoe, Sara, to the author, 8 March 1998.

8 Fox, G. F., to the Commissioner of Crown Lands, 8 Decembner 1961, Kapiti Caretakers Correspondence Collection, DOC (Wgtn).

9 *Evening Post*, 18 December 1997.

10 *Kapiti Observer*, 26 March 1959.

11 *Ibid.*, 17 October 1973.

12 Director-General, Department of Lands and Survey, Memo, 'Kapiti Island', 14 March 1984, file 7/5/2(3), DOC (Wgtn).

13 *Evening Post*, 13 March 1997.

14 Elder, Norman, 'Waimahoe', MS papers 699, ATL, p. 213.

CHAPTER ONE
THE SHAPE OF THE LAND

1 Alpers, Antony, *Maori Myths and Tribal Legends*, Longman Paul, 1985, p.138.

2 'Simmons, D. R., *The Great New Zealand Myth*, A. H. & A. W. Reed, 1976, pp. 21, 30.

3 Conversation with Peter Daniel, 11 May 1997 (tape).

4 Moore, P. R. and Francis, D. A., 'Geology of Kapiti Island, Central New Zealand', *New Zealand Geological Survey, Record 28*, 1988, p.13.

5 Cockayne, L., 'Report on a Botanical Survey of Kapiti Island', *AJHR*, 1907, C-8, pp. 14, 15.

6 Worthy, T. H. and Holdaway, R. N., 'Quaternary fossil faunas from caves in Takaka Valley and on Takaka Hill, northwest Nelson, South Island, New Zealand', *Journal of the Royal Society of New Zealand*, 24(3) September 1994, p. 365, 366.

7 Anonymous, 'Kapiti Island', MS papers 1101, ATL; and Buchanan, J., 'Notes of a Ramble at Kapiti', MS papers 292, p. 3, ATL.

8 J. L. Bennett to R. Stidolph, 1 June, 30 June 1917, Diana Stidolph Collection.

9 Stevens, Graeme, *On Shaky Ground – A Geological Guide to the Wellington Metropolitan Region*, Geological Society of New Zealand, Guidebook No. 10, 1991, p. 102.

10 Stevens, Graeme, *Lands in Collision – Discovering New Zealand's Past Geography*, Science Information Publishing Centre, 1985, pp. 104, 110.

11 Stevens, *On Shaky Ground, op. cit.*, p. 102.

12 *Ibid.* pp. 102, 103.

CHAPTER TWO
THE WITHERING BLAST

1 Adkin, G. L. 'On the nomenclature of the Waikanae River, Western Wellington', *Journal of the Polynesian Society*, 50(4) December 1941, p. 238.

2 Stevens, Graeme, *On Shaky Ground – A Geological Guide to the Wellington Metropolitan Region*, Geological Society of New Zealand, Guidebook No. 10, 1991, p. 102.

3 Carkeek, W. C. *The Kapiti Coast*, A. H. & A. W. Reed, 1966, p. 1.

4 Commissioner of Crown Lands, H. W. Mackintosh, to A. S. Wilkinson, 13 March 1939, includes an account of the battle attributed to Hari Wi Katene, a Ngati Toa elder, Diana Stidolph Collection.

5 Te Rauparaha, Tamihana, *Life and Times of Te Rauparaha*, Peter Butler (ed.), Alister Taylor, 1980, p. 42.

6 Wakefield, Colonel William, Diary, 1839-42, MS papers 2102, pp. 83, 84, 89, 90, ATL.

7 Wakefield E. J., *Adventure in New Zealand*, John Murray, 1845, Volume One, p. 131 (facsimile edition, Wilson & Horton, undated).

8 Taylor, Rev. Richard, 'Journal and Register of Baptisms, Marriages and Burials 1842, 1843', MS papers 2000, p. 15, ATL.

9 Wilkinson, Amy, *Kapiti Diary*, Masterton Printing Co. Ltd, 1957, p. 129.

10 Lovell, Sylvia, 'Storm', Kapiti typescript, Ray Lovell Collection.

11 McNab, Robert, *The Old Whaling Days*, Golden Press, 1975 (original edition 1913), pp. 154, 155.

12 Caretakers Annual Report for the year ending 31 March 1934, Kapiti Caretakers Correspondence, DOC (Wgtn).

13 Caretakers Report for July 1939, Kapiti Caretakers Correspondence, DOC (Wgtn).

14 Conversation with Raewyn Empson, Technical Support Officer, Wellington Conservancy, Department of Conservation, 10 November 1997 (tape one); Gabites, Isobel, *Wellington's Living Cloak – A Guide to the Natural Plant Communities*, Wellington Botanical Society and Victoria University Press, 1993, p. 87.

CHAPTER THREE
A VERY VIGOROUS VEGETATION

1 Stevens, Graeme, *Lands in Collision – Discovering New Zealand's Past Geography*, Science Information Publishing Centre, 1985, p. 110.

2 Adkin, G. L. *Horowhenua*, Department of Internal Affairs, 1948, p. 112.

3 Dieffenbach, Ernst, *Travels in New Zealand*, John Murray, 1843, p. 108.

4 Wakefield, E. J., *Adventure in New Zealand*, John Murray, 1845, Volume One, pp. 400, 401 (facsimile edition, Wilson & Horton, undated).

5 Wakefield, Colonel William, Diary 1839-42, 'Extract from Report of Committee on New Zealand', p. 18, MS papers 2102, p. 18, ATL: Rhodes, William Barnard, 'Log of the *Eleanor* 1839-41', 31 October 1839, MS Micro.59, ATL; Wakefield, E. J, *op. cit.*, p. 56.

6 Wakefield, E. J., *op. cit.*, p. 400.

7 Sheep were brought to Mana Island in 1834 by John Bell of Sydney, see McNab, Robert, *The Old Whaling Days*, Golden Press, 1975, p. 71. Some were later taken to Kapiti, see Knocks, John A, 'Reminiscences of Early Wellington and Mana Island, 1832-1840', MS papers 1117, p. 2, ATL.

8 Fuller, Stephen, 'A History of the Flora and Introduced Fauna on Kapiti Island', in Olive Baldwin (ed.), *The Celebration History of the Kapiti District*, Kapiti Borough Council, 1988, p. 260; Buchanan, J., 'Notes of a Ramble at Kapiti', MS papers 292, ATL.

9 Greville R. P., 'Kapiti Island', Survey Office Plans 14958 and 14959, Land Information New Zealand, Wellington Office.

10 Department of Lands, Memorandum 13557, 1 November 1911, in Kapiti Caretakers Correspndence, DOC (Wgtn).

11 Fuller, *op. cit.*, p. 261.

12 Cockayne, L., 'Report on a Botanical Survey of Kapiti Island', *AJHR*, 1907, C-8, p. 15.

13 Under-Secretary, Department of Lands and Survey to J. L. Bennett, 3 July 1913, in Kapiti Caretakers Correspondence Collection, *op. cit.*

14 Elder, Norman, 'Waimahoe', MS papers 699, p. 210, ATL.

15 Fuller, *op. cit.*, p. 261.

16 Assistant Under-Secretary, Department of Lands and Survey to J. L. Bennett, 26 November 1914, in Kapiti Caretakers Correspondence Collection, *op. cit.*

17 *Ibid.* (This was an early conservation organisation which had no connection with the Royal Forest and Bird Society, founded in 1923.)

18 *New Zealand Gazette*, No. 93, 31 August 1916, p. 2891.

19 O'Neill to Bennett, *op. cit.*, 29 November 1917.

20 O'Neill to Bennett, 18 July 1917; Brodrick to Bennett, 29 January 1918, Kapiti Caretakers Correspondence Collection, *op. cit.*

21 Wilkinson, A. S. and the late Amy, *Kapiti Bird Sanctuary – A Natural History of the Island*, Masterton Printing Co. Ltd, 1952, p. 29.

22 *Ibid.*

23 Adkin, G. L., Diary, 25 February 1921, MONZ (goats); Fuller, *op. cit.*, p. 260 (cattle and sheep).

24 Wilkinson, *op. cit.*, p. 30.

25 *Ibid.*

26 A. S. Wilkinson to L. D. Haggett, Secretary, Native Plant Preservation Society, 29 August 1939, Kapiti Caretakers Correspondence Collection, DOC (Wgtn).

27 Gabites, Isobel, *Wellington's Living Cloak – A Guide to the Natural Plant Communities*, Wellington Botanical Society and Victoria University Press, 1993, p. 91.

28 Cockayne, *op. cit.*, p. 15.

29 Reeves, W. P., *New Zealand*, Adam & Charles Black, 1908, p. 191.

30 Wilkinson to Haggett, *op. cit.*

31 This figure appears to be an extrapolation of data based on possum research in the Orongorongo Valley as described in Robert Brockie, *A Living New Zealand Forest*, David Bateman, 1992, p. 76.

32 Conversation with Colin Miskelly, Technical Support Manager, Wellington Conservancy, Department of Conservation, 20 November 1998.

CHAPTER FOUR
A GLIMPSE OF GONDWANA

1 Converstion with Colin Miskelly, Technical Support Manager, Wellington Conservancy, Department of Conservation, 3 November 1997 (tape).

2 Bishop, Nic, *Natural History of New Zealand*, Hodder & Stoughton, 1992, p. 10.

3 Holdaway, R. N. and Worthy, T. H., *New Zealand Geographic*, 12, 1991.

4 *Ibid.*, p.18.

5 Stevens, G., McGlone, M., and McCulloch, B., *Prehistoric New Zealand: The Birds*, Heinemann Reed, 1988, pp. 97-99.

6 Wakefield, Jerningham, E, *Adventure in New Zealand*, Volume One, John Murray, 1845, p. 423 (facsimile edition, Wilson & Horton, undated).

7 *Ibid.*, p.58 (kereru), p.81 (tui), p. 228 (pukeko), p. 259 (kaka).

8 *New Zealand Heritage*, Hamlyn House, 1978, p. 659.

9 Hill, Susanne and John, *Richard Henry of Resolution Island*, John McIndoe, 1987, p. 288.

10 Wilkinson, A. S. and the late Amy, *Kapiti Island Bird Sanctuary – A Natural History of the Island*, Masterton Printing Co. Ltd, 1952, p. 34; conversation with Colin Miskelly, *op. cit.*

11 Drummond, James, 'The Kapiti Island Bird Sanctuary', Annual Report of the Commissioner of Crown Lands (Appendix V), *AJHR*, 1908, C-1, p. 83.

12 Hill, Susanne and John, *op. cit.*, p. 310.

13 *Ibid.*, pp. 308, 309.

14 Wilkinson, *op. cit.*, p. 32.

15 *Ibid.*, p. 33.

16 *Ibid.*, p. 48.

17 Jolly, Jim, 'Little Spotted Kiwi: Paradise Regained or Paradise Lost?', *Forest and Bird*, 16(1) 15-17, February 1985.

18 Wilkinson, *op. cit.*, pp. 34, 35.

19 *Ibid.*, p. 36.

20 *Ibid.*, p. 86.

21 Converstion with Raewyn Empson, Technical Support Officer, Department of Conservation, Wellington Conservancy, 10 November 1997 (tape one).

22 Conversation with Shane Treadwell, 10 April 1997 (tape).

23 Empson, Raewyn, 'The Eradication of Rats from Kapiti', Statement of Evidence (undated), p. 10.

24 *Ibid.*, p. 15.

25 Baldwin, Olive, *Weka Rescue*, Fields Publishing House, 1997, p. 10.

26 Ian Logan, General Manager of Animal Control Products, to the author, May 1997.

27 Raewyn Empson (tape), *op. cit.*

28 Converation with Alan Saunders, Mainland Island Ecologist, Department of Conservation, 28 October 1997 (tape).

29 Logan, *op. cit.*

30 Miskelly, *op. cit.*

31 Gregorie, David, 'Jurassic Islands', *Kapiti Observer*, 1 September 1997.

CHAPTER FIVE
THE NEW FRONTIER

1 Buchanan, J., 'Notes of a Ramble at Kapiti', MS papers 292, ATL.

2 Kapiti Marine Reserve, Draft Conservation Management Plan, Department of Conservation, November 1997, p. 9.

3 Rippon, Peter, 'A Survey of Kapiti Island', *Dive*, 9 (6) 12-15, 1987.

4 Baxter, A. S., 'Kapiti Island: Sub-Tidal Ecological Survey', 1987. Ministry of Agriculture and Fisheries, Central Fishery Management Area (Napier), Internal Report No. 87/2; 'Kapiti Island: Marine Recreational Survey', 1987, *ibid.*, No. 87/3.

5 *Kapiti Observer*, 28 September 1987.

6 Baxter, 87/2, *op. cit.*

7 Conversation with Peter Daniel, 14 February 1997 (tape one).

8 *Kapiti Observer*, 29 January 1979.

9 *Otaki-Waikanae Weekly News*, 27 March 1958.

10 Baldwin, Olive (ed.), *The Celebration History of the Kapiti District*, Kapiti Borough Council, 1988, p. 270.

11 Conversation with Nolan Best, 24 February 1987 (tape).

12 *Otaki-Waikanae Weekly News*, 5 December 1957.

13 *Otaki-Waikanae Weekly News*, 6 February 1958.

14 *Ibid.*

15 Marine Reserves Act, 1971 (long title).

16 *Marine Reserves*, Department of Conservation Information Paper, October 1995, p. 8.

17 *Kapiti Mail*, 27 November 1991.

18 *Marine Reserves*, *op. cit.*, p. 7.

19 Kapiti Marine Reserve, Draft Conservation Management Plan, *op. cit.*, Appendix 7.

20 *Ibid.*, p. 13.

21 *Kapiti Observer*, 16 June 1997.

22 *Kapiti Observer*, 23 June 1997.

CHAPTER SIX
MOTU RONGONUI

1 McEwen, J. M., *Rangitane – A Tribal History*, Reed Methuen, 1986, pp. 13, 21.

2 *Ibid.*, pp. 14, 24; Ballara, Angela, 'The Occupation of Te Whanganui a Tara', in *The Making of Wellington*, David Hamer and Roberta Nicholls (eds), Victoria University Press, 1990, p. 13.

3 Best, Elsdon, 'The Land of Tara,' *Journal of the Polynesian Society*, Volume 26, 1918, pp. 1, 2, 6.

4 Reed A. W., *A Dictionary of Maori Place Names*, A. H. & A. W. Reed, 1974, p. 38.

5 McEwen, *op. cit.*, pp. 24, 25; conversation with Joe Tukapua, 16 May 1997 (tape).

6 Williams, Herbert, *A Dictionary of the Maori Language*, Government Printer, 1971, p. 96.

7 Carkeek, W. C., *The Kapiti Coast*, A. H. & A. W. Reed, 1966, p. 159.

8 Williams, *op. cit.*

9 Cowan, James, 'Kapiti Island – Origin of the Name' (Information from Hone Wairere, 1911), MS papers 39, Item 40, ATL.

10 McEwen, *op. cit.*, p. 38.

11 *Ibid.*, pp. 39, 40; Carkeek, *op. cit.*, p. 160.

12 Belich, James, *Making Peoples – A History of the New Zealanders*, Allen Lane and the Penguin Press, 1996, pp. 130-133

13 Ballara, *op. cit.*, pp. 9, 10.

14 Wi Parata at the Ngarara Hearing, Maori Land Court, 1890, as quoted in Carkeek, *op. cit.*, p. 10.

15 Barratt, Glynn, *Bellingshausen – A Visit to New Zealand: 1820*, Dunmore Press, 1979, p. 46.

16 Te Rauparaha, Tamihana, *Life and Times of Te Rauparaha*, Peter Butler (ed.), Alister Taylor, 1980, p. 10.

17 Maori Land Court, Otaki Minute Book No. 2, 1 April 1874, p. 437.

18 Burns, Patricia, *Te Rauparaha – A New Perspective*, A. H. & A. W. Reed, 1980, p. 11.

19 Carkeek, *op. cit.*, p. 17.

20 Travers, W. T. L., *The Stirring Times of Te Rauparaha*, Whitcombe & Tombs, 1906, p. 110.

21 Maori Land Court, *op. cit.*, p. 438.

22 Smith, S. Percy, 'Maori History of the Taranaki Coast', *Memoir of the Polynesian Society*, Volume One, 1910, p. 397.

23 Te Rauparaha, *op. cit.*, p. 29.

24 Testimony of Ropata Hurumutu and Rapihana Te Otaota, Maori Land Court, Otaki Minute Book, No. 2, Rangatira – Kapiti No. 4, 18 April, and 20 April 1874.

25 Smith, *op. cit.*, pp. 397, 398.

26 This explanation, attributed to Hari Wi Katene of Ngati Toa, was described by H. W. Mackintosh, the Commissioner of Crown Lands, in the letter to A. S.

Wilkinson, 13 March 1939, p. 6, Diana Stidolph Collection.

27 Downes. T. W. *Old Whanganui*, Parkinson & Co., 1915, pp. 139-144.

28 Cowan, James, *Pictures of Old New Zealand: The Partridge Collection of Maori Paintings*, Whitcombe & Tombs, 1930, p. 186.

29 Taylor. N. H., 'Map of Kapiti Island – Showing Geology, Distribution of Bush and Sites of Historic Interest', 1929, ATL.

30 Cowan, James, 'Kapiti Island', Report to the Tourist Department, *AJHR*, 1907, C-8a, p. 3.

CHAPTER SEVEN
AN ISLAND EMPIRE

1 Te Rauparaha, Tamihana, *The Life and Times of Te Rauparaha*, Peter Butler (ed.), Alister Taylor, 1980, p. 33.

2 *Ibid.*

3 McNab, Robert, *The Old Whaling Days*, Golden Press, 1975, p. 161.

4 'Huge task to return heads, says expert' (David Simmonds), *Evening Post*, 19 August 1997, p. 2.

5 Carkeek, *op. cit.*, p. 47.

6 McNab, Robert, *Historical Records of New Zealand*, Government Printer, 1908-1914, Volume One, p. 635.

7 Welch, Denis, 'Where the Whales Are', *Listener*, 10 May 1997, p. 26.

8 Wakefield, E. J., *Adventure in New Zealand*, Whitcombe & Tombs, 1955, p. 146.

9 McNab, *op. cit.*, p. 10.

10 *Ibid.*, p. 5.

11 *Ibid.*, p. 13.

12 *Ibid.*, p. 10.

13 Old Land Claim 1-43 (37), National Archives.

14 Wakefield. E. J., *Adventure in New Zealand*, John Murray, 1845, Volume One, p. 125 (facsimile edition, Wilson & Horton, undated).

15 Knocks, John A., 'Reminiscences of Early Wellington and Mana Island', ATL, MS papers 1117, p. 3, ATL.

16 Buick, T. L., *An Old New Zealander*, Whitcombe & Tombs, 1911, p. 198.

17 Testimony of Edward Bolton, Maori Land Court, Ngarara, 5 March 1890, Otaki Minute Book No. 10, p. 410.

18 Burns, *op. cit.*, p. 134.

19 McNab, *The Old Whaling Days, op. cit.*, pp. 15-17.

20 Te Rauparaha, *op. cit.*, p. 36.

21 Burns, Patricia, *Te Rauparaha – A New Perspective*, A. H. & A. W. Reed, 1980, pp. 158, 159.

22 Te Rauparaha, *op. cit.*, pp. 40-42.

23 Campbell, Alistair Te Ariki, *Pocket Collected Poems*, Hazard Press, 1996, p. 59.

24 McNab, *The Old Whaling Days, op. cit.*, p. 18.

25 *Ibid.*, pp. 36, 37 and Appendix A.

26 Montrésor. C. A., *Leaves from Memory's Log-Book*, Allen, 1887, p. 70; McNab, *The Old Whaling Days, op. cit.*, p. 18.

27 McNab, *The Old Whaling Days, op. cit.*, p. 159.

28 Stack, Rev. W. J., as quoted in Burns, *op. cit.*, p. 171.

CHAPTER EIGHT
THE CRUCIBLE

1 Carkeek. W. C., *The Kapiti Coast*, A. H. & A. W. Reed, 1966, pp. 162, 165.

2 'Shore Whaling', Porirua Museum History Series (compiled by Kelvin Day), No 1., 1986, p. 7.

3 Wakefield, E. J., *Adventure in New Zealand*, John Murray, 1845, Volume One, p. 329 (facsimile edition, Wilson & Horton, undated).

4 Wilson, James G., *Early Rangitikei*, Whitcombe & Tombs, 1914, pp. 1, 2.

5 'The passing of an old whaler – death of Mr Stenton Workman', *Evening Post*, 23 May 1904.

6 Old Land Claims OLC – 1/185, Case 90, Final Report (Enclosures 1, 2 and 4). National Archives.

7 Burns, Patricia (ed. Henry Richardson), *Fatal Success – A History of the New Zealand Company*, Heinemann Reed, 1989, pp. 84-87.

8 Wakefield, E. J., *op. cit.*, p. 110, 111.

9 *Ibid.*, p. 129, 130.

10 Knocks, John. A. 'Reminiscences of Early Wellington and Mana Island 1832-1840', MS papers 1117, p. 5, ATL.

11 Wakefield, Colonel William, Diary, 1839-1842, MS papers 2102, p. 159, ATL.

12 Wedde, Ian, *Symmes Hole*, Penguin Books, 1986, p. 192.

13 Old Land Claims OLC – 1/129, Case 70a, Final Report (Enclosure 3), National Archives.

14 Knocks, *op. cit.*, p. 2; McNab, *The Old Whaling Days*, Golden Press, 1975, p. 228.

15 McNab, *ibid.*, 1975, p. 229.

16 *Ibid.*, p. 333.

17 Rogers, Lawrence M. (ed.), *The Early Journals of Henry Williams, New Zealand, 1826-40*, Pegasus Press, 1961, pp. 455, 453.

18 Burns, Patricia, *op. cit.*, pp. 51, 61.

19 McNab, *op. cit.*, pp. 334, 336.

20 Barrett, Alfred, *The Life of the Rev. John Hewgill Bumby*, John Mason, London, 1843 (Second edition), p. 146.

21 McNab, *op. cit.*, p. 338.

22 'Journal of Reverend Octavius Hadfield, 1839' MS papers, 896, ATL.

23 Burns, Patricia, *Te Rauparaha – A New Perspective*, A. H. & A. W. Reed, 1980, pp. 196, 197.

24 Orange, Claudia, *The Treaty of Waitangi*, Allen & Unwin and the Port Nicholson Press, 1987, pp. 72, 73.

25 *Ibid.*, p. 90.

26 *Ibid.*, p. 81.

27 Belich, James, *Making Peoples – A History of the New Zealanders*, Allen Lane and the Penguin Press, 1996, p. 206.

CHAPTER NINE
THE TRANSIENT NATURE OF ALL EARTHLY THINGS

1 Wakefield, Edward Jerningham, Diary, 18-23 March 1840, MS papers 2208, ATL.

2 Taylor, Rev. Richard, 'Journal and Register of Baptisms, Marriages and Burials, 1842-1843', MS Papers 2000, p. 16, ATL.

3 Rogers, Lawrence. M. (ed.), *The Early Journals of Henry Williams, New Zealand 1826-40*, Pegasus Press, 1961, p. 460.

4 Cairns, Bob, 'Notes on an Archaeological Survey of Kapiti Island', c. 1980-1985, Archaeological Section, Science and Technology Division, Department of Conservation, Wellington; *Manawatu Daily Times*, 10 January 1919; Adkin, G. L., Diary, 26 February 1921, MONZ.

5 Maori Land Court, Otaki Minute Book No. 2, Kaiwharawhara Hearing, 17 April 1874. Testimony of Henare Te Heierau, p. 466.

6 Barrett, Alfred, *The Life of the Rev. John Hewgill Bumby*, John Mason, 1845, p. 146.

7 Carkeek, W. C., *The Kapiti Coast*, A. H. & A. W. Reed, 1966, p. 167.

8 McNab, Robert, *The Old Whaling Days*, Golden Press, 1975, pp. 230, 231.

9 *Ibid.*, pp. 164, 165.

10 Dieffenbach, Ernst, *Travels in New Zealand*, John Murray, 1843, Volume One, p. 109.

11 Wakefield, Colonel William, Diary 1839-42, MS papers 2102, p. 89, ATL.

12 Maori Land Court, Wairarapa Minute book No. 1, Waiorua – Kapiti No. 5, 27 April 1874; Testimony of John Nicol, p. 59.

13 *Ibid.*, Testimony of William Jenkins, pp. 61, 62.

14 Taylor, *op. cit.*, p. 16.

15 Rhodes, William Barnard, 'Log of the *Eleanor*, 1839-41', 31 October 1839, MS Micro 59, ATL.

16 Knocks, John. A., 'Reminiscences of Early Wellington and Mana Island, 1832-1840', MS papers 1117, p. 2, ATL.

17 *Ibid.*, p.4.

18 Simcox. F. S., *Otaki*, A. H. & A. W. Reed, 1952, p.132.

19 Taylor, *op. cit.* pp. 16, 17.

20 Wakefield, William, *op. cit.*, p. 89.

21 Maori Land Court, Wairarapa Minute Book No. 1, *op. cit.*, p. 61.

22 *Ibid.*, p. 73.

23 Hansard, G. A., 'An account of the work of H. M. S. *Acheron* in New Zealand waters', MS Volume 157, Hocken Library, University of Otago, Dunedin.

24 *Dictionary of New Zealand Biography*, Volume One, Allen & Unwin and the Department of Internal Affairs, 1990, p. 504; Browne, Cyril, 'Bill Jenkins, Kapiti Coast Pioneer', *Otaki Historical Society, Journal*, 1984 (7) p. 21; Maclean, Chris and Joan, *Waikanae – past and present*, Whitcombe Press, 1988, p. 169.

25 Purchase deed, 3 December 1839, Case 383a, OLC-1/928, National Archives.

26 Report of the Commissioner, Case 90a, OLC-1/185, National Archives.

27 Wakefield, William, *op. cit.*, p. 90.

28 Taylor, *op. cit.*, p. 15.

29 OLC-1/929, National Archives.

30 Transcript of Te Rauparaha's evidence before Land Commission, 12 May 1843, Case 383a, OLC-1/928, National Archives.

31 *Ibid.*, Spain's decision.

32 Simcox, *op. cit.*, p. 138.

33 Extracts from Mr Ronaldson's Journal, 1847, in Downes, T. W., *Old Whanganui*, Parkinson & Co., 1915, p. 282 (facsimile edition, Capper Press, 1976).

34 Attorney General's memo, 23 July 1849, Case 383a, *op. cit.*

35 *Ibid.*, Extract from the Minutes of the Proceedings of the Executive Council of New Munster, 1, 8 August 1850, case 383 a, OLC/928.

36 Cowan, James, "Kapiti Island – Report to the Department of Tourist and Health Resorts', *AJHR*, C-8a, 1907, p. 4.

37 Brown, Margaret, 'Andrew Brown of Kapiti', *New Zealand Society of Genealogists*, Parts II, III, MS papers 4280, ATL.

38 Heath, Barbara and Balham, Helen, *The Paremata Story*, Paremata Residents Association, 1994, p. 27.

39 Sheep Inspector's Report, Wellington and West Coast, *Wellington Provincial Government Gazette*: Volume 8, No. 39, 1861, pp. 260, 261, Volume 21, No. 32, 1874, p. 193.

40 *Ibid.*, Volume 10, No. 1, 1863, p. 3.

41 Testimony of Wi Parata, Maori Land Court, Otaki Minute Book No. 2, Waiorua – Kapiti No. 5, 21 April 1874.

42 Ron P. Brown's recollections published in: Baldwin, Olive (ed.), *The Celebration History of the Kapiti District*, Kapiti Borough Council, 1988, p. 167.

43 *AJHR*, 1879, Volume II, H-9, p. 3.

44 Simcox, *op. cit.*

45 Anonymous, 'Kapiti Island', 13-18 April 1876, MS papers 1101, ATL.

46 Map of the Principal Triangulation in the Province of Wellington, 1872, ATL.

47 Buchanan, *op. cit.*

48 Wilkinson, A. S. and the late Amy, *Kapiti Island Bird Sanctuary – A Natural History of the Island*, Masterton Printing Co. Ltd, 1952, p. 24.

49 Maori Land Court, Otaki Minute Book No. 2, Waiorua-Kapiti No. 5, 24 April 1874, p. 74.

CHAPTER TEN
BIRDS OR PEOPLE?

1 King, Michael, *The Collector: Andreas Reischek – A Biography*, Hodder & Stoughton, 1981, p. 110.

2 *Ibid.*, pp. 110-11.

3 Arnold, Rollo, *New Zealand's Burning: The Settlers' World in the Mid 1880s*, Victoria University Press, 1994.

4 Buller, Sir Walter, *A History of the Birds of New Zealand*, E. G. Turbott (ed.), Whitcombe & Tombs, 1974, p. 56; Phillips, W. J., *The Book of the Huia*, Whitcombe & Tombs, 1963, pp. 57, 63, 95.

5 Potts, T. H., 'Out in the Open – A Budget of Scraps of Natural History, Gathered in New Zealand', *Lyttelton Times*, 1882, p. 35 (originally presented in a paper read before the Philosophical Institute of Canterbury in 1872).

6 Galbreath, Ross, *Walter Buller – The Reluctant Conservationist*, GP Books, 1989, pp. 125-127.

7 Bevan, Thomas, 'Reminiscences of an Old Colonist', *Otaki Historical Society, Journal*, 5 (1982), p. 87.

8 Johnston, Judith, 'The New Zealand Bush: Early Assessments of Vegetation', *New Zealand Geographer*, 37(1): 19-24, 1981.

9 Galbreath, *op. cit.*, p.165.

10 *Ibid.*, pp. 176, 177.

11 *Ibid.*, p. 182.

12 *Ibid.*, pp. 190-192.

13 *Ibid.*, p. 212.

14 Buller, Sir Walter L., 'Notes on New Zealand Ornithology, with an Exhibition of Specimens', *New Zealand Institute, Transactions and Proceedings*, Volume 28, 1895, pp. 326, 327.

15 Ross Galbreath to the author, 30 March 1998.

16 Buller, 'Notes on New Zealand Ornithology', *op. cit.*

17 Field, H. A., Survey Notebook, MS 740, ATL. (This contains a personal diary from 27 May to 26 November 1893. See entries for 9 July, 13 August, 2 November and 8 November.)

18 Conversation with Jean Dobson, 24 April 1997; *AJHR*, 1897, Volume III, 1–3c, p. 2.

19 'Island of Kapiti', *AJHR*, 1904, G-8, p. 1; Simcox, F. S., *Otaki*, A. H. & A. W. Reed, 1952, p. 138.

20 The combined total of land leased on Kapiti by the Macleans (2646 acres), Charles Lowe (1238 acres) and C. B. Morrison (405 acres) was 4289 acres – 86 per cent of the island's total area of 4990 acres. When this is added to land owned by Europeans (the Browns had title to 617 acres at Wharekohu and Field and the Macleans owned 12½ acres each at Rangatira), it shows that only 59 acres (1.12 per cent of the total area) was not owned or leased by Europeans. See 'Island of Kapiti', *AJHR*, 1904, *op. cit.*

21 Maclean, Chris and Joan, *Waikanae – past and present*, Whitcombe Press, 1988, pp. 58, 59.

22 *AJHR*, 1897, Volume III, *op. cit.*

23 W. H. Field to Charles Lowe, 27 August 1897, W. H. Field, Letterbooks, Volume 3, MS 0729, p. 666, ATL.

24 Field, W. H., Letterbooks, Volume 4, *op. cit.*, p. 548, ATL.

25 Hemi Kuti, Native Affairs Committee, Minutes of Evidence, 15 December 1897, *AJHR*, Volume III, 1–3c, pp. 2, 3.

26 *Ibid.*, p. 6, Hanikamu Te Hiko and Raiha Puaha examined.

27 *Ibid.*, p. 7, Heni Te Rei examined.

28 Field, H. A., Survey Notebooks, MS 742, 1897, ATL. (This contains a diary covering the period from 1 September to 31 October. Relevant entries are 9, 13 and 14 September.)

29 Stafford, Treadwell and Field to the Chairman, Native Affairs Committee, *AJHR*, Volume III, 1897, 1–3c, p. 2.

30 *NZPD*, Volume 100, 1897, p. 915.

31 *Ibid.*

32 *Ibid.*, p. 925.

33 *Ibid.*, pp. 927, 928.

34 New Zealand Statutes, 1897, No. 28, 'Kapiti Island Public Reserve Act', pp. 68, 69.

35 Sinclair, Keith, *A History of New Zealand*, Penguin, 1991, p. 192.

CHAPTER ELEVEN
MARKING TIME

1 Phillips, W. J., *The Book of the Huia*, Whitcombe & Tombs, 1963, pp. 77, 24.

2 Sheridan, P., Chief Native Land Purchase Officer, 'Return showing particulars in respect of the Island of Kapiti', *AJHR*, 1904, G-8, pp. 1–3.

3 *Ibid.*, p. 1.

4 Field, W. H., Letterbooks, Volume 6, p. 469, 22 September 1900, MS Group 60, ATL.

5 Seddon to Field, 25 September 1900, Field Family Papers, MS Group 60, MS papers 0113, 2/78, ATL.

6 Field, W. H., Letterbooks, Volume 6, p. 497, 1 October 1900, *op. cit.*

7 *AJHR*, 1904, G-8, pp. 1, 2.

8 *Ibid.*, p. 3.

9 Conversation with Jean Dobson, 16 April 1997 (tape).

10 *Evening Post*, 4 February 1949.

11 Greville, R. P., Map of Kapiti Island, Survey Office Plans SO 14958, 14959, 1912, LINZ (Wellington).

12 Galbreath, Ross, *Working for Wildlife – A History of the New Zealand Wildlife Service*, Bridget Williams Books and the Historical Branch, Department of Internal Affairs, 1993, p. 12.

13 Secretary, Wellington Acclimatisation Society, to the Colonial Secretary, 16 May 1900, IA 1 52/71, National Archives.

14 *Ibid.*, Declaration under the Animals Protection Act, 25 May 1900.

15 Roche, M. M., 'Securing Representative Areas of New Zealand's Environment; Some Historical and Design Perspectives', *New Zealand Geographer*, Volume 37(2), October 1981, p. 73.

16 Galbreath, *op. cit.*

17 Donne, T. E., Superintendent, to the Minister for Tourist and Health Resorts, 21 September 1905, IA 1 52/71/1, National Archives.

18 *Ibid.*, margin note.

19 Cowan, J., 'Kapiti Island', *AJHR*, 1907, C-8a, pp. 2, 4.

20 *Ibid.*

21 Ell, H. G., to Donne, T. E., 22 January 1906, IA 1 52/71/1, National Archives; 'Outlook Extreme', *Listener*, 12 December 1998, p. 20.

22 Hill, Susanne and John, *Richard Henry of Resolution Island*, John McIndoe, 1987, p. 303.

23 *Ibid.*

24 Wilkinson, A. S. and the late Amy, *Kapiti Island Bird Sanctuary – A Natural History of the Island*, Masterton Printing Co. Ltd, 1952, p. 24.

25 Field, W. H., Letterbooks, Volume 13, p. 166, *op. cit.*

26 *New Zealand Free Lance*, 30 March 1907.

27 *New Zealand Times*, 3 April 1907.

28 Cockayne, L., 'Report on a botanical survey of Kapiti Island', *AJHR*, 8 May 1907, C-8, p. 1.

29 *New Zealand Times*, 3 April 1907.

30 Dingwall, Paul R., 'Harry Ell's Vision in Nature Conservation', *Landscape (Journal of the Department of Lands and Survey)*, Volume 10, November 1981, p. 27.

31 Cockayne, *op. cit.*, p. 15.

32 Application to the Maori Land Court, Aotea District, Waiorua Kapiti Island, March 1998, 'Chronology of Waiorua Kapiti'.

33 Cowan, *op. cit.*, p. 1.

34 Maclean, Chris and Joan, *Waikanae – past and present*, Whitcombe Press, 1988, p. 41.

35 Cowan, *op. cit.*, p. 4.

36 Maclean, *op. cit.*, p. 184.

37 Conversation with Rewa Webber, 16 October 1998 (tape).

38 Henry, R., to Under-Secretary, Department of Lands, 21 April 1910, Lands (and Survey), file 4/53(1), DOC (Wgtn). Until 1913 it was known as the Department of Lands.

39 Drummond, James, 'The Kapiti Island Bird Sanctuary', Annual Report of the Commissioner of Crown Lands, Appendix V, *AJHR*, 1908, C-1, p. 83.

40 Hill, *op. cit.*, p. 300.

41 *Ibid.*, p. 305.

42 *Ibid.*

43 *Ibid.*, p. 312.

44 'Kapiti Island proposed boat harbour', 1910, Marine Department, MD 3677, National Archives.

45 Henry, Richard, 'On Kapiti Island – Cats, Rats, Goats, etc.', 22 June 1911, MS papers 387, Hocken Library.

46 Hill, *op. cit.*, p. 310.

47 *Ibid.*, p. 307.

48 *Ibid.*

49 Henry, to Under-Secretary for Lands, 30 October 1910, 4/53(1), DOC (Wgtn).

50 Henry, to Under-Secretary for Lands, 31 March 1911, *ibid.*

51 Memo to W. C. Kensington, Under-Secretary, Department of Lands, 1 November 1911, Kapiti Caretakers Correspondence Collection, DOC (Wgtn).

52 Henry, 'On Kapiti Island', *op. cit.*, p. 3.

53 Field, W. H., Letterbooks, Volume 9, p. 24, ATL.

54 Parliamentary Question from W. H. Field, Supplementary Order Paper, 9 August 1911, Question 107, IA 1 52/71/1, National Archives.

55 Field, W. H., Letterbooks, Volume 16, p. 352, *op. cit.*, ATL.

CHAPTER TWELVE
GETTING STARTED

1 Murdoch, James, to the Minster of Internal Affairs, 10 July 1911, Department of Lands and Survey, file 4/53(2), DOC (Wgtn).

2 Commissioner of Crown Lands to Under-Secretary, Department of Lands, 6 July 1911, *op. cit.*

3 Bennett, J. L., to Under-Secretary, Department of Lands, 9 August 1911, *op. cit.*

4 Adkin, G. L., Diary, 25 February 1921, MONZ.

5 Phillips, W. J., *The Book of the Huia*, Whitcombe & Tombs, 1963, pp. 67-78.

6 Under-Secretary, Department of Lands and Survey, to Bennett, 2 July 1913, 4/53(2), *op. cit.*

7 Ell, H. G., to Minister of Lands, 14 June 1912, Kapiti Caretakers Correspondence Collection, DOC (Wgtn).

8 Sanderson, E. V., 'Kapiti', February 1914, p. 1, IA 1 52/71, National Archives.

9 *Ibid.*

10 *Ibid.*, p. 2.

11 Sanderson to the Minister of Lands, 19 February 1914, IA 1 52/71, *op. cit.*

12 Massey, W. F., to Sanderson, 27 February 1914, *ibid.*

13 Secretary, New Zealand Forest and Bird Protection Society, to the Minister of Internal Affairs, 24 March, and 15 April, 1914, *ibid.*

14 Phillips-Turner, E., 'Kapiti Island', 1 June 1914, *ibid.*

15 Under-Secretary, Department of Lands and Survey, to Bennett, 17 December 1914, Kapiti Caretakers Correspondence Collection, DOC (Wgtn).

16 Conversation with Rewa Webber, 16 October 1998 (tape).

17 *Dominion*, 9 May 1916.

18 Dalgety and Company Limited to Bennett, 10 September 1915, Department of Lands and Survey, 4/53 (1), DOC (Wgtn).

19 Assistant Under-Secretary, Department of Lands and Survey, to Bennett, 18 May 1916, *ibid.*; Greville, R. P., to Under-Secretary, Lands and Survey Department, 23 November 1916, *ibid.*; Secretary, New Zealand Forest and Bird Protection Society, to the Minister of Internal Affairs, 21 October 1914, *ibid.*

20 Ell, H. G., to the Acting Minister of Lands, 10 October 1916, Department of Lands and Survey, 4/53 (2), DOC (Wgtn); Bennett to Assistant Under-Secretary, Department of Lands and Survey, 4 January 1917, *ibid.*

21 Memorandum to Bennett, 30 August 1916, Kapiti Caretakers Correspondence Collection, DOC (Wgtn).

22 Under-Secretary, Department of Lands and Survey to Bennett, 23 May 1917, *ibid.*

23 Myers, M., Bell Gully Bell and Myers, to Under-Secretary, Department of Lands and Survey, 21 June 1917, *ibid.*

24 Assistant Under-Secretary, Department of Lands and Survey, to Bennett, 9 July 1917, *ibid.*

25 Manager, Dalgety and Company Limited, to the Chief Accountant, Department of Lands and Survey, 31 August 1917, Department of Lands and Survey, 4/53 (2), DOC (Wgtn).

26 Kirk, H. B., 'Report on Kapiti Island as a Plant and Animal Sanctuary', 16 January 1919, Department of Lands and Survey, 4/53 (1) DOC (Wgtn).

27 Stead, E. F., to Under-Secretary, Department of Internal Affairs, 22 November 1920, IA 1 52/71, National Archives.

28 Thomson, J. A., to Under-Secretary, Department of Internal Affairs, 23 February 1920, IA 1 52/71, *ibid.*

29 Vosseler, F. W., to the Department of Lands and Survey, 15 December 1921, Department of Lands and Survey, 4/53 (3), DOC (Wgtn).

30 Bennett, to Under-Secretary, Department of Lands and Survey, 20 December 1921, *ibid.*

31 Under-Secretary, Department of Lands and Survey, to Bennett, 23 December 1921, *ibid.*

32 *Evening Post*, 22 December 1921.

33 Sanderson, to Sir Thomas Mackenzie, 27 November 1922, MS papers 0444/116, ATL.

34 *Evening Post*, 10 January 1922.

35 *Ibid.*, 16 January 1922.

36 *Ibid.*, 28 February 1922.

37 *Dominion*, 1 March, *Waikato Times*, 2 March, and *New Zealand Times*, 3 March 1922.

38 *Dominion*, 7 March 1922.

39 *Ibid.*, 21 March 1922.

40 *Evening Post*, 4 April 1922.

41 Galbreath, Ross, 'Sanderson, Ernest Valentine', *Dictionary of New Zealand Biography*, Volume 4, Auckland University Press and the Department of Internal Affairs, 1988, p. 450.

42 Commissioner of Crown Lands to Bennett, 16 May 1922, Kapiti Caretakers Correspondence, DOC (Wgtn).

43 Commissioner of Crown Lands to Mrs John Webber, *ibid.*

44 Galbreath, Ross, *Working for Wildlife – A History of the New Zealand Wildlife Service*, Bridget Williams Books and Historical Branch, Department of Internal Affairs, 1993, pp. 13, 14.

45 Sanderson to Mackenzie, 31 October 1922, MS papers 0444/116, ATL; Mackenzie to Sanderson, 14 November 1922, *ibid.*

46 Sanderson to the Secretary, New Zealand Forestry League, 29 November 1922, *ibid.*

47 Galbreath, Ross, 'Founding Forest and Bird – The First Meeting', *Forest and Bird*, February 1998.

48 Sanderson to Massey, 17 April 1923, Department of Lands and Survey, 4/53 (3), DOC (Wgtn); Minister of Lands to Sanderson, 11 May 1923, *ibid.*

49 *New Zealand Times*, 13 August 1923.

50 *Evening Post*, 2 October 1923.

51 Secretary, New Zealand Native Bird Protection Society, to Commissioner, Lands and Survey Department, 25 August, 1924, MS papers 0444/152, ATL.

CHAPTER THIRTEEN
THE GOLDEN YEARS

1 Maclean, Chris, *Tararua – the story of a mountain range*, Whitcombe Press, 1994, pp. 133-138.

2 *Dominion*, 7 April 1924.

3 Joyce, Horiana and Dennis, Jonathan, 'The Singing Tahiwis', *Otaki Historical Society, Journal*, 1998, (21), pp. 45-50.

4 Conversation with Bryan Vickerman, 23 September 1998.

5 *Otago Daily Times*, 23 January 1926.

6 Andersen, Johannes Carl, Diary 'Kapiti', 1924, MS – 0053, pp. 69-78, ATL.

7 Wilkinson, A. S., Diary, 1925-26; 15, 19 January 1925, Diana Stidolph Collection.

8 *New Zealand Gazette*, 15, 26 February 1925.

9 Wilkinson, Diary; 20, 21 and 29 January 1925, *op. cit.*

10 Wilkinson, A. S. and the late Amy, *Kapiti Bird Sanctuary – A Natural History of the Island*, Masterton Printing Co. Ltd, 1952, p. 29.

11 Weggery, W. H., to Sanderson, 8 February 1927, MS papers 0444/152, ATL.

12 Wilkinson, *Kapiti Bird Sanctuary – A Natural History of the Island, op. cit.*, p. 30.

13 Secretary, New Zealand Native Bird Protection Society to Commissioner, Department of Lands and Survey, 24 June 1925, MS papers 0444/152, ATL; Commissioner of Crown Lands to Secretary, New Zealand Native Bird Protection Society, 7 August 1925, *ibid.*; Wilkinson, Dairy, June 1925, *op. cit.*

14 *Evening Post*, 21 November 1925.

15 Secretary, New Zealand Native Bird Protection Society, to Commissioner,

Department of Lands and Survey, 30 November 1925, MS papers 0444/152, ATL.

16 Commissioner of Crown Lands to Secretary, New Zealand Native Bird Protection Society, 14 December 1925, *ibid*.

17 Wilkinson, A. S., 'Kapiti Island Plants 1924–1942', Diana Stidolph Collection.

18 Sanderson, E.V., 'Kapiti Sanctuary', 27 September 1926, MS papers 0444/152, ATL.

19 Conversation with Sylvia Lovell, 1 August 1997 (tape).

20 Lovell, Sylvia, 'Kapiti', typescript, 'The Captain', Ray Lovell Collection.

21 Fletcher, A., to Sanderson, 3 February 1927, MS papers 0444/152, ATL.

22 Secretary, New Zealand Native Bird Protection Society, to Under-Secretary, Department of Lands and Survey, 17 February 1927, *ibid*.

23 Stidolph to Sanderson, 5 March 1927; Sanderson to Stidolph, 7 April 1927; Stidolph to Sanderson, 14 April, 6 May 1927, *ibid*.

24 Thomson, J. Allan, to Under-Secretary, Department of Internal Affairs, 9 March 1927, IA 1 25/103/75, National Archives.

25 *New Zealand Times*, 3 March 1922.

26 *Evening Post*, 18 March 1925.

27 Under-Secretary, Internal Affairs to Under-Secretary, Lands and Survey, 17 February 1927, IA 52/71, National Archives.

28 Commissioner of Crown Lands to Wilkinson, c. February/March 1927 (part of letter with actual date missing), Kapiti Caretakers Correspondence Collection, DOC (Wgtn).

29 Sanderson to Under-Secretary, Internal Affairs, 23 April 1927; Sanderson to Commissioner, Crown Lands, 5 May 1927; and Secretary, New Zealand Native Bird Protection Society, to Sir Thomas Mackenzie, 18 May 1927, all in MS papers 0444/152, ATL.

30 Wilkinson, A. S., Diary, 29 March – 12 April 1927, MS-2403, ATL.

31 Wilkinson, Diary, 3 May – 15 May 1927, *ibid*.

32 Sanderson to Wilkinson, 24 June 1927 and Wilkinson to Sanderson, 2 July 1927, MS papers 0444/152, ATL.

33 Conversation with Nancy Jordan, 2 October 1998 (tape).

34 Sanderson to Halcombe, 1 May 1928, MS papers 0444/152, ATL.

35 *Evening Post*, 19 October 1927.

36 Field, W. H., to Wilkinson, A. S., 24 October 1924, Letterbooks Volume 29, p. 111; 8 December 1926,

Letterbooks Volume 30, p. 219; and 18 January 1928, Letterbooks, Volume 30, p. 782, MS Group 60, ATL.

37 Lovell, Sylvia, 'Kapiti', typescript, 'Vice-Regal', Ray Lovell Collection.

38 Wilkinson, *Kapiti Bird Sanctuary – A Natural History of the Island*, *op. cit.*, Foreword.

39 Conversation with Sylvia Lovell, 1 August 1997 (tape).

40 *Ibid*.

41 *International Exhibition of Nature Photography*, 16 October – 30 November 1935, Diana Stidolph Collection.

42 Lovell, Ray, 'Descendants of John Stanley Crighton Wilkinson', p. 5, Ray Lovell Collection.

43 Lovell, Sylvia, 'Kapiti', typescript, 'Around the Island', *op. cit.*

44 Conversation with Sylvia Lovell, *op. cit.*.

45 Conversation with Jim Webber, 4 October 1998 (tape).

46 Conversation with Rewa Webber, 16 October 1998 (tape).

47 *Dominion*, 11 June 1938.

48 Webber, Rewa, *op. cit.*

49 Conversation with Sylvia Lovell, *op. cit.*.

50 Conversation with Sylvia Lovell, 15 August 1997 (tape).

CHAPTER FOURTEEN
HOME, HEART & SOUL

1 Conversation with Rewa Webber, 16 October 1998 (tape).

2 *Dominion*, 22 June 1939.

3 President, New Zealand Native Bird Protection Society, to Under-Secretary, Department of Lands and Survey, 17 June 1940, MS papers 0444/152A, ATL.

4 Heenan, J. W., to Sanderson, 19 June 1940, *ibid*.; *Dominion*, 12 October 1951.

5 Conversation with Nancy Jordan, 2 October 1998 (tape).

6 Sanderson to Mrs Webber, 19 September 1940, MS papers 0444/152A, ATL.

7 Utauta Webber to Sanderson, 26 September 1940, *ibid*.

8 Sanderson to Mrs Webber, 6 November 1940, *ibid*.

9 Sanderson, Memo, undated (c. November 1940), *ibid*.

10 Conversation with Nancy Jordan, *op. cit.*

11 Baldwin, Olive (ed.), *The Celebration History of the Kapiti Coast District*, Kapiti Borough Council, 1988, p. 79; Hughes, G. W., Caretaker's Report for November 1943, Kapiti Caretakers Correspondence Collection, DOC (Wgtn).

12 Conversation with Peter Daniel, 14 February 1997 (tape).

13 Lovell, Sylvia, 'Kapiti', typescript, 'Visitors come and go', Ray Lovell Collection; conversations with Sylvia Lovell, 1, 15 August 1997 (tapes).

14 Sanderson to Hughes, 19 March 1945, MS papers 0444/152A, ATL.

15 Conversation with Nancy Jordan, *op. cit.*

16 *Ibid*.

17 Minister of Internal Affairs to the Secretary, Forest and Bird Protection Society of New Zealand, 14 January 1946, MS papers 0444/868, ATL.

18 *Evening Post*, 20 September 1946.

19 Assistant Under-Secretary, Internal Affairs, to Commissioner of Crown Lands, (as the top page of this letter is missing the exact date is unknown although its contents suggest c. 1946), Lands and Survey 4/53 (1), DOC (Wgtn).

20 Fox, G. F., Caretaker's Report for the Year Ending 31/3/1952, Kapiti Caretakers Correspondence Collection, *op. cit.*

21 Galbreath, Ross, *Working for Wildlife – A History of the New Zealand Wildlife Service*, Bridget Williams Books and Historical Branch, Department of Internal Affairs, 1993, pp. 73-78.

22 Commissioner of Crown Lands to Fox, 21 July 1954, Kapiti Caretakers Correspondence Collection, DOC (Wgtn); Controller, Wildlife Division, Internal Affairs, to the Commissioner of Crown Lands, 29 July 1954, *ibid*.

23 Fox, G. F., Annual Report for the Year Ending 31/3/1956, *ibid*.

24 Fox, G. F., Annual Report for the Year Ending 31/3/1959, *ibid*.

25 Conversation with Doug Williams, 12 November 1998 (tape).

26 Commissioner of Crown Lands to Fox, 13 December 1954, Kapiti Caretakers Correspondence Collection, DOC (Wgtn).

27 Fox to Commissioner of Crown Lands, 1 October 1952, *ibid*.

28 Conversation with Doug Williams, *op. cit.*

29 Director-General, Department of Lands and Survey to Commissioner of Crown Lands, 19 March 1954, 4/53 (5), DOC (Wgtn).

30 Acting Commissioner of Crown Lands, to Director-General of Lands, 23 January 1963, *ibid*.

31 'Purchase of Maori Land – Kapiti Island', handwritten memo, 30 April 1963, *ibid*.

32 Conversation with Jim McIntyre, 16 April 1997 (tape).

33 *Ibid*.

34 Commissioner of Crown Lands to Director-General of Lands, 21 October 1963, 4/53 (5), DOC (Wgtn).

35 Commissioner of Crown Lands to Director-General of Lands, 2 March 1965, *ibid.*

36 Maori Trustee, Department of Maori Affairs to Director-General, Department of Lands and Survey, 3 May 1965, *ibid.*

37 Commissioner of Crown Lands to the Director-General of Lands, 11 May 1967, *ibid.*; conversation with Peter Daniel, *op. cit.*, in which he recalls a conversation with Mike Webber's wife to this effect.

38 Commissioner of Crown Lands to Director-General of Lands, 6 December 1971, 4/53 (5), DOC (Wgtn).

39 Director-General of Lands to the Commissioner of Crown Lands, 17 February 1972, *ibid.*

40 Director-General of Lands to the Minister of Lands, 30 May 1972, *ibid.*

41 Director-General of Lands to Commissioner of Crown Lands, 2 June 1972, *ibid.*

CHAPTER FIFTEEN
WINDOW ON ANOTHER WORLD

1 Fox, G. F., to the Commissioner of Crown Lands, 1 May 1962, Kapiti Caretakers Correspondence Collection, DOC (Wgtn); Caretaker's Annual Report for the year ending 31 March 1963, p. 5, *ibid.*

2 *Ibid.*, p. 4; *Dominion*, 24 October 1973.

3 Wilkinson, A. S., to Miss Wilkins, 31 March 1942, Kapiti Caretakers Correspondence Collection, *op. cit.*

4 Fox to the Commissioner of Crown Lands, 5 February 1962, *ibid.*

5 Fox to the Commissioner of Crown Lands, 21 December 1965, *ibid.*

6 Notes of a discussion between Fox and the Commissioner, 27 February 1962, *ibid.*

7 *Dominion*, 24 October 1973.

8 Esler, A. E., 'The Vegetation of Kapiti Island', *New Zealand Journal of Botany*, 1967(5), p. 356.

9 Esler to the author, 2 May 1998.

10 Discussion Paper – 'Opossum Control, Kapiti Island', September 1981, Department of Lands and Survey file 8/5/359/1, p. 2.

11 Atkinson, I. A. E., 'Effects of possums on the vegetation of Kapiti Island and changes following possum eradication', DOC Investigation No. 1001, 1992, p. 4.

12 Conversation with Peter Daniel, 14 February 1997 (tape).

13 Bell, B. D., and Atkinson, I. A. E., 'Opossum Research on Kapiti Island', *Forest and Bird*, February 1976, pp. 12, 13; Falla, R. A., 'Opossums on Offshore Islands', Workshop Discussion on Marsupial Research and Management (1977), in Bell, B. D. (ed.), *Proceedings of the First Symposium on Marsupials in New Zealand*, Victoria University Zoology Publication, No. 74, 1981, p.269.

14 Minutes of the Kapiti Island Advisory Committee, 15 April 1977, p. 5; Department of Lands and Survey 4/53(6), DOC (Wgtn).

15 Pracy, L. T., 'Opossums: Kapiti Island 1980', pp. 1, 2, 5 and 6; RES 7/5/2, DOC (Wgtn).

16 Atkinson, Ian, to the author, 15 June 1999, p. 2.

17 Sherley, G. H., *Eradication of Brushtail Possums on Kapiti Island, New Zealand: Techniques and Methods*, Department of Conservation, Science and Research Series No. 46, 1992, p. 4.

18 Conversation with Geoff Alexander, 27 March 1997 (tape one).

19 Cowan, P. E., 'A proposal for the eradication of possums for Kapiti Island', Ecology Division, DSIR, June 1982, p. 2.

20 Conversation with Peter Daniel, *op. cit.*

21 *Ibid.*; conversation with Geoff Alexander, *op. cit.*

22 Sherley, *op. cit.*, p. 27.

23 Conversation with Geoff Alexander and Bill Collins, 27 March 1997 (tapes one and two); Bob Cairns, 'Kapiti Island' 1997 (tape one).

24 Atkinson, I. A. E., 'Kapiti possum study: vegetation surveillance 1978-1982', Botany Division, DSIR, May 1982, p. 1.

25 Shields, Margaret, to Minister of Forests, 26 April 1984, Department of Lands and Survey, 7/5/2(3), DOC (Wgtn); conversation with Geoff Alexander and Bill Collins, *op. cit.*; conversation with Peter Daniel, *op. cit.*

26 Cowan, P. E., as cited in Sherley, *op. cit.*, p. 13.

27 Cairns, *op. cit.* (tape two).

28 Sherley, *op. cit.*, p. 27.

29 Lovegrove, Tim, 'Interim reports to the Wellington District Office of the Department of Lands and Survey on the present status of the stitchbirds on the Kapiti Island Nature Reserve', December 1983, June 1984.

30 Daniel, Peter, 'Monthly Report, Kapiti Island', August 1987, Kapiti Caretakers Correspondence Collection, DOC (Wgtn).

31 Atkinson, 1992, *op. cit.*, p. 41.

32 Daniel, 'Monthly Reports, Kapiti Island'; November 1986 to October 1987 and January 1989 to December 1990, *op. cit.*

33 *Ibid.*, March 1987.

34 Lovell, Sylvia, Kapiti typescript, 'Wellington to Paraparaumu', Ray Lovell Collection.

35 Conversation with Rewa Webber, 16 October 1998 (tape).

36 Daniel, 'Monthly Reports, Kapiti Island', November 1984, February 1986, *op. cit.*

37 *Ibid.*, February 1986.

38 *Ibid.*, March 1986.

39 *Kapiti Observer*, 12 January 1987.

40 Maori Land Court of New Zealand, Aotea District, Waiorua Kapiti No. 6, Application for Partition, Minute Book – September 1990, p. 10.

41 *Ibid.*

42 Waitangi Tribunal', Wai. 52, Index to the Record of Inquiry, 22 July 1996.

43 Conversation with Raewyn Empson, Technical Support Officer, Department of Conservation, 10 November 1997 (tape one); conversation with Ani Parata, 18 December 1997 (tape).

44 Internal Memo, 23 December 1976, file 4/53(3), Lands and Survey Department, DOC (Wgtn).

45 Daniel, 'Monthly Report, Kapiti Island', May 1989, *op. cit.*

46 *Evening Post*, 12 January 1952.

47 Fox, annual report for year ending 31 March 1966, Kapiti Caretakers Correspondence Collection, *op. cit.*

48 Visitor preferences (Department of Conservation and Heylen Research, 1994) as quoted in 'Kapiti Island Nature Lodge', Concept Plan, Tourism Resource Consultants, May 1995, p. 10.

49 Conversation with Rewa Webber, *op. cit.*

50 Boffa Miskell, 'Assessment of Environmental Effects of Proposals on Crown Land at the Northern End of Kapiti Island', August 1997, 6.3.4.

51 Swan, Jamie, 'Ecotourism – Creating a Sustainable Visitor Experience', Massey University, 1997, p. 55.

52 Aitken, Graeme, 'Kapiti Island – Overview of Treaty of Waitangi claims on Crown owned land', Wellington, 1997, p. 38.

53 'The Commissioner of Crown Lands formal decisions on applications for use of the Crown land at the northern end of Kapiti Island', 27 November 1997, p. 6.

54 *KEA News*, February 1999.

55 *Kapiti Mail*, 26 December 1997, 30 April 1998.

56 Wyllie, Tutekawa, speech on Kapiti Island, 20 December 1997 (tape).

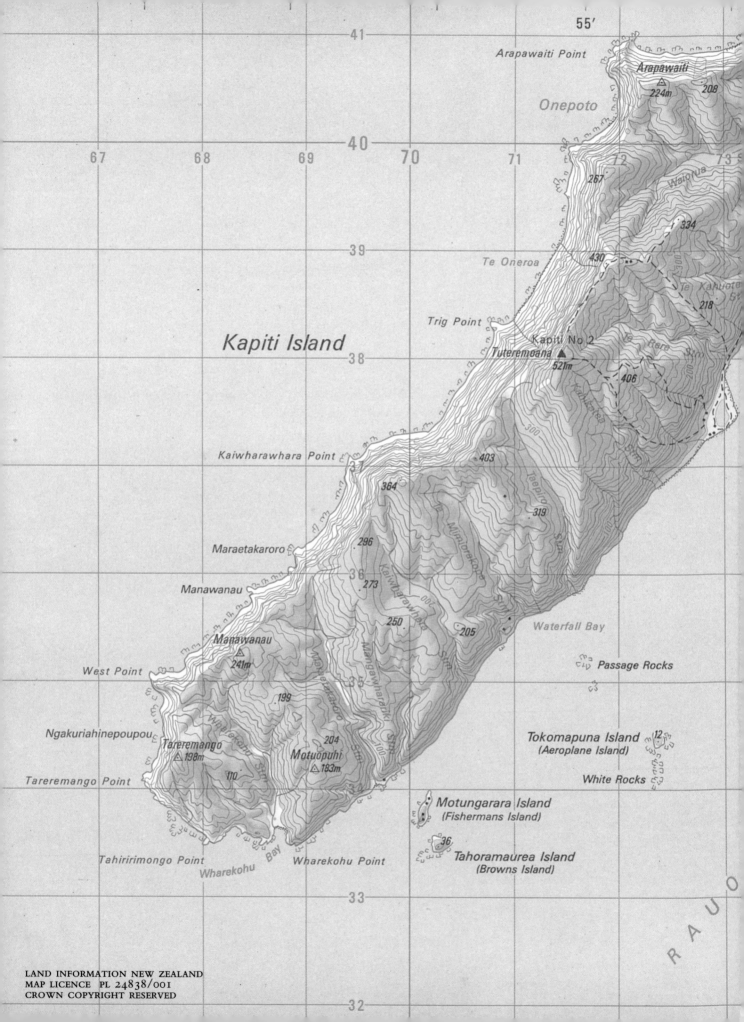

55'

41

40

67   68   69   70   71   72   73

Arapawaiti Point

Onepoto

Arapawaiti
△ 224m   208

267

Waiorua

334

39

Te Oneroa

430

Te Kahuoteran 5tm

Trig Point

218

Kapiti No 2

Kapiti Island   38

Tuteremoana ▲
521m   Te Bere Stm

406

Kaiwharawhara Point   37   403   300

364

Te Minitorakau Stm

319

300

Maraetakaroro   296

Te Kaiwharawhara Stm

36   273

Kaipiro Stm

Manawanau

250   205   Waterfall Bay

Manawanau
△ 241m   Passage Rocks

West Point

199   Mangawharariki Stm

Ngakuriahinepoupou   204   Tokomapuna Island   12
Tareremango   Motuopuhi   (Aeroplane Island)
△ 198m   △ 183m
110   White Rocks

Tareremango Point   34

Motungarara Island
(Fishermans Island)

36   Tahoramaurea Island
(Browns Island)

Tahiririmongo Point   Wharekohu   Wharekohu Point
Wharekohu   Bay

33

32

R A U O